3.00 net

ORDEAL OF FAITH

ORDEAL OF FAITH:

The Crisis of Church-Going America,

1865-1900

By

Francis P. Weisenburger

Professor of History
The Ohio State University

PHILOSOPHICAL LIBRARY

New York

Printed in the United States of America

PREFACE

When the people of Ohio were presented with their first state constitution in 1802, it was reported that many did not like it because there were "no pictures in it." Some individuals may have the same reaction to this volume, but the lack in this case is due wholly to economic factors. Some, moreover, may wish for more sophisticated writing which often sacrifices accuracy to the smart overstatement or deals flippantly with matters of serious concern to many worthy people, but such is not the author's conception of the historian's responsibility.

The work is frankly intended as a synthesis of much widely scattered knowledge. Use has been made, accordingly, not only of letters, memoirs, and contemporary newspapers and periodicals, but of countless monographs. Where the author of a special study has the unquestioned confidence of the historical profession, his mature conclusions have generally been accepted in this work, for professional scholarship is surely a cooperative venture. The extensive research of many students in the files of periodicals like *The Catholic World, The Congregationalist,* and various sectional editions of the Methodist *Christian Advocate* has greatly reduced the task of this writer.

The author has accumulated large files of notes dealing with church statistics, institutional churches, revivals, immigrant religious activities, and reform movements, as well as with the functioning of the churches as centers of worship, fellowship, and educational efforts. In this volume, however, limitations of space have commanded a definite adherence to the restricted scope of the work.

Heartfelt personal thanks must be given to a number of friends who have read all or parts of the manuscript—Professors Harold J. Grimm, Eugene H. Roseboom, Warner F. Woodring, Henry H. Simms, Francis R. Aumann, Paul Varg, and Foster Rhea Dulles. For encouragement expressed in various ways, sincere appreciation is extended to Merle Curti, Carl Wittke, H. Paul Hudson, D. Luther Evans, Lawrence F. Hill, Everett Walters, Thomas D. Clark, James H. Rodabaugh, Jeannette Nichols, Clayton Ellsworth, and Charles E. Cuningham. To Mrs. Rose Morse, Assistant Director of the Philosophical Library, especial gratitude is due for her aid in the publication process.

Francis P. Weisenburger

TABLE OF CONTENTS

INTRODUCTION

Over a century ago (in 1835) Alexis de Tocqueville expressed the observation that religion had come to be a more vital force in the United States than in Europe.[1] At any rate, everyone intimately acquainted with the development of the great Republic certainly has had occasion to note the large part played by religious forces. The late Professor J. Franklin Jameson in his presidential address before the American Historical Association in 1907 declared that there is merit in the contention that religious history might give the most complete insight into American character, for only a relatively small group in the United States has ever been much concerned with literature, philosophy, music, and the plastic arts. He elaborated:

> . . . Not that all or even most Americans have been religious, but there have been religious men in every class, every period, every sub-division of America. . . . Millions have felt an interest in religion where thousands have felt an interest in literature or philosophy, in music or art. Millions have known little of any book save one, and that one the most interesting of religious books, the most influential, the most powerful to transform. Doubtless they were occupied mainly with the tasks of daily life. . . . But no view is truthful that leaves out of account the ideals which animated these toiling millions, the thoughts concerning the universe and man which informed their minds.[2]

In the more than half a century since Dr. Jameson's address, much has been written both in general and church history. Certainly today there is no paucity of printed material relating to the details of America's religious past. Every large library fairly groans under the weight of shelves crowded with religious periodicals and histories of dioceses, presbyteries, synods, conferences, and other church bodies. Numerous scholarly monographs have laid substantial foundations for an accurate appraisal of the religious heritage of the United States. A number of general histories of religion in America (especially those by Sweet, Latourette, Garrison, Rowe, and Sperry) have not been without their substantial contributions. Yet, a distinguished American historian, Henry Steele Commager, has declared: "As yet we do not have any satisfactory history of religion in America."

Part of the difficulty has been that religious organizations have been so numerous, with the multiplicity of sects in the United States, that a scholarly analysis based on reliable sources has seemed a colossal, if not impossible, task. The clerical historian, moreover, has often lacked the interest and the objectivity to deal with groups other than his own denomination. Furthermore, he has often felt incompetent to integrate American religious history with the social and intellectual forces of the past. Academic historians, on the other hand, have often been so alienated from organized religious life as to shun its history as relatively unimportant, or at best, as foreign to their concern. Some, moreover, have no doubt sought to avoid the bitterness of religious controversy. A prominent newspaper correspondent, Paul S. Mower, has asserted that he learned early in his career as a reporter to refrain if possible from any discussion of Catholics, Christian Scientists, and Jews, some of whom would misinterpret anything that was written so as veritably to stir up a hornet's nest.[3] However that may be, various persons in all churches have at times resented even the slightest implication of criticism relating to their household of faith. Yet, the mature person—Catholic, Protestant or Jew—is usually receptive to an impartial approach to truth, and the present writer has earnestly endeavored to present this account of American religious history in a spirit of rigid objectivity.

To bring the whole story of American religious history within the confines of a single volume is manifestly impossible. The present effort, therefore, is confined to a discussion of a central aspect of American religious development from 1865 to 1900. This was an era of rapid scientific progress, urban growth, and intellectual adjustment, and the last quarter century of it has been aptly termed by Professor Arthur Meier Schlesinger, Sr. of Harvard University as "A Critical Period in American Religion."[4]

Certainly, drastic changes associated with the New Geology, the evolutionary hypothesis, comparative religions, the Higher Criticism of the Bible, among other influences, had a very significant impact on the thought and life of the American churches. The impact of this crisis, as analyzed by a representative of Roman Catholicism, Bishop John L. Spalding of the diocese of Peoria, Illinois, was explained thus:

> The wavering of religious belief has unsettled all other things so that nothing seems any longer to rest upon a firm and immovable basis. The new theories are in the air, and precautionary measures are ineffectual, at least with regard to society in general. . . . The old Protestant controversy is as obsolete as the dress of the Pilgrim Fathers. . . . The old disputes will doubtless survive for a time, and individuals and even classes may be helped by them, but the real issue so far as the active mind of the age is concerned, has already been transferred to quite other grounds, and it is our immediate and urgent duty to fit ourselves for the new conflict, which is not between the Church and the sects, but between the Church and infidelity.[5]

Allan Nevins, then of Columbia University, in an introduction to a volume dealing with American Free Thought during this period, called attention to Matthew Arnold's famous contrast between Hellenism which stressed "an unclouded clearness of mind" and Hebraism which emphasized "strictness of conscience." Nevins pointed out the need for a resolving of the tensions between the two in order to secure a well-rounded national character.[6] Unquestionably, never in American history were such tensions greater than in the period under discussion. In the present volume an effort has been made to summarize the conflicts in American religious thought and life as they existed in 1865, and then to trace through the life stories of hundreds of individuals the adjustments which were made to changing currents of thought and action. In a very real sense the basic struggle was over by 1900, and the story of the conflict of faith in church-going America since 1900 seems to be largely an interesting development of patterns determined during this period.

Many thoughtful people of our day have often been appalled at the amazing religious illiteracy of many Americans. Andrew D. White, the eminent first president of Cornell University, declared in his *Autobiography* that his experience had taught him that he should never desire revolutionary changes in religion, for, he asserted, "Such changes, to be good, must be evolutionary, gradual, and in obedience to slowly increasing knowledge." Whatever may be the truth found in such a statement, the present author trusts that the volume here presented may be a modest contribution to the "increasing knowledge" of all Americans concerning the basic struggles of faith on the part of those who participated in the organized religious life of late nineteenth century America. Though the illustrations used are representative rather than exhaustive in scope, it is hoped that they may be somewhat stimulating to those fairly familiar with the history of the American churches as well as somewhat enlightening to the less well-informed but intelligent "average citizen."

CHAPTER I

A CHURCHGOING, TOLERANT AMERICA

On the evening of Lincoln's assassination, April 14, 1865, an Ohio businessman, Rufus Dawes and his wife, destined to be the parents of a Vice President of the United States, were on a belated honeymoon in Washington. They had tickets to "Our American Cousin" at Ford's Theatre for that night and looked forward to seeing President Lincoln in the audience. But, the young wife was weary from much sightseeing, and they decided to postpone the opportunity to see the President until Sunday. Then, they planned to go to the New York Avenue Presbyterian Church which Lincoln "scarcely ever failed to attend."[1] Fate decreed that Lincoln's death should preclude any chance of their seeing him in life, but the incident is but one illustration of the fact that in those years America was definitely a churchgoing nation.

This aspect of American life was deeply imbedded in long established traditions. Much of the vigor of thought and culture in the Republic had been derived from the New England Puritanism. The Yankee heritage had stressed an immediate responsibility of the individual to God. But, man does not live unto himself alone, and the Church had been central in the constant striving for the establishment of the "holy community" after the manner of the Geneva of John Calvin.[2] Intimately intertwined with the prevailing culture, Congregationalism had been more than a sect, indeed "a social reform movement with a complete ideology."[3]

By 1865, the religious unity of New England life had been shattered by the rise of the Baptists, Methodists, Universalists, and Unitarians,[4] and by the large influx of Roman

Catholics.⁵ Yet, the prevailing power of the New England
churches was indicated by James Russell Lowell, when he
wrote in August 1865, "I shall never be a poet till I get out
of the pulpit, and New England was all meeting house when
I was growing up."⁶

Everywhere, the churches of America were varied in doctrine, organization, and religious practice; but, beneath the
differences there was a widespread area of agreement which
gave a vital core to American social and cultural life. A
recent president of the American Historical Association has
pointed out that after 1865, "the traditional Christian approach was still dominant . . . Orthodox doctrine taught the
reality of original sin, but it also taught men to believe in
their ability to struggle against sin and in the possibility of
redemption."⁷

An important historian and political scientist with an
international reputation, Goldwin Smith, was to summarize
the situation in 1891:

> We must remember that, whatever may be our philo-
> sophic school, we are still living under the influence of
> theism, and most of us under that of Christianity. We
> have inherited a Christian or a theistic code of ethics,
> and characters cast in a corresponding mold. This is
> particularly the case with regard to those gentler virtues
> the reverence for which is the special protection of the
> weak against the strong.⁸

When President Charles Eliot of Harvard at a Commencement Address at Smith College in 1879 had asserted
that it "is a common opinion that interest in the great themes
of God and immortality, and life and death, has died out,"
he was strongly challenged by publicists such as E. L. Godkin of the *Nation,* who affirmed that interest in them was as
strong as ever.⁹

At any rate, at Harvard itself, the traditional religious
services, but with an emphasis on generally accepted ethical

and spiritual values, were maintained. Until 1886 there was compulsory attendance for undergraduates at daily prayers and Sunday services. After 1886, when attendance became voluntary, an effort was made to make religious ministrations more meaningful. Daily worship was enriched by a full choir of men and boys, and a new hymn book and book of readings, adapted to the needs of young men, came into use. Special services arranged for Thursday afternoons were attended by many, and a staff of University preachers, available also for religious counseling, was appointed. These included men of broad but towering spirituality, Edward Everett Hale, Alexander McKenzie, Phillips Brooks and George A. Gordon.[10] Hale who gained a niche in the history of American literature by his authorship of *The Man Without a Country* was a Unitarian but not one (as the orthodox complained in regard to some others) whose message had become literary expressions of "pale negations" such as echoed a fundamental "skepticism." Hale believed emphatically that the Church constitutes the "body of Christ" and that Unitarianism must "articulate first, last, and always that it was at work 'in the name of our Lord Jesus Christ.' " To him every Christian minister "must be in close touch with life and give his chief attention to the difficulties of life, for which the teachings of Jesus Christ were a true panacea, something that could cure every evil and without which nothing could be cured."[11] To him, Unitarianism was a tested faith that made life tolerable for "care-wrung men, fear-worn women," to whom God had "made clear the mystery of godliness" and to whom "the heavenly life of the Brother—the chosen son" of God must ever be an inspiration.

With such Unitarians, members of more orthodox bodies found much common ground. Lyman Abbott who had served both Congregational and Presbyterian congregations, believed that Unitarianism "was not merely nor mainly an endeavor to substitute one dogmatism for another." It was in part a protest against "a too mathematical and scholastic" doctrine of the Trinity—a protest which, it seems to some of us, rejected, with scholastic formularies, "some valuable and vital truth." Abbott felt that the Unitarian system of theology could not survive but that "its insistence on a simplicity of faith and on a substitution of ethico-spiritual for dogmatic tests of character" had made itself felt in every Christian church.[12]

Another Harvard preacher was the famed Phillips Brooks, who had been christened in a Unitarian church but had been reared in an atmosphere of liberal Episcopalism and had become a leader of Broad Church tendencies in that Church. Accordingly, his power was based on no sectarian emphasis as, according to one student, he gave to Harvard students "a gift of unsurpassable richness," stressing in a never to be forgotten way that "if the material forces of life are not to wreck the world, the spiritual forces must hold them in check, indeed control them."[13]

At Wellesley no sectarian influence was apparent, but when Alice Freeman (Palmer) started to teach there in 1879, required prayers twice daily led by teachers, daily Bible classes, and Sunday services conducted by visiting ministers were part of the regular order of life.

Alice Freeman later became President of the college, and her secretary came to write of her strong religious motivation:

"Underneath her cheerfulness, her keen sense of humor, her thoughtfulness of others, her joy in all that make life lovely, there ran a current of confidence and unhesitating trust in her Heavenly Father. She consequently never appeared perplexed. . . ."[14]

At Smith College in the years around 1882-3, students were expected to attend morning worship every day except Sunday in Social Hall, and on Sundays family worship in the various dwelling houses was followed by attendance at church and by a vesper service later in the day.[15] Elsewhere in New England colleges the formal expression of religious life was not dissimilar.

Even at state universities such as the University of Michigan there was a surprising unanimity in religious expression. Of course, there were the various denominational churches in Ann Arbor, but in 1874, for example, the Y.M.C.A. was active, and each of the four undergraduate classes held its own prayer meetings. During that winter, every evening the largest University lecture room was full for religious meetings, and in the town itself there were five daily prayer meetings (one for ladies, one for business men, etc.) with a union preaching service in the evening. When Lucy Salmon, later to be a noted professor of history at Vassar, left Ann Arbor, she wrote:

> There is so much warm sympathy here among the Christian students and professors that it seems almost easy sometimes to be a Christian and I shall dread going away, but I suppose there is the same feeling among Christians everywhere only I have not cared so much about finding how great it is. . . .[16]

At Western Reserve College (then located at Hudson, Ohio) in the 1870's a morning prayer meeting at eight o'clock every day, a required church service on Sunday, and a student missionary society gave corporate unity to the college religious life. The more zealous religious students conducted Bible classes in neighboring country school houses on Sunday afternoons.[17] Colleges farther to the south and west were not without similar activities.

Outside of college communities, denominational loyalties were often subordinated to an emphasis on common beliefs and practices. One expression of this was in the great interdenominational revivals in various cities such as those of Dwight L. Moody and Ira D. Sankey. People of many faiths attended, and the audiences were often numbered in the thousands.[18]

An effort to bring together "members of different communions in fraternal Christian intercourse and in the discussion of themes of a common doctrinal and practical import," found expression in the Evangelical Alliance. It had been founded in London in 1846, and a vigorous American branch which fostered many cooperative enterprises was organized in 1867. The greatest international gathering of the Alliance finally met in New York City in 1873, after delay because of the Franco-Prussian War (1870-1). The meetings brought together scholars like Professor Dorner of Tübingen, ecclesiastics like the Dean of Canterbury, internationally known preachers, and believers from all parts of the world such as the noted Indian convert, Narayan-Sheshadri.[19] Subsequent gatherings were held in Washington (1887) and in Chicago (1893). Later, the movement developed into the Federal (later National) Council of Churches.

At the grass roots level also religious comity was widely in evidence. William Jennings Bryan's parents were Baptists, but when the boy found an especially congenial church home among the Presbyterians, he was permitted to join that denomination.[20] In Kansas, William Allen White (around 1880) was accustomed to attending a Disciples Sunday School at 9 o'clock, the Presbyterian one at noon, and that conducted by the Methodists at 2:30.[21] Champ Clark, later speaker of the House of Representatives, from Missouri, tells us that his wife was an Old School Presbyterian while he was a Disciple (as his parents had been). Clark and his wife attended church with each other (the children being baptized as Presbyterians) and religious argument was shunned.[22] Henry Watterson, eminent Kentucky journalist, was born into the Presbyterian Church, received lay baptism as a babe in a Roman Catholic church from a zealous Irish nurse when he was seemingly near death, and was married in the Disciples Church.[23] Richard Owen, prominent Indiana scientist (and son of Robert Owen) was a Presbyterian, but when in his later years he found no church of that denomination in New Harmony, he worshipped in the Episcopal Church and on occasion filled the pulpit of the Methodist Church.[24]

Roscoe Pound, born in 1870, and later Dean of Harvard Law School, came from a family of mixed religious antecedents (Methodist, Universalist, Presbyterian, and Quaker). The parents never affiliated with any church and exhibited broad tolerance in allowing the children to follow their own consciences (a policy which the son said got them nowhere). For a time the son attended a German Methodist Sunday School; later he became associated with the Episcopalianism of his wife; and in his later years he was to join the Society of Friends.[25]

In the opening of the newer sections of the West, common religious interests are illustrated by the case of the rush to Oklahoma (after 1889), where vast tracts previously reserved for Indians, were opened to "boomers" who raced to find the most promising parcels of land. Missionaries were on hand to accompany the movement, and services at first were held on street corners, in unoccupied store buildings or in some homesteader's sod house. The quiet insistence of one or more women who sensed the need for religious expression sometimes led to the holding of Sunday School classes in smaller communities. Such "Gospel Songs" as "Beulah Land," "Bringing in the Sheaves," and "Let the Lower Lights Be Burning" were used, tattered old hymn books having been collected from many homes. A significant occasion in the life of the community, it brought together young and old alike, the youths riding their ponies and families with many children arriving in lumber wagons.[26] Lonely people in a new location often seemed starved for religious expression and turned out on the hottest days to pack a church when a visiting home missionary was present.[27] Denominational differences were inevitably minimized as the settlement would join in a pioneer community religious service.[28]

Oliver Wendell Holmes, a Unitarian, had often been a regular attendant at Episcopal services at Pittsfield where the rector was "doing admirable work in the most catholic, unsectarian way," and he sometimes attended the Baptist

Church at Beverly "not without edification."[29] An intellectual Unitarian such as Moorfield Storey could good-humoredly assert that he was wholly tolerant of the "Anglican regularities" of his wife.[30] Even a rather radical Unitarian like Wendell Phillips had come to recognize the practical benefits of orthodox Congregationalism. By 1880, he had come to believe that whatever had been narrow and inhumane in its doctrines could not have been the "main character" of its teaching, for otherwise the New England known far and wide for its generous, energetic, hopeful, independent spirit, "ready for every good work, and willing for every necessary sacrifice" during the nineteenth century could not have emerged.[31]

Many Roman Catholics exhibited a large degree of tolerance, though not many were prepared to go so far as Chief Justice Roger B. Taney of an old Maryland Catholic family who earlier in the century had refused to permit clerical interference with the education of his daughters in the Episcopal faith of their mother.[32] Charles J. Bonaparte, prominent Marylander and a grand nephew of Napoleon I, was an aggressive Catholic who gloried in the increase in numbers of the Catholic Church. Yet, even he was somewhat tolerant, and his beloved wife each Sunday attended the Protestant Church of which she was a member. Among the French of Louisiana, a rather easy-going religious liberalism was sometimes expressed. The well known Civil War leader of the Confederacy, General P. G. T. Beauregard, had earlier written to a friend that he had come to believe that anyone of any religion would attain salvation if he lived a good life and believed in God. When Beauregard died in 1893, a friendly priest conducted services at the home, commenting that the General had deep religious feelings but had not been very regular with formal religious practices.[33]

Walter Rauschenbusch, born to pious German Baptists in Rochester, New York, and destined to be a beacon light of the Social Gospel in American Protestantism, was a boyhood friend of Edward J. Hanna, later to be Roman Catholic

Archbishop of San Francisco. When Rauschenbusch went abroad to study, he took time to visit his old friend, who was a student for the priesthood in Rome.[34]

When Archbishop John Ireland of St. Paul had reached the height of his influence, Robert J. Burdette who had known him as a Civil War chaplain and who had become a popular orator and as a Baptist preacher "the physician of the merry heart," could write to him:

> My dear Archbishop Ireland—For you are my Archbishop, aren't you. I was a private soldier . . . when the entire brigade called you its Chaplain. And time and promotion has not moved you from the place you then held in a soldier's heart. There was a boy's love and reverence then, there is the reverence and a love of a man today. This is your birthday. . . .[35]

Roman Catholics in large cities sometimes attended Protestant services, after Mass, to hear a famed Protestant preacher, and in turn an eloquent Irish-American prelate like Cardinal Gibbons of Baltimore might find an occasion that a large part of his congregation was made up of non-Catholics who had come for the uplift of a stirring uncontroversial sermon on a theme like, "Am I My Brother's Keeper?"[36]

Gibbons, rather daring in the adjustments which he had made as a missionary bishop in North Carolina, had in those days ventured to preach in a Methodist pulpit, with a Methodist choir, and a Protestant version of the Bible. Indeed, Gibbons was sometimes inclined to be all things to all men, for, as his first biographer suggests, he not only was a man of many moods but seemed like "several men in one." Gibbons could write a popular, appealing *Faith of Our Fathers* (1876) which won many converts to Catholicism.[37] But, he was also the author of *Our Catholic Heritage* (1889), in the introduction to which he made it clear that he had nothing to say against any Christian denomination which at least affirmed the divine mission of Christ. Of such, he said, "I would gladly hold out to them the right hand of fellowship, so long as they unite with us in striking a common foe." Understandably a Presbyterian clergyman at Princeton University hailed this as "another sign of the growth of an American spirit in the Roman Church."[38] Moreover, although some of the Catholic clergy might not relish the observance of a religious occasion of Puritan origin,[39] Gibbons in 1881 issued an invitation to the laity and clergy of the archdiocese of Baltimore to attend Mass as a proper means of celebrating the national Thanksgiving Day.[40]

Indeed, it often seemed that when an individual had been imbued definitely with the values of the Classical-Judaeo-Christian tradition and earnestly sought to make them effective in his life, it was difficult for sensitive persons of another denominational allegiance to disavow a basic spiritual kinship. All this had meant a decided change from the century before the Civil War. In the eighteenth century a Presbyterian stone mason in Scotland had been tried and perhaps excommunicated for helping to build an Episcopal Church. But John LaFarge, the gifted artist, who was inextricably but hardly devoutly attached to Roman Catholicism, found bigotry foreign to his nature, and his respect for the beliefs of others was illimitable. Hence, his "religiously attuned" mind found artistic expression in innumerable churches which he decorated with superb skill,[41] and much of his best work was in Protestant churches like Trinity Church, Boston and the Church of the Ascension, New York.

Propinquity often seems to dissolve ecclesiastically implanted sentiments, for, as one observer noted:

> When a Roman Catholic boy has been captain of a High School nine or eleven, and has depended for school victories which are much dearer to him than prizes or scholarship, upon the fidelity to duty of a Protestant companion, it is impossible for him to believe that his

Protestant play fellow is doomed to eternal torment because he has not been confirmed in the Catholic communion; and it is equally impossible for the Protestant
to regard his captain as a child of the Scarlet Woman
and a citizen of the Modern Babylon.[42]

Joseph H. Twichell, long the vigorous and gifted pastor
of the liberal Asylum Hill Congregational Church, Hartford,
Connecticut after 1865, had during the Civil War been the
chaplain of an extremely rough regiment. Under such rigorous activity, Twichell's closest friend had been a Jesuit
chaplain, Father J. B. O'Hagan, and the two had often
shared a blanket in the field. Such mutuality of experience
seemed practically to dissolve for the two the importance
of their ecclesiastical differences. When O'Hagan became
President of Holy Cross College, Worcester, Massachusetts,
the two remained close friends, and Twichell's fellow towns-
man, Mark Twain, became a third member of the intimate
group. For Twain to visit O'Hagan was to enjoy a merry
time with "a most jolly and delightful" friend, and the close
relationship was clearly indicated by their ability to jest
among themselves about matters of popular prejudice which
divided many worthy people. Twain could write that he was
wholly informed about the machinations of Jesuits, for he
had read the Sunday School books, and that he accordingly
knew full well that O'Hagan was snaring Twichell and him
into his den in order to skin the two and make religious
parchment out of them after the ancient style of the Jesuits
since the days of Loyola, but that he was taking the chance
and trusting in Providence![43]

Agnes Repplier, later an essayist of considerable reputation, was a Catholic who often wrote on matters which non-
Catholics knew little about or were inclined to misunder-
stand. But, in her home community of Philadelphia, she
became a friend of the able Rev. William Furness, noted
Unitarian minister. Honesty compelled her to recognize

him as spiritually entitled to be considered "a saint," though understandably she admitted that she was "loath to acknowledge Unitarian saints."[44]

The fluidity of American social life meant that potential religious barriers were often disregarded. Cardinal Gibbons on one occasion was a guest at a private dinner party in Baltimore where other members of the group included Rev. William Paret, Protestant Episcopal Bishop of Maryland, and Dr. James S. B. Hodges, rector of St. Paul's Episcopal Church.[45]

A cultivated Presbyterian minister and author like Henry Van Dyke could later write movingly of his long friendship with Maurice Francis Egan, distinguished Catholic essayist:

> He was a firm Catholic and I an equally firm Presbyterian, but ecclesiastical differences never divided us. No doubt he would stretch the doctrine of 'invincible ignorance' enough to give me a good hope, and certainly I made the doctrine of 'prevenient grace' include him. . . .[46]

The experience of the Protestant family in Wisconsin in which Robert M. LaFollette was one of the children, was not unlike that of thousands of other families of pioneer days who had found that necessity compelled cooperation and tolerance among those of different racial traditions and religious faiths. Latent bigotry evaporated in an atmosphere of neighborliness.[47]

While a professor at Notre Dame, South Bend, Indiana, in the 1880's, the Catholic essayist, Maurice F. Egan, circulated freely among persons of different faiths and found little religious prejudice. Among social leaders there was Mrs. Clem Studebaker, wife of the well known industrialist of the period. Egan found her a valiant Methodist "who loved good books and was interested in all subjects that lead to righteousness." At the hospitable Egan home, "The Lilacs," no narrow prejudices limited the guest list which might include an Episcopalian High Church rector and the progressive Roman Catholic, Bishop John L. Spalding, who on one occasion engaged in a stimulating discussion of Unitarianism.

In many communities, those of different faiths enjoyed sociability and a type of Christian fellowship with those of other churches. People would turn out in a community to patronize the highly esteemed "chicken pie socials" of the Methodists, the suppers where the Baptists served tempting pies, the dramatic offerings (such as Longfellow's "Box of Pandora") of the Episcopalians, and the lucrative bazaars or fairs sponsored by the Catholics.[48]

Throughout the country, works of charity of Roman Catholic orders were widely recognized and often enthusiastically supported by non-Catholics. Frequently this spirit was reciprocated, as when the renowned Unitarian minister of Syracuse, New York, Samuel J. May, died in 1871. He was distinguished for his activities among the poor, and the Catholic Sisters of Charity in the community attended the grave-side ceremonies at the time of his burial.[49]

Cardinal Gibbons, moreover, had no hesitation in responding to Protestant efforts to enlist his aid in supporting what he agreed was worthy moral effort. In 1888, he endorsed a petition to Congress, sponsored by a New York Protestant minister, asking for a law against Sunday work in relation to government mail, for military services, and interstate commerce. Again, in Maryland when the Sunday laws began to be relaxed he joined with Protestant ministers in protesting the "lowering of the moral tone of the Lord's Day."[50]

As Protestants came to know individual Catholics more intimately, old prejudices tended to disappear. Immediately after the Civil War, one who had been an Irish Catholic boy in the elementary and grammar schools of Lowell, Massachusetts, later declared that the teachers were of the strictest Puritan mold with the severest notions of duty and a distrust of every aspect of Catholicism. Catholic boys who were absent from class to serve Mass on Good Friday were publicly reprimanded and punished at the school.[51] But two decades later a Catholic lad at Newport, Rhode Island, found the teachers to be "of the good old New England variety," of a type who showed "full consideration" for Catholic religious beliefs.[52]

Many Roman Catholic leaders on their part had worked zealously to promote cordial relations with other Christian groups. In Philadelphia, September 1887, at the Centennial celebration of the American Constitutional Convention, Cardinal Gibbons offered prayer, although Bishop Henry C. Potter of the Episcopal Church of New York had also been associated with the ceremonies. Gibbons had consulted other Catholic leaders, and the Holy See had reacted favorably to his participation.[53]

Father Edward McGlynn of New York, a controversial figure in the history of Catholicism in America, went so far as to contribute a statement at a memorial service for Henry Ward Beecher in which he said that no one knew so well how "to minimize the differences that seem to separate us" as Beecher.

One of the foremost leaders in an effort to increase mutual respect and toleration among Christian peoples was Bishop John J. Keane, rector of the Catholic University of America and later Archbishop of Dubuque, Iowa. In May 1890, he delivered a lecture at the University of Notre Dame on "Christian Patriotism," in which he urged toleration with the motto, "Union in essentials, tolerance in non-essentials, charity to all,"[54] a slogan which was especially being emphasized by German Reformed theologians in Pennsylvania.[55]

Later in the same year (October 23) he appeared in his sacerdotal robes to give the Dudleian lecture from the pulpit of Appleton Chapel, Harvard University. He did not hesitate to announce the two hymns (though both were composed by Protestants and are usually identified with Protestant services), "Nearer My God to Thee" and "Rock of

Ages," and dismissed the congregation with the customary apostolic benediction.[56] This aroused wonderment in some Catholic circles. Bishop Keane considered a request to preach at Cornell University, but Bishop McQuaid of the diocese of Rochester had asked him not to speak at Cornell, and Bishop Keane finally declined the invitation. He did, nevertheless, give a Yale Law School lecture in New Haven (February 1892) on "The Church and the Social Problems of the Day."

Keane also caused consternation in some Catholic circles by preaching a funeral sermon in his prelatial robes in the Senate Chamber in Washington (June, 1892) over the body of Senator John S. Barbour of Virginia, a non-Catholic. When this was reported to the Cardinal who was Prefect of the Congregation of the Propaganda in Rome, inquiry was made in the United States as to the circumstances. Cardinal Gibbons, who loved to use the pageantry of the Church "to display its beautiful ceremonies and to have heard its holy truths," strongly defended Keane. Barbour, it was stated, belonged to no Protestant church, had a Catholic wife, attended Mass on Sundays, and had indicated an intention of becoming a Catholic. There is no evidence that Vatican authorities were not satisfied.[57]

Keane had extensive additional associations with non-Catholic organizations, lecturing at Brooklyn Institute of Arts and Sciences on "Leo XIII and the Social Problems of the Day" (January, 1892) and "The Great Lessons Taught by History" (January, 1893). During February 1893 he again lectured at Cambridge, Massachusetts, and in June, 1893, Harvard bestowed upon him an honorary doctorate. When Dr. Philip Schaff, a German-born Presbyterian scholar of Union Theological Seminary, New York, who was known for his ecumenical views and his disdain for exaggerated or false notions concerning Catholic doctrine, made a visit to Washington, D. C. he took time to call on Keane. Reporting the incident, Schaff explained, "He came out and embraced me. Was not that remarkable?"[58]

Keane's tolerant interfaith efforts reached a high point when he was instrumental in securing Catholic participation in the World's Parliament of Religions at the Columbian Exposition in Chicago in the fall of 1893. Archbishop Ireland was also favorably inclined, and the powerful influence of Cardinal Gibbons was secured.[59] The Roman Catholic Archbishops in the United States, after much discussion, had in November 1892, instructed Keane to arrange for twenty Catholic speakers to expound Catholic doctrine during the sessions. Keane took a prominent part in the meetings.[60] Rev. John H. Barrows, Presbyterian minister, who was the key figure in this Interfaith Parliament, later exclaimed:

> Those who saw the Greek Archbishop, Dionysius Latas, greeting the Catholic Bishop Keane, with the apostolic kiss on the cheek and words of brotherly love, those who heard Bishop Keane relate how Archbishop Ireland and himself finding that they were unable to enter the Hall of Columbus on account of the throng, went to the Hall of Washington and presided over the Jewish Conference; . . . and the scores of thousands who beheld day after day the representatives of the great historic religions joining in the Lord's Prayer, felt profoundly that a new era of religious fraternity had dawned.[61]

Accounts like this were exaggerated in some Catholic circles where extreme consternation was expressed regarding this fraternization with non-Catholics. Finally Pope Leo XIII ruled in 1895 against further participation of Catholics in interfaith gatherings. A year later Keane was removed from the rectorship of the Catholic University of America on the grounds that a definite time limit had to be established for the office, but the action was commonly considered as a rebuke to "liberal" prelates.[62]

Keane, as Rector, was succeeded by Thomas J. Conaty, one who was not definitely conservative or liberal. He had taken no active part in interfaith movements but he had read a paper, "The Relations of the Catholic Church to Temperance" at a Unitarian Church Conference in 1894 and another paper, "The Roman Catholic Church and the Educational Movement" at the Pan-American Congress in Toronto in 1895.[63] He, moreover, in practice had repudiated the view of extremely conservative Catholic clergy who shunned participation in constructive community enterprises with non-Catholics. As a priest in Worcester, Massachusetts for fourteen years (1873-1887) he had served on the local school board and for twelve years on the Board of the Worcester Free Library.

A leader of American life of Jewish background such as Henry Morgenthau who was destined to become United States Minister to Turkey, found that the sources of the burning idealism of his youth had been fed by the fire of various spiritual teachings. The Jewish precepts taught him by the rabbi who led the congregation in which he was reared; the inspiring association which he had enjoyed with a saintly New York Quaker doctor; the noble messages to which he had listened as they were preached from Christian pulpits like that of the Presbyterian, Dr. John Hall; and the "austere and lofty" Ethical Culture philosophy of Dr. Felix Adler—all these had helped to mold a useful and enlightened personality.[64]

The widespread acceptance of certain basic attitudes often meant that those within the fold of the Church in America—especially within Protestantism—could without undue difficulty find a religious haven which seemed to meet their individual needs. Thus, George H. Putnam, destined to be a noted publisher, when he returned to New York in 1865 after service in the Union army, was a Baptist who had done some chaplain's work in the field.[65] But, he had reacted against Baptist Calvinism and was attracted by the preaching of Dr. Edward A. Washburn, "a scholarly and fairminded" rector at Calvary Episcopal Church, who had been reared as a Congregationalist. Occasionally he heard

Dr. Samuel Osgood (1812-1880), a conservative Unitarian, who was soon (1870) to enter the Episcopal fold. For a time he also participated in the First Unitarian Society where Dr. Henry W. Bellows, "clearheaded and wide-minded" and with a sense of humor emphasized spiritual values from an intellectual viewpoint. He also drew much satisfaction from the sermons of the theologically radical Octavius B. Frothingham of Third Unitarian Society.[66]

The German-born John Augustus Roebling, noted suspension bridge builder, was somewhat of a Universalist in his views and his wife was a Lutheran, but the family maintained a pew in the First Presbyterian Church, Trenton, "to enhance the family respectability."[67]

As will be indicated later, many persons distressed by the "arid rationalism" of Unitarianism, by the rather scholastic theology of the Calvinistic Presbyterians and Congregationalists, by a distaste for Methodist revivalism, by the appeal of the *Book of Common Prayer,* or by the social prestige of many Episcopal churches, made the transition into the Episcopal Church.[68] At other times and places, some of Congregational, Presbyterian, Episcopalian, or Lutheran antecedents were carried into the Methodist or Baptist folds by the practical vigor or the emotional appeal of the evangelistic services of those religious bodies.[69] Thus, the parents of Frances Willard, temperance reformer, had been Congregationalists in Ohio, but the only church available in Janesville, Wisconsin, was one on a Methodist circuit, and they and their daughter became enthusiastic Methodists.[70]

But, when Methodism became increasingly a more prosperous and less emotional communion, some "old timers" among them, with a nostalgia for the old ways, found a spiritual home in groups like that which became the Church of the Nazarene.[71] And, when some left the older churches to embrace Christian Science, an Episcopalian bishop could tolerantly express the belief that the new faith seemed to be performing a type of work which "the historic churches have sometimes neglected to do."[72]

This flexibility of American religious life made for great charity in regard to the views of others. It came to be widely recognized that each denomination has "its own peculiar merits, and has rendered to the community and the Church of Christ its own peculiar service." Thus in 1887, a leading Congregationalist found that Episcopalianism "by its historic continuity and its liturgical order" had contributed much; the Presbyterians had manifested "a unique power to educate in Christian truth" those who already had received the gospel; Methodism "by its system of circuit riders, its emotional theology, and its free-pew system" had done great evangelistic work in city, village, and country; while the Congregationalists had maintained a large degree of freedom for the individual church and pastor.

It is not strange then, when Bishop William Lawrence was consecrated as Episcopalian bishop of Massachusetts in Trinity Church, Boston in October, 1893, the sermon by Bishop Henry Benjamin Whipple of the diocese of Minnesota (who himself had been christened a Presbyterian) embodied a plea for the reunion of all Christians including Unitarians. Following him, the Archbishop of Zante, Greece, of the Eastern Orthodox Church, stressed the Protestant and Catholic characteristics of Episcopalianism and its responsibility in the movement toward church unity.[73]

Before Catholic officials definitely frowned on inter-faith meetings a rather remarkable brotherly spirit was sometimes shown. Thus, at a Congregational Church in New Haven, Connecticut the Men's Club of the church on one Sunday night presented a discussion of, "Ways in which Protestants and Catholics can Cooperate." A local Catholic priest sat in the pulpit with the pastor, and the discussion was led by two New Haven judges, one a Catholic and the other a Protestant.[74]

One who worked tirelessly for greater church cooperation and eventual unity was William Chauncy Langdon, Protestant Episcopal clergyman, who organized a number of scholars into a group seeking union of the Episcopal,

Presbyterian, and Congregational churches. At his funeral in 1895 in Grace Church, Providence, Rhode Island, thirty-five clergy of eleven different denominations partook of communion together.

Yet, these harbingers of Christian understanding were not the only forces on the religious scene. Before his death Langdon had been keenly disappointed at the unfavorable attitude of the Protestant Episcopal General Convention of 1895 toward the Union which he devoutly sought. Furthermore, in every large communion there were intelligent and sincere men of good will whose carefully considered convictions limited their sympathy for inter-faith movements. There were also large numbers of Protestant bigots and narrow-minded Catholics whose ill-informed prejudices effectively checked any latent spirit of brotherhood.

CHAPTER II

ROOTS OF ANTICLERICAL INDIVIDUALISM

In the United States, various influences that had deep roots in the traditions of the Western World were, actually or potentially, a challenge to the authority of the Church. The struggle between freedom and authority was an age-old one. If the Church secured the unquestioned conformity of its followers, undoubtedly its external strength was like that of a mighty army subject to a military-like discipline. But, if such discipline proved inflexible, the role of the seer and prophet (never wholly suppressed in the Jewish-Christian tradition) might be lost, and the Church might seem to some like a great museum, cherishing merely the treasures of the past.

The Protestant Reformation had challenged the authority of the Medieval Church, but the most gifted Reformation leaders had insisted that authority in religious life was necessary to the corporate life of Christianity. Zwingli, Luther, and Calvin all had sought, as they thought, to purify the Church, and not wholly without reluctance did they finally participate in the founding of new ecclesiastical organizations.[1] Calvinism and Lutheranism were, under the circumstances, led to establish their own norms of church discipline. Yet, a strong impetus had been given to the severe criticism of church authority when it seemed to violate the insights of individual conscience.

Moreover, in those areas of the United States where traditions of German pietism or of Methodism were strong, the churchly precedents of the older religious bodies were, in some respects, minimized to even a greater degree. Pietism had been a protest of individualism against institutionalism

and continued to emphasize personal religious life rather
than conformity to external standards, although doctrines
were not challenged.[2] Similarly, Methodism stressed a "me-
thodical" Christian life rather than church traditions, although its ecclesiastical power could often be effective indeed.

Early New England had been the abode of a church-
dominated society which had sent its own dissenters like
Roger Williams and Anne Hutchinson into exile. Puritan
leaders, like Calvin before them, had realized that unbridled
individualism and sectarianism leads often to fanaticism and
to a fragmentation of the witness of the Christian community.[3] Yet, in the long run, the Protestant idea of "justification by faith," involving a personal experience between
the individual and God tended to impair seriously the institutional authority of the Church. As pointed out elsewhere,
this combined with the individualism which the rugged aspects of New England life had tended to foster, contributed
to the development of the Puritan principle which insisted
on the right of self-expression "uncorrupted by privilege,
unfettered by authority, and untrammeled by tradition."

In areas where New Englanders had settled this had
sometimes borne fruit in a variety of "isms," some of them
of a rather extravagant sort. Needless to say, some came to
regret the apparent religious instability which resulted.[4]
Characteristic of this dissatisfaction was the remark of a Congregational minister at Hartford, Connecticut, in 1882, following the presentation of some rather liberal views by a
brother, "The advanced ground taken would compare with
that of an architect who should now propose an improvement in St. Peter's at Rome by the addition of fifty bay-
windows." Unitarianism, moreover, grounded in New England dissidence had gone even further. Some of the results
were indicated by E. L. Godkin, Irish-born editor of the
Nation, who had been attracted to the Third Unitarian
Society of New York City by his own "profound weariness
of doctrines." The gifted pastor, Octavius Brooks Frothing-

ham, seemed, however, to represent the bitter fruits of
private judgment unchecked by the insights of traditional
religion. Godkin complained in 1866 that Frothingham had
become increasingly "a snappish dialectician," boring one
with as much dogmatism as to what ought not to be believed as any orthodox preacher did in his insistence on
what one ought to believe. Godkin felt that Frothingham
discussed "nothing but opinions," giving one a definite impression of the profound narrowness of so-called "progressive radicals."[5] In the same year, Samuel Bowles, renowned
editor of the Springfield (Massachusetts) *Republican* went
to hear him but found him "bitter and severe" on even the
Unitarians.[6] Even to his sophisticated cousin, Henry Adams,
Frothingham's faith had seemed to become mere "skepticism."[7] Eventually this skepticism overtook Frothingham
himself, for by 1881 he had given up his church work asserting that it "appears to lead to nothing, and may have been
grounded upon mistaken premises." Among such troubled
souls there seemed to be a spiritual confusion resulting
from their search for the fruits of the Tree of Knowledge
through liberal inquiry and for the fruits of the Tree of Life
which would bring spiritual certitude.

Some endeavored to find an answer for the problem of
certainty by seeking an authority which would speak with
unequivocal assurance. There were those, both within the
Episcopal and the Roman Catholic Churches, who found
such authority in the beliefs of their organizations in Apostolic Succession.

One such individual was Edward Abbott, brother of the
influential Congregationalist, Lyman Abbott. Ordained a
Congregational minister in 1863, he became an Episcopalian
(1878), serving long as rector of St. James' Church, North
Cambridge, Massachusetts. He placed great emphasis on
the Church "as a Divine Institution, with a divinely appointed threefold ministry, and divinely constituted Sacraments." Another individual of somewhat similar views was
Ferdinand C. Ewer, who in 1871 organized the Anglo-Catho-

lic congregation of St. Ignatius, New York City, as one which would emphasize the Apostolic tradition and Catholicity rather than almost unlimited private judgment within the Episcopal Church.

Among some in the Episcopal church, for whom Apostolic Succession was a precious doctrine, a drift toward Rome —which made emphatic insistence on its own historic continuity—had been definitely noticeable, but was less significant than during the earlier Oxford Movement.[8]

Yet, many Episcopalians placed little emphasis on dogmatic ideas of Apostolic Succession. Phillips Brooks emphatically denied that the Christian Church had started with anything but the simplest organization. Hence, the Episcopal Church, he insisted, did not claim "for the churches of the Episcopate the sole ministry of Christ." To him it was evident that church order was not intended "to be a fixed and definite and final system all arranged at the beginning and doomed to be obligatory throughout all generations." He could not subscribe to a theory of apostolic succession which so narrowed the Church to a certain type of organization as to make of her "but a sect" with "her face backward toward the past." For him, whenever in a Church there was found "Christ's continual personal presence with His people," there was the true Apostolic Succession.[9] Some, moreover, who valued the historic continuity of their Church as a check on the vagaries of a particular generation, insisted that the Church's strength was intimately linked with "liberty of opinion" and "mutual respect." Some of these were inclined to protest when the Bishops of the Episcopal Church issued, in October 1894, a pastoral letter urging the clergy to shun certain dangerous "novelties." To some lay persons this seemed to mean that the imagination must not be allowed to "stray beyond the intellectual horizon of the Dark Ages."

To many earnest laymen of other Christian bodies the idea of Apostolic Succession made no appeal. Thus, Jacob Riis, Danish-American journalist and zealous Methodist layman, who greatly influenced Theodore Roosevelt toward a concern for the less fortunate "Other Half" of an American city, confessed that he just could not "put up" with this doctrine.[10]

In the nineteenth century, and perhaps especially in the United States, the conflict between religious authority and individual freedom was a problem which also concerned Roman Catholics. The tension, moreover, had often resulted in a definite resistance to Catholic discipline. No one illustrated this more definitely than James Gordon Bennett (editor of the New York *Herald*) who died in 1872, after having received the sacrament of Extreme Unction of the Church. Born in a devout Catholic family in Scotland, he had been designated for the priesthood by his father. In the United States he came to be a strong opponent of what he considered both Protestant and Catholic bigotry. Long before the Civil War he had assailed the "ridiculous superstitions" of Rome and the tyranny exercised over the Irish of New York by the bishop "and a Bourbon knot of ignorant, uneducated priests." He had written of the Virgin Mary and of the Eucharist in a way that was shocking to non-Catholics and "as a Catholic," he had called upon the clergy of New York to emerge "from the darkness, folly, and superstition of the tenth century."[11]

A Catholic who apparently had extremely independent inclinations wrote in *The Forum* in 1886 indicating his opposition to the Pope's *Syllabus of Errors* (1864) which had denounced liberalism and modern views of progress. This writer asserted that persons holding such views did not belong in the United States but in "some tranquil isle in the Doldrums," and that if it seemed that Catholics in the United States would ever "approve of the Pope's anathema of modern civilization," laws would have to be passed "to check the growth of Catholicity in this country." But, the writer gave assurance that such action would never be necessary, for American Catholics intended to do their "political thinking" for themselves.

Such independent-mindedness in political matters often
gave rise to evidences of anti-clericalism, for the line of demarcation between matters strictly pertaining to faith and
morals and those of purely secular concern has often been
difficult to define. One case which tended to dramatize some
of the tensions involved was that of Father Edward
McGlynn, popular priest of one of the largest Roman Catholic churches of the time in New York City, St. Stephen's on
East Twenty-ninth Street.[12] As early as August 1881, *Harper's Weekly* had referred to him as "a scholar and linguist
of high attainments" and one of the most effective Catholic
orators in the United States. At the same time it endorsed
the suggestion that he be made Bishop of the diocese of
Nashville, Tennessee. St. Stephen's parish had faced severe
problems of poverty, and McGlynn had been attracted to a
possible solution found in the economic views of Henry
George, exponent of the Single Tax. McGlynn's views incurred opposition as early as 1882 when he had made
speeches in favor of the Irish Land League. He had also
opposed the establishment of a parochial school in his parish.[13]

The situation led to the Prefect of the Propaganda in
Rome ordering McGlynn's suspension from his priestly duties unless Archbishop McCloskey of New York should rule
otherwise. McCloskey secured a promise from McGlynn that
he would make no more speeches for the Land League,
McGlynn writing privately that he did this, not because he
acknowledged any right on the part of anyone to forbid such
action, but because he realized the practical power of his
ecclesiastical superiors to impair and even destroy his usefulness to the Church.[14] Later, when Henry George ran for
mayor of New York in 1886, McGlynn was one of the
speakers for him at a meeting in Chickering Hall. McGlynn
believed that he had a right as an American citizen to speak
on domestic matters, but the new Archbishop, Michael A.
Corrigan, felt differently. At the same time, Thomas Scott
Preston, Vicar-General of the archdiocese of New York, par-

ticipated in the political fray to the extent of writing a formal letter condemning the candidacy of George and declaring his principles "unsound, unsafe and contrary to the teachings of the Church." Preston was the son of a successful insurance company executive who had turned from the Episcopalian ministry to Catholicism and had seemed to some Catholics to be "more Catholic than the Pope" in his extremely zealous and uncompromising enforcement of ecclesiastical discipline.

Shortly after the election, in which George was defeated, the Archbishop, without mentioning Henry George, issued a pastoral letter, as he believed that his duty demanded that he be prompt "in discerning dangerous movements" and in "sounding timely alarms." McGlynn now gave an interview to the New York *Tribune* defending George's principles as not contrary to the teachings of the Church. Corrigan then suspended McGlynn for the remainder of the year.[15] The Vatican soon ordered McGlynn to Rome to give an account of himself, but he replied that grave reasons including heart trouble prevented him from complying and that, in any case, his views were well known. Corrigan then extended McGlynn's suspension until Rome should act. Henry George at once raised the question as to whether an American citizen because of his position as a Catholic priest could be held to answer before a foreign tribunal for his concern with American politics. Father Sylvester L. Malone, pastor of St. Peter and St. Paul Church in Brooklyn, emphatically denied that the Archbishop had any right whatever to interfere with McGlynn in the expression of his political opinions or that McGlynn was accountable to Rome for his views on political economy. On January 14, 1887 McGlynn was removed from his pastorate. Feeling ran high in the parish.[16] McGlynn's successor, Father Arthur Donnally, with the support of a police captain ordered two of McGlynn's assistant priests out of the church. On the first Sunday of Father Donnally's pastorate, the engineers refused to build the fires, and the choir and altar boys went on strike.[17] The anger of many

Catholics at McGlynn's removal was aroused, and on March 29, he delivered a fiery address on, "The Cross of the New Crusade" at the Academy of Music, largely to an audience of his former parishioners. A number of New York priests were on the platform. Archbishop Corrigan deemed this to be a source of scandal. The priests were reprimanded and several of them ultimately were disciplined by such means as a transfer to a less desirable parish, and this led to further outbursts in the press on both sides.[18]

Corrigan wrote privately that the episode marked *"organized* opposition to Episcopal authority" on the part of various priests and that a knife was necessary to deal with the "ulcer." In May, Corrigan informed McGlynn that he must go to Rome within forty days or be excommunicated. McGlynn refused, and a great parade, estimated by some at over 75,000—mostly Catholic workingmen—demonstrated in favor of McGlynn.[19] In an interview McGlynn denounced the "engineers of the Roman machine" and made rather contemptuous reference to "the whole army of lackeys and flunkies, both lay and cleric, who surround the Pope with a barbaric pomp scarcely equalled by that of any imperial despotic court." A large mass meeting of Catholics, claiming to be 100,000 in number, sent a telegram to Rome, denouncing the threatened excommunication. McGlynn insisted on a liberty of interpretation of his priestly vow of obedience, but Frederic R. Coudert, a prominent lawyer, expressed the view that the vow permits "no exceptions" or "reservations," since it is "absolute." The liberal Bishop John Moore of St. Augustine, however, was a stronger supporter of McGlynn,[20] and Moore enlisted the sympathies of the influential Archbishop Ireland of St. Paul, although the latter was very conservative on matters of private property and had no sympathy with Henry George's views.[21] In July, Corrigan issued a statement that McGlynn had incurred excommunication. This seemed to goad McGlynn to further measures, as he engaged in speaking tours for the Anti-Poverty Society, although Corrigan had forbidden Catholics to attend its meetings.[22]

On July 31, he spoke in the Brooklyn Opera House on "The New Know-Nothingism and the Old," denouncing Catholic authorities in the United States and in Rome. Corrigan now sought to have George's *Progress and Poverty* placed on the Roman Catholic list of forbidden books, the *Index*. But the astute Cardinal Gibbons deemed this a step toward unwise restriction of economic discussion, and Archbishop Ireland and he were active in trying to influence the Roman Curia toward a liberal policy. In February 1889, authorities in Rome announced that the works of Henry George were worthy of condemnation, but that this pronouncement need not be published. Apparently a compromise, this action enabled Corrigan to feel that Rome had vindicated his emphatic views on George's writings, but Gibbons could find comfort in the fact that Corrigan could not publicly reveal his triumph.

McGlynn continued his activities. In November 1891, he addressed at Cooper Union a Sunday evening audience of Irish Catholics who cheered wildly his every sharp criticism of Monsignor Preston, Archbishop Corrigan, and even the Pope. McGlynn went so far as to predict that in another generation "the bitterest opponents of the Catholic Church" would be the children and grandchildren of those who were then thronging its churches. The *Independent* commented that the struggle involved "not dogma so much" as ecclesiasticism and predicted that more liberty would "be allowed by the ecclesiastical authorities of the Roman Catholic Church, or it will alienate its supporters in this country."[23]

McGlynn's economic views were submitted to Archbishop Francesco Satolli who had come to the United States as a papal representative, and he turned over McGlynn's statement to four Catholic University of America professors. They found nothing in the statement contrary to faith and morals, and McGlynn was restored to his priestly functions in December 1892.[24] Even then, the fiery Irish-American could hardly be restrained. In the next year (during which summer he made the long-delayed trip to Rome) he wrote for *The Forum* that Catholic bishops had "had practically a free hand to govern despotically both clergy and people and to lay upon them what burden they pleased and to refuse them justice and even a hearing," with recourse to the Vatican the only remedy and that means generally a physically impossible one. McGlynn claimed that bishops had often been "so spoiled by the possession of despotic authority" that they had not carried out the spirit of the reforms provided by the Pope, but that the situation was being remedied by the appointment of an Apostolic Delegate in Washington, D. C., one who possessed great modesty, ecclesiastical learning, "and an open, perspicacious, and logical mind."

McGlynn's independent spirit and his loyalty to Henry George were constant. When George died in October 1897, a great funeral service was held at the Grand Central Palace, New York City. A liberal Episcopalian minister and lifelong friend read the Episcopal service and offered prayer, followed by eulogies by the Congregationalist, Dr. Lyman Abbott, and the Rabbi Gustav Gottheil. Then Father McGlynn with obvious sincerity referred to the familiar Scriptural statement, "There was a man sent of God whose name was John," and expressed the belief that he was not mocking Scripture when he asserted that another man had been sent from God whose name was Henry George. The next morning a further service was conducted by two Episcopalian clergymen and Father McGlynn.[25] McGlynn was indeed a stormy petrel in ecclesiastical circles, but his influence was doubtless enhanced by the fact that his moral character was above reproach. A Catholic editor had felt impelled to meet boldly charges against his moral character, for he had known McGlynn as "one of the most scrupulous and purest men that ever lived."[26]

In any organization difficulties often arise as to whether

undesirable conditions should be publicly aired to secure a correction of them or whether the problems should be minimized in the interests of harmony and unified efforts. Occasionally a priest would express vigorous, perhaps intemperate, views regarding a situation which he did not approve. An example is Father Valentine F. Schmitt, who assumed the pastorate of St. Joseph's Catholic Church, Washington, D. C., in 1887. He maintained that evidence showed that the parish, in charge of the Jesuits since 1871, had been maladministered by them and he spoke pointedly about the matter. Offense was taken by the Jesuits, and Cardinal Gibbons required Schmitt to write a letter expressing regret for what were deemed unjust and uncharitable remarks, and he was further obliged to promise not to repeat the alleged offense.[27]

Until 1908, Roman Catholicism in the United States was organized on a missionary basis in the United States, and parishes and parish priests in the traditional canonical sense were not recognized until 1918. Moreover, in a country of frontier aspects, the canon law would have been difficult of application in many respects. These factors, combined with a certain individualism in American life and a certain contentiousness on the part of some first-generation German and Irish-Americans led to other quarrels between dissatisfied priests and their bishops. One instance was that of Father E. M. O'Callaghan of Youngstown, Ohio who in 1870 went incognito to Rome to represent certain dissatisfied clergymen who were distressed by alleged instability of tenure. At about the same time (1869) in a diocese of strong German-American influences, Milwaukee, forty English-speaking priests had met and pledged themselves to do all they could to obtain "parochial rights."[28] Sometimes the friction was so great that the mediation of the tactful Cardinal Gibbons was employed, as in bitter disputes between Bishop Rupert Seidenbush, Vicar Apostolic of North Minnesota and his clergy (1887) and between Bishop Richard Gilmour and the Grey Nuns in Toledo, Ohio (1887), and the same bishop

and a dissatisfied pastor, Father Quigley, in the same city.[29]
Bishop Gilmour thought that he had to deal with a lot of
"very small, but very noisy men in Toledo." When the
bishop had summoned Quigley to Cleveland, then the seat
of the diocese, the latter had refused to go, and the controversy had been taken to the civil courts.[30]

Another aspect of the conflict between ecclesiastical discipline and freedom was found in the careers of certain
Catholic journalists. Outstanding among them was the orthodox, fiery David Samuel Phelan, a priest with journalism
as an avocation. Editor for about half a century after 1863
of the *Missouri Watchman,* he considered himself a defender of the clergy against episcopal arbitrariness. Having
attacked an appointment by Archbishop John J. Kain as one
lowering the intellectual level of the hierarchy, he was reproved (1893) by the Archbishop. Phelan retorted that
Kain had come fom a slave state, hence had to be instructed
as to how to rule free men. Evidently Archbishop Ireland
compromised the difficulty.

Within the Catholic church in America there were other
influences which stressed freedom rather than docile conformity. Father Walter Elliott, a prominent Paulist priest,
had preached a sermon in St. Paul, Minnesota in December
1889, stressing the point of view that American ideas of
manhood were not so much those of loyalty, obedience, and
uniformity, but those concerned with a worthiness to be
free. Related ideas of American freedom expressed in
Elliott's *Life of Father Hecker* (1890) caused additional concern among conservative Catholics.[31]

Another liberal bishop, John L. Spalding of Peoria, had
irritated the traditionalists by his advanced views of the
importance of the scientific mind.[32]

Perhaps no more emphatic view on the part of a distinguished Catholic clergyman expressing the need for
change rather than tradition in religious procedure could
be cited than that of Archbishop Ireland. Speaking in October 1893, on the silver anniversary of Gibbons' service as

bishop, he discussed "The Church and the Age," proclaiming that "routine" had come to be "fatal" and that "the common" was really "exhausted senility," hence the Church must help to provide "the new, the extraordinary."[33]

Even among the Mormons (Church of the Latter Day Saints of Jesus Christ) there was resistance to clerical domination. Under the leadership of Joseph Smith and Brigham Young, the Church had developed a closely integrated economic and social organization.[34] Tithes and cooperative efforts had helped to build the substantial foundations of Mormon life. Mormonism was thus "a self-contained theocracy" with an effective, highly centralized economic system. The coming of non-Mormons ("Gentiles") especially with the building of the transcontinental railroad prompted Brigham Young to set up the Zion Cöoperative Mercantile Institution to which practically all retailers were forced to sell out. Young's will appeared to be law, and social conditions were conducive to the exercise of absolute authority. But this absolutism was carried too far.[35] Opposition began to express itself. By 1868, there developed even within Mormonism a "New Movement," also called "The Reformation."[36] Among the leaders was the English-born convert, William S. Godbe (1833-1902), who came to oppose polygamy and the restrictions imposed upon the life and thought of the Mormon people, especially in matters definitely temporal in nature. These dissenters were often called "Godbeites," some of whom were interested in the development of the nearby mining resources, which the Church refused to allow its members to tap.

The broader aspect of the movement involved a protest against Young's doctrines that the world was on the road to ruin and that the Mormon priesthood in effect should do the thinking for the people. By 1877, many loyal Mormons, moreover, were reacting in favor of greater individualism and against a system to elevate the poor and depress the well-to-do economically. One scholar tells us, "However much they may have differed from the Gentiles in their

social values, the Mormons were not substantially different
in their economic values."[37] A genuinely reformed Mormonism did not emerge.[38] Yet, to some extent, the demand for
reasonable initiative bringing its personal economic rewards
triumphed, though the Mormon cooperative life continued
to function in the social sphere.[39]

In the meantime, polygamy had proved a divisive and
deteriorating influence. Perhaps two-thirds of the Mormons
were devoted to Young and his elders and were known as
"Orthodox Saints"; about one-third were Liberals or "Hickory Mormons" and opposed polygamy.[40] During the 1880's
the stiffening attitude of the United States government in
its opposition to polygamy helped to restrict the power of
the theocracy. By 1889, it was reported that Bishop Andrew
Cahoon of Salt Lake City, after serving a term in prison for
polygamy, had renounced his faith, refusing to be considered
a rebel against his country. But, in 1890, President Wilford
Woodruff of the Mormon Church issued the famous "Mani-
festo," officially abandoning polygamy.[41]

In politics, Mormon church leaders had dominated the
life of the area under the territorial regime. With the coming of statehood (1896) there was no intention of abandoning such control and friction developed. The Church insisted that the Mormon priesthood must give approval to
candidates of the political parties. Resistance to this led to
the disciplining of a number of the brethren. Thus, in
1898, Apostle Moses Thatcher was deprived of his apostle-
ship because of his refusal to follow the Church's will in
this respect.[42]

CHAPTER III

WHY SOME CHURCH PEWS WERE EMPTY

Obviously, no sharp line can be drawn between those who were outside the influence of the Church because of scruples primarily intellectual and those who shunned its activities for other reasons. On the other hand, many had been alienated from the Church for reasons of a moral or social nature, and during the nineteenth century the trend continued. Among these were:

1. Those feeling that they had not, perhaps could not, attain the moral or spiritual requirements for church membership. This included many obviously wicked or profligate persons in a community but also many sensitive souls who felt that they had never experienced a "personal experience of salvation." Another aspect of the situation has been expressed by a leading authority on Puritanism, who tells us that an important factor in its decline over three centuries was that it made demands on the individual which were so exacting that later generations simply "could not longer stand the pace."[1] One such generation was that following the Civil War.

2. Those alienated by the devastation of war and by sectional bitterness which seemed to repudiate the practical implications of the "Golden Rule."

Certainly the Civil War and "the Tragic Era" thereafter, a veritable "Age of Hate," brought definite losses to the cause of organized religion. The war itself had impaired the leadership of the churches, as pastors had left their charges in order to serve as chaplains, and in both North and South a large portion of the male lay leadership had been called to service in the field. In the South, moreover, religious edifices had been destroyed by invading armies; congregations had been demoralized; and bitter enmities obscured the teachings of ethical religion.

Thus, between 1860 and 1865, the Methodist Church in the South had declined thirty per cent in membership. Losses of wealth in slaves and in property destroyed or confiscated; the disruption of educational institutions; the practical collapse of itinerary—all contributed to the Church's problems in that region.[2]

The situation in the South is broadly indicated by the conditions existing in South Carolina. There, in 1868, of seventy-three Episcopal parishes before the War, only fifty-three survived, and only ten held services regularly. Bishop Thomas F. Davis, blind and shabby, lamented, "I am the dying bishop of a dead diocese."[3]

Even in those border slave states which had officially remained loyal to the Union, the churches had been seriously affected. There, animosities were extremely bitter, as neighbors who had favored the Confederacy and those who had been Unionists eyed each other with studied antagonism. In Kentucky, the intensity of political feeling sometimes prompted the church member and even the church officer to "forsake attendance upon divine service, given up even an outward show of holy living, and betake himself to drinking and swearing. . . ."[4]

The breakup of the chief Presbyterian denomination (Old School) into northern and southern branches at the outbreak of the Civil War, and the acrimonious dispute over rights to church buildings and property had seriously weakened that Church in some border states like Kentucky.[5] Bitter rivalry, moreover, between leaders of Northern and Southern Methodist churches was accompanied by the establishment of many Northern Methodist churches in border and southern towns and villages.[6] A Southern scholar, with at least a suggestion of continuing resentment, tells us that Northern Methodists, "the most uncompromising clerical gladiators," steeped in "the new isms of the age," made a new invasion of the South "to remake the people in the image of Thaddeus Stevens."[7] In 1872, a Northern Methodist paper termed Southern congregations "pro-slavery, man-stealing, Negro-whipping, whiskey-drinking, Ku Klux churches." Such invective did not remain unanswered in Southern circles. Robert L. Dabney, renowned Presbyterian leader, shouted: "I do not forgive. I try not to forgive. What! forgive those people, who have invaded our country, burned our cities, destroyed our homes, slain our young men, and spread desolation and ruin over the land! . . ." An extremist, Dabney opposed even "fraternal correspondence" with Northern Presbyterian groups, and when efforts were made toward unity with the Northern brethren he could engage in a vitriolic harangue for three hours. Under such circumstances, conciliatory forces fled in terror, as they found that he "stripped every leaf from the olive branch and made it a rod to beat us with." Obviously, he was an example of the way in which hate could dominate at least the moods of sincere, religious men, and fortunately he represented but one aspect of the mind of the post-war South.[8] The very unsullied integrity, rigid conscientiousness, and utter selflessness of such men, according to a latter commentator in the *Nation* merely "added to the harm they were able to do by keeping their countrymen out of the great spiritual currents." Under such circumstances, some Southerners turned from religion and found what solace they could in drinking, a practice which the strain of war service had definitely encouraged. Accordingly, "Grogshops grew up in many country settlements or crossroads and peppered the bigger cities."[9]

3. Those alienated by the seeming hypocrisy of church members and the apparent separation of religion and ethics. Thus in Indiana, the children of a zealous Roman Catholic father, among them Theodore Dreiser (the novelist), rebelled against religion in part because the father seemed to feel that if the forms of worship were maintained, God would take care of the family. Accordingly, as the father

seemed to take less family responsibility, Theodore Dreiser
came to look upon Catholicism and poverty as going hand
in hand to produce a denial of the good things of life.[10] A
nine year old girl in the Presbyterian Sunday School in
Johnstown, New York, quit attending there in outraged
indignation when she carefully learned all of the Shorter
Westminster Catechism with the promise of a prize, only to
find that the reward was a chance to memorize the eighteenth
psalm by the following Sunday.[11]

Many who looked upon the activities of Daniel Drew as
a kind of financial "piracy" were greatly irritated by his
role as Methodist layman and benefactor.[12] In the 1870's the
scandals of the Grant Administration seemed to show some
ethical failure on the part of the Church, for some involved
were not inconspicuous church people.[13] Don Piatt, editor
of the weekly *Capital* in Washington, D. C., outraged by the
revelations of the period, felt that there was no disguising
the fact that the materialistic nation was "rapidly outgrow-
ing religion."[14]

The importance of religious faith for ethical conduct
was not strengthened in the popular mind by the acts of
various persons closely associated with organized faith. Thus,
Albert Cardozo, Vice President of the Spanish-Portuguese
Synagogue in New York City, was a devoted parent and
active in various charities. A brilliant man, he was Justice
of the Supreme Court of New York, but in that position he
did not prove strong enough to resist the temptations offered by the Tweed Ring. He joined with other justices in
countenancing illegal naturalizations, mostly those of new
voters who would do the will of Tammany Hall. At Tweed's
behest, he granted a receivership to Jay Gould's Erie Railroad, and in assigning refereeships he turned over hundreds
of them to a nephew and over a hundred to a son of Tweed.
A legislative investigation led to his resignation, for he was
clearly guilty of malfeasance in office. His son (later United
States Supreme Court Justice), Benjamin Cardozo, was re-

ligious in spirit but came to abstain from attendance at orthodox services.[15]

4. Those not indifferent to religion or spiritual matters who were alienated by the long, dull sermons and by the failure of some churches to present a service of spiritual vitality and inspiration. *Harper's Weekly* raised the following questions in 1867:

> . . . Do not long sermons drive many from hearing the Word altogether? Have not the seeds of fatal disease been sown in the long hours passed in that icy-cold and draughty stone church? Have not some of the poor children, who, after being exhausted in a Sunday-school, are placed, without being permitted to sleep . . . up in those hard-seated galleries for other long hours, been brought to dread the name of a church? . . .

A few years later a leading Middle Western newspaper suggested, "Either the churches will have to change much or coming man will not attend them."[16]

James Parton, the famous biographer, declared in 1867 that in some fashionable New York City churches the sermons "laboriously prepared and earnestly read . . . contained not the most distant allusion to modern modes of living and sinning, had no suitableness whatever to the people or the time, and from which everything that could rouse or interest a soul living on Manhattan Island in the year 1867 seemed to have been purposely pruned away."[17]

James A. Garfield, who had been a local preacher in the Disciples Church, occasionally found a sermon that was very instructive and "free from cant and hypercriticism," but after hearing a Presbyterian minister in 1878 preach "a goodish feeble sermon," he wondered whether nearly all modern sermons—regardless of the creed of the preacher—did not tend to inanity.[18]

An observer at the very end of the century spent much

time over a period of a year attending church in several towns near Boston. He believed that not more than one-eighth of the population stayed away from church entirely, yet not more than one-half of the people were actively identified with any church. Modern diversions seemed not to be the reason for declining church attendance, and mere liberality of doctrine did not seem to be the answer, for the more liberal the doctrinal teaching the smaller proportion of men in attendance. Men seemed to be present in greater numbers when the preacher seemed abreast of practical modern life and did not appear to be living "in a world that no longer has an existence."

5. Those disgusted by narrow denominationalism and religious bickerings. In the 1890's a writer found that in Middleboro, Plymouth county, Massachusetts, then a fair example of the better class of New England towns, religious activities were so divided among Congregationalists, Roman Catholics, Baptists, Methodists, Episcopalians, Unitarians, Perfectionists and Adventists that none had the support that was desirable. Every edifice was of wood; most of the congregations were in debt; and on a typical Sunday less than 1200 persons (or 3 out of 20) attended the fifteen churches. The Protestant churches had become practically "religious clubs," and the result was a confusion of dreary services varied by sensational programs to attract a crowd, with one-half of the women and four-fifths of the men of the community being essentially lost to organized Christianity. Where a grim Congregational deacon was unsure that his wife was of the "elect," and she was distressed by the fact that her husband had not been immersed, the result was that the boys of the family spent Sunday trotting the horses.

Similarly it was found that in Fall River, a manufacturing town then of about 90,000 people, there were forty-nine churches (including mission chapels and separate Sunday schools), served by twenty-eight clergymen. The Catholics had fifteen of the churches (with two more large ones in process of construction) where about forty Masses were said on Sundays. But denominational rivalry made for little effective work on the part of the Protestant churches. Of 25,000 people who were classed as Trinitarian Protestants, only about 5,000 attended church services regularly, about as many as attended the two largest Catholic churches.

Within churches like those of Lutheranism there were sometimes persons who were irked when they were not permitted to entertain pietistic non-Lutheran clergymen. Some such persons (who frequently had somewhat liberal theological and social views as well) withdrew or were excommunicated. Among Swedish-Americans this withdrawal later led to the formation of the Swedish Mission Covenant Church.[19] Sectarianism in the rural districts especially contributed to a situation which will be considered as the next social reason for alienation from the Church.

6. Those, discouraged with the Church, because of a decline of rural areas, especially in New England, where the loss of accustomed support and leadership was particularly noticeable. As population declined in many rural areas after 1865, no longer were there in many small communities strong, vigorous churches "uniting the intelligence, the resources, the society of an entire village and township in uplifting worship, hearty good-fellowship, dignified social life, and aggressive Christian work." In Waldo county, Maine, it was found that in 1892, 4850 out of 6987 families did not attend church; in Oxford county, 4577 out of 7288 families. Part of the problem was rooted in theological niceties and excessive individualism, but the superfluous sects constituted "the gnarled and knotty branches" and "artificial and unreal sermons" became "the blighted and bitter fruit." To cope with the problem definite efforts were made toward greater strength through a union of scattered Congregational congregations of a county or district into a single church with a resident pastor.

7. Those caught up in the impersonal and often class-conscious atmosphere of urban life. The rise of metropolitan districts which meant the spiritual isolation of great num-

bers of people, including country boys or girls in city room-
ing houses and the very poor cramped into tenement houses.
In 1867 it was asserted that everything in and around many
fashionable New York churches proclaimed them "a kind of
exclusive ecclesiastical club, designed for the accommodation
of persons of ten thousand dollars a year, and upward." In
the 1880's Lyman Abbott expressed concern at the migration of churches from the crowded downtown districts. He
believed that not ten per cent of the wage workers in New
York City were regular attendants at any Protestant service.
To him, "heathenism" was gaining in New York, Chicago,
Cincinnati, St. Louis, Philadelphia, and other cities. In the
prosperous residential districts, the churches prospered, but
churches where the rich and poor worshipped together were
few indeed. In New York "the saints seemed to go to heaven
in first and second class carriages."[20]

In Fall River, Massachusetts in 1894 some of the more
prosperous factory workers asserted that they had tried to
associate with the church life of the Protestant churches on
the hill but that their wives had been deeply hurt by the
cold treatment given them so they had abandoned church
attendance. In 1896, the labor leader, Samuel Gompers, declared that in the churches the real God was "the Almighty
Dollar."[21]

Washington Gladden, liberal minister of First Congregational Church, Columbus, Ohio, found that wage-earners
were often conscious of their less than fashionable clothes as
they attended middle-class churches. A little later he sum-
marized the experience of many years, as he concluded that
many of America's toiling millions were embittered against
the Church, with "no faith in it, and no expectation" that
any good would come out of it.[22]

Even a middle class college student might experience
the sting of social exclusiveness. Harold L. Ickes, later Secretary of the Interior, as a student at the University of Chicago, went once or twice to the Hyde Park Presbyterian

Church, but he later declared that he felt like he was trespassing on the privacy of an aristocratic club.[23]

A noted Catholic writer in 1879 expressed alarm at the rising threat of Socialism among the Catholic poor in the tenement areas of the cities where the cramped life was conducive to a loss of religion. He thought that educated Catholic young men of the favored economic classes needed to show less fortunate ones the Catholic way of life.[24]

A practical balance between the material and the spiritual was often difficult to maintain. As the country prospered, beautiful and costly churches were inevitably erected, but to many this seemed to suggest an over-stressing of material things. Although not necessarily alienated from the Church, many Catholics, according to one who served as a popular but stormy priest, were disturbed when priests and bishops gloried in their roles as successful administrators rather than as spiritual instructors, comforters, and guides of their flocks. Sometimes costly cathedrals and pastoral residences came to be preferred "to the less tangible conversion of the sinning and the erring, the comforting of the sorrowing, the helping of the poor."

8. Those of immigrant background for whom there were special problems of adjustment. Some who had come to America for freedom and economic advantage felt that they had been emancipated from the religious traditions of the Old World. One of the most extreme of these, Karl Heinzen, who had been born in a devout Roman Catholic family in a predominantly German Catholic region along the Rhine, long before his first residence in the United States (1847) had broken abruptly with organized religion. In the United States until his death in 1880, he was an outspoken supporter of a materialistic philosophy and a fanatical opponent of the Church, monarchy, and Communism.[25] (Most of the Germans, however, were Lutherans, Catholics, or members of the Reformed or pietistic groups. Many of these were very clannish, a factor which often intensified church loyalty.)

In the Catholic Church much friction developed between the English-speaking Irish and the German Catholics. Many Germans felt that the Irish population had furnished far too large a proportion of the bishops of the Church.[26] Extremists in both camps contributed to the bitterness of the situation, and in the 1880's and 1890's a movement for greater recognition of foreign-speaking Catholics, especially the Germans, in the administration of the Catholic Church in America, led to a fierce conflict over so-called "Cahenslyism."[27]

During the period after 1865, and especially after 1882, tens of thousands of Italians, moreover, had come to the United States. In Italy Catholicism had been deeply embedded in the traditions of the country, but amidst the poverty and the political and religious conflict of the homeland, religion had often been an emotional affair finding only nominal expression in practical life. The question of the temporal power of the Pope had tended to create many anti-clericals, some of whom came to America. Education, moreover, had been very meagre in old Italy, so that in America by 1888 there were thousands of Italians in New York City who did not know the Apostles' Creed.[28] Their poverty, and their crowded living conditions in tenement areas, moreover, had made religious activities among them difficult indeed. Archbishop Corrigan of New York had reported that of 50,000 Italians in New York only 1200 went to Mass.

Italy had not always been known for the saintliness of its priests, and the best among them had often remained in Italy. When in the United States, Italians started to attend Mass they were often irritated by the leadership of English-speaking priests, and when Italian priests were sought to help minister to them, there were other difficulties. At one time it was found that two hundred Italian-Americans had been confirmed by a heretical bishop and that of twelve priests in charge of them in New York City, ten had been expelled from Italy for crimes. At times, moreover, Italian

priests were woefully neglectful of pastoral duties.[29] When
it had been suggested that special Italian Roman Catholic
parishes should be created, Archbishop Corrigan of New
York stated in 1883 that such a plan faced three difficulties:
(1) Italian immigrants ordinarily did not go to church;
(2) They lived dispersed in all parts of the city; and (3)
They gave little or no financial support to the Church.[30]
In regard to the last factor, not only were the Italians in the
United States extremely poor, but they had commonly been
used to state-supported or endowed churches in the homeland, and had been accustomed to gorgeous vestments, mar-
ble statuary, and well trained voices as a part of the service
without contributing to the financial support of the Church.
Eventually, the problem was solved, but the period of transition meant definite losses to Catholicism in America.

The tensions were particularly marked among Bohemians or Czechs who had lived under the political domination of the Catholic Hapsburgs of Austria. Among the Irish
and Poles the Church had seemed like a precious bulwark
against foreign tyranny, but among the Bohemians it had
sometimes seemed like a power in league with the forces
of reaction. Hence, in America, when Bohemian Catholics
sometimes tasted the sweets of freedom, they reacted against
religious control in what seemed to be essentially secular
matters. Thus, in Cleveland in 1870, when the priest of a
local church opposed an insurance and fraternal organization, over half of the Czechs withdrew from the church, and
many became followers of the agnostic, Robert Ingersoll.[31]

Among Poles, there was some opposition to the degree
of domination of the Catholic Church exercised by Irish-
Americans. In Pennsylvania in particular this led to demands for local control of church properties. Some seceded
from the Roman Church, and after the turn of the century
(1904) became organized as the Polish National Independent Catholic Church.[32] In 1886 dissension in Pittsburgh had
led to an attempt on the life of a Polish priest, and in the
same year in Toledo, Ohio, an effort to kill a priest with

a home-made bomb had resulted in a riot, in which three persons were killed.

9. Those who found the churches seemingly illiberal in their social attitudes on matters such as Sabbath observance and the use of intoxicants. Thus, a boy of seven who attended two services on Sunday morning and perhaps another in the afternoon and then returned home to read his Sunday School paper might find the rest of the day dull indeed. Denied the opportunity of playing outside the house, he might stand at the French doors of the living room filled with envy toward some of the children of the "Godless" who were allowed to play hop-scotch in the sunshine. Such a youth by his late 'teens had come to associate church-going with "oppressiveness."[33] Certainly many reacted against the attitude which condemned even the most innocent family diversions on Sunday and insisted on "restraints and repressions" which involved often the serving on Sunday of only cold foods (such as rice, baked apples, bread and butter, meat and cheese) which had been prepared the day before. Sometimes even the pet dog of a family would be reproved if he greeted his youthful master too excitedly on a Sunday morning.[34] Many Germans reacted unfavorably to the Puritanical attitudes of many Protestant churches both toward Sabbath observance and beer drinking.[35] (Often, however, they belonged to churches which also opposed Puritan views.) Non-Germans were often irritated by similar tendencies. A noted foreign correspondent, Paul Scott Mower, has told us that as a boy in Bloomington, Illinois, his family used no intoxicants but a little brandy kept for medicinal purposes, yet his mother (the daughter of a Methodist lay preacher) objected to the effort of the Sunday School superintendent to get him to take a teetotal pledge.[36]

10. Those not hostile to the Church but inclined to be indifferent to it in the wake of an increasing secularism. In part this was an aspect of the vigorous active tempo of American life that tended to crowd out the other-worldliness often associated with the life of the churches. This was

especially noted on the frontier, as the new settlers pressed energetically to establish new homes and the workaday world frequently obscured a consideration of the meditative life. Amidst the boisterousness of a mining camp, the saloon and the gambling den had certainly provided discouraging competition for the missionary preacher.[37]

One observer stated his conviction that three-fourths of those who never read the Bible or entered a church had such an attitude because they were engrossed with material affairs or found church-going a bore. Their apparent skepticism was "a kind of dogmatic materialism," for they would take as little time to examine and would be as much bored by "Spinoza or Darwin as Moses or St. Paul." Their attitude was based upon the convenience of lethargy toward matters of the mind as well as of the spirit.

Also tending to stimulate an indifference towards church-going was the gradually increasing tendency to devote much of Sunday to "the visiting of summer resorts, ball games, and the Sunday theatre."[38] A Catholic priest in New York state in the years around 1880 found that Protestant boys often spent the day on excursions or in fishing or boating, and that their Catholic chums were naturally tempted to go along and miss attendance at Mass.[39]

The appearance of Sunday newspapers, the marked increase in the use of railroads and street cars on Sunday, and the growth of a seven day week for the operation of various industries, were other evidences that Sunday was being used for various activities besides church-going.[40] A trend of the times was indicated in 1895, when the Maine Methodist Conference's Committee on Sabbath Observance recommended that the day be not crowded with so many services as to weary worshippers and that "such recreation as brings real rest to the body and soul be not prohibited." This report was not accepted by the Conference, as one of the brethren declared that "the committee was knocking the foundations out of the Methodist church, and it was drifting to hell."

By the end of the century, among other distractions were the country clubs, of which there were hundreds by 1900, almost all of them established since 1885. (Some of them, however, had restrictions on Sunday golf.)

Another factor was the further trend, which had developed over a period of many generations, toward intellectual and cultural activities at best only indirectly related to the mission of the church.

For the well-to-do, especially, the riches of a secular culture encroached increasingly on church-going activities. Thus, as young people William C. Whitney and his wife Flora had both been devout. As a girl she had been a Sunday School teacher in the Old Stone Presbyterian Church, Cleveland, and had taken such a personal joy in its services that she had written in 1869 of her utter dependence upon Christ.[41] Whitney had been raised in a home of genial but devout Congregationalism, and as a young business man in New York had been active in Calvary Episcopal Church. He had acquired a habit of inviting friends for evenings and Sunday afternoons to his bachelor quarters to discuss the Bible and religion. Often they attended Calvary Church in a body, and then the two ministers of the church would conduct a discussion of the sermon at Whitney's residence. Good Friday noon would find him with business associates at Old Trinity, Wall Street, where the sanctuary would be crowded, with hundreds standing in the aisles. But as Whitney became a dominant figure in the New York business world and his wife one of the reigning hostesses of the day, secular interests gradually became dominant. By the 1890's at their luxurious home Sunday evenings were often spent in the enjoyment of the best in music. Joseph Hoffman performed on the piano; Paderewski and Kreisler displayed their genius; and Nordica and Melba pleased all with the glorious beauty of their voices. By 1904, an intimate friend could say of Whitney that he was not religious but lived by a "good code." This friend, William Graham Sumner, was himself an example of the trend toward secularization on the cultural level. For a time an Episcopalian clergyman in the New York area, in 1872 he left to become a renowned professor of political and social science at Yale.

For the rank and file of Americans there was, moreover, during the nineteenth century (indeed until about 1926) a steady increase in the membership of fraternal organizations which included secret societies of various kinds. Embracing a wide variety of moral, social, and humanitarian objectives, these lodges often seemed to give positive support to the work of organized religion. Yet, their ritualism and symbolism, not infrequently presented with the use of an altar, and their employment of secret oaths were sometimes considered as, in a way, in competition with the churches. Catholics, Missouri Synod Lutherans, and United Presbyterians were often strenuously opposed to various of the fraternal organizations. Yet, millions of Americans gave allegiance to the societies, and in a somewhat pluralistic culture, its fraternal groups received from many a devotion which religious leaders often sought to have more exclusively reserved for the Church.[42]

CHAPTER IV

THE AGE OF ROCKS AND THE ROCK OF AGES

(1) *The Impact of the Scientific Method.*

The Medieval Mind in which Faith and Reason had seemingly been brought into perfect harmony had gradually yielded to the spirit of the Renaissance and then to the intellectual currents of the Modern Age. The Copernican system of astronomy had revolutionized western thought by showing that the earth was not, scientifically considered, the center of the Universe. It appeared that Man's place of supreme importance in the world of nature had been seriously called in question. Gradually there had emerged through the work and influence of men like Roger Bacon, Francis Bacon, Isaac Newton, Antoine Lavoisier, Joseph Priestley and others an emphasis on the experimental method of science. In the eighteenth century cultural and scientific thought had found expression in the Age of the Enlightenment and Reason, and Rationalism and Deism (the latter a religion of nature without Revelation) had been accepted by many of the educated classes of Europe.[1] Such ideas had made their impress on men of education in America, as is shown clearly in the views of Jefferson, Franklin, and even Washington. Toward the end of the eighteenth century this had meant that many intellectual persons were inclined to deny Divine Revelation and to espouse Deism or some other form of skepticism.[2] Some of the Southern aristocracy and parts of the New England college world had temporarily embraced the free-thinking spirit. Generally this was more intimately connected with the idea of Reason than with the method of science, and to a large degree it was a passing phase.[3] During the nineteenth century before 1850, much

Free Thought had been associated with an emphasis on Nature as well as Reason, in opposition to the Revelation as found in the Scriptures.[4]

Much of the seeming conflict between religion and science was to develop out of new knowledge of geology and anthropology. But, a nineteenth century Positivist who attacked religion on broader grounds was John William Draper, noted chemist and author of the *History of the Conflict of Religion and Science* (1874). Born in England, he was the son of a Catholic father who became a Methodist district superintendent.[5] Long associated with New York University, in his much discussed volume, he insisted that religion and science were basically in conflict, for religion conserved its power through the organized Church, while science sought to destroy the Church's pretensions by indicating the human origins of all religious institutions. To him the Church was everywhere opposed to free scientific inquiry. Draper concluded that Christianity would disappear, as Roman paganism had done, leaving science with its "grander views of the universe, more awful views of God."[6] Yet, Draper was not a scientific materialist, for he believed in the immortality of the soul and thought that science would ultimately justify that belief. In his own day even the title of Draper's book was criticized "on the ground that religion is a personal element entirely, and with this, of course, science can never be in antagonism."[7] Even Draper's obvious hostility to ecclesiastical organizations seems to have been tempered in practice, for his wife who had been raised a Roman Catholic, became a liberal Anglican after their marriage, and he was personally on friendly intimacy with many liberal clergymen. Draper was even known to have expressed the belief that, while no reconciliation between science and religion was possible for the Roman Catholic (whose Church has placed his *History* on the Index),[8] there might be one for the Protestant with the emphasis on private interpretation of Scripture.[9]

The New York *Nation* was scarcely less bitter than

Draper toward what it considered the conflict between
Catholicism and science. In 1874, it pointed out that in
Ireland, Catholic alumni of the Catholic University there
had prepared a solemn memorial complaining of the almost
total lack of scientific instruction at that University, and it
contended that this tended to show much light "on the relations of the Catholic Church to education everywhere." The
article asserted that some Catholics might accept scientific
truths, but the daily practice of scientific investigation resulted in "acquiring intellectual habits and making use of
tests which the church considers signs of a rebellious and
therefore sinful temper." It further contended that the
Church lost all control over its members who entered the
field of science, for, "Her weapons are the jest of the museum
and the laboratory, and her lore the vain babbling of the
ignorant or blind." Mathematics and astronomy appeared to
be the only fields of science in which Catholic laymen could
attain distinction without losing the favor of the clergy.

A Catholic writer, asserting that his confidence in the
reputation of the *Nation* for not abusing Catholics had been
shaken, came to the defense of his Church. He maintained
that, although the Catholic Church did "not consider it its
primary end and aim to advocate the interests of science, it
always has and still does favor its advance. True, it will not
allow what it considers divine truth to be called in question
by its adherents. There is not a fact of science which Catholics may not accept. There is a *theory* or two which *may*
possibly conflict with its teachings."

Godkin, editor of the *Nation,* replying in the same issue,
quoted from the Papal Encyclical of December 8, 1864 which
had denounced in a rather comprehensive way many modern views. Godkin asserted, "Complete liberty, and constant
and open-minded diligence in the collection of facts, are the
beginning and end of all scientific processes." He thought
that the history of the Catholic Church "bristles with illustrations of her hostility to this liberty." He further contended "that any Catholic scientific man who strictly com-

plies with the decrees of the church is untrustworthy, and that, if he does comply with them, he is *pro tanto* a bad Catholic, and will go to hell. . . ."[10]

The selection of Washington D. C. in 1885 as the site for the new Catholic University of America evoked praise from the New York *Times* which expressed the hope that the teaching there would be "broad and liberal, not shunning any of the truths of science or of history merely because it is the custom to avoid them in most Catholic schools. . . ."[11]

If to some Catholicism seemed on the defensive, in view of the increasing prestige of science, some deemed liberal Protestant clergymen almost too eager to embrace the scientific method as an aid to true religion. At any rate, such a liberal Congregational clergyman as Theodore T. Munger (1830-1910), long pastor after 1885 of the United Church of New Haven, Connecticut,[12] in 1888 optimistically expressed the "gains from science" of which religion was the recipient. He found that Science had: (1) Deepened reverence; (2) Taught religion to think according to the laws of cause and effect; (3) Delivered religion from superstition; (4) Put religion on the track of the truth that moral laws are really natural laws; and (5) Helped to deliver religion from the habit of defending traditional beliefs because of their apparent usefulness. Doubtless there was much validity in this analysis, but a later generation was to detect that, while excessive traditionalism might do damage to faith because of obscurantism, faith might also be impaired because liberal religion often became so emancipated from tradition and from its time-honored insights that its message became increasingly secular and social.[13]

Toward the end of the century a more moderate exposition than Draper's of the relation between science and religion was written by the President of Cornell, Andrew D. White. With the assistance of a Cornell professor of History he published *The Warfare of Science with Theology in Christendom* (1896). White wrote privately to a leading his-

torian of the period that he proceeded on the "fundamental
thought as illustrated from history" that Religion has never
had any reason for trouble with science, but that ecclesiasticism, which to a certain extent was necessary "to give
protection and form to Religion in its worldly relations,"
in practice had "constantly developed in a way contrary to
the best science and philosophy."[14] White made an age, the
Medieval, rather than an institution, the object of his criticism, condemning religion only when it exhibited essentially medieval characteristics. He believed that social evolution would gradually mitigate the conflict between science
and religion with the gradual unlocking of the secrets of the
universe.[15]

White's volume became widely popular. One scholar tells
us that it captured "the anticlerical sentiment of the *fin de
siecle* 'nineties" and provided for a generation a platform
for crusading "against Roman Catholicism, Protestant fun-
damentalism, and ecclesiasticism generally." One Catholic
writer has recently told us that this was "an age of agnosticism, liberalism, and subjectivism; of false notions of the
development of dogma; of misdirected attempts to reconcile
science and religion and to bring the Church into harmony with the intellectual, moral, and social needs of the
time. . . ."[16] Certainly it was a period of tensions and efforts
at readjustment. At Cornell, one writer for the student paper
many years earlier had complained that a student there had
found no difficulty in believing in the reality of miracles
until he had heard White lecture on "Demonology."[17]

White himself was a liberal Episcopalian, and he reported that he received letters of approval of his book from
Christian leaders, including an Anglican and an Episcopalian bishop.[18] A recent scholar believes that President
White apparently failed to realize "that if religion itself is
subject to the determinisms of Nature," it necessarily loses
its potency to bring "transformations for righteousness in
men's lives" and that he failed to "recognize the primacy of
Christian love."[19]

At the laying of the cornerstone of the first building of the Catholic University of America in May 1888, the liberal John L. Spalding, Bishop of Peoria, Illinois, expressed the viewpoint of advanced Catholic thought, saying in part:

> The scientific habit of mind is not favorable to child-like and unreasoning faith, and new views of the physical universe which the modern mind is forced to take, bring us face to face with new problems in religion and morals, in politics and society.[20]

Needless to say, some Catholics were far from enthusiastic about such a declaration.

At the World's Parliament of Religions at Chicago in 1893, moreover, a noted Catholic priest, Father d'Arby of Paris, France, had emphatically declared, "We love science; the office of science in religion is to prune it of fantastic growths. Without science religion would become superstition." Such statements were hailed by a leading humanist as an assurance that the religion of the future would be free from Pharisaism, narrowness, and aspects irreconcilable with scientific truth.

A leading professor at Wesleyan University in Connecticut, moreover, in 1890 expressed the view of many intellectually inclined churchgoers:

. . . "True science is the reading of the truths of the eternal One through his works and the Christian religion is founded upon the reading of his truths through his revelation. If both are true they cannot disagree. . . . For what is science, except the attempt to discover the laws of nature? And what are the laws of nature, except the modes of divine activity? . . ."[21]

(2) Geology

Long before organic evolution had challenged the thought and faith of educated men, the New Geology had

raised obstacles to a literal acceptance of the Biblical account of a Special Creation. At first the matter had attracted
the attention of scientific men almost exclusively. The significance of fossil remains, changes in the earth's structure,
and other geological data had come to the consideration of
scientists as early as the sixteenth century, and in the early
years of the American Republic, James Hutton (1726-1796),
a Scotchman of Edinburgh, had correlated aspects of the
problem. Epic-making of course was Charles Lyell's *Principles of Geology,* which insisted that the earth had arrived
at its existing stage through a long process of slow evolution.
Thereupon, furious contention on both sides of the Atlantic
had developed for a generation over the conflict of the geologist's view of terrestrial origins with the literal Old Testament version. The acceptance of the newer scientific viewpoints was a slower process in the United States than in
Great Britain. Among the British scientists, after Richard
Kirwan's *Geological Essays* (1799), no one of responsible
professional status contended for the literal creation story.[22]

In New England, Benjamin Silliman, Edward Hitchcock,
and James Dwight Dana, all of whom were devout Congregationalists who accepted the prevailing Calvinistic theology
and the traditional inspiration of the Scriptures, attempted
to reconcile the new geologic knowledge with religious orthodoxy. Silliman who taught at Yale until 1853 endeavored
to show that geology demonstrated the work of the Creator
which contributed to His glory. To Silliman, however, the
Bible was a guide to moral excellence rather than a textbook
of science, and he followed European scientists like the
French Georges Cuvier in interpreting each day of the
Genesis story as a geologic period of indefinite duration.
While his views had been received with favor by intellectually inclined clergymen, he had been criticized by the skeptical Thomas Cooper of South Carolina as yielding his
"common sense to clerical orthodoxy" and, on the other
hand, by the conservative Professor Moses Stuart of Andover
for his departure from Biblical literalism.[23]

Hitchcock, who was a Congregationalist minister, wrote

a volume on *The Religion of Geology* (1851) endeavoring to show that the character of God could be seen in the principles of science, and that geology strengthened faith by manifesting the working of the Divine Plan. Dana, Silliman's son-in-law, followed in the same viewpoint, and for many an impressive harmony of scientific and religious thought had been established.

Dana believed that the new doctrines of science had a tendency to spread infidelity, but that, as they came to be understood, it could be seen that science could have nothing to "say on moral and spiritual questions" but fulfilled its highest purpose in manifesting more and more the glory of God.[24]

Of greater reputation was the Swiss-born Jean Louis Agassiz, the son of the last of a long line of Protestant clergymen, and long professor of natural history at Harvard. To him all nature gave manifestations of the divine purpose, as he pointed out through his studies that changes through which animals go during the embryonic stage coincide with "the order of succession of the fossils of the same type in past geological ages."

Gradually these viewpoints reached the rising generation of students and then a wider circle of intellectually interested persons. At Princeton, for example, the Swiss-born Arnold Henry Guyot (1807-84), who had come to America at the urgent bidding of his friend Agassiz, endeavored to reconcile scientific views with devout faith. In his *Creation, or the Biblical Cosmology in the Light of Modern Science* (1884) he presented the vast picture of creation as one involving during the first three Biblical days the formation of the suns and planets and during the second three days the creation of the earth with its flora and fauna.[25] The slow development of thought in relation to this attempted reconciliation of science and theology was evidenced by the career of a younger contemporary, Charles W. Shields (1825-1904), a minister who had become professor of the harmony of science and religion at what is now Princeton University in 1865. Shields, after years of study and reflection, aban-

doned Guyot's seemingly forced efforts at harmony as spe-
cious and illogical. He urged a truce between science and
theology until new knowledge would wipe away all discrepancies in a perfect blending of various aspects of truth.

The relation of geology to Biblical truth continued to
concern intelligent laymen, but for those of open mind
the conclusions seemed well-nigh inevitable. Thus, in
1867, a prominent New Yorker, a vestryman in Trinity Episcopal Church, spent a couple of hours in the School of
Mines of Columbia University with the well known geologist, John S. Newberry. As a result he confided to his diary
that there seems to be no answer to the viewpoint of the
geologists as to the gradual development of terrestrial struc-
tures. He personally felt that such findings should not be
accepted reluctantly, but should be looked upon as an
awful enforcement of the "infinity of Creative Power."[26]
Thus, a certain adjustment was being made in a matter of
crucial significance for Western thought, for, as one historian, quoting W. H. Lecky, tells us:

> . . . the direct antagonism between science and theology
> which appeared in Catholicism at the time of the dis-
> coveries of Copernicus and Galileo was not seriously felt
> in Protestantism till geologists began to impugn the
> Mosaic account of the creation. . . .[27]

Yet, the adjustment was made, and soon there were geologists like the devout Presbyterian professor at Indiana
University, Richard Owen, who found no difficulty in reconciling his religious views with the new science.[28] On the
other hand, when the old orthodoxy proved inflexible, bitterness and heartbreaks were not unknown. Edward F. B.
Orton, a young Presbyterian minister who was teaching at
Albany State Normal School, in 1859 had been arraigned
for heresy by the Albany presbytery. Washington Gladden,
the famous Congregational clergyman, who came to know
Orton intimately, at the end of the century commented on
the intellectual climate of the period:

What was the nature of the divergence charged against him I do not know; it may, very likely, have been some conflict between his science and the traditional interpretation of the Book of Genesis. This was a time when strenuous efforts were made to reconcile Genesis with geology; such books as Hugh Muller's 'Testimony of the Rocks' and Pye Smith's 'Scripture and Geology' held fast to the historical and scientific accuracy of the early chapters of Genesis and sought to make them agree with the facts of modern science. Of course it was a hopeless undertaking; those chapters do not tally with the testimony of the rocks and it is not improbable that Edward Orton said so. . . .

At any rate, Orton resigned his teaching position, and after an interval as principal of an academy in Orange County, New York, he accepted a position as professor in Antioch College, Yellow Springs, Ohio in 1865. The situation which resulted has been well described by Dr. Gladden:

. . . Antioch College was in those days one of the most promising of the western institutions, and the call was a distinct promotion for Dr. Orton. But it was, at this time, under Unitarian control, and the acceptance of a professorship in it signified the identification of the professor with that denomination. To his good Presbyterian father, who had then retired from the ministry and was dwelling in retirement in northern Pennsylvania, this was a terrible calamity—almost a tragedy. He could not regard his son's action in any other light than that of apostasy; for a long time he could neither be reconciled nor comforted. At length, however, he was persuaded to visit Yellow Springs, and after a few weeks spent in the home of his son, the father returned to his own house greatly reassured and quieted. One cannot help pitying the good man in his agony of soul over the departure of his son from the orthodox fold, yet one must wonder at the blinding power of a theological prejudice, which

could fill the heart of a father with mortal fear for the
fate of a son with a faith as firm and a character as
Christlike as that of Edward Orton.[29]

Orton became President of Antioch College, later (1873-
1881) President of what came to be called the Ohio State
University, and finally State Geologist of Ohio (1882-1899),
but his experience had alienated him from the older religious orthodoxy, although according to Gladden, not at all
from "his hold on the fundamental verities of religion."

One, however, who became completely alienated from
organized religious life, after a period of earnest devotion
to it, was Lester F. Ward, destined to be one of the founders
of modern sociology.[30] Ward was long (1865-81) associated
with the United States treasury department. Scientifically
inclined, he joined the Geological Survey in 1881 and eventually became a recognized authority in paleontology. This
interest was definitely related to his becoming an ardent
advocate of monistic and evolutionary interpretations of
social development based on ethical and humanitarian, but
not orthodox religious, viewpoints.[31]

Even conservative Presbyterian orthodoxy, as represented
by Princeton Theological Seminary, however, long before
the end of the century, had definitely accepted the implications of the New Geology. In April 1891, Professor Benjamin
B. Warfield wrote:

> Man seems to have existed on the globe at least ten
> or fifteen thousand years; how much longer let the in-
> vestigations of the future search out for us. Theology
> at all events has nothing to gain or lose by the result. . . .
> Theologians will look to the exegetes of the book of
> nature to read her this riddle and will rest in their re-
> sults.[32]

Thereafter, in informed circles, opposition to the New
Geology was an expiring cause.

CHAPTER V

DARWINISM AS A CHALLENGE TO ORTHODOXY

The idea of development in the physical world had early been present in the history of Western thought. Over many centuries, however, it had remained largely dormant. Then it had become implicit in the contentions of the New Geology and in cultural changes associated with the beginnings of an acceptance of some of the views of the Higher Criticism of the Bible. Yet, more revolutionary to the thought of the late nineteenth century was the concept of organic evolution.[1] Those whose theology had been worked out in a very detailed way, as was especially the case of the Catholics and Calvinists, soon saw the implications of the new biological theories for the time-honored views. The argument of design in the universe, as popularized by the English theologian, William Paley, had long been accepted in Protestant circles as a basis for definite proof of theism. This seemed imperilled, as did the established views of Adam's fall, the depravity of man, the Atonement, and immortality. This came at a time when urban growth, woman's rights, and other changes were altering American society, so especial concern, often inarticulate, became evident, as "the ultimate security" of fixed religious beliefs in a world of change now seemed endangered.[2] Thus, Charles Darwin's *Origin of Species* (1859) which was to symbolize the whole evolutionary controversy, "fired a shot," the effects of which were eventually heard round the theological world. According to one present day authority, by undermining the fixity of concepts regarding "species—plant, animal, and human, Darwin exposed mind, morals, and therefore, the whole scope of social relations to change and, ultimately, to naturalism."

At first, Darwin's views were, of course, of primary interest to scientific men. Yet, their views were at length to have great effect on theologians and church-goers in general, who were in many instances unwilling to ignore the scientific viewpoint. In the early years of the controversy in the United States, Louis Agassiz, James Dwight Dana, and Asa Gray were those of outstanding influence.[3] Agassiz, the descendant of a long line of Swiss Protestant ministers, was a man of obvious sincerity who opposed Darwin's claims on what he believed to be conclusive scientific grounds. His fundamental postulates had been formed over a period of years, and perhaps it was difficult for him to alter his basic views. Although he cared little for dogma, he was a convinced theist who found in Nature a constant revelation of God.

Asa Gray, distinguished Harvard botanist, had received from Darwin an early account of his proposed work and so was probably the first American scientist to have any pre-publication knowledge of Darwin's research. Gray was a convinced theist, who accepted the historic Nicene creed and considered himself a conscientious exponent of the Christian faith. Both Agassiz and Gray believed in the existence of absolute truth. Gray held that this was not affected by Darwinism, while Agassiz found some variance between it and his own views of absolute truth. Gray was at first not a complete convert to Darwin's views, in keeping with the caution of the true scientific spirit, but he soon moved from an attitude of receptive interest to one of definite acceptance. He endeavored to defend Darwin's theism, and the compatibility of natural selection with the argument from design, and he refused to agree that the origin of species should be left in the realm of the supernatural.[4]

The third scientist, James Dwight Dana, also a profoundly religious man, occupied a middle position between Agassiz and Gray. Long a professor at Yale, he took no prominent part in the controversy.[5] Yet, his position was definitely indicative of the trend of thought. He was first an opponent of the theory, then a cautious advocate, and finally a convinced supporter.

After the scientific world, the larger circle of intellectually inclined people in the colleges took up the question. New England colleges at that time almost without exception had a definitely religious emphasis, and the same situation generally prevailed elsewhere. Naturally, there was opposition to the acceptance of a theory which in the view of some implied no "aid or need of a Deity."

At first religious periodicals were almost uniformly opposed to any concessions to the new hypothesis. *The Biblical Repertory and Princeton Review,* scholarly vehicle of Presbyterian thought, and the *Methodist Review* as early as 1860 had spoken out strongly against it.

In the early stages of the controversy the churchmen attacked Darwinism definitely on scientific grounds, claiming: lack of proof that species had really evolved; no record in geological remains of the fossils of the missing links; the sterility of hybrids; the inability of man-made varieties to survive in a state of nature; and, to them, the more plausible explanation of natural phenomena provided by the idea of special creation.[6] At first these critics did not accuse Darwin of a definite attempt to further atheism. Rather they charged him with ignoring or treating lightly the traditional evidences for design and making merely "complimentary allusions to the Deity." Very early, however, some asserted that atheism, though unavowed, was really implicit in Darwin's work.

Yet, in 1864, Professor P. A. Chadbourne, a future president of Williams College, declared that he did not see a tendency toward atheism in the theory. Professor William North Rice of Wesleyan University wrote an article in *The New Englander* (1867) declaring his belief in the special creation of species (at that time espoused by Dana), and against Darwin's position, but he protested against the bitterly aggressive tone of many theologians of the time.[7] Dr. A. P. Peabody of Harvard in *Christianity, the Religion of*

Nature (1863) had asserted that as for the first tree, the first bird, the first elephant, the first man,—each was a miracle. Yet, in the next year (1864) in an article in *Bibliotheca Sacra* he showed a sympathetic view of Darwinism denying that it was antagonistic to Christianity.

The insinuations in the 1860's that atheism was involved in the implications of Darwinism gave way in the 1870's to direct charges that Darwin deliberately sought to advance atheism.[8] Darwin's *Descent of Man* (1871) definitely linked man with the evolutionary process and seemed to imperil, to an increased degree, Christian dogma. Professor Herman Lincoln of the Baptist Theological Institute at Newton, Massachusetts, repeated the arguments of Agassiz against Darwinism, and Dr. Luther T. Townsend of Boston University also wrote in utter rejection of the theory. Dr. Howard Crosby, classical scholar and Presbyterian minister, lent the prestige of his position as Chancellor of the New York University to identify the new theory with Greek materialism.

Very influential was Enoch Fitch Burr who had been made lecturer on the scientific evidences of revealed religion at Amherst College in order to combat Darwinism. Among his works were *Pater Mundi: or the Doctrine of Evolution* (Boston, 1873) which linked evolution with stark materialism. (Apparently, however, his lectures tended to make evolutionists of the students, and they were discontinued.) Asa Mahan, President of Adrian College, Michigan, in lectures at Ohio Wesleyan University made the issue one of anti-theism against theism. In 1872 President Randolph S. Foster of Drew Theological Seminary (and later a Methodist bishop) denounced Darwinism as "undisguised atheism," although he recognized that the evolutionary theory itself was not "essentially atheistic."

For those who put firm trust in the literal truth of the Bible, the Creation story itself was an effective answer to the new theory. Some claimed that if the Creation story were rejected along with it would go the contributions of "Paul and the New Testament in general."[9] In line with this, one of the most noted theologians of the period, Charles Hodge of Princeton Theological Seminary, editor of the *Princeton Review,* came forth at the age of seventy-seven with a popular exposition of the theme that theism and Darwinism could not be reconciled. Published as *What Is Darwinism?* (1874), it endeavored to overthrow the defenders of evolution by proclaiming that the Bible asserts that those who reject Holy Writ are lost to reason or morals, or both. In his zeal Hodge, according to some, had abandoned the attitude of fairness for which he was known, asserting that Darwin denied design in nature, hence in spite of Darwin's professed belief in God, his theory was atheistic.[10]

Hodge was followed by John T. Duffield, professor of mathematics at Princeton, who was also a Presbyterian minister. He wrote in similar vein as did the illustrious classical scholar, Tayler Lewis, also a Presbyterian, who insisted that the Bible and Darwinism were in "polar opposition" to each other.

The attitude generally of the Catholic Church in America was shown by the *Catholic World* which expressed in 1869 the view that the more light that was thrown upon the matter the more glaring would become the "absurdity" of the theory. A writer in the *Catholic Advocate* (Louisville, Kentucky) even suggested that Darwin had to his pecuniary advantage perpetrated a huge hoax upon the learned world (1871). Other articles in the *Catholic World* insisted that the Creation story was still the authentic account of man's origin. In that publication and in his own *Review,* Orestes A. Brownson was tireless in his denunciation of every phase of Darwinism.[11] Brownson furthermore, demanded no compromise with the new geology and biology, denouncing such a concession as a regression from the teachings of Thomas Aquinas.[12]

Religious leaders were especially irritated at those whom they deemed "the shallow and blatant opposers of Christianity," who espoused the new views. They, moreover, strongly attacked provocative defenders of Darwinism like Haeckel,

Tyndall, and Spencer. Thomas Huxley visited the country in 1876, delivering lectures on the evidences for evolution, and Spencer did the same in 1882, and the former especially received sarcastic denunciation in the religious press.[13]

Gradually, however, a more receptive attitude toward evolutionary views became evident. Newton Mann (1836-1926), who was the supply pastor of the Unitarian church in Cincinnati in 1859, preached a sermon on "The Implications of Darwin's Philosophy" which may have been the first forecast of some of the effects of evolutionary theories on American religious trends. He maintained that this constituted a break in the whole history of thought, for special creation, original sin, and the old idea of redemption were outmoded. At that time, however, such a sermon was too revolutionary even for liberal Unitarians.[14]

A little later, however, Minot Judson Savage (1841-1918), who had built the First Congregational Church of Hannibal, Missouri, into the largest congregation of that denomination in Missouri became sorely troubled by an intellectual struggle in which evolutionary views played a part. He therefore welcomed a pastorate at the Third Unitarian Church of Chicago (1873-4), followed by one at the Church of the Unity, Boston (1874-96), and the Church of the Messiah (later, the Community Church), New York (1896-1906). He was probably the earliest American clergyman to attain prominence by an unqualified defense of evolutionary views. In his sermons he steadfastly maintained that the idea of scientific, social, and religious evolution enhanced and ennobled the essential values of Christian belief and conduct, rather than debasing or destroying them. In 1876 he wrote *The Religion of Evolution*. At Massachusetts Agricultural School at Amherst, a young man from Vermont feared that he might lose his faith, as fellow students discussed Darwin and Huxley, and one bragged that he was an atheist. But the young man picked up a paper bound edition of Savage's book and found renewed faith in God and the Bible.

Such was the experience of Daniel Willard, later noted president of the Baltimore and Ohio Railroad.[15]

Savage's successor at the Third Unitarian Church of Chicago (1874-77) was Edward Payson Powell who became the author of *Our Heredity from God* (1887), dedicated to "all those who, like the author, have lost faith in authoritative Revelation, in hopes that they, like himself, may find satisfaction in the revelation of Eternal Life and Truth which is steadily unfolded to us by Science."

Even in Unitarian circles, however, the struggle continued. In 1875 a writer in the *Unitarian Review* had condemned Darwin for discarding the rich treasures of theism for a "hotchpotch of semi-arabesque scrawls, presenting only delusory appearances of meaning." Yet, another Unitarian, Jenkin Lloyd Jones, began publishing in 1872, Sunday School lessons for liberal churches, emphasizing the evolution of man, and the blossoming of Christianity into a universal religion of ethical theism. Others of similar views, like John White Chadwick, for forty years (1864-1904) pastor of the Second Unitarian church of Brooklyn, New York, welcomed the doctrine of evolution. The influential Henry Ward Beecher had in a Sunday morning sermon, March 11, 1860, indicated his personal inclination to accept the doctrine of evolution. Yet, he was careful not to venture far in advance of his intellectually inclined congregation, and not until almost twenty years later did he begin the systematic advocacy of evolution as a positive aid to evangelical faith. Eight sermons published as *Evolution and Religion* (1883) were widely read.[16]

One who did much to influence thinking in America regarding evolution, although he had little direct effect on the orthodox churches, was Francis E. Abbot (1836-1903). His faith was rooted in free present intuition, in the spirit of Emerson. He developed a system of scientific theism, based on evolutionary views, but his individualism alienated him from Unitarianism and then from The Free Religious

Association. No important figure followed his leadership, and he committed suicide in 1903.[17] In more orthodox circles, some who did not accept evolution as definitely demonstrated, now contended that if it were true, atheism was not a necessary corollary. They endeavored to reject mechanistic views of evolution and to combine the idea of a Divine Creator with the view of an evolutionary process of growth to show a new cosmic Providence.[18] The old "carpenter theory" with anthropomorphic ideas of a designer was rejected in favor of the principle of design working through the orderly principle of law.

Two approaches were evident in the attempts to achieve a compromise between science and religion. Some, like Andrew P. Peabody of Harvard, asserted that there could be no real conflict between science and Christianity, for both came from the same source, and God had surely put his seal on nature as well as on Holy Writ. To Peabody, "The hieroglyphics of nature must needs correspond to the alphabetic writing of revelation, which may interpret and supplement, but cannot supercede or falsify them." Another approach was to hold to the ancient idea of the duality of truth with the view that Christianity and science, resting on different foundations and dealing with different subject matter, had nothing to do with each other.

Some, recalling the allegorical adaptations of the Creation story to the new geology, searched the Scriptures to find intimations of the evolutionary hypothesis. James McCosh and Arnold Guyot of Princeton found such evidence in Genesis. McCosh, Scottish-born president of Princeton, who had entered upon his duties there in 1868, published his *Christianity and Positivism* (1871). Of unquestioned orthodoxy and of fervent religious zeal, McCosh had an international reputation as a thinker and educator. He now professed acceptance of the evolutionary hypothesis, though he insisted that man's unique spiritual qualities pointed to his special creation rather than to his origin by natural selection.[19] In his *Religious Aspects of Evolution*

(1888) he came to emphasize the factors modifying evolution,—light, life, sensation, instinct, intelligence, and morality. These, he believed, were created by an "immediate fiat" of God, thereby continuing the divine process of creation.

Another Calvinist, George Frederick Wright, Professor of the Harmony of Science and Revelation at Oberlin College, proclaimed Darwinism as the "Calvinistic interpretation of nature," involving a true doctrine of design and rescuing natural history "from empiricism and positivism."[20]

John Bascom, president of the University of Wisconsin from 1874 to 1887, was one who was ready to pay respect to Darwin and Huxley so long as they dealt with the lower forms of life, but he found it impossible to accept their discussions in relation to men.[21]

Among those of the German Reformed faith, John Summers Stahr (1841-1915), long professor and later President of Franklin and Marshall College, had written for a denominational journal as early as 1872, stoutly affirming that evolution and the doctrines of genuine Christianity were not in conflict. Similarly, John Benjamin Drury (1838-1909), long a Dutch Reformed pastor in New York state, wrote *Truths and Untruths of Evolution* (1884) cautioning his clerical brethren that true religion was not served by an attempt to deny such facts relating to evolution as had been established by true scientific methods.

St. George Mivart, an English Catholic, and a firm critic of the theory of natural selection, was an evolutionist, and both in Catholic and in Protestant circles after 1871 he contributed definitely to the discussion of the Darwinian controversy in America. He frankly asserted that the influence of Darwin in respect to the question "whether the world is the outcome of a blind, irrational, and immoral energy, or whether it is the work of God" was probably greater than that "of any writer since St. Paul." He insisted that the existence of human reason made the conception of an undesigned universe an absurdity. To him Darwinism had wonderfully stimulated biological research but was philosophically "a retrogression," for it ran contrary to what he deemed obvious—that evolution is a "divinely ordered process." Later, Mivart was condemned by the Church for other views.

During the eighteen eighties and nineties, as Catholic liberals expressed advanced views, including those which came to be associated with "Americanism," Father John A. Zahm of Notre Dame University and others worked zealously in advocating the scientific probability and theological acceptability of the evolutionary theory. They contended: (a) That evolution was scientifically more valid than the idea of special creation; (b) That the evolution of Adam's body was a defensible hypothesis; (c) That the Church Fathers, especially St. Augustine, had been evolutionists.

In conservative Catholic circles Archbishop Corrigan of New York and others strenuously opposed such views, and they carried the issue to Rome. There, they were able to have Zahm's *Evolution and Dogma* (1896) visited with a rebuke from the Congregation of the Index. Father Zahm had been a leading teacher of science at Notre Dame since 1873, but his statements regarding the origin of man's body were not approved, and he was ordered to withdraw *Evolution and Dogma* from circulation. The doctrine advanced by Zahm was never expressly condemned as heretical. The decree of the Congregation of the Index, moreover, was never published. Yet, the action taken was publicized in the United States by the conservatives and tended to announce that while the theory was acceptable as applied to plants and animals, as applied to man, it was not.[22] As time went on, Conservative Catholics sought to preserve the Zahm precedent, but much of informed Catholic opinion in the United States was to accept evolution as "not opposed to Catholicism" but as a process by which God works "through secondary causes which He instituted." Such a view holds that "Materialism is a philosophical explanation of the universe which has nothing in common with evolution," as explained by Catholic scholars.[23]

The weekly *Independent,* most influential religious paper in the Protestantism of that day, with more than six thousand clergymen receiving it, was a pioneer in giving a cautiously sympathetic appraisal of evolution. It took the theme that evolution did not endanger theism, and it offered attempts at a reconciliation of evolution and the Scriptures.[24] The idea of evolution, however, made for such a marked change in thought processes that it was only slowly accepted.

An influential publicist of the time was (Flavius) Josephus Cook (1838-1901) who for almost twenty years after 1875 delivered the Monday lectures at Tremont Temple, Boston, to great throngs of the intellectually inclined who wished to know about the latest trends of scholarship as affecting science and religion. He always spoke in an oracular manner that carried conviction. After Huxley had delivered lectures in 1876 on evolution, Cook was one of many ministers who took up the theme. He insisted in a way that comforted the orthodox that what scientists and philosophers were saying was either incorrect or was wholly compatible with revealed religion. A journal like the *Nation* took definite exception to some of his remarks, deeming them superficial and pretentious in so far as they invaded the province of the scientist.

A prominent vestry man of Trinity Church, New York, who had had no difficulty in accepting the New Geology as modifying literal ideas of the Creation story, found (1871) in Darwin's *Descent of Man* not a scintilla of scientific evidence. He believed the whole thesis untenable, for he held that higher species could no more be descended from the lower "than gold from lead."[25] As late as 1886, moreover, in the wake of the evolutionary hypothesis the House of Bishops of the Episcopal Church issued a Pastoral Letter deploring "the flood of infidelity which is sweeping over our land."[26]

Three important popularizers of the theory of evolution in non-clerical positions were Edward L. Youmans, Joseph Le Conte, and John Fiske, and all had a profound influence in church-going circles. Youmans (1821-87) as a scientific lecturer to lyceum audiences, as an editor of popular but authoritative works by scientists like Darwin, and as the editor after 1872 of *Popular Science Monthly* (later the *Scientific Monthly*) did much to acquaint Americans with trends in science, including evolution.

Joseph Le Conte (1823-1901) was a Southerner of New England antecedents. Of deep personal piety, he early accepted the theory of evolution. Long a geologist at the University of California, he emphasized the rational factor on the human level, and relegated the importance of natural selection to the pre-human period. Thus, he rejected Social Darwinism, and, much influenced by the philosophy of idealism, he looked to God operating through physical laws and in the soul of man, and found in Jesus Christ the culmination of the evolutionary process. His theology was not that of the old orthodoxy, but for many he seemed to present a satisfactory adjustment between science and the ethical insights of Christianity.

Of primary importance was John Fiske, philosopher, historian and popular interpreter of science.[27] Fiske as a youth in Middletown, Connecticut had joined a conservative Congregational church and had been much interested in religious activities. But the reading of the works of Gibbon and Humboldt had stirred religious questioning. His own pastor was narrowly dogmatic and not very helpful. Scholarly clergymen at that time sometimes explained fossil remains which pointed to animal origins as a part of the work of Satan who had distributed them so as to confuse men as to the divine truth revealed in Genesis. Having read Buckle's *History of Civilization in England,* Fiske had abandoned dogmatic Christianity in the summer of 1859.[28] By 1860, as a student at Harvard, he wrote to his mother that he had become a Positivist. He had continued to attend church, as required by Harvard regulations but lost a scholarship because he was too often absent from morning prayers. Having read Draper's volume, he came to look upon theoretical Christianity as "sublime" but its history as one of decep-

tion, superstition, misery, and blood-shed, in reality "a gi-
gantic swindle" that had caused its power in the eighteenth
and nineteenth century to dwindle "almost to nothing."[29]

But, his views gradually moderated. Occasionally he
loved to go to Petersham, Massachusetts and play the organ
for the Sunday service at the Unitarian church. Soon he
was lecturing in Boston on the "Critical Attitude of Philosophy Toward Christianity." He felt that he was throwing a
"blaze of new light" on the complete harmony of true Christianity and the deepest philosophy. He rejected miracles, but
by March 1872 he was convinced that his views when thoroughly understood disarmed opposition and were accepted
"by the most truly religious part of the community of
whatever sect."

President Charles Eliot had invited him to give a series
of lectures on the philosophy of evolution at Harvard. This
Fiske had done in the fall of 1869, and while some opposition asserted itself, he was reappointed for 1870-1. Yet, in
1872 even the liberal Eliot felt that he could not invite Fiske
to give the Lowell Lectures in Boston, because the provision for their establishment required that the lecturer believe in the Divine Revelation of the Old and New Testament. Eliot stated that he personally could not declare his
belief in such a Revelation as generally interpreted, and he
did not believe that Fiske could.

In 1874 his *Outlines of Cosmic Philosophy* appeared.
Fiske endeavored to show that no real issue existed between
religion and science. In his various writings over a period
of years Fiske held that the difficulties had arisen because
of the Augustinian idea of a transcendent God, actuated by
human passions, utterly remote from the universe and acting
intermittently to suspend the so-called natural laws; because
of the disassociation of natural law and divine action; and
because of a conservative fear that the new ideas would lower
man's spiritual outlook. To Fiske, evolution brought a final
reconciliation of science and religion, for it explained the
development of truth in each, and it presented God not in

anthropomorphic terms localized in space but as infinite
and immanent in the world of nature.[30] Fiske insisted that
this cosmic theism involved higher religious and ethical
ideals than those of orthodox theology. Having overthrown
some of the "semi-barbaric mythology" of Christian symbolism Fiske claimed that the evolutionist held firmly to
the religious and ethical principles for which Christianity
was chiefly valued even by those who clung to its traditional
forms. To Fiske both the medieval saint and the modern
scientist were seekers after righteousness, the former yearning to become "like his highest concrete conception of
human excellence, ideally embodied in Christ" while the
scientist sought to live rightly by "entire conformity to
the requirements of nature."[31]

In 1879 Fiske resigned his position as librarian at Harvard and "entered upon a life career as perhaps the most
popular lecturer on history America has ever known,"
though for some years his chief interest found focus in science and philosophy. By this time Fiske looked upon Positivism as a philosophy from which he utterly dissented.[32]
Fiske, emphasizing as he did a theistic position had much
more influence than avowed freethinkers and thus did
more than they to break down rigid orthodoxy.[33]

Fiske thoroughly enjoyed his career as a lecturer. Sometimes he talked on American History, and sometimes on
science. His letters abound in references to lecture and
preaching engagements. At first (1879-80) his audiences
were often very small, as at Dayton and Cleveland, Ohio.
In the latter place only 35 attended, but he captivated the
audience and paved the way for future successes and popular fame.[34]

In 1884 he lectured at Concord at the School of Philosophy, expressing his faith in the immortality of the soul.
This became a favorite theme with him. Thus, in August
1884 he preached to a large audience of summer boarders
and farmers at the Unitarian Church in Petersham, Massachusetts on the subject. One farmer told him that he could

have sat on the floor for five hours in order to listen "to such beautiful doctrine."[35] The material was published as *The Destiny of Man Viewed in the Light of his Origin* and was a great success. Later, a son of a Presbyterian minister and one who became a liberal philosopher of religion, Henry N. Wieman, recorded that he had read Fiske's volume in his father's small library in a little Missouri town at the age of fourteen and had then become an evolutionist.[36] A Presbyterian minister at Albany, New York was captivated by the volume and deemed the author the "Evangelist" of the age.

Fiske was especially welcome at Unitarian churches throughout the country,—at Portland, Oregon where crowds came to hear him expound on "The Mystery of Evil;" at Tacoma, Washington; at New Orleans; at Brooklyn; at San Jose, California; at Minneapolis, and elsewhere. On other occasions he preached at liberal Congregational churches and at Gunsaulus' undenominational church in Chicago. On one occasion when he preached in a great Gothic structure with the "finest stained glass" windows in the country and was assisted by a magnificent choir and organ, in 1893, he found real exuberation in being a "parson" and he felt "just a wee bit near to heaven."

Representative Episcopalian clergymen found much to commend in his works. In 1892, William S. Rainsford, noted pastor of St. George's Church, New York, wrote to congratulate Fiske on his having made clear to thoughtful Christians the great unity of purpose "running through all life and all time." In 1899 Rev. William G. Thayer, head of the well known St. Mark's School, wrote in endorsement of every word in *Through Nature to God,* as he found it especially helpful for idealistic young men of scientific interest who had feared that sooner or later they might be compelled to admit that a personal God was intellectually absurd.

Within the main stream of American Protestantism perhaps no clergyman had greater influence in winning an acceptance of the evolutionary idea than Henry Ward Beecher and his successor, Lyman Abbott. Beecher, most noted preacher of his day, as pastor of Plymouth Congregational Church, Brooklyn, had taken a stand in acceptance of the evolutionary views as early as 1880. Beecher's *Evolution and Religion* (1885), however, expressed views that he felt might be embarrassing to some of his clerical brethren so he had already withdrawn from the Association of Congregational ministers in October 1882.[37] In 1881, Abbott had become editor-in-chief of what had been generally known as "Mr. Beecher's paper," *The Christian Union*. By 1882, Abbott was writing that the theory might be incompatible with some church and Biblical views but it was "certainly not atheistic, nor even un-Christian."[38] Abbott was soon, through sermons, editorials, and rather notable books developing a conception of evolution acceptable to many orthodox Protestants. His books included *The Evolution of Christianity* (1892) and *The Theology of an Evolutionist* (1897). The latter, phrased in epigrammatic style (with borrowings from many other authors) stressed an optimistic interpretation of the role of evolution. Much influenced by the Scottish writer and lecturer, Henry Drummond, who had written *Natural Law in the Spiritual World* (1883) and *The Ascent of Man* (1884), Abbott found in evolution a sturdy defense for faith in immortality. Some believed that Abbott was a power in winning skeptics back to the Christian fold, but the editor of the Episcopalian *Church Standard* deemed *The Theology of an Evolutionist* "a dreadful book." Moreover, when in 1895, Abbott was commencement speaker at Northwestern University, his address on "Evolution" was so liberal in its implications as to make some hearers squirm in their seats.

At any rate, theistic evolution was a soothing doctrine to many in a world of change, and in the Middle West, Washington Gladden performed a role not unlike that played by Abbott in the East, in preaching the optimistic implications.

Evolution was fundamentally a scientific question, but

interpreted so as to conserve moral values,[39] it gradually was increasingly accepted in the colleges. The tension involved in this was illustrated in the case of an intellectually inclined Catholic, Maurice F. Egan, who in the period after 1878 was one of an informal group of ten or twelve college students in Philadelphia. Two had become agnostics, and the other non-Catholic members held to their belief in revealed religion in spite of Darwinism, although they had become unsettled in their views. Egan treated evolution as a hypothesis, not a dogma, and felt that he was not hampered, as were many Protestants, by a literal interpretation of the Scriptures. But some of the group considered him a less than orthodox Catholic.[40]

One of the most influential teachers of his time was Charles Edward Garman (1850-1907), son of a Congregationalist minister and for over a quarter of a century professor of philosophy at Amherst College. Among his interests was that of reconciling Darwin's theory with man's moral and spiritual life.[41] A not uncommon experience of college youths was that they slowly and "without perceptible crisis or violent wrench with the past" accepted the evolutionary views. Such was the case of Edgar S. Brightman, destined to be a leading Methodist religious teacher, who as a boy had strenuously resisted any attempt to reconcile the contributions of Moses and Darwin to human thought.[42] On the mature level a similar change took place in the thinking of President Bascom (previously mentioned) who came to distinguish between "mechanical" and "spiritual" evolution, the latter being the work of a creative force which is "the embodied wisdom and love of God." Bascom, now stressing the immanence of God, found in evolution the very touchstone of religion and the key to new interpretations of the social and spiritual life of man.[43]

In general, the South was extremely cautious in accepting evolution. Professor Alexander Winchell had been a lecturer on geology and biology at Vanderbilt University, Nashville (1875-78). Among his views were those later

published in a book, *The Pre-Adamites* (1880) in which he
asserted that Adam was the progenitor of Caucasians only,
the black and brown races having been in existence for some
centuries previous.[44] A devout church member, Winchell
was known as an advocate of the theory of evolution as explained in his *The Doctrine of Evolution* (1874). His views
were distinctly theistic, and he found even in "natural selection" the design of the "Author of Nature—God."[45] Yet,
conservative Methodist opinion was unfavorable to the retention of Winchell, and his contract was not renewed in
1878. Officially, this was done on grounds of economy, but
Winchell looked upon it as "ecclesiastical proscription."[46]

A more serious storm developed later in the Columbia
(S. C.) Theological Seminary (Presbyterian) in 1884, where
James Woodrow (uncle of the future president, Woodrow
Wilson) was Professor "of Natural Science in Connexion
with Revelation." Woodrow in an address to the Alumni
denied any real conflict between the Bible and science, insisting that the concept of evolution was conducive to a
more profound reverence for God's plan of creation. He believed that Adam's body had probably been the result of
an evolution from the body of some lower animal. After
much conflict, he was removed from his teaching position,
but he soon became associated with the University of South
Carolina, eventually becoming President, and he continued
to be an influential figure in Southern Presbyterianism.

The Woodrow episode occurred at a time when no
southern institution of higher learning included a course
on evolution in its curriculum.[47] Yet, before the end of the
century numerous ministers and instructors in the South
were open supporters of the evolutionary theory.[48] Here, as
in other parts of the country, there were of course great
numbers of religious people whose religious experience was
so deeply grounded that they found little reason to be disturbed by controversies over evolution.[49]

At any rate, by the end of the century leading educational leaders of Christian background had come to accept

the principle of evolution as no more a matter of uncertainty than the law of gravitation. As early as 1891, a prominent Methodist, who was a professor in the field of science, asserted that one could easily count on the fingers of one hand "all anti-evolutionists who are competent to have an opinion on the subject."[50]

In the adjustment that had taken place within the bounds of evangelical Protestantism, the efforts of Congregationalists had been more important than those in any other denomination. Henry Ward Beecher, Lyman Abbott, Newman Smyth, Theodore T. Munger, Francis Johnson, Henry Churchill King, and George Frederick Wright had been especially influential, along with leaders in other religious groups.

During the same period a more mature reconciliation of evolution and theology had been achieved. Now, some were dissatisfied with the easy identification of the evolutionary process and the message of Christianity after the manner of John Fiske. Thus, a distinguished Methodist scholar, Borden P. Bowne, who fifteen years before had pictured the dark despair which evolution brought in its train through a philosophy of naturalism,[51] now wrote (1893) for a denominational periodical that evolution in the scientific sense, "is a perfectly harmless and not over-important doctrine." He elaborated, "In itself it is as good as any other, and, when proved, or in so far as proved, it is better than any other. It is equally plain that most of the conclusions drawn from it do not follow. The mass of what passes for evolution in popular literature and discussion is bad metaphysics, worse logic, and hearsay science."[52]

CHAPTER VI

BIBLICAL CRITICISM AND COMPARATIVE RELIGIONS

Biblical Criticism

Another challenge to the faith of the churches was the rise of Biblical Criticism, including the "Higher Criticism," which cast further doubts on the verbal inerrancy of the Scriptures. From the time of the Reformation occasionally writers had challenged traditional views regarding certain aspects of Holy Writ, and modern Old Testament criticism had definitely gotten under way in Germany after 1780. At about the same time new conclusions were being drawn concerning dates, reliability, and kindred questions affecting the New Testament.

As early as 1850 advanced scholars in the United States had come to the conclusion that the writings of the Hebrews and early Christians must be tested by critical standards, as in the case of other literature. New England Unitarians had early taken advanced positions. John G. Palfrey contended that Genesis was a later compilation from at least two independent sources in his *Lectures on Jewish History and Antiquities* (1840), and Andrews Norton had rejected the Mosaic authorship of the Pentateuch (1844).[1]

Much of the meticulous scholarship involved was carried on for many years, especially on the continent of Europe, by those who felt lightly or not at all the restraint of ecclesiastical authority. In 1860, Benjamin Jowett, renowned Professor of Greek at Oxford, had written that true inspiration must be such as conforms "to all well-ascertained facts of history and science" and that the Gospel ought not, instead of warring on the vices of mankind, oppose itself "to one of the highest and rarest of human virtues—the love of truth."[2] Soon, Rowland Wilson in England had been tried by an ecclesiastical court and found guilty of heretical views about Biblical inspiration, but the verdict was set aside by the court of appeal, the judicial committee of the Privy Council.

In the meantime, in 1862, Bishop John William Colenso (1814-83), Anglican bishop of Natal in South Africa, had published the first of a series of critical treatises on the Pentateuch and the Book of Joshua. Colenso had translated parts of the Bible into the Zulu language, and the puzzling queries put to him by the natives had strengthened him in his dissatisfaction with traditional interpretations. At length he was excommunicated and deprived of his bishopric, but he received widespread moral and financial support in England.

Colenso, in the view of his supporters, had demonstrated mathematically that it would have been impossible for as many persons to have satisfied their thirst from a single well or have subsisted in a barren wilderness for forty years, as the Scriptural writings asserted.[3]

In the United States in 1865, the House of Bishops of the Episcopal Church endorsed the excommunication of Colenso and authorized a letter to the clergy and candidates for clerical orders, emphasizing the condemnation of such views as those of Colenso.[4]

A few years later in England, Matthew Arnold took an advanced position, which his father, the famous Dr. Thomas Arnold of Rugby, in some respects a liberal churchman, had always avoided. The older Arnold had never criticized the authority of Holy Writ, but the author of *Culture and Anarchy* now published *Literature and Dogma: An Essay Towards a Better Apprehension of the Bible* (1873) and *God and the Bible: A Review of Objections to Literature and Dogma* (1875). In these an effort was made to demonstrate that the Bible must not be considered a scientific account of the spiritual history of man.[5] In Germany, scholars like Julius Wellhausen rejected (in a work first published in 1878) the time-honored view that Moses was the author of the Pentateuch, and he endeavored to reconstruct much of the history of the Jewish religion.[6]

To the devout, the Bible was "the Sacred Page," and in Scotland, espousal of the new views led to the dismissal of William Robertson Smith, a learned philologist, archaeologist, and Biblical critic from his professorship at Free Church College, Aberdeen.

In the United States, as elsewhere, the popular view was that the Scriptures were inspired, hence inerrant. Daniel Willard, later the distinguished President of the Baltimore and Ohio Railroad, was a not untypical American boy, raised in Vermont, who later recalled how he considered the Bible handed down by God himself with every word and comma in keeping with the divine wish.[7]

In view of this climate of opinion, textual criticism of the Biblical narrative, was deemed almost a form of sacrilege. Accordingly, in commenting on apparent inconsistencies as to the number of men in an army (as in Kings and in Chronicles) or as to details of certain incidents in the different Gospels, it was common practice to dismiss such discrepancies as the mistakes of copyists or the errors of translators. At least, it was claimed, the *original* form (no longer in existence) had been directly inspired, hence it was inerrant.[8] The Hebrew and Greek texts were deemed especially reliable, and, accordingly, educated ministers were faithful students of the two languages.

The progress of the new scholarship, nevertheless, led to troubled times for theological professors, ministers, and intelligent laymen. When one's faith had rested confidently in the Bible as an Infallible Book it was shockingly disconcerting to have the higher critics raise troublesome questions. Protestant churches which did not stress, or perhaps believe in (as did Roman Catholics and some others) the authority of a church organization claiming continuity from apostolic times, looked upon this trend as a particularly dangerous one.

At the time of the Reformation, all theologians, Catholic and Protestant, except a relatively few rationalistic ones had accepted the authority of Scripture in matters of doctrine and morals. This was looked upon as so unquestioned that the Lutheran Augsburg Confession had not even contained an article affirming it. But, the average man seeks firm authority for guidance in unseen things; generally he feels relaxed if he can be told what to believe.[9] Accordingly, part of the tension in the late nineteenth century was due to the fact that some Protestant groups had definitely developed more iron-clad theories of verbal inerrancy than had been held in the sixteenth century when Luther had looked upon the Scriptures as an infallible guide to faith and practice but had felt no hesitation about criticizing details in Biblical views. To him, whether Moses wrote the Pentateuch was inconsequential, and he definitely preferred Kings to Chronicles.

Many of the scholars who expressed adherence to the new conceptions were godly men, but preachers and parishioners alike were disturbed by their statements that some books of the Bible could not have been written by the persons who had been considered their authors; that David had composed only a few of the Psalms; that the story of Jonah was really a parable; and that discrepancies existed in the story of the life of Christ as recorded in the different Gospels. Reverent scholars who did much pioneer work in advancing the cause of Biblical scholarship were Moses Stuart (1780-1852) long professor at Andover Theological Seminary, and Edward Robinson (1794-1863) of Union Theological Seminary.[10]

Among Unitarians with their traditions of freedom that often tended toward rationalism, a commonly held position was that expressed in 1871 by Rev. Samuel J. May, noted pastor of the Unitarian Church, Syracuse, New York. He said that "to assert and maintain the infallibility of the Bible" was "as absurd and dangerous as to assert and maintain the infallibility of the man who occupies the papal chair." Yet, in the Bible were to be found "the highest, the sublimest moral and religious precepts, and the most glorious revelations of the character of God and of the nature and destiny of man."[11]

In more orthodox circles Leicester Ambrose Sawyer, an accomplished scholar in classical and oriental languages and an early advocate of Biblical criticism, recognizing the change in his personal views, had as early as 1859 secured a letter of withdrawal from the Congregational ministry to become an independent Christian preacher.

Many who came to accept the claims of some of the Higher Critics hesitated to assert them openly for fear that they would be deemed purveyors of dangerous doctrine. The situation was well expressed in 1869 in a private letter from the poet, Oliver Wendell Holmes, to Rev. Frederic H. Hedge, then Professor of Ecclesiastical History at Harvard Divinity School:

> It is strange how we read these [Bible] stories, like children, until some wiser teacher shows us the full-grown meaning they hide under their beautiful simple forms. . . . The truth is staring the Christian world in the face, that the stories of the old Hebrew books cannot be taken as literal statements of fact. But the property of the church is so large and so mixed up with its vested beliefs, that it is hopeless to expect anything like honest avowal of the convictions which there can be little doubt intelligent church men of many denominations, if not all, entertain. It is best, I suppose, it should be so, for taking idolatry and bibliolatry out of the world all at once as the magnetic mountain drew the nails and bolt of Sindbad's ship, and the vessel that floats much of the best of our humanity would resolve itself in a floating ruin of planks and timbers. . . .[12]

A prominent Congregational clergyman later recalled sitting at a table at the Massasoit House in Springfield, Massachusetts in 1875 with about a score of ministers of his de-

nomination, as they discussed whether it would be judicious
to tell their congregations that a verse in 1 John (not included in the later Revised Version) was an interpolation.
All the other ministers agreed that the verse was spurious
but that ordinary people would be vexed by the knowledge.
Many of the period realized the force of Tennyson's warning:

> Leave thou thy sister when she prays,
> Her early Heaven, her happy views;
> Nor thou with shadow'd hint confuse
> A life that leads melodious days.[13]

Accordingly, many clergymen and teachers emphasized
the traditional values of Biblical religion, and as in the case
of Rev. Endicott Peabody, the headmaster of Groton School
in Massachusetts, did not interest themselves "in details of
the Higher Criticism or lower skepticism."[14] Theodore L.
Cuyler, for thirty years (1860-90) pastor of the Lafayette
Avenue Presbyterian Church, Brooklyn, New York, and one
of the influential spiritual leaders of his day, took a similar
conservative stand. As a pastor emeritus he could give thanks
that no gales of higher criticism had ever ruffled a feather of
his faith "in the perfect inspiration, the perfect infallibility,
and the perfect authority of the Bible."
Intelligent men and women who had made no careful
study of scriptural backgrounds very often agreed with the
sentiments of President Grover Cleveland:

> The Bible is good enough for me: just the old book
> under which I was brought up. I do not want notes or
> criticism, or explanations about authorship or origin, or
> even cross-references. I do not need or understand them,
> and they confuse me.[15]

The conservative viewpoint was firmly supported by the
highly influential Dwight L. Moody, who of course made

no claims to extensive scholarship. To press home his position, Moody pictured a layman who once carried to his
liberal pastor a badly mutilated Bible, explaining, "I have
cut out all that you say is fable and allegory and folk lore
and also the mythical and so-called unauthentic parts, and
here is what is left."

Moody emphasized his own position:

> . . . I have said that ministers of the Gospel who are
> cutting up the Bible in this way denying Moses to-day
> and Isaiah to-morrow, and Daniel the next day and Jonah
> the next, are doing great injury to the Church; and I
> stand by what I have said. I don't say that they are bad
> men. They may be good men, but that makes the results
> of their work all the worse. . . . They are emptying the
> churches and driving the young men of this generation
> into infidelity.

When a liberal clergyman asserted that the account of
Jonah and the whale was a myth, newspapermen asked
Moody to state his opinion. His brief reply was widely re-
ported: "I stand by Jonah."[16]

At first among students in the colleges and the more
widely read of the citizenry, however, there began to be a
fundamental change from a strict literalism. William Allen
White, the noted Kansas editor of later years, as a boy in
Kansas (around 1880) had realized that his father who "set
great store by the Bible as literature and as a code of
morals" had little use for its theological implications. About
a decade later, as a young man in Emporia the son attended
a young men's Bible class in the local Presbyterian Church,
taught by "a marvelous teacher." There, White received
his first glimpse of Biblical criticism, as the teacher asserted
that the book of Jeremiah was probably written by two
or three men, that the Gospels probably appeared first in
writing a hundred years after Matthew, Mark, Luke, and

John were dead, and that Moses had made mistakes in chronology.[17]

William Kelly Wright, later a well known Protestant scholar, the son in Illinois of a devout Presbyterian mother and a Congregationalist father, was introduced to Biblical criticism guardedly at Lake Forest Academy and then unreservedly at Amherst College by scholars of deep religious convictions. John W. Buckham, who attended Andover Theological Seminary in the late 1880's, was there first introduced to Biblical criticism, and later he professed great relief at learning that the stories of Eden and the Flood had no such claim to divine inspiration as the prophecies of Isaiah, the Sermon on the Mount, and the Epistles of St. Paul.[18]

Henry Ward Beecher often stimulated his hearers by somewhat unorthodox theological views, and he did much to popularize views which repudiated the verbal inerrancy of the Scriptures. Yet, in 1882 he expressed a fairly conservative viewpoint as to the Bible, when he stated, ". . . in the main . . . I accept the first chapter in the Confession of Faith of the Presbyterian Church as being a very wise and very full and very admirable definition of my views of the Bible." On this question, as on other matters, Beecher was not a scholar or a close reasoner.[19] The liberal movement was hastened by widely circulated volumes such as those by Rev. Washington Gladden, pastor of the First Congregational Church, Columbus, Ohio, a man of deep spiritual convictions who frankly accepted what he deemed to be the inescapable conclusions of modern scholarship. Gladden preached to a congregation of strong intellectual inclinations, including numerous university professors, and college and medical students. Many had become aware of the discrepancies and contradictions in the Biblical text, and in view of the common assertion that "a single error in the Bible rendered it worthless," some were on the verge of casting it aside.

If the literate public did not read books dealing with the

Higher Criticism there were men like Robert G. Ingersoll,
(1833-99), the son of a Presbyterian minister in Dresden,
New York and one who became an able lawyer and attorney-
general of Illinois and who popularized the results of scholarly activities by expressing them in popular parlance. Ingersoll, able lawyer and peerless orator, took delight in expos-
ing what he deemed the foibles of his youthful Biblical
instruction by speaking to huge crowds on themes such as,
"Some Mistakes of Moses." With him, humor and comedy
were matchless weapons. He ridiculed the Biblical statement
that Joshua had made the sun to stand still, and when
clergymen like the Rev. Henry M. Morey and the Rev. De
Witt Talmadge contended that the truth of this could be
explained by refraction Ingersoll urged a little "reflection"
instead.[20]

Facing such a situation, Gladden had felt "deeply pained
by the growing contempt for the Bible." Accordingly, he
had first presented a series of Sunday evening lectures trac-
ing the origin of the Bible, and large congregations had
turned out to hear his message.[21] Although some of Gladden's congregation were at first troubled by his presentation
of the problem, at the end of the series, his church members were virtually unanimous in approval. The lectures were
later published in book form as *Who Wrote the Bible? A
Book For the People.* Gladden asserted that his aim was "to
put into compact and popular form, for the benefit of intelligent readers, the principal facts upon which scholars
are now generally agreed concerning the literary history of
the Bible." He denied the verbal inerrancy of Scripture but
asserted that the "same divine influence which illumines
and sanctifies its pages is waiting to enlighten our minds
that we may comprehend its words, and to prepare our
hearts that we may receive its messages."[22] The book was
widely used in Bible Classes and by the Young Men's Christian Associations.[23] Later, he presented a second series of lectures, a supplement to the first, and these were published too

in book form, this time under the title *Seven Puzzling Bible Books.*

Gladden realized that many people were troubled by any deviation from a rock-like standard of belief, and in many conservative evangelical churches he was deemed worthy of the most strenuous opposition.[24] Yet, he believed that in the long run, his approach was one of constructive guidance. At any rate, the eminent sociologist, Edward A. Ross, long associated with the University of Wisconsin, later confessed that intellectual difficulties had prompted him to abandon organized religion, and rigid Biblical interpretation had played its part in this renunciation. He tells us that as a college senior he had attended five services on Sunday, including three Bible School sessions. But, in 1888, when the International Sunday School lessons switched from the New Testament back to Genesis, he gave up his adult class, for he could not teach as facts, what he had come to believe to be legends.[25]

David Graham Phillips, later noted novelist and "Muckraker," was raised in a devout Methodist home. But, at Princeton in the late 1880's, he boasted that at fifteen he had examined "all of the claims to the inspiration of the Scriptures and found them valueless." Yet, the influence of his early environment in "Bible-reading" Madison, Indiana continued to affect his values in a permanent way and made him consider modern industrial communities as "downright indecent" in their disregard of what he deemed basic human considerations.[26]

A later eminent theological professor, Eugene W. Lyman, of New England Congregational background, asserted that the writings of Gladden had essentially solved the problem of the Higher Criticism for him before he had entered college.[27] Generally, however, ideas of Biblical criticism made slow progress, especially in the South.[28] Even in New York City and in relatively liberal Congregational circles, in 1897 a Sunday evening lecture by Dr. Lyman Abbott, successor

to Henry Ward Beecher at Plymouth Church, expressing
doubts as to the historical accuracy of the Book of Jonah
and viewing it allegorically, created strong repercussions.
The Manhattan Association of Congregational ministers
thereafter almost unanimously declared its emphatic dissent
from such handling of the Holy Scriptures and deplored the
probable effect of such teaching.

In a period of transition, new viewpoints were indeed
soul-distressing, and James H. Breasted (b. 1865), destined
to be one of the world's great Egyptologists, gave up his
studies for the Congregational ministry and turned to secular scholarship under the impact of the New Scriptural interpretations. His philosophy came to be that of a reverent
humanist.[29]

The Presbyterian Church was widely recognized as one
of high educational standards and as one whose Scottish
antecedents had left to it an absorbing interest in theological
and Biblical questions. A system of church government,
moreover, that required conformity to doctrine throughout
the national organization, permitted no easy solution (as was
quite generally true of Congregational churches) of allowing individual congregations to follow their own theories
of Biblical inspiration. Presbyterians, moreover, on the
whole did not find refuge (as was quite generally done in
many Episcopal churches) in a ritual emotionally satisfying to those of widely different views on questions of the
"higher criticism." Hence, the most nationally significant
heresy trials of the period were found in this denomination.
The trials were significant of both the strength and weakness of this Church, for they demonstrated its tremendous
zeal and meticulous scholarship as well as the narrowness
and unimaginativeness of some of its leaders. The time-honored Westminster Confession of Faith of 1646 had not specifically required a belief in a *verbal* inspiration of Holy
Writ, but had provided that the Old Testament in Hebrew
and the New Testament in Greek, "being immediately inspired by God, and by his singular care and providence, kept

pure in all ages, are therefore authentical."[30] Thus, higher critics in the Presbyterian Church were on very vulnerable ground. Even conservative scholars, however, had come to accept the actuality of discrepancies as to figures and dates of the Old Testament and as to details in the New Testament. The problem presented itself as to how these were to be accounted for without surrendering the Bible as an inspired guide for human life. Two frequently suggested ways were: (1) To attribute the errors and discrepancies to the copyists' carelessness in transcription; (2) To alter the conception of divine inspiration so as to leave room for error through human transmission in matters not pertaining to "teaching, reproof, correction, and instruction in righteousness."[31]

Conservatives naturally preferred the former, though they were on hardly tenable ground from the standpoint of the Confession which stated that Providence had kept the Scriptures "pure in all ages." Such conservatives, however, tended to contend for their views as a test of orthodoxy. For a period, nevertheless, Biblical scholarship as presented in the *Presbyterian Review,* by a kind of agreement alternated in successive numbers between conservative and liberal viewpoints. But, at length the conservative scholars at Princeton Seminary found themselves in fundamental disagreement with Professor Charles Augustus Briggs (1841-1913) of Union Seminary.[32]

As early as 1870, Briggs had publicly repudiated conservative theories of inspiration, and in later books,—*Biblical Study* (1883), *Messianic Prophecy* (1886) and *Whither?* (1889), had taken advanced positions, though seemingly within the widely accepted bounds of toleration.[33] One Presbyterian colleague reported in 1889 that *Whither?* was selling like "hot cakes," and that the theological world had "not been so lively for many a day." Briggs' position gradually aroused increasing opposition, partly because he did not seem to emphasize the faith-arousing and conscience-stimulating power of the Scriptures, though he succeeded intellectually in rescuing some young men from deep skepticism regarding the Bible as a guide to faith and life.[34]

At length a storm broke when Briggs, who had long been professor of Hebrew and cognate languages at Union Theological Seminary, a Presbyterian institution in New York City, became professor of Biblical Theology in the same institution.[35] In his inaugural address in January 1891, Briggs gave a notable exposition of "The Authority of Holy Scripture" or "The Bible, the Church, and the Reason" as "historically three great fountains of divine authority." To some, he seemed to be minimizing the importance of the Bible.[36]

Briggs was a very learned man, and he was not unaware of the fact. Lyman Abbott later commented that one of Briggs' serious offenses was that he knew more about the Hebrew Bible than most of his opponents, "and he knew it, and they knew that he knew it."[37] Most observers today agree that he had "an irritating way of claiming to know more than his judges, and the offense was greatly magnified by the fact that the claim was valid."[38] Dr. Philip Schaff, also of Union Seminary, and a man of broad tolerant views, who was one of the foremost church historians in America, wrote:

> Dr. Briggs stated his views on the authority and in-spiration of the Scriptures and the higher criticism in such a defiant and exasperating tone against what he called bibliolatry, that the inaugural address sounded like a manifesto of war, and aroused at once a most determined opposition on the part of the conservative and orthodox press. It is this aggressive style and manner which brought on the trouble.[39]

Harper's Weekly reported that Briggs' address seemed to be more dogmatic and irritating than his real opinions and that it evidenced "a very combative temper" which obscured his fundamental "accord with his brother orthodox Christians." It was stated by friends of Briggs, moreover, that before the delivery of the Inaugural, they had remonstrated with him, when he had shown the address to them, but that he seemed intent on shocking his hearers.[40]

Perhaps an aggressive champion was needed at this time to focus attention on the crucial issues, but the situation did not promote the peace and unity of Protestant fellowships. The public press gave wide attention to the controversy. Rev. Allen Macy Dulles, Presbyterian minister at Watertown, N. Y. and father of the later Secretary of State, assailed the inaugural address as vague and ambiguous, and there was general condemnation of it in the religious press.[41]

Briggs, in spite of his patent lack of humility, stood in a sense for what many believed to be a cause far greater than Briggs himself, "that liberty of investigation which believes that the reverent study of the Word of God must be hampered by no prohibitions of stereotyped opinion" and that such study, properly conducted will lead to "larger and serener faith."[42]

Throughout the Presbyterian Church many definitely expressed sympathy for Briggs. Not untypical of these was Rev. S. G. Anderson, esteemed pastor of Westminster Church, Toledo, Ohio, and he was not branded as a heretic by members of his flock. Two prominent professors at the Presbyterian McCormick Seminary in Chicago publicly defended Briggs' position, and a noted scholar at Oxford, Professor Samuel R. Driver, thought the address both "harmless and excellent." The noted Rev. Charles H. Parkhurst, Presbyterian minister who later crusaded against Tammany Hall, said that Briggs' offense was that he did not satisfy those who had become "more enamoured of a formula than of that which the formula vainly attempts perfectly to express."[43]

On the other side were many clergymen, lawyers, and plain people who feared that the old beliefs which they loved and cherished were hanging in the balance. Some grimly faced Briggs and his supporters with a fierce intolerance such as has characterized much of religious history.

At the annual meeting of the governing body of the Presbyterian Church, the General Assembly, at Detroit in 1891,
a paper, signed by Briggs' colleagues deprecated the dogmatic and irritating tone of his inaugural and other writings
but declared that in their judgment he was a devout student
of the Bible. In spite of a strong plea on the floor of the Assembly for a delay that a conference might be had with
the Directors of the Seminary, the Assembly vetoed the appointment. This action was rejected by the Seminary directors on the grounds that Briggs was being transferred from
one professorship to another and that such internal man-
agement did not properly come under the Assembly's judicial cognizance.[44] The case involving alleged heretical doctrine regarding the Scriptures on the part of Briggs was
first tried before the relatively liberal New York presbytery. By this time, Briggs was disclaiming some interpretations placed on certain passages of his Inaugural. *The Independent* asserted that if he had been as careful in what he
had said in his inaugural as in what he was now saying in
his defense "he would have saved himself much criticism."
The presbytery dismissed the charges against Briggs late in
1891 by the overwhelming vote of 94:39. The attitude of
the presbytery was based on views of Broad Churchmanship.
Declining to endorse specifically Briggs' views, the presbytery desired that the Church should be broad enough to include men of his beliefs.[45] The case, after further controversy, was sent by the General Assembly back to the New
York presbytery.[46] This presbytery again acquitted him of
the heresy charges in January 1893. Upon appeal to the General Assembly meeting in Washington D. C., there was an
accentuation of the bitter antagonisms. John Meigs, renowned headmaster of the famed Hill School in Pennsylvania, was one of twenty-one members of a special Judicial
Committee appointed to study the matter. Deeply disturbed,
Meigs wrote to his wife, "Pray for my guidance and my
help!" Meigs was aware that it was Briggs' personality that

had aroused relentless enmity so that his views were "hooted or sneered at by unfriendly judges" in a most unchristian manner.[47] Meigs was one of six who presented a minority report, while fifteen offered a majority report, resulting in Briggs' conviction and his suspension from the Presbyterian ministry.[48]

In the meantime, the Directors of Union Seminary made it wholly free of ecclesiastical control, while renewing the declaration of their individual loyalty to the Presbyterian Church.[49]

Eventually Briggs was accepted into the Episcopal priesthood in 1899, but all did not greet this hospitality to a suspended clergyman with equanimity. The New York *Sun* commented that Ingersoll had done trifling damage to the Christian faith in comparison with that done by "infidels" with "the authority of special scholarship." An Episcopalian rector of St. Peter's Church, Westchester, later stated that he believed the burning of his church and an attempt to set fire to a barn on his farm were inspired by hostility to him because he had successfully opposed Briggs' ordination in St. Peter's Church. Benjamin F. De Costa, a New York Episcopalian clergyman, was so dismayed by what he deemed a surrender to unsound principles in the reception of Briggs into the Episcopal Church that he became a Roman Catholic, and after the death of his wife, a priest in that Church.

Joseph Choate, a leading lawyer and an Episcopalian, later a U. S. ambassador to Great Britain, told one of Briggs' leading legal opponents, a prominent Presbyterian corporation lawyer, "I cannot see what you are after, unless it be to wreck the Presbyterian Church, so that your firm may have the business of reorganizing it."[50]

It is interesting to note that Briggs, primarily an Old Testament scholar, was conservative in most religious matters, and was later much disturbed by persons who, following the Higher Criticism of the New Testament, were prone to question the Virgin Birth of Christ.

A present day Presbyterian Church historian evaluates thus the position of Briggs in American theological development:

> . . . He who in his prime had been widely—and quite incorrectly—regarded as a dangerous religious radical, found himself in old age left far behind by the very forces in American religious thought which he had done so much to stimulate in their earlier and more formative period. In his last years there was about him a kind of heroic loneliness. And yet with his life long interest in what we have come to call ecumenity, and in his demand for a Christianity which should be both scientific and evangelical he was, in some respects, once again in advance of his times.[51]

The very fact that the Presbyterian Church held such deep concern for the basis of a sound faith commended it to many of its people, who determined to struggle for its recovery from what seemed to many to be a trend toward obscurantism. Philip Schaff, the indefatigable church historian and Biblical scholar, had already declared that, on the whole, no denomination suited him better, for "perfection is not to be found on the earth." Yet, he felt that the General Assembly was "certainly on a wrong track in trying to impose a new test of orthodoxy" when "the best spirit of the age" was towards greater liberty.

Many leading clergymen such as the noted Dr. John Hall of the Fifth Avenue Church, New York, had felt (as President James McCosh of Princeton was reported to have said) that Briggs needed to be answered but that heresy-hunting was not the answer. Hall's son had broader views than his father and considered leaving the Presbyterian communion, but his father's counsel of moderation prevailed.[52]

In the meantime, however, heresy-hunting became an active pursuit. One who was destined to endure greater personal hardships than Briggs as a result of his views was

Henry Preserved Smith (1847-1927), professor of Old Testament at Lane Seminary (Presbyterian) in Cincinnati. His temperament was conservative, and he had selected teachers of that type during his scholarly studies at the Universities of Berlin and Leipzig. Yet, he had become honestly convinced of the truth of the Higher Criticism.[53] To safeguard the peace of the Church, however, he had refrained from giving any considerable publicity to his opinions. The bringing of charges against Briggs impelled him to come publicly to the latter's defense. Thereupon, he too was tried for heresy (denial of the verbal inspiration of the Bible) and was suspended from the ministry of the Presbyterian Church. At first the Board of Trustees at Lane Seminary declined to receive Smith's resignation from his teaching position. The General Assembly, however, brought pressure in 1893, and the resignation was accepted.[54] For five years thereafter he was without official position (having failed in an appeal to the General Assembly of 1894), until he received an appointment at Amherst College in 1898.

A third Biblical critic who ran afoul of conservative opinion was Arthur Cushman McGiffert (1861-1933) who had been a student of the well-known scholar, Adolph Harnack, in Germany. Ordained to the Presbyterian ministry in 1888, he served thereafter at Lane Seminary, and beginning in 1893 at Union Theological Seminary, New York. In 1897 he published *A History of Christianity in the Apostolic Age* in which he expressed doubt as to whether Jesus intended to institute the Lord's Supper as a perpetual rite. To the Pittsburgh presbytery this was a "scandal" which called into question the validity of one of the sacraments of the Church. Eventually, to avoid further controversy, McGiffert became a Congregationalist.[55]

Many of those trained even in conservative seminaries began to accept newer viewpoints. Thus, while in Princeton Theological Seminary, Louis Bayles Paton (1864-1932) prepared a thesis on "The Historical Character of the Book of Chronicles," as a result of which research he abandoned

the conservative point of view. In 1892, he began life long
service as a teacher at Hartford Theological Seminary, and
in the same year he transferred from the Presbyterian to
the Congregational ministry.

Professor Schaff had earlier asserted: . . . "Surely the
great Presbyterian Church of the United States . . . is orthodox and conservative enough, and can afford to be tolerant
and liberal without running any risk. She has too much
intelligence, good sense, and solid piety to be thrown off
her balance. . . ."[56] As time went on, various leaders sought
to restore that balance. Henry Sloane Coffin, a member of
a prominent New York family, as a boy of sixteen, had been
much interested in the Briggs trial. After an education at
Yale, at Union Seminary, and in Scotland, he had entered
the Presbyterian ministry. Destined to be one of the most
influential clergymen of his generation, in his first charge
at Bedford Park, Brooklyn in 1900, he had preached on
"The Seat of Authority in Religion," rejecting as impossible
the conception of the verbal inerrancy of the Scriptures.[57]

In the same year (1900) there died the aging William
Henry Green, professor of Hebrew at Princeton Seminary.
By temperament, training, and personal conviction he had
been a defender of traditional Biblical scholarship. But even
he had to admit that the slaughter of 500,000 soldiers on one
side in a single encounter between Jewish tribes might indicate an error in textual transmission. Increasingly there came
to be acceptance of the more liberal views such as those
held by Francis Brown (1849-1916), who had been a favorite
pupil of Briggs, and had succeeded him as Professor of
Hebrew and cognate languages at Union Seminary in 1890.
He was not given to daring hypothesis, but his inexhaustible
diligence, absolute fairness, scrupulousness in weighing evidence, and care in arriving at conclusions made him an able
and dependable leader of liberal Presbyterian forces. By
1902, the liberals in the Presbyterian Church (through the
influence of such men as Brown and Henry Van Dyke)
secured the adoption as part of a new "Brief Statement of

the Reformed Faith" of a viewpoint which did not demand verbal inerrancy.[58] The Scriptures were declared to be "the faithful record" of God's revelations and the only infallible guide to "faith and life."

Changing attitudes were very noticeable over a period of twenty years in other denominations. In the early 1880's, among Congregationalists at Yale, it was generally assumed that Higher Criticism was a passing phase and that conservative views would inevitably prevail.[59] As late as 1886, "nothing was said yet in any Congregational seminary about the Higher Criticism of the Bible." Andover, Oberlin, Hartford, Chicago, and Bangor Seminaries were devoted to the traditional views.[60]

During the period of transition an important mediating figure was George Frederick Wright, a Congregational minister and distinguished geologist, who served at Oberlin as professor of New Testament language and literature (1881-92) and of the harmony of science and religion (1892-1907). For almost forty years, moreover (1883-1921), he was editor of *Bibliotheca Sacra,* a medium for the expression of scholarly religious viewpoints of moderately conservative trends.

In Baptist circles, and with an influence that extended widely through the colleges and Chautauqua groups, William Rainey Harper (1856-1906), Hebrew scholar and dynamic President of the University of Chicago, was especially noteworthy. In his earlier years, he later admitted, he had studied the Bible endeavoring to find the means "to convince others that it was only an ordinary book, and very ordinary at that."[61] A zealous churchman and Sunday School superintendent, in the face of bitter criticism, he stood out as a defender of the Higher Criticism, and one authority tells us that he "did more than Matthew Arnold to educate the general public to a recognition of the principle that scholars must be free to study the Bible like any other book."

Also highly influential was William Newton Clarke (1841-1912), Baptist clergyman and professor of Christian Theology at Colgate Seminary after 1890. His spiritual autobiography later appeared as *Sixty Years With the Bible* (1909). In it he declared:

> I have described the change by saying that I passed on from using the Bible in the light of its statements to using it in the light of its principles. At first I said, The Scriptures limit me to this; later I said, The Scriptures open my way to this. As for the Bible, I am not bound to work all its statements into my system; nay, I am bound not to work them all in; for some of them are not congenial to the spirit of Jesus and some express truths in forms which cannot be of permanent validity.

Also influential in Baptist circles and moving in the same direction as Clarke was Augustus H. Strong, long President of Rochester Theological Seminary.

Following the Civil War period, intellectual viewpoints in the Methodist Episcopal Church North had been definitely conservative. Such a leading Biblical scholar as James Strong (1822-1894) taught his classes at Drew Seminary, New Jersey without any substantial concession to the higher criticism. He believed in the Mosaic authority of the Pentateuch, that there was one Isaiah and that Paul wrote the Epistle to the Hebrews. He was followed by Robert William Rogers, who taught at Drew from 1893 to 1925, accepting fully the newer critical view of the Old Testament, yet exercising such tact that he escaped the church censure which was visited upon some of the Old Testament scholars within the Methodist fold.

Milton Spencer Terry (1840-1914), head of the work in Hebrew and Old Testament exegesis at Garrett Biblical Institute, Evanston, Illinois, attended lectures on Biblical criticism in 1887. Becoming convinced of the truth of some of the newer viewpoints, he revised his own ideas and over a period of many years courageously withstood attacks from those within his denomination who were vigorously opposed to change.

In New England, William Fairfield Warren (1833-1929), first president of Boston University, became convinced of the validity of the new approach to Biblical teaching and secured devout but open-minded teachers who helped guide a generation of seminary students through the troubled seas of intellectual change. Perhaps the foremost of these teachers was Borden Parker Bowne (1847-1910), head of the philosophy department for thirty-five years. He defended his colleague, Hinckley Gilbert Thomas Mitchell (1846-1920), Biblical critic, when the latter was accused of unorthodox views in 1895, because of a denial of the Mosaic authorship of the Pentateuch. Officials of the Church cautioned Mitchell further in 1899, but later (1905) his appointment was not renewed, and he subsequently taught at Tufts College.

Even in a liberal denomination which had many churches in typical American communities there was resistance to changing views. Thus, Orello Cone, a distinguished New Testament scholar, who taught at St. Lawrence University (1865-1880), was often assailed in his own denomination (Universalist) as a "destructive" influence because of his scholarly views, but he steadfastly refused to be involved in public controversy.

At the very time that Briggs, in the face of vigorous protest, had been accepted in the Episcopal ministry, scholars of his advanced views were to be found in no seminary of that Church except the Episcopal Theological School in Cambridge, Massachusetts. Over a period of about a quarter of a century the Cambridge institution had been the only one in the denomination which freely accepted and taught the Higher Criticism of the Scriptures. Not one member of its faculty was brought to trial for his views, but bishops generally steered their candidates for the ministry to more conservative instruction.

Even in New York City, R. Heber Newton, pastor of All Souls' Church (1869-1902), who became the foremost liberal preacher of the denomination, ran into serious opposition because of his lecture-sermons some of which were published

as *The Right and Wrong Uses of the Bible* (1883) . In this
he referred to "primeval sagas" and "the traditions" relating
to Biblical figures like Abraham and Isaac. 25,000 copies
of the first edition sold in one year. Formal charges were
brought against him claiming that he had violated his ordination vows. The astute bishop, Henry C. Potter, for the
time being solved the problem by persuading him to dis-
continue his lectures early in 1884, as he thought that public
opinion was as yet unprepared for them. In 1891, twelve
New York clergymen appealed to the Bishop to undertake
an investigation of Newton's teaching, but once again, Potter
pigeonholed the charges. Phillips Brooks believed that Newton's sermons were "calm, serious, and conscientious." He
wrote privately (1883) that he believed nothing could "begin to equal the mischief which must come from the dishonesty of men who refuse to recognize any of the new
light which has been thrown upon the Bible, and go on re-
peating assertions about it which, if there is such a thing
as proof, have been thoroughly and repeatedly disproved."[62]

By the end of the century the slow change in opinion
was shown by an Encyclical Letter issued by the Lambeth
Conference (1897) at which various Anglican bodies
throughout the world were represented. It acknowledged
that critical Bible study by a competent scholar was necessary "to the maintenance in the church of a healthy faith,"
but it warned against the dangers of inquiry which were
not "protected by the guard of reverence, confidence, and
patience."[63]

Slowly, even some of the older Bible professors presented
newer viewpoints without wholly realizing it.[64] By the end
of the century a relatively conservative professor at Yale
University, George Park Fisher, who served there as professor of ecclesiastical history in the Divinity School (1861-
1901), addressing the International Congregational Council
in 1899 expressed a viewpoint that was receiving ever wider
acceptance:

"The whole of the Bible is not authoritative, but the

Bible as a whole is. The whole of the Bible is not authoritative, the soul of the Bible is. . . ."[65]

More conservative patterns, however, were recognizable in Roman Catholicism. Cardinal Newman in 1884 had published an article in the British periodical, *The Nineteenth Century,* admitting incidental errors in Scripture that were unrelated to faith and morals.[66] But, among Roman Catholics in the United States, such views were not well received. Later, Cardinal William O'Connell, Archbishop of Boston, recalled how in the 1880's as a student in the American College, Rome, there was much discussion of the Higher Criticism, "mostly in Germany, from a group of clever agnostics whose plain purpose was to destroy completely the fundamentals of the Christian faith by a well-planned attack upon the whole system of divine revelation. . . ." He commented that such "so-called discoveries" had received immense applause from Protestants who little dreamed that Protestantism would be undermined by the process, but that Catholicism had resisted the trend and time had proved the "falsity" of the premises and the "shallowness" of the scholarship of the Higher Critics.[67]

In November 1893, Pope Leo XIII, in one of his longest encyclicals, the *Providentissimus Deus,* silenced Roman Catholic higher critics, as he defined the doctrine of the Church on the "Study of Holy Scripture." He asserted that it could not be admitted that "the sacred writer could have erred" or that "divine inspiration extends only to what touches faith and morals." According to this view, as one Catholic historian has expressed it, "As for self-sufficient professional students of the Bible, their closed minds precluded anything like the attainment of objective truth."[68] This involved an insistence that the Roman Catholic Church alone could speak with finality on Biblical knowledge and that under her guidance all truth could be harmonized so that natural phenomena and divine revelation would present no irreconcilable aspects. Accordingly, Pope Leo XIII in 1902 appointed a Bible Commission to pass on controversial points of Scriptural learning, but the door was closed against the acceptance of "modernist" interpretations by a new encyclical "Pascendi" (1907), which squelched so-called Modernism and its alleged errors.

Pope Leo's encyclical of 1893 had disturbed many Catholic scholars, especially in the Old World. The distinguished Alfred Loisy, in his inaugural address at the Catholic Institute of Paris in 1892 and in an essay published during the following year, had denied the absolute inerrancy of the Holy Scriptures and the Mosaic authorship of the Pentateuch. Such views were emphatically rejected by the Pope's encyclical of 1893. Loisy a month later wrote to his friend, Archbishop Ireland, of St. Paul, that the Pope's views of divine inspiration did not trouble him, but that apparently historical exegesis had no right to exist if its findings were predetermined.[69] Later, he was excommunicated (in 1908).

Similarly, Monsignor Louis Duchesne, a noted French scholar, was not without his influence in American Catholic circles. As a professor at the Catholic Institute of Paris (1877-85) he had taught church history according to the canons of the so-called scientific criticism. Later, he had been the author of numerous volumes, including a preliminary presentation of *Les Fastes episcopaux dans l'ancienne Gaule* in 1895. This aroused animosity among the traditionalists by disputing such local claims as that Mary, Martha, and Lazarus had once landed at Marseilles. Subsequent writing ran afoul of the *Index,* and in January 1912, a visitor found him with his head between his hands, weeping bitterly, for he was loyal both to his ideas of the validity of historical method and to the Church of his fathers in which he had taken Holy Orders. Americans learned that he had soon made formal submission to the Church. His later researches, *L'Eglise au VIe siecle,* were published after his death.

In Protestant circles, doubtless the changing attitudes in many colleges and seminaries and more liberal views among the reading public in general had reacted upon each other to produce a widespread change in the climate of opinion. Only a few were prepared to follow the iconoclastic trends of those like Dr. Octavius B. Frothingham who in his Unitarian Sunday School on West Fortieth Street, New York City, around 1870, had enthralled the young people by a weekly talk, "usually a fable." There, the children had been introduced to the Bible as partly history and partly the myths of a primitive people.[70]

Yet, those who read the "quality" magazines of the time had become familiar with the views of writers like Elizabeth Stuart Phelps who wrote in 1882 in the *North American Review:*

> We are to regard the Bible, not as a splendidly wrought sarcophagus, but as the bed of a deep and magnificent ocean, wherein is hid treasures that the life of a man, or a race, may dive for and not exhaust.[71]

By 1886, moreover, an intellectual Baptist could write that one grievance against his beloved Church was its rigid and literal views of Biblical interpretation which had become "hard and mechanical."

The sermon-lectures and published works of men like R. Heber Newton and Washington Gladden (previously discussed) had influenced many. Two other individuals, moreover, were among those who did much to alter popular views. One, William Rainey Harper, served as a professor at Yale for almost a decade after 1881. He was a Biblical scholar who contributed much to publications in his field. This included a discussion extending over two and a half years on the Mosaic authorship of the Pentateuch. Harper took the point of view of advanced Biblical criticism, while the conservative scholarly W. H. Green of Princeton Seminary espoused the traditional viewpoints.[72] But, even before going to Yale, he had established at the Baptist Union Theological Seminary in Chicago a summer course in Semitic languages and Biblical studies which within a decade became the parent of thirty similar courses throughout the country. At Yale, students filled the largest lecture hall to hear his Bible lectures. For several years he gave a series of Bible lectures in one of the largest New Haven churches with 1,200 persons crowding the building, and he repeated the series in New York, Philadelphia, and Boston. Each year, moreover, he gave a Bible lecture once a week for the women of New Haven. For a year he went every other Sunday to Vassar College to speak, and he frequently spoke at other women's colleges. At Lake Chautauqua he also gave Bible courses for a number of summers.

After 1890 Harper became associated with the new University of Chicago, serving as President until his death in 1906. An influential Baptist clergyman, when Harper was being considered for presidency at Chicago, accused Harper of unorthodox views and endeavored to secure his subscription to ideas of Biblical literalism.[73] Harper, however, made crystal clear the fact that his Biblical views were not those of the old literal orthodoxy, and the freedom that was permitted him brought a discussion of the new Biblical criticism for the first time to the front pages of Middle Western newspapers.[74] Tireless, he carried his convictions to the public in various ways, even serving as superintendent of the Hyde Park Baptist Sunday School, Chicago from 1897 to 1905.

A second individual who strongly influenced liberal Protestantism toward less rigid views of Biblical tradition was Lyman Abbott. A foremost present day authority on American church history has asserted that no modern religious leader has wielded a more lasting influence.[75] For a generation, an editor, writer, and preacher, at first his views were those of New England orthodoxy. When he published *Old Testament Shadows of New Testament Truths* (1870), he proclaimed that he was dealing with "veritable history," as he accepted the destruction of Sodom and Gomorrah, the fiery serpents and other features of the Biblical account as actual facts. As editor of the new *Illustrated Christian*

Weekly beginning in 1871, he denounced (1876) John Fiske's "dogmatic skepticism" coming with the Tübingen school of Biblical criticism, and an article by Felix Adler on "The Evolution of Hebrew Religion."[76]

In 1876 Abbott became editor of the *Christian Union* (later the *Outlook*), continuing in that position until 1922. His position now became more liberal, as he was now no longer under responsibility to the secretaries of the conservative American Tract Society which published the *Illustrated Christian Weekly*. Indeed, already in the summer of 1876, he was telling a convention of Sunday School teachers at Lake Chautauqua that the Bible was not a book but a library that had been produced over a period of a thousand years and that in studying and teaching it, account must be taken of the times, the people, and the temperament of the writer involved in the Biblical narrative.[77] Soon (1879) he was writing that the Bible was not "a complete and systematic revelation of all truth" or even of all truth bearing "on moral and spiritual problems." By 1889, in a sermon he warned against the use of the Bible as a basis for knowledge of "geology, or chronology, or physiology, or even theology."[78]

During the winter of 1896-7, Abbott presented a series of Sunday evening lectures at Plymouth Church, Brooklyn on the Bible as literature. Young people from other churches joined the crowds which sometimes were so large that people were turned away. Misleading accounts were published in some of the papers throughout the country, creating a storm of criticism from orthodox circles. Abbott developed the same theme for a Lowell Institute lecture series (1899-1900). In these lectures, later presented in *The Life and Literature of the Ancient Hebrews* (1901), he unreservedly accepted the Higher Criticism but endeavored to show that this did not impair spiritual values. To him the significance of Old Testament stories depended upon their ethical content rather than their basis in historical fact.

Abbott frankly admitted that his work was not that of

basic research but of popularization, acknowledging his debt
to the well-known scholarly contributions to the Higher
Criticism as well as to earlier popular summaries by Gladden and others.

Abbott had now come to espouse views which he had
attacked thirty years before, and he now received bitter criticism from conservative Christians who looked upon his work
as an effort toward the "destruction of the Bible," a work
resulting in more support "for the devil than Ingersoll"
could secure.

In Protestant circles, what came to be termed Fundamentalist groups clung tenaciously to the conservative views,
but the trend of opinion in the most prominent Protestant
churches and colleges was illustrated by a comment in *Harper's Weekly* in 1898. Discussing a recently published letter
written by Thackeray, a "pious man and a Christian" to his
daughters, it was stated that the English novelist had indicated that he did not believe literally in the six days' cos-
mogony and some of the Mosaic writings. *Harper's Weekly*
observed that "the number of those who think Thackeray's
conclusions about the Bible were mistaken is less than in
his day, and seems likely to diminish from decade to decade
in the generations to come."

A Methodist scholar in 1893 had expressed the viewpoint
of many of the thoughtful leaders of that Church:

> The narratives in both Old and New Testaments fur-
> nish valuable lessons, and, in whatever light they are
> viewed, are worthy of respect and credence for instruc-
> tion in life and manners. The substance of revelation re-
> mains the same, no matter what the names of the chosen
> prophets. . . . A critical change in the order and number
> of the kings of Judah need not be revolutionary to the
> most orthodox conception of our Lord's Messiahship. . . .
> If Methodism is to be distinguished for its life rather than
> its creeds, it will not be affected hurtfully by a scholarly
> investigation of the sacred records. . . .[79]

There was widespread concern, however, that many would abandon the personal spiritual enrichment that had come from regular reading of the Bible, if it seemed no longer an inerrant textbook of science as well as a guide to life. But, President Harper, a frank defender of the Higher Criticism, counselled against such a temptation:

> For relief from temptations of every kind, whether of life or thought; for a help which may always be obtained; for a rock on which firm standing-ground may be gained—go to the Bible; not as to some talisman possessed of magic power, but as to a book containing story after story which tells of God's dealings with man; to a book containing precept after precept, richer in truth than any other of the world's possessions—a book which will guide your thought unfailingly to the only source of all wisdom—to God.[80]

Comparative Religions

Much of the external strength of religious organizations was often related to their insistence that they alone had the saving faith that would bring admission to Heaven. "Outside of the Church there is no salvation" had been a widely accepted doctrine of Christian bodies. But there was often an important explanation associated with it,—that for valid reasons some outside the Visible Church were in reality members of the Invisible Church of the redeemed.

In a country like the United States with its many faiths, there was widespread religious toleration. Cardinal Gibbons who manifested great liberality in his attitude toward Protestants and who was considered one of the most tolerant of Catholic ecclesiastics, nevertheless, could emphasize the Roman viewpoint that it was definitely the religious institution with a "Divine Mission and Unerring Authority."[81] Gibbons elaborated this position in an article, "Introductory Remarks to the Pope's Encyclical," in the *American*

Catholic Quarterly Review, October, 1894. Gibbons stated
that one could not "be with Christ unless he be with His
true Church," the authority of which Christ had set up "in
Peter and his successors." The New York *Independent* took
exception, declaring that it gave the Cardinal credit for
more charity than his words suggested, for he certainly believed that many Protestants were "with Christ" and not
against him.[82]

On another occasion Gibbons would not arrange for
priests of his archdiocese to explain Catholicism in what was
planned as an especially arranged service at the Christian
(Disciples) Temple, Baltimore.

Within Protestant circles conformity to correct doctrine
was widely regarded as a prerequisite to a saving faith. Thus,
when Franklin K. Lane, later to be the distinguished Secretary of the Interior under Woodrow Wilson, was a young
man, he had looked forward to Christian work as a Presbyterian minister. His views, however, were rather unorthodox,
and a Presbyterian clergyman suggested that with such
views he might find a career in Unitarianism. This thought
was almost terrifying to the youthful Lane, for it seemed
to suggest that he was definitely outside the fold of God's
own people and that nothing but Eternal Damnation awaited
him.[83]

Even in Congregationalism, destined to be one of the
liberal groups in American Protestantism, a bitter quarrel
developed after 1880 over the "Andover Controversy." At
Andover Seminary in Massachusetts a group of theological
professors had endorsed the idea of a "second probation."
Orthodoxy insisted on a knowledge of Christ's Gospel as
a prerequisite to salvation, but the Andover men suggested
a second chance after death for those who had been denied
acquaintance with the Gospel on earth.[84] Bitterness developed in Congregationalist circles because some conservatives
wished to deny foreign missionary appointments to those
who would not make a clear cut distinction between the

saved and the lost. If one believed that the unrepentant were not destined for eternal punishment, it was claimed, the "vital nerve" of the missionary enterprise would be cut. Yet, intelligent Orientals were sometimes repelled by Christianity when it insisted that their ancestors who had not heard of Christ were everlastingly doomed.[85]

As early as the period around 1820, Unitarians had tended to break down what they deemed the "moral enormity" in the old views of the Atonement, associated with seemingly arbitrary aspects of the idea of salvation. Emerson and the Transcendentalists had challenged the traditional views of God, Jesus, Christianity, and the sacraments.[86] All of this had paved the way for a greater tolerance for those outside the Christian fold who had been commonly designated as "heathen."

Travel had often broken down provincialisms, and Richard Henry Dana Jr., who had written *Two Years Before the Mast* (1840) on a trip around the world (1834-6), noticed a "close resemblance" between Buddhist worship in Canton and that which he had observed at the Roman Catholic cathedral in Havana, Cuba. The removal of the idols from the Buddhist temple, and the putting in their place of the furniture of the cathedral would have made, he thought, for marked similarity. He noted, moreover, that all travellers seemed to be impressed with the same similarity between Buddhist and Catholic worship, and asserted that some early Jesuits had ascribed the common element to the work of the devil, counterfeiting true religion. Some people attributed the similarity to the common traditions of the patriarchal age.[87]

One who did much to popularize a more inclusive religious spirit was the gifted Unitarian minister, James Freeman Clarke (1810-88), long a Boston clergyman. He considered himself to be a convinced believer in Christian faith and piety, but he sought to show the elements of goodness and truth in other faiths. His *Ten Great Religions* (Part I,

1871; Part II, 1883) became a religious classic in liberal-minded circles.[88] James A. Garfield, as a Congressman, read the first part of it. As one who had been a Disciple of Christ local preacher, he now wrote to another leader of the denomination that he thought that they had "taken too narrow a view of the subject of religion." He had come to the conclusion that "the absolute truths of religion" must be as old as the race, and books like Clark's tended to widen one's horizon and make him more liberal.[89]

Much influenced by the studies of Max Mueller, younger Transcendentalists who became associated with the Free Religious Association used the empirical method in an effort to show the basic common affirmations of the various world religions. Samuel Johnson contributed a three volume *Oriental Religions and Their Relation to Universal Religion* and a pamphlet by Thomas W. Higginson, *The Sympathy of Religions,* written in 1855, became a popular tract of the times.

One who did much to popularize such views in college halls was Charles Carroll Everett (1829-1900), Unitarian theologian who became dean of Harvard Divinity School in 1878. As a professor at Harvard, as early as 1872 he had offered perhaps the first course in comparative religions to be presented in the United States. Men of all faiths were his students, and persons of widely different backgrounds later looked back upon him "as the greatest intellectual and spiritual inspiration of their lives."[90]

Experience with other groups sometimes developed toleration. Andrew D. White, President of Cornell University and minister to Russia and Germany, in his travels was impressed with Mohammedan fanaticism "as one of the great misfortunes of the world," but he found in Mohammedan worship much of "simplicity, directness, and reverence." This, he felt, did not diminish his preference for Judaism and Christianity which he felt had come to be "purer than ever before," although he had come to believe that modern thought was "absolutely fatal to the claims of the various churches, sects, and sacred books to contain the only or the final work of God to man."[91]

Much of modern scientific investigation was conducive to tolerance. As one scholar has expressed it:

> Anthropologists established stages in the growth of the religious sentiment. Deluges were found in the legend of Gilgamesh, and the epics of creation in Chaldean remains. Much to the consternation of faithful believers, crucifixions and atonements were discovered in 'pagan' cults of old, and counterparts of patriarchal Abrahams emerged from the back wash of near eastern rivers. Even the hallowed pronouncements of the prophets, hallowed though they remained, bore disturbing resemblances to the experiences of Sumerians, Akkadians, and long-deceased gentlemen of Egypt in the Old Kingdom.[92]

Such views soon became known in all parts of the country. William Allen White, the famous Kansas editor, tells how as a youth in Emporia in the 1880's, he was troubled about religious matters, and one hot summer night fell into conversation with a well-dressed man who told him not to fret about the Virgin Birth and miracles, which he said were found in other religions, but to look to Jesus as the greatest hero of all time whose life and death had slowly changed the course of history.[93]

While to some a study of comparative religions made for lessened certitude, others like Dr. J. G. K. McClure, who was later president of McCormick (Presbyterian) Seminary in Chicago, found that it had given to Christianity "an established conviction of its own pre-eminence," and "a new assurance of its adaptation to all mankind." To him, a new understanding of Christ and the Scriptures had given Christ a transcendent place in the minds of men.

For Phillips Brooks a study of other religions had deepened his Christian insights, and this had later been furthered by his travels in the Orient. Near the close of the Civil War, Brooks had written in his note-book: . . . "Mohammed has done vast harm. I should dishonor God if I did not believe that Islam has done good."[94]

In 1883 in a trip which included a visit to India and Ceylon he found, as he thought, much both in Brahmanism and Buddhism that threw light upon the idea of the "new" or "second" birth in Christian thinking. Buddhism in Ceylon had for him "a look of intelligence and decency after the horrible squalor and coarseness of Hinduism." Yet, he could not look upon Buddhism at all as "a great spiritual religion, with any chance in it for the salvation of the world." For him both primitive Buddhism which had a controlling ethical purpose and modern Buddhism which had become an "elaborate ceremonialism" with a developed "mythology" were devoid of theism, hence lacking in any dynamic faith.

The World's Parliament of Religions in Chicago (1893) brought together representatives of the world's major faiths in a spirit of mutual consideration adopting as a motto the words from Malachi, "Have we not all one Father? hath not one God created us?" Lyman Abbott writing in the *Outlook* looked upon this as a useful corrective to old views often sedulously cultivated "that all forms of religion but our own are a mixture of ignorance and superstition." He found in each religion a message for some period and some part of the human family as it proclaimed some resplendent truth—as in the case of Christianity—often dimmed by superstition. Yet he still believed that "all thoughtful Christians" would find in the religion of Jesus Christ the real answer to the soul's quest of other peoples.[95]

A more uncompromising position had been taken at the World's Parliament of Religions by W. C. Wilkinson of the University of Chicago:

The attitude of Christianity toward religion other

than itself is an attitude of universal, absolute, eternal, unappeasable hostility, while toward all men its attitude is an attitude of grace, mercy, peace for whosoever will.[96]

Rev. John H. Barrows, Presbyterian minister, who more than any other individual had been responsible for the success of the World's Parliament of Religions, in 1899 surveyed sympathetically the situation as to non-Christian faiths in Asia.[97] He carefully showed the blessings conferred by Israel on mankind, the good that is found in Mohammedanism, the salutary doctrines of incarnation and sacrifice in early Hinduism (though the popular Hinduism of the time he deemed a grossly corrupt retrogression), and the positive contributions of Buddhism and Confucianism.

Yet, according to a scholarly reviewer Barrows's catholic spirit did not curb his realistic appraisal, for

> The picture that he draws of the corruptions of heathenism today is as dark and repulsive as that depicted by Paul in the first chapter of Romans; and his intense conviction that Asia needs above all else the gospel of Christ finds in these lectures, abundant and emphatic expression.[98]

Indeed, Barrows believed that a comparative study of religions would show that Christianity's adaptability to universal acceptance meant that it more than probably would ultimately prevail. Yet, he held that the times demanded less "destructive" and more "constructive" teaching with less emphasis on the "non-essentials" of western theology.[99]

Certainly the Gospel was being offered more definitely in a spirit of love, however, than when Dr. Lyman Beecher had addressed the American Board of Foreign Missions in 1827, branding heathenism, Romanism, despotism, and crime all as "resources of the adversary" which must be overthrown.[100] In increasing degree viewpoints were developing that soon would prompt Charles Cuthbert Hall, President of Union Theological Seminary (New York), in 1903-4 to address crowded congregations of cultivated Hindus in India, treating non-Christian faiths as a stage in the spiritual development of a people seeking after God. These yearnings, to him, contained "flickering and broken lights of God, which shall be purged and purified and consummated through the absolute self-revelation of the Father in Christ Incarnate."[101]

CHAPTER VII

THE NEW SOCIOLOGY AND ECONOMICS
AND THE SOCIAL GOSPEL

Closely associated with some of the psychological trends which had important implications for sociology and economics was the viewpoint of Dr. Oliver Wendell Holmes, physician, poet, novelist, and essayist. In his psychological novels such as *Elsie Venner* he indicated how inherited tendencies and physical limitations seem to restrict freedom of the will. Accordingly, his sociological viewpoint became one that looked upon some types of criminals as meriting pity rather than punishment. Such a position was one which looked upon much of the suffering and evil of the world as of basically physiological origin, and had reactionary, aristocratic implications as to the role of heredity in providing a natural elite for society.

This coincided with the social and economic theory which had been a heritage of the pre-Civil War years and which taught that poverty was inevitable, and that misery at best should be dealt with by a program of guarded and well-labeled philanthropy.[1]

Similar trends were becoming clearly discernible in the social application of Darwinism in the writings of Herbert Spencer, which carried over the principle of the "survival of the fittest" into the social and economic field and justified the theory of *laissez faire*.[2] In a world of competition and struggle, it was argued, the ablest and most efficient would survive. Business leaders such as Andrew Carnegie, James J. Hill, and John D. Rockefeller found this admirably fitted to their views of the proper direction of affairs in an age of iron, steel, railroad combinations, and business monopoly.[3]

The most vigorous and influential follower of Spencerian philosophy was William Graham Sumner who had left the ministry of the Episcopal Church to be a professor at Yale.[4] He combined into an imposing synthesis three important currents of Western capitalistic thought: the Protestant ideal of the industrious and frugal man (apparently a representative of the "fittest" to survive in the evolutionary struggle), the Ricardian view of *laissez-faire,* and the scientific determinism of evolutionary thought. While not an uncritical follower of Spencer, Sumner came to have powerful influence as he preached "the predestination of the social order and the salvation of the economically elect through the survival of the fittest."[5] Thus, "in a generation, social Darwinism developed from a shocking piece of 'atheism' to the principal justification for existing society, promulgated from platform and pulpit."[6]

This might seem like a far cry from the Christian doctrine of brotherly love, but it was essentially the viewpoint of such a leading Baptist as John D. Rockefeller. His son, John D. Rockefeller, Jr., moreover, after the turn of the century took pains to explain that the growth of any large business was merely a process involving the survival of the fittest. To him, this was simply the operation of the laws of nature and God, which provided that the beauty and fragrance of the American Beauty rose were only attainable by the sacrifice of the early small buds which grew around it.[7]

The American heritage of Christian humanitarianism was not wholly consistent with such ideas. Herbert Spencer indeed had sought to reconcile idealism with evolution by looking forward to a time when egotism would yield to altruism. But Spencer and Sumner often expressed views which seemed Nietzschean in their implications, and Lester Ward, born in Joliet, Illinois, the son of an itinerant mechanic and a clergyman's daughter, made a sharp dissent. Like others of his day, he markedly differentiated physical evolution and mental, human evolution greatly modified by purposive action.[8]

James T. Bixby, while pastor at the Yonkers, New York, Unitarian Church, published in 1891 his *Crisis in Morals,* rejecting Herbert Spencer's theory of pleasure and pain as wholly inadequate to explain man's moral nature including the factor of conscience. He insisted that altruism was as inherent in the make up of the Universe as self-interest. In 1893, Thomas Huxley had heartened the religious world in his Romanes Lectures by proclaiming that the development of man's moral nature which involved a checking of the ruthlessness of Nature was independent of the cosmic process.[9] Henry Drummond's lectures of 1894 on the *Ascent of Man* also stressed self-sacrifice as quite as important as self-fulfilment. Benjamin Kidd, an Englishman, wrote *Social Evolution* (1894) stressing the need for competition, the irreconcilability of self-interest and the social good, and the need for religion as a non-rational means of modifying excessive egoism. Religious people, however, were not prepared to relegate their faith to a definitely non-rational level.[10]

George Harris, Andover Seminary theologian, showed in his *Moral Evolution* (1896) that four main attitudes had developed in relation to the connection between evolution and morality. One attitude looked upon nature as ruthless, hence evolution and ethics were antagonistic. Another deemed the two independent, for mental and moral factors operated on a higher level than physical life. A third looked upon the two as identical, both parts of a cosmic process. The fourth attitude, which was one shared by Harris, looked upon the two as harmonious though not identical and stressed the need for a blending of self-interest and altruism.[11]

Some writers endeavored to develop social ideals without stressing the relation of them to scientific views of the universe. Emphasizing the social implications of Christianity they were the forerunners of a movement to be known as the Social Gospel. A pioneer work was that by a Congregational minister, Josiah Strong. In *Our Country* (1885) he took an advanced stand in regard to the application of Christian principles to such problems as monopoly, labor, and urban living. It was translated even into Oriental languages and became a best seller. Later, a Kansas minister, Charles M. Sheldon, raised the question as to what Christ would do in the America of the 1890's, and the answer, *In His Steps* (1896), was a grass roots, novelized effort to express Christianity in concrete form. By 1925 over twenty-three million copies in English had been sold.[12]

For many years, however, a Church like the Methodist, with a long tradition of concern for the poor and lowly, showed little interest in economic and social changes in society, and in church circles generally conservative patterns were overcome only slowly and with great difficulty.[13] Furthermore, until well into the twentieth century, the Catholic Church, with its large laboring class membership, was looked upon as a decidedly "conservative" force in economic matters. Pope Leo XIII's famous encyclical, *Rerum Novarum* of May 1891, heralding new emphasis in Catholic social teaching, was for a long time received with little enthusiasm in the United States.[14]

Those who represented an intellectual approach to the cause of Social Christianity were in general agreement that unbridled competition needed to be curbed and that the social fatalism of Spencerian philosophy did not provide the answer to America's needs. Some professional economists held similar views of the excesses of laissez-faire individualism. Hence, forward-looking economists like John R. Commons and Richard T. Ely found common ground between the world of the churches and that of the professional economists, and at one time more than sixty clergymen were members of the American Economic Association.[15] Undoubtedly the proponents of the Social Gospel had a tremendous effect on American thought, as their lectures and books influenced thousands and even hundreds of thousands of people. A new emphasis was given to American Protestant Christianity, and at the local level in thousands of

American communities, intellectual ground was broken for the later Progressive Movement.

Yet, the Social Gospel as an effort to carry the ethical principles of Christianity into a secular world always confronted the danger that it would lose its distinctly religious moorings and become, in fact, a form of secularized social service. Indeed, as evolution, Biblical criticism, and theological changes upset the old traditions, many whose inspiration for altruism had been rooted in the inspiration of a Christian congregation, tended to find in new social and economic activity the principal expression of their spiritual interests. Thus, Henry Carter Adams, born (1851) to the family of a Congregational minister, and imbued there with a compelling sense of social responsibility and of ethical concern, went to Andover Seminary to secure ministerial training. But he had early been "plagued by doctrines," and by 1876 had made the irrevocable decision to enter economics as a avenue for the implementation of his ethical and humanitarian ideals. In that spirit he served notably in a long career as professor of Political Economy at the University of Michigan after 1887.[16]

Similarly, Edward A. Ross, long professor of Sociology at the University of Wisconsin and one of America's leading sociologists during the early twentieth century, had had a strict Presbyterian boyhood. In college he had taken religion very seriously and had sometimes attended five services on Sunday. He was superintendent of one Sunday School, a teacher in another, and a member of a third. Later study in Berlin convinced him that theology was "a sky-scraper founded on cobwebs." He still found in the cardinal Christian principles the means of great consolation and good will, but his life work was devoted to sociology, and he refrained from participation in church activity.[17]

Lester F. Ward (1841-1913), one of the most important of American sociologists and sometimes called the "American Aristotle," as a young man associated with the Treasury Department at Washington, had found the churches an important part of his early life there. Sometimes he attended services twice on Sunday, and his young wife and he had found great enjoyment in reading the Bible together. As time went on, he had become a leader in a lyceum meeting on Sunday to discuss intellectual matters, and his views came to find more unorthodox expression.[18] Gradually he entered with enthusiasm into the conflict between theology and science, as he had become a thorough-going secularist, who found in science and education the answers to the problems of man and society.[19] For him *Dynamic Sociology* had displaced theology.[20]

Among those whose views crystallized into definite movements to advance the frontiers of humanitarian effort were Edward Bellamy and Henry George, both of whom were products of pious home environments and had intense spiritual convictions. Bellamy, the son of a Calvinistic Baptist minister in Massachusetts, spent a happy boyhood marked by simple, Christian living. At fourteen he had joined his father's church (April 1864), and he continued his membership there until after his father's resignation as pastor in 1882. His own religious philosophy became very liberal, being greatly influenced by Emerson, the Neoplatonists, and the religions of India. Thus, the author of *Looking Backwards, 2000-1887* (1888) which influenced thousands in their social thinking had left the ranks of organized religion. He had found the outlet for his deeply spiritual purposes in his interest in a program for the improvement of humanity.[21]

Henry George, author of *Progress and Poverty* (1879) and exponent of the Single Tax, was the son of a deeply devout Episcopalian family in Philadelphia, the father being a publisher of church and Sunday School books for the denomination.[22] Going to California as a youth, George had joined a Methodist church in 1860. There he fell in love with Annie Fox whose grandfather had been a prosperous Irish Catholic contractor. Annie and her sister Teresa had been educated at a convent, and Teresa became a nun. As

Henry George and his wife became increasingly interested in social reform, organized religion became less important to them. The latter often attended Episcopalian services with her husband's family, and she had her children baptized as Catholics only in deference to her sister's wishes. Yet, she disassociated herself from church membership. George left his children free to choose their own religious expression, and he worshipped in any church when occasion offered. Busy with his program of social reform, however, more often he did not take time to worship in any. Even among those intimately associated with the promulgation of the Social Gospel in the churches, there was a noticeable tendency to stress less the function of worship and to emphasize more and more the task of social reform. Thus, Walter Rauschenbusch who had been reared in a German Baptist family of genuine piety came increasingly to read less theology and more economics and to stress social education and action as a part of the evangelistic mission of the Church. Yet, Rauschenbusch never lost sight of the need for vitalizing personal faith if success were to be attained in "Christianizing the Social Order."[23]

A more marked reaction occurred in the career of George Davis Herron. As pastor of the Lake City, Minnesota, Congregational Church and then the First Congregational Church at Burlington, Iowa, he became a leading advocate of the Social Gospel. He found, however, that his relations with organized Christianity became increasingly tenuous in succeeding years. Having become professor of applied Christianity at Iowa College (later Grinnell) he criticized existing institutions so scathingly that he alienated many of his most devoted supporters. After the turn of the century (1901) his Socialist views influenced him to deem Jesus' philosophy of life as "inadequate to the Social Revolution," and by 1910 he had even dropped the Christian phraseology.[24]

Similarly, William S. Rainsford (1850-1933) who developed St. George's Episcopal church, New York City, into one of the great institutional churches of the country and the largest and most active parish in the denomination, gradually lost his enthusiasm for traditional religion. His preaching tended to emphasize enthusiasm for the love of Jesus and service to one's fellows, but became so increasingly free from dogmatic affirmations that in 1912 at his own request, he was deposed from the ministry.[25]

A somewhat different experience but one which ended similarly was that of Terence V. Powderly, foremost leader of the important union organization, the Knights of Labor. Born to devout Irish Catholic immigrants in Pennsylvania, he had been taught to believe that the Church was of divine origin. As he had endeavored to organize the Knights to advance their economic interests, an oath had seemed necessary to protect the workingmen from representatives of hostile employers. Many priests deemed this a restriction on the individual in making an unhampered recital of his sins in the confessional, and some Knights of Labor were denied the sacraments in certain parishes. Powderly earnestly endeavored to placate the priests who opposed the Knights and his own union associates. Often, for his pains he was deemed by some priests to be far from faithful to Catholicism, and some Knights of Labor leaders looked upon him as truckling to clerical domination.[26] His experience over many decades, according to his own story, convinced him that some priests were tyrants by nature, not hesitating to "launch the curse of Rome" on those who resisted subserviency. He asserted, "Such a priest was never slow to point to any misfortune befalling one who refused to yield to his wish, will or whim as the vengeance of God for disobeying the priest."[27] Powderly reported that his faith in God was never shaken, but his experience caused him to believe that a priest was not the intermediary between man and his God. Cardinal Gibbons eventually influenced Rome to refrain from a definite condemnation of the Knights of Labor,[28] but Powderly apparently was slowly disillusioned by the conduct of others. Powderly's own account may be exaggerated, but if the basic facts are correct, his experience was a harrowing one. In 1871, it had been reported that he was a "Mason," and he was not permitted to attend Mass at the Scranton cathedral, on one occasion the usher at the door using some physical force to eject him from the building. When he had gone to confession, an irate priest in the presence of others had denounced him as a "blackguard" and had declared that his soul would "roast in hell" if he did not "quit that society."[29] Over many years he felt that his faith in the Church had been so seriously impaired that he left the Church of his fathers in 1901.[30]

The Challenge of Social Christianity

Many active churchmen gradually came to believe that a more effective expression of their faith was needed in the every day life of the world. A line of demarcation between personal and "socialized" religion, in reality, had seldom been employed by religious leaders. Generally, some emphasis had been placed, at least since the days of the prophet Micah, on the obligation "to do justly, and love mercy" as well as "to walk humbly" with one's God.[31] In the nineteenth century, Presbyterians were generally conservative on social questions, yet each congregation usually had its duly appointed "deacons" whose duties embraced care for the poor of the parish. Among all religious groups the faith of many found expression in works of mercy and benevolence. Yet, as a distinction had commonly been drawn between the "saved" and the "unregenerate," charities of church-going Americans frequently seemed not to extend much beyond the organized "household of faith." Furthermore, with the growth of industrial cities, the neighborly sympathy and generosity of rural communities often found no counterpart amidst the anonymity of urban centers.

Seemingly, the way had been prepared for a new emphasis upon humane activity by the liberalizing of New England theology with a greater faith in the worth of the common man. Congregational pulpits had gradually devoted less time to the decrees of an "angry God" and the soul-searchings of the "elect" and more attention to the practical piety that the times seemed to demand. Some Unitarian leaders had gradually moved from "a faith in universal moral order" to a "faith in social benevolence" and an emphasis on individual freedom. Increasingly, liberal preachers obviously endeavored less to prepare men for heaven than to bring heaven to man on earth. The very individualism of much of this leadership, however, generally did not contribute to cohesive organization for a common end, though many persons were influenced by the new emphasis on social thinking.

At an ever accentuated pace, moreover, economic development stimulated industrialization and urbanization, resulting in impressive material and intellectual gains but also in vexatious problems for organized religion and morality. The flight of great numbers of middle-class Protestants from the older sections of the leading cities presented a challenge as to whether the faith of organized Protestantism could survive in those areas.[32]

In the meantime, the arrival of tens of thousands of immigrants who crowded into the cities presented a difficult challenge to Roman Catholic leadership. Yet, the problem was resolutely faced, and often beautiful churches were erected which mediated what little there was of dignity and loveliness in the lives of these struggling city dwellers.

Even before the Civil War, leaders among the Protestant clergy had challenged the prevailing complacency associated with the view that the lot of the poor was due to idleness, disease, debauchery, and inherent worthlessness.[33] The Y.M.C.A. had been established to combine a ministry of an individual and social nature.

Gradually interdenominational missions and the pioneer institutional churches were established. This melioristic attitude, however, was not a refutation of that fact that before 1876 "Protestantism presented a massive, almost unbroken

front in its defense of the social status quo." Then the rude
shock of the bitter industrial disturbances of 1877, 1886, and
1892-94 affected many Protestant leaders who were brought
face to face with inadequacies in the old self-reliant, individualistic traditions of rural America.

Yet, the two outstanding Protestant clergymen of the period, Phillips Brooks and Henry Ward Beecher, were fundamentally conservative in social outlook. Brooks, born to
social and economic security, could write in 1887, "Excessive poverty, actual suffering for the necessities of life, terrible as it is, is comparatively rare."[34]

Beecher who often loved to shock his expectant hearers
with some startling opinion and then qualify it so as to
reassure them of the "soundness" of his opinion, gave approval to labor unions but so opposed them in much of
their practical operation as to make a "good union" appear
almost functionless. Personally he enjoyed a large salary
and enviable revenues from royalties, newspaper syndicate
fees, and lecture appearances, and indulged rather extravagant tastes for driving expensive horses and carrying uncut
gems in his pocket. Yet, he could point out to strikers in
1877 the virtue of patient acquiescence in poverty:

"It is said that a dollar a day is not enough for a wife
and five or six children. No, not if the man smokes or drinks
beer. . . . Water costs nothing; and a man who cannot live
on bread is not fit to live."

In 1878 the *Congregationalist* branded the wandering
unemployed as "profane, licentious, filthy, vermin-swarm-
ing thieves, petty robbers, and sometimes murderers, social
pests and perambulatory nuisances" and suggested the revival of the whipping post for them.[35] Gradually, however,
the religious press took a more favorable attitude toward
industrial workers and unions. Stirring books by an optimistic Congregational clergyman, Josiah Strong, stressed
the alternative of social catastrophe or regeneration in a
spirit of fervent evangelism. His best-selling *Our Country*
(1885) became a veritable *Uncle Tom's Cabin* of city re-

form. Concrete details of revolting conditions in urban life shocked many people who read books like Helen Campbell, *Prisoners of Poverty* (New York, 1889), and Jacob Riis, *How the Other Half Lives* (New York, 1890).

The conscience of church-going America was stimulated by such disclosures to establish missions in the slums, give support to the Salvation Army (imported from Great Britain in 1880), develop recreational facilities, and build social settlement houses.

Ideologically, however, as late as 1880, preachers and professors still taught that laissez-faire was grounded in the laws of God and nature, that the worker's position must be raised by saving and good habits—not by labor organization or state action—and that misery was always a punishment for vice.

Practical experience in industrial areas and the teachings of various English, German, and other European economists, however, increasingly challenged the old classical economic views. Socially-minded clergymen then combined with economists in the academic world in establishing the American Economic Association as a revolt against the old doctrines.

For a time, however, evolutionary ideas, as interpreted by Herbert Spencer, contributed to a conservative reaction. The former clergyman, William Graham Sumner, developed ideas of Social Darwinism to justify social and economic ideas of the survival of the fittest. Under this view, laissez-faire was deeply rooted in the very nature of the physical world.

Liberal clergymen, however, came to be much more definitely influenced by the evolutionary views of John Fiske who stressed man's cooperative traits, and they were also much affected by the writings of Lester F. Ward, the sociologist, on purposive cooperation.[36] Richard T. Ely, the noted economist, moreover, struck a responsive chord when he appealed for a new ethical and Christian spirit in formulating the goals of economic thought. The widely read writings of Henry George, Edward Bellamy, and Henry D.

Lloyd, furthermore, made a deep impression, even when their own specific objectives were not approved.[37]

Gradually even conservative clergymen assumed a defensive and apologetic rather than a complacent position. Less and less were they inclined to point to a supposed economic and spiritual necessity for human suffering and to endorse the old iron law of wages. More and more they tended to urge the poor to be patient in the struggle for economic improvement and to urge employers to grant higher wages as a Christian act which would thwart the efforts of those fostering trade unions and even Socialism.

A transitional figure in the middle 1880's was the well-known Brooklyn Congregational clergyman, A. J. Behrends, who defended great wealth and handsome profits but indicated the important responsibilities of the prosperous. While still affirming that defects of character were the main causes of poverty, he was willing to grant that hardships did arise from social conditions, and he mentioned as possible remedies improved public education, liquor control, and even inexpensive housing. *The Baptist Quarterly Review* deemed him too lenient with radical opinion.

Soon there arose clergymen who were not satisfied with defending existing institutions with moderate changes to stave off radical demands. These new liberals were definitely concerned with the search for an improved social order. To them, individual regeneration was not enough, and they endeavored to find specific proposals to improve the life of organized society. Optimistic and retaining much of traditional American individualism, they appealed especially to middle class people who gradually abandoned the rigid economic views of mid-nineteenth century Protestant thought. Especially congenial to the growth of this type of Social Christianity were three viewpoints of the liberal theology of the period: (a) The immanence of God; (b) The organic character of nature and human life; (c) The ideal of the Kingdom of God on earth.[38]

Perhaps most influential was Washington Gladden, after

1882 for more than thirty years pastor of the First Congregational Church of Columbus, Ohio.[39] Owing much to the thought of Horace Bushnell, Frederick Robertson, and John Ruskin, he, like other pioneers of what was later called the Social Gospel, began with no preconceived economic theories, but asserted the validity of Christian principles for the whole of life.[40] Gladden's ideas gradually developed so that he came to a firm insistence on labor's rights of collective bargaining and was moved to advocate some adequate form of profit-sharing to resolve the tension between capital and labor. Finding no ultimate solution for the problem either in the older individualism or in socialism, he gradually recognized the need for greater governmental intervention. His personality, his plain speaking with the use of practical illustrations, and his genuinely religious spirit brought him extraordinary influence.[41]

In the earlier years of the new Social Christianity perhaps second in influence to Gladden was R. Heber Newton, liberal New York Episcopalian. A careful student of the period holds that Newton was more drastic than Gladden in his advocacy of eventual social change but less advanced in his position regarding immediate results.

Of outstanding influence also was Walter Rauschenbusch who as a young clergyman in 1886 had accepted the pastorate of the small Second German Baptist Church near the tough "Hell's Kitchen" area of New York City's west side. Working on a meagre salary in the midst of struggling German immigrants he acquired invaluable experience in meeting the needs of men in a most unpromising environment. There, he supported Henry George for mayor of New York and worked with the journalist-reformer, Jacob Riis, in behalf of playgrounds and fresh air centers for tenement children.[42] Acquiring a knowledge of the philosophy of men like Tolstoi, Mazzini, Marx, Bellamy and others, he began to emphasize the ideal of a "Kingdom of God" on earth. He found that many church-goers avoided social work as not an essential part of Christian service, but in his study of the

Bible he came to feel that he needed to devote more study to economic problems and less to theological niceties in preparing for greater usefulness to the cause of religion.

A friendship with two New York Baptist clergymen of similar theological and social views, Rev. Nathaniel Schmidt and Rev. Leighton Williams, led to the organization in Philadelphia (1892) of the "Brotherhood of the Kingdom," a fellowship devoted to the moral and spiritual ideals of Jesus in both individual and social life. Annual summer conferences at a rural retreat in the Hudson Valley were held for a number of years. Prayer, discussions, and addresses with a service at sunset, comprised the procedure. Social, ethical, and theological problems relating to such matters as corporations, the single tax, the family, evolution, and Biblical criticism were thoroughly discussed. Local chapters of the Brotherhood were also founded in a number of cities.[43]

Rauschenbusch became a professor associated with Rochester Theological Seminary in 1897, and there over a period of years he was to develop a wide influence in the crystallizing of the social thinking associated with the Social Gospel.[44]

Many other leaders were not without important influence in the movement.[45] A few became avowed Christian Socialists. Thus, William Dwight P. Bliss, attracted by the position of the Episcopal Church in relation to social reform, left the Congregational ministry and sought (1886) as an Episcopal clergyman to further ethical, non-violent methods for the socialization of all productive property. In 1896, however, he gave up his active ministry.[46]

The most uncompromising Christian Socialists, however, were followers of Rev. George D. Herron.[47] Attention has already been called to his stormy clerical and political career which finally led to his departure from the ministry.[48]

Among religious bodies the Protestant Episcopal Church "gave birth to the first and most effective Social Gospel organizations." Here, a rather aristocratic church group exhibited deep social concern, partly because of its large membership in cities where economic problems were acute. Important also were the influence of English Christian Socialism, the leadership of able bishops, and a disciplined organization which still retained some of the medieval ideal of society guided by the Church.[49]

Congregationalists were doubtless second in importance in their activities in the early Social Gospel movement, under clergymen like Josiah Strong and Washington Gladden. The free, independent organization of Congregationalism; its heritage of Genevan and New England traditions which stressed the control of worldly affairs by ministerial guidance; its advanced educational leadership; its new theology permeated by a spirit of humanitarianism; its large following in the industrial Northeast and Middle West,— all explain the vitality of the movement in Congregational circles.

The Baptists made significant contributions to the movement through able leaders like Walter Rauschenbusch and Leighton Williams. Yet, the traditional emphasis of the denomination on a clear cut separation of church and state, the large rural membership especially in the conservatively-minded South, and the increasing influence of rich laymen like John D. Rockefeller dampened enthusiasm for a movement to rebuild society.

Although individual Presbyterians had been much interested in social questions, as an organization they showed the least interest in the Social Gospel of any of the major Protestant churches. Members and, even more so, influential lay leaders belonged especially to conservative social and economic groups, and the Church's Calvinistic traditions and strict church government had followed far less than New England Congregationalists the pathway of the reformer and the innovator.

In view of its traditional interest in the poor and lowly, the early lagging of interest among Methodists in the Social Gospel may seem surprising. To some extent their energies had been expended on what they deemed moral concerns such as Reconstruction, Mormonism, temperance, and Sabbath observance. Their traditions, moreover, had stressed the virtues of frugality and hard work. A large part of the membership lived on farms, not in industrial centers, and in the cities the influence of the newly acquired wealth of important business men who were members of the denomination was increasingly significant. Liberal intellectuals and industrial workers, furthermore, were not relatively important groups within Methodism, and its revivalistic tradition pointed to individual repentance for sin rather than social reform as the remedy for evils of the day.

At the end of the century three distinct attitudes toward Social Christianity were noticeable. Significant headway had been made, as has just been pointed out, by those who emphasized positively the social mission of Christianity. In various denominations, candidates for the ministry were being taught social doctrines greatly influenced by the newer trends in thinking. A leading Methodist, Borden P. Bowne, had given moderate allegiance to Social Christianity in his *The Principles of Ethics* (1885). In this he had rejected the older concept that the state should be limited to police duty, but he had cautioned against more extreme "current social agitation." Newman Smyth, a liberal Congregationalist, had published a text book of Christian ethics in 1885 in which he had abandoned the inflexible, simple dogmas of the earlier period for concepts of evolutionary Christian thinking. The exponents of Social Christianity were more influential than their numbers might have indicated, and, as highly articulate individuals, gave a religious impetus to the rising Progressive Movement and made a permanent impression on the thought of Protestant America.

The second attitude was one which continued to emphasize individual salvation as the major objective of the Church. To some extent it was the viewpoint of many who believed that the task of the Church was to transform and instruct individuals and send them forth as a saving leaven

in society. Many believed that the Church lost influence as
excellent churchmen of differing views came to engage in
bitter conflict when the Church became too specifically involved in controversial social and economic problems. Such a
deeply intrenched conservative position was typically expressed by a resident of Terre Haute, Indiana, writing in
The Presbyterian and Reformed Review in 1893. The writer
insisted that the Church could not champion Henry George's
land theories or those of the Knights of Labor, for the
Church must not take sides in a question not purely moral.
Rather it was bound to avoid embroilment in social cleav-
ages so as to condemn selfishness in all classes. The writer
contended that this did not mean the avoidance of social
obligation, as he explained:

> There never was a time when benevolence was more
> emphasized by the Church than at present. . . . This
> benevolence reaches the sick, the hungry, the naked, the
> ignorant and the churchless.[50]

This viewpoint seemed to many to be subject to two
objections. First, the failure of religious people to demonstrate their religious precepts in the everyday world had
resulted in social evils which could only be met by concerted
action. Second, the limits of a "purely moral" question appropriate for church concern might be so restricted that the
Church would avoid speaking out on some of the most
degrading social sins of the time. In regard to the first objection, a liberal Episcopal clergyman, Rev. Richard Heber
Newton, had found the most flagrant dishonesty in business
practices in New York City and had demanded not only a
revival of ethical religion among church-going business
leaders of the metropolis, but trade associations to imple-
ment the effort to raise ethical standards.[51]

As to the second point, even a conservative Presbyterian
scholar, Benjamin B. Warfield, had been appalled by the
revelations of degradation in New York City areas revealed

in the pages of Jacob Riis, *How The Other Half Lives* (1890) and *Children of the Poor* (1892). Warfield believed that the "gravest and most formidable condonations of skepticism and atheism are found in just such specific facts." He felt that the time had come when morals would "more and more compel recognition in economics as well as in politics," and he mentioned with obvious approval that "Consumers' leagues" were being organized, the members pledging themselves not to deal with firms that refused to pay a living wage.[52]

A purely individualistic Gospel always carried with it the danger of protecting comfortable parishioners from the fact that many congregations had often taken on certain aspects of an exclusive club and of shielding them from the evidences of moral failure in a nominally Christian society. William S. Rainsford when he had begun a remarkable ministry of institutional Christianity at St. George's Protestant Episcopal Church, Manhattan, found that Admiral Alfred Mahan, noted author of books on naval power, withdrew from the congregation, and at times J. P. Morgan, the senior warden, was aroused to opposition.[53]

The continuing emphasis on individual salvation indeed was deeply intrenched. Throughout much of rural America the "Social Gospel" was at best little more than a vague intellectual concept. The changing theological views which were implicit in the principles of some of its advocates were widely regarded with suspicion in agrarian and small town circles. Except in unusual cases, moreover, pastors in such communities faced the immediate problems of the poverty and crudity of many of their own people, and their preaching of the "Social Gospel" was likely to be the old time religion with an emphasis on neighborliness and generosity. In 1888, the Bishops of the Methodist Episcopal Church, aware of the condition of their people, issued an Address urging evangelism and stressing the true spiritual doctrines of the Church as remedies for the "labor problem."[54]

In the South the old religious atmosphere was especially

dominant. Before the Civil War, Southern insistence on divine sanction for the prevalent status of the races had definitely silenced anti-slavery views in the churches and had stamped a conservative character upon all social thinking among religious people. The Presbyterian Church with an impressive influence among middle-class people continued to emphasize with great effectiveness the obligations of vital family religion and Christian stewardship.[55] The Methodist Church South had separated from the Northern brethren partly because of a belief that the Church should avoid politics and confine her activities to her "Scriptural" mission. The deep-seated individualism and the rural isolation of much of the South, moreover, tended to insulate it from newer social movements. Pastors continued to preach the Golden Rule as a never-failing remedy for human ills, although some began to feel toward the close of the century that a wider approach was imperative as mill towns arose utilizing the cheap labor supply. In 1899, the Rev. Henry P. Gibbs, a Methodist minister in northern Mississippi, aroused by the poverty, degradation, and immorality of the people in the local mill towns, published a revealing series of articles on "The Factory and Its People" in a secular magazine. Shortly thereafter, he was brutally assaulted by a mill official and died not long afterwards, and a deep conspiracy of silence, interrupted only occasionally by a bold humanitarianism, continued to preclude any real discussion of the plight of the worker.[56]

Progressive leaders of the Church in the South, however, began to be sensitive to the charges that organized religion seemed concerned only with the life beyond. Methodists who had once made a definite appeal to the poorer classes came to feel that the lowly were being alienated from the Church. Accordingly, social work which avoided local antagonisms was undertaken. New charitable and humanitarian organizations were founded, church homes for widows and orphans were established, and local churches compiled "poor lists" as an aid to the charitably disposed. Yet, until after 1900, organized Protestantism in the South made no substantial effort to concern itself with social and economic problems, or to establish social clubs in poor neighborhoods, or even to build kitchens, social halls, and gymnasiums as a part of their ministry to their own congregations.

In the North, in the meantime, earlier trends toward city mission activity, and settlement houses and institutional churches were further developed.

As a means of combining individualistic Christianity with social service, the Salvation Army, introduced from England as early as 1879-80 in Philadelphia, had its distinctive service. In the next year George S. Railton visited New York with seven "Hallelujah Lasses," and he helped organize twelve corps in various cities. His recall to England, however, led to five years of dissension which ended with the coming to America (1886) of Ballington Booth and F. L. Booth-Tucker, son and son-in-law of the founder, and Mrs. Ballington Booth. Numerous converts were secured, and they were encouraged to join the regular churches, which in turn gave support to the Army, and it secured the legal right to hold out-of-door services.[57]

In 1886 Ballington Booth and his wife broke with the Salvation Army to form the Volunteers of America, similarly organized but with a patriotic aspect and a connection between each post and a church in its vicinity.

Many came to believe that a mature Christianity was a proper blend of individualistic and social religion. A prominent Columbus, Ohio Methodist minister who later served within Congregationalism, wrote in 1900 that actually it was the "whole Gospel" which needed to be preached, "the heavenward side" with its theology and concern for the relations of God and man, but also the Social Gospel. Primary, he held, were "the philosophic and revealed biblical bases of man's duties both godward and manward," these in every well-balanced scheme of preaching always being the first to be taught and emphasized. But, as in the case of Jesus, these became the foundation for that preaching which pointed up one's duties to one's "fellow-men, to the visible kingdom of God on earth, and to society at large."[58] Perhaps much of the power of Washington Gladden and of Lyman Abbott was based on their appreciation of this need for balance. Generally they concerned themselves on Sunday morning with the task of developing spiritual power in the individual parishioner while the Sunday evening discourse often dealt with new intellectual or social challenges.

A third attitude toward Social Christianity was that of various Adventist groups, who generally minimized the importance of social reform because of their pre-millennial doctrines which distinguished them from post-millennialists who looked to the gradual coming of the Christian Kingdom. Followers of William Miller, the "Millerites" in the 1830's and 1840's had looked for the imminent literal appearance of Christ, the ascent of the saints into heaven, and the descent of the wicked into hell.[59] The dramatic tension associated with the eager awaiting of the Second Coming at a certain day and hour had disappeared with the failure of the great expectations to be realized. Yet, less excited believers in Pre-Millennialism came to be found not only in the Seventh Day Adventist and other Adventist denominations but also among certain leaders of the churches like the Episcopal, Baptist, Lutheran, and Reformed. An interdenominational meeting of those sharing this belief was held in the Episcopal Church of the Holy Trinity, New York City, in October 1878. These people, looking forward to a day of judgment, were naturally intensely evangelistic.

In the Adventist sects various writers produced much Scriptural-based literature, often with a wealth of quotations, condemning organized society as having embraced the spirit of the Anti-Christ, and picturing the entire contemporary social horizon as "shrouded in a horror of great darkness."[60] Profoundly pessimistic, this viewpoint particularly attracted the suffering poor who saw no hope in social change and sought escape from economic misery through belief in a divine cataclysm which would destroy the world and its "worldly leaders" and elevate the "saints" to heavenly bliss.[61] Yet, the main trend in Protestantism was the more conventional individualistic Gospel, with, as has been shown, an increasing concern for social responsibility.

While Social Christianity increased in importance in American Protestantism, especially in areas where "Yankee Reformers" were active, a recent scholar comes to the conclusion that in the same region both clerical and lay Catholics were almost wholly passive to social reform. This author asserts, for example, that in Boston, Catholic leaders deemed voluntary poverty a religious virtue and involuntary poverty a consequence of disobedience to God's law. A Boston priest is quoted as warning reformers in 1880 that those who sought to abolish want were conspiring against the divine plan. The assertion, moreover, is made that the Archdiocese of Boston failed to send a single priest into the ranks of social reform, 1880-1900, though some gave support to the temperance movement. John Boyle O'Reilley and James Jeffrey Roche, both Irish-born and both influential in determining the policies of the Boston *Pilot,* an Irish Catholic paper, seemed radical to many Catholics. Yet, we are told that on economic issues, both "side-stepped and back-stepped to keep in line with policy made in Rome," and that after the Pope's encyclical, *Rerum Novarum,* Roche "reversed O'Reilley's and his own radical assumptions to return to the passive doctrines which flowed from the concept of Christian charity."[62]

The same authority also concludes, that, as the Catholic dock hand awaited the Day of Judgment which would bring heavenly bliss to the faithful, the Jewish sweatshop worker held in mind the coming of the Messiah to lead his Chosen People to the Promised Land. In New England only one Jewish rabbi, an extremely unorthodox one, Solomon Schlindler, of Boston took an active part in social reform. In 1893 he was dismissed from the leadership of his congregation, partly because his ideas of economic equality failed to appeal to members of the synagogue who had wrung success, in the economic sphere, by hard work and self-reliance.

Nevertheless, in organized religion in the United States before 1900 the seeds had been planted of a more flourishing faith in the social implications of religion. In American Protestantism no one represented this development more than Walter Rauschenbusch. As we have seen, his early Baptist training had been imbued with a deeply devotional spirit, and he believed that such experiences were highly significant for the development of good citizenship.[63] But, the experience which he underwent during the depression of 1893 dismayed him as he heard "human virtue cracking and crumbling all around." Hence, he sought to transmute the spirit of personal religion into every aspect of social relations. For him, as for Jane Addams in connection with her settlement work, the Social Gospel was a veritable "Renaissance of Christianity" along humanitarian lines.

If, as a Catholic scholar has pointed out, leaders of the Catholic Church in the United States were rather lacking in vigor in carrying out even the moderate views of the Pope's *Rerum Novarum,* they did tend to exhibit more vigor than he formerly believed to be the case as they advanced the compulsory arbitration of labor difficulties. In the Methodist and Presbyterian Churches, moreover, conservative views on economic issues were slowly feeling the impact of challenges which were to find expression in the vigorous Social Action pronouncements of their denominations in the twentieth century. In 1886, a Presbyterian minister declared that he had once preached in the Pullman, Illinois, Presbyterian Church but, "by the help of God," would never do it again, for the word monopoly seemed to be written "in black letters over the pulpit and pew," and even the organ seemed to give forth the same refrain.[64] Thus, the old economic order was imperceptibly weakening in its hold on Churchgoing America.[65]

CHAPTER VIII

FROM PURITANISM TO PRAGMATISM

For many of the colonial Fathers in America, theology and not secular philosophy was the discipline which intellectually lighted the pathway of life. Scotch-Irish Calvinists, moreover, maintained a rather tenacious adherence to this religious standard. The Calvinism of the Puritan Fathers, however, had been somewhat modified, especially by the influence of the French humanist and Platonist, Peter Ramus.[1] Accordingly, the Puritans were not so dependent on Biblical revelation as they appeared to be, and an almost gradual transition to deism and natural religion in New England was almost unconsciously accomplished. One step along this way was symbolized in the career of the gifted Jonathan Edwards who was one leader in an effort to absorb into the Puritan tradition a type of religious individualism and pietistic revivalism. The movement came to be known as the "Great Awakening," and divided the "New Lights" who supported the religious revivals from the "Old Lights." This was a landmark between the organized conformity of 1630 and New England individualism of three centuries later. The religious life of New England thereafter was no longer a unity, for emotion and reason, as well as individualism and tradition were no longer integrated in the cultural pattern. In Rhode Island, Roger Williams came to preach religious liberty, and by the time of the American Revolution, philosophical liberalism was beginning to express itself in deism, Unitarianism, and Universalism.

Unitarians, influenced by the Enlightenment's emphasis on reason, had come to teach the strict and simple unity of God, the essential humanity of Jesus (though most of them

believed that he was more than a man and truly a Saviour),
the native dignity of man, and God's aid to man's every
good effort toward salvation. Among them there soon developed differing opinions as to the reliance to be placed on the
Holy Scriptures and on reason when the two seemed to be
in conflict, the renowned William Ellery Channing holding
that reason was to be followed, while Professor Henry Ware,
Jr. of Harvard Divinity School taught the supremacy of
Holy Writ. Eventually Channing's view became prevalent
in Unitarian circles.[2]

In the meantime, a third basis for religious truth, in addition to the Scriptures and reason, began to be emphasized.
This was intuition, which was one element in the influence
of German thought on American ideology.

Even before the end of the eighteenth century American
clergymen had been influenced by German Biblical scholarship and the teachings of Immanuel Kant. After the close
of the Napoleonic wars, Americans like George Bancroft,
Edward Everett, and George Ticknor had gone to Germany
to study, although generally they were not much interested
in German philosophy. Coleridge and Carlyle were apparently important transmitters of German thought (especially
Kant) to Americans through their writings. At any rate,
there emerged the philosophical movement known as Transcendentalism, which had many roots,—Platonic and pre-
Socratic philosophy, European Mysticism, New England theological trends, various English and French writers and
poets,—and in its later stages, Oriental philosophers and
Germans poets and philosophers. American Transcendentalists read avidly seeking congenial ideas in the minds of
others and findings inspiration in the writings of men like
Schleiermacher who sought intuitive sanctions for religion.[3]

Unitarianism had been in part a rational protest against
Calvinist dogmatism, but by 1835 it had become almost a
cult of "sobriety and decorum," and there arose those who
were unhappy with what Emerson called "the corpse-cold

Unitarianism of Brattle Street and Harvard College."⁴ Thus, New England youth revolted against stereotyped liberalism, and Transcendentalism, not "primarily a philosophy or a reform movement" but essentially "a mental and spiritual attitude" emerged. It sought to find the source of all truth within the nature of man, and each Transcendentalist was at least potentially a mystic.⁵

Many Unitarians would have no traffic with the seemingly non-rational emphasis of Transcendentalism, and Andrews Norton, noted Biblical scholar, who was sometimes called "the Unitarian Pope" deemed it "infidelity," which then meant a denial of Scriptural authority.⁶ All of this conflict illustrated something of the tension which had been present from early years in New England. The Puritans had believed that the saved individual received an influx of divine spirit and was joined to God by a direct infusion of his grace, but they had guarded against a tendency to fanaticism which was apt to follow when persons insisted that they had received instruction from an inner voice or from the presence of God in the landscape. Jonathan Edwards himself had represented something of the Puritan zeal for excitement as expressed in the "Great Awakening," but he had been opposed by those who had demanded that zeal and emotion be rigorously restrained.

The Unitarian protest against Transcendentalism was then that of worldly caution, self-control, and social conservatism which insisted that not dogma but restraint and sobriety were the bases of a stable society. For them, the Church, no longer bound to the rigors of Calvinism, but transmuting to society the traditional values of Biblical Christianity, was a basic institution.⁷

But, Emerson, a spokesman for Transcendentalism, believed that every man had an inward and immediate access to God which he chose to call the "Over Soul" and which embodied beauty, love, wisdom and power existent everywhere in nature. Emerson, accordingly, had abandoned the

ministry in 1832, and had come to pursue actively the vocation of a student of Transcendentalism, a scholar outside
the Church.

Some early Transcendentalists had endeavored to carry
the inspiration of the new movement into the organized
Church and three leaders have not inappropriately been
called "Christian Transcendentalists."[8]

One who in a way sought to bridge the gap between
liberal Unitarianism and Transcendentalism was William
Ellery Channing whose heritage was a combination of the
reasoning spirit of the Enlightenment, the Puritan concept
of personal piety, and humanitarianism. Channing had begun
his career as one with a faith in a universal moral order,
and he personally to the end of his career believed that
miracles were a necessary part of historic Christianity which,
if reduced to a set of abstract ideas, ceased to be "the power
of God unto salvation." Yet, gradually he found, with real
wistfulness that reason and humanitarianism had tended to
uproot his faith, which had been nourished in a soil enriched by the distinctive aspects of the Christian Gospel. In
practice, much of his preaching had denied such unique
qualities, and he had even worked hard to prove that the
substance of Christianity and natural religion was identical.
From liberal Unitarianism he had gone over to a faith in
social benevolence and then to the faith of romantic Transcendentalism in individual freedom.[9]

Thus, Channing came to feel a concern about the mystical flights of Transcendentalism if unchecked by the insights of historical experience.[10] Many others felt that a
younger contemporary, Theodore Parker, was moving too
far along paths of dubious merit. By 1845, Unitarians had
come to look upon Parker as one who had repudiated even
liberal Christianity.[11] Emerson's writings were rather obscure for the average man, but Parker on a Sunday spoke
regularly to more than 4,000 people and carried the Gospel
of Transcendentalism to immense throngs of thoughtful
people. He denounced Unitarianism as inconsistent in its

rationalistic approach by clinging to miracles, and sought to develop religion along naturalistic lines. A later President of Cornell, Andrew D. White, asserted that Parker, more than any other individual, had strengthened his "theistic ideas and stopped any tendency to atheism."[12] In reality Parker's position was even more extreme than that of the deists, for he repudiated the permanence and universality of even natural theology. Essential religion was piety which was independent of all theology.[13]

But Parker betrayed a fundamental ambiguity, for he was avowedly a Transcendentalist maintaining that ultimate truths were to be known through the mind rather than by means of the senses, for they transcended experimental proof. Yet, as a man of encyclopedic knowledge, more and more he tended to bury his intuitive insights under an avalanche of facts which he had presented, supposedly to clarify the insights. Thus, gradually intuition yielded to a scientific accumulation of data. Church-going America would not long find in this an answer to its spiritual quest.

In a sense, Transcendentalists had sought to make "literature a substitute for religion, and religion a substitute for philosophy," and two deeply religious souls in the Transcendentalist camp, Orestes A. Brownson and Sophia Ripley, had sought refuge in Catholicism.[14]

Brownson, as he had studied Kantian idealism which had been a main source of Transcendental philosophy, had found in its divorcing of Pure Reason and Practical Reason a fundamental defect for an adequate theory of knowledge. Eventually he rejected German philosophy as leading to subjectivism and pantheism, and ultimately to skepticism and atheism.

Thus, by the period after the Civil War, the Unitarian emphasis on reason, the Transcendentalist emphasis on intuition, and the scientific emphasis on the accumulation of facts, had tended to separate theology from its earlier intimate connection with philosophical studies. Philosophy became increasingly secularized in American thought, and, depending less and less upon Scriptural and other religious sanctions, constituted at least a potential threat to the intellectual bulwarks of church-going America.

Yet, the change was slow, and at the close of the Civil War in most colleges the little philosophy that was offered was usually taught by the President, sometimes with the collaboration of an ordained minister. Thus, at Williams College, for example, in the late 1890's President Carter taught with proper piety a course using as a text Flint's *Theism.* Around 1870, philosophy and theology were still so closely identified that the most extensive courses in philosophy were given in the divinity schools.[15] With the establishment of graduate schools at Johns Hopkins and elsewhere, divinity schools became the conservators of theological traditions.[16] On the other hand, philosophy became increasingly secularized in American thought, especially as evolutionary concepts placed great emphasis on natural processes.[17]

Against such trends conservative Protestant religious thinkers insisted upon metaphysics as necessary for logical thought, and to many of them Scottish "Common Sense Realism" appeared most congenial to the preservation of religious values.[18] According to this view, certain fundamental truths were reached, not by any deductive or inductive processes, nor by "revelation," but by "common sense." Some representatives of this school held that all experience rested upon four "common sense" truths: (1) Reality—that real existence implies substance and is not a succession of mere appearances; (2) Duality—that substance is of two essentially different kinds, mind and matter; (3) Personality —that mind exists as intelligent, voluntary, self-conscious entities; (4) Immortality—that persons are fitted for existence independent of the body and so for life after death.[19]

John Dewey relates that when he was a student at the University of Vermont in the late 1870's, philosophy teaching under the sensitive and cultivated Professor Henry A. P. Torrey followed the "Common Sense" school. Later, Torrey confided to Dewey that to him pantheism seemed "the most satisfactory form of metaphysics intellectually" but that it unfortunately ran "counter to religious faith."[20]

The advocates of a "Common Sense" approach opposed the pantheists who looked upon the world as having no being of its own, and the positivists or sensationalists, who held that all knowledge comes through the senses.

Espousing "duality," Common Sense philosophers insisted that mind and matter are distinct and incapable of being resolved into one another, although acting and reacting on each other. In opposition to duality were two main philosophical trends: (1) Materialism; and (2) Various kinds of idealism.[21]

Materialism was so appealing to many that one historian of philosophy tells us that the whole period was characterized by a striking "trend toward materialism and naturalism."[22] Some of the older generation, such as Chief Justice Salmon P. Chase, avoided intellectual difficulties by refraining from reading that which was disturbing to their established views.[23] One who went to Germany to study philosophy in the 1890's later stated that students deemed it "almost a sacred duty to suppress all the spiritual initiatives of the human soul," a situation which he believed left lasting "intellectual and moral scars."[24]

Materialists, according to their intellectual opponents, held that nature acts not "from a conscious design, but according to an immanent necessary instinct." Leading proponents of materialism held that all mental phenomena is of physical origin and the only immortality is that associated with the disintegration of the body so as to enrich the soil for later generations. In opposition to this, religionists held that materialism could not account for consciousness, for free will, for idealism, or for life itself.[25]

A variant form was "idealistic materialism" which endeavored to avoid the objections to stark materialism by claiming to affirm the reality of both mind and matter. Yet, it looked upon consciousness as simply a concomitant phenomenon of a series of mechanical changes, and conservative religionists looked upon it as basically materialistic and anti-religious in its conception of mind.

One related trend in the philosophic movements of the period was found in the career of Spanish-born George Santayana (1863-1952) who began to teach philosophy at Harvard in 1889. As a boy in Spain he had learned his Catholic catechism and prayers and through the example of his devout relatives he had come to love the forms and ceremonies of the Church. Yet, his parents, who were nominally Catholics, regarded "all religion as a work of human imagination" and prayers, penances, churches, and concepts of immortality as inventions of "rascally priests." During his boyhood and his college days at Harvard, Santayana had become intellectually estranged from Catholicism, yet he still revered the tenderness and beauty which he found in the Catholic tradition.[26] At Harvard, Santayana taught that right does not depend on might, nor ethics on religion. He professed a kind of "animal faith," and held that brutal nature could not absolve man from his obligation to actualize ideals of beauty and good.[27] He drew no fundamental distinction between moral and aesthetic values, and for the orthodox, he had left out religious faith in his aesthetic appreciation of a world whose naturalistic aspects he frankly accepted.[28]

Other philosophical viewpoints which contradicted duality included those of the idealists, among whom were:

(a) The Transcendental Idealists.

Although Kant was not an idealist, he had contributed to the development of this trend by denying that anyone could know ultimate reality, things in themselves (or noumena). Further developments had taken place in this line of thought in the teachings of Fichte, Schilling and Hegel. Hegel's "dialectic" had seemed to bring all things into unity, and in revised form had many followers in late nineteenth century America. Many conservative religionists could not accept the Hegelian idea as to the origin of the universe in the "absolute idea." This idea, according to the traditionalists, was "neither mind, nor matter, heaven nor earth, God nor man; that is . . . nothing."[29]

(b) Psychological Idealists.

These, following in the line of thought of Bishop Berkeley, insisted on the personality of God and also of men. God, to them, is the supreme free Spirit, comprehending, yet standing over and against the individual free spirits of men. Conservative theologians held that their essential denial of the material world did violence to religion by making life in the physical world an illusion.

In the latter decades the trend in American intellectual circles was away from the "realism" of McCosh and others. One who endeavored to mediate between realism and the new idealism so as to avoid the dangers of pantheism for a vital religious faith was Laurens P. Hickok, liberal Presbyterian minister and for a time President of Union College, Schenectady. He has been called "the ablest American dialectician of his day," but his "Constructive Realism" carried with it strong pantheistic and idealistic implications so as to arouse concern among the conservatively orthodox. His position was, nevertheless, a half-way house along the road from the older realism to the increasingly popular idealism, as was that of George T. Ladd of Yale.

Another who assisted in the transition was Professor George S. Morris who carried over from his early training the Scotch Common Sense view of the reality of the external world. Yet, he insisted that the truth of German idealism (Hegelianism) had been "demonstrated" as a guide to the good life. In America, the philosophical world was reacting against sensational empiricism and was eagerly following the writings of the British idealists, Thomas Hill Green, the two Cairds, John Watson, and Lord Haldane. As a student under Morris at Johns Hopkins, John Dewey was much influenced by this trend.[30] Morris's principal work, however, was at the University of Michigan where his teaching was "friendly to moral and religious pieties."

One who for a brief time was associated with Morris was George H. Howison, who long served as professor of philosophy at the University of California. There he taught his idealistic philosophy with a religious zeal.[31] Howison's idealism was not of the kind which denied the significance of individual persons.[32]

As Scotch-Common Sense Realism receded in popularity, the liberal religious world rapidly accepted idealism as "the bulwark of English-speaking Protestant piety."[33] Indeed, both the world of liberal Protestantism and the philosophical thinkers of the universities seemed to embrace the new idealism with unabashed abandon. Professor Ralph B. Perry who became a distinguished professor of philosophy at Harvard tells us that as a student at Harvard in the late 1890's the idealism of Josiah Royce seemed "impregnable and irresistible," following in a notable succession those who adhered to the "great cult of Kant." A later professor of philosophy at Johns Hopkins, Arthur O. Lovejoy, testifies similarly that at that time Royce seemed to give the "most coherent and adequate expression" to reigning philosophical ideas. A young scholar returning in 1896 from study in Germany to become Professor of Philosophy at Brown looked upon himself as a "critical realist" but he was much impressed with the way in which Royce's idealism was attracting the most attention in the field of philosophy.[34]

A student at the University of Minnesota (1889-1893) found that the most distinguished members of the faculty "threw their influence in favor of religion." Among these were President Cyrus Northrop and Williston S. Hough, professor of philosophy. The latter was a neo-Hegelian, and the texts used were standard works of idealistic philosophy, Royce, *The Spirit of Modern Philosophy;* Jacob G. Schurman, *The Belief in God;* and Edward Caird, *The Evolution of Religion.*[35]

So widespread was the acceptance of absolute idealism that liberal theological journals presented review after review of volumes defending "spiritual monism." This was the doctrine that all existence is spiritual, since it is the offspring of God and expresses God who alone is the perfect personality, acting himself out in the universe and training human personalities through ethics and religion for divine fellowship. It was hailed as evolutionary in theory, searchingly ethical in effect, and profoundly religious in spirit.[36] When James Iverach delivered a series of lectures of similar import at New York University, they were commended as "clear, calm, judicial."[37] Professor Robert M. Wenley of the University of Michigan in appraising the Gifford Lectures by James Ward of the University of Cambridge welcomed the published work as a "most valuable" book, pointing out that perhaps the author had gone too far in treating Herbert Spencer "almost with pity" as one trained as an engineer and never able to come really "into sight of a philosophical problem."[38]

Professor Frank C. Sharp of the University of Wisconsin proclaimed that Josiah Royce's latest book, *Studies of Good and Evil* (N. Y., 1898) was nothing less than "brilliant," as its "ethical idealism" espoused "an interpretation of the universe whose significance lies in the ethical ideals that its processes realize." Royce explained that the finite self is part of the larger Self who includes within himself all conscious life and who suffers with suffering humanity.[39] Similarly, a reviewer praised John Watson's *Christianity and Idealism* (N. Y., 1897) for laying firm hold on "the ultimate question," the reconciliation of the facts of the Christian revelation with a unitary (monistic) explanation of the universe which was also rational in "the sense of being spiritual."

The later distinguished Harvard professor of philosophy, William E. Hocking, found as a student at that university that Royce, as an exponent of idealism, manifested "intellectual majesty and moral greatness." At a meeting of philosophers in 1895, Howison (although differing somewhat from Royce in his views) went so far as to declare that idealism was the one "great tenet," the very basis of philosophy itself, on which they were all agreed.[40] This was in spite of the obvious naturalistic trends of the period.

The appeal of the idealistic synthesis was so great, moreover, that it was applied not only to philosophy but to society, literature, art and religion. President Augustus H. Strong, Baptist President of Rochester Theological Seminary, endeavored to adjust the new viewpoints to traditional theological concepts in *Christ in Creation and Ethical Monism* (Philadelphia, 1899). President William DeWitt Hyde of Bowdoin College, furthermore, tried to relate the new idealism to the practical life of the individual in *Practical Idealism* (N. Y., 1897). He asserted that the Incarnation of Jesus tended to give "concrete and individual expression" of God, as was needed to give deliverance from the emptiness of pantheism, but the heart of the doctrine centered not in Jesus as an individual but in the spirit of love which was poured forth from the Infinite God upon and through Jesus.

Henry C. King of Oberlin went so far as to announce the bankruptcy of philosophical materialism.[41] Yet, soon after 1900, just as idealistic philosophy had seemingly routed all opposition, its decline became evident. The optimistic climate of American middle class opinion had been conducive to the sentimentalism involved in the dominant thought forms of the period. Already, however, a student like W. E. Hocking was finding that he had been attracted to Royce's views without being wholly persuaded by his argument.[42] Arthur O. Lovejoy who became a noted philosopher felt impelled to renounce absolute idealism for what he later called a "Temporalistic Realism." Charles A. Strong, son of the previously mentioned A. H. Strong, found as a youth that, in correcting proofs of his father's work on theology he was so repelled by the "unnaturalness" of the suppositions which theologians made in order to reconcile conflicting Biblical stories that he had found that he could not become a minister. Long a professor of psychology at Columbia and a friend of Santayana, he held that nature was morally indifferent, caring not for human good or human suffering, a view far removed from the ethical idealism which his father had espoused.[43]

At Harvard, William James was influencing many students in a way which helped to break the spell of absolute idealism. Americans were a rather sentimental people, for whom the glow of absolute idealism had had its appeal, but they were also a very practical folk, and James's pragmatism began to come into vogue. This stressed practical consequences as a basic test of truth. Many had been profoundly influenced long before 1900 by James's *Principles of Psychology* (1890). A later professor at the University of Wisconsin was subsequently to assert that he was perhaps first led to question the validity of absolute idealism by a visit of James to the University of California in 1897.[44]

In 1906 a well known Columbia University philosopher was to write of "the remarkable diminution in the influence of the Kantian philosophy during the past decade," as the average university student seemed to consider idealistic philosophy "not simply unconvincing, but decidedly on the wrong track."[45]

As absolute idealism receded in popularity while empiricism and pragmatism attracted increasing attention, one who sought to develop a viewpoint which would conserve religious values was Borden P. Bowne, long head of the philosophy department at Boston University. His training in Germany had been under Lotze in idealism of the monist type. Bowne was not a monist and moved from "objective idealism" to what he called transcendental empiricism. He held that man's experience is not limited to the senses and emphasized the importance of the pragmatic in ethical theory. Unlike James and Royce, the latter of whom had early in life divested himself of any connection with a "visible religious body," Bowne was definitely church-minded. Stressing the reality of the Self which he insisted was free from bondage to inanimate nature, his philosophy which made distinct appeal to church-going America was at length called Personalism.

Other contemporaries were moving in a somewhat different direction. Gradually John Dewey drifted away from Hegelian idealism and came to be greatly influenced by James.[46] As will be indicated later, James's views were congenial to the religious spirit, for he held that there is an area of human experience into whose fundamental meaning science can never penetrate. He presented as proof the evidence of tragedy and evil.[47] Somewhat later, Dewey's "instrumentalism" and various forms of "naturalism" were to challenge rather directly the validity of many traditional religious insights. But, that is a part of the story of the twentieth century.

Psychological Thought

Before the Civil War, psychological ideas in the United States were largely based on the time-honored "faculty psychology" which had close associations with theological and philosophical principles. The basis of this was found in concepts of mind developed by Jonathan Edwards on principles laid down by John Locke. This appeal to introspection involved extended study of the understanding, affections, motive, power, and will. Naturally there were differences of opinion and of emphasis on the part of various proponents of these views. Closely related to this was "Mental Philosophy," with texts by men who served as orthodox college presidents, finding a wide use in American colleges. Among such texts were *Human Intellect* (1868) by Noah Porter of Yale; *The Principles of Psychology* (1869) by John Bascom, later President of the University of Wisconsin; and *Psychology* (1886) by James McCosh of Princeton.[48]

The new psychology of the later nineteenth century, however, had its roots in the German physiology of sensation blended with British philosophy of empiricism and associationism. In America, the prevalent social emphasis on that which was useful demanded a "shirt-sleeve" psychology, hence the German-British antecedents of American psychological thought were modified on the American scene.[49]

To indicate briefly the trends of the time it is instructive to look at the careers of G. Stanley Hall, William James, and John Dewey, all of whom came from definitely religious home environments. Hall was born in Massachusetts, and as a student at Williams College in the 1860's, he had taught a Bible class in a nearby manufacturing village and had gone on to Union Theological Seminary for ministerial training. He, however, had developed unorthodox tendencies, and when he had preached his trial sermon, his mentor had omitted criticism but had fallen on his knees to pray for the young skeptic. Hence, after a candid talk with Henry Ward Beecher, Hall had left the theological seminary and had gone to Germany for study. Later, completed his theological course, took a Ph.D. at Harvard, and went to Germany to pursue work in physics, physiology, and experimental psychology. His work, particularly at Johns Hopkins and at Clark University, was based upon the experimental approach, and for some there developed a seemingly irresolvable conflict between this empirical method and the "revealed" doctrine of the Church. Hall retained in his very fibre some of the values of the church-going society in which he had been reared, and he was strongly repelled by such attitudes as sex flippancy. The wife of his younger years was a deeply religious woman and active church member (as had been his beloved mother). Hall dutifully accompanied the family to church on Sundays and seems to have listened with nostalgic pleasure to the Bible stories which his wife conscientiously told to the children of the family. Yet, his personal religion was no longer that of the old orthodoxy; it was rather than of scientific evolution.[50]

William James (1842-1910) was the grandson of William James, a merchant and leading citizen of Albany, New York, who had been an ardent, orthodox Presbyterian. Henry James, son of the older William James, had rebelled against the traditional Calvinism. To him institutional religion became unimportant. He had sought a personal revelation of God and had become an ardent Swedenborgian rejoicing in the emphasis of that faith on "the immanence of God in the unity of mankind."[51] Thus, the younger William James was heir to a strong religious bent, and in his career he felt a decided compulsion to reconcile the spiritual aspirations which were a part of his very being, with the scientific approach to which his professional life was devoted.

As a young man in the late 1860's, he had suffered from ill health, melancholia, and philosophic doubt. For a time, he later confessed, he was saved from pervasive fear that might have led to insanity, only by clinging to the affirmations of Scriptural texts like, "The eternal God is my refuge," and, "I am the resurrection and the life."

Eventually psychology and philosophy became his fields of special interest, and, like Hall, he was a pioneer in the establishment of a psychological laboratory. Religiously, he had no sectarian affiliations, and organized, institutional religion did not command his allegiance, although for a time he was a regular attendant at the Harvard College chapel. James's understanding of psychology pointed to man's need for God. In such a belief James found a necessary preliminary to action. Indeed, to him anything short of theism was irrational.[52] With an emphasis in his philosophy on the importance of experience and the will, he came to study the psychology of religion, by investigating the fruits of religion in actual life. Part of his findings were published after the turn of the century as *The Varieties of Religious Experience* (1902), which had the effect of emphasizing the mental states associated with religion rather than its doctrines or external forms. Thus, whatever may have been James's contribution to American religious life, it was not along the line of direct support of organized church life. His grandfather had found personal religion and the organized expression of it in the Presbyterian Church; his father had found personal religious experience in Swedenborgianism; but William James found in religion, as a scientific study, a paramount "interest" of his life, devoid of any "living sense of commerce with a God." Essentially removed from the corporate expression of religion in his own life he found that the Divine was represented by "impersonal and abstract concepts" which but faintly moved him in comparison with the sense of communion with God which moved and inspired many in church-going America.[53] Accordingly, he could write privately (1890) that he doubted whether anyone on earth was "a more genuine enemy" than he was of what the Catholic Church stands for internally. though he said that he found the practical expression of Catholicism an entirely different matter.[54]

John Dewey was a third representative of the new psychological trends of organized religion. His parents were active members of the First Congregational Church of Burlington, Vermont, his father having served as a church officer and his mother being active in Sunday School and local missions work. He had been a regular attendant at Sunday School and public worship, had joined the church at the age of eleven, had taught a Sunday School class, and had become the first president of the Young People's Society of the congregation.

At the University of Vermont, however, Dewey had gradually come to abandon the older philosophical and psychological concepts which separated God from Nature and the soul from the body. After he had gone on for graduate work at Johns Hopkins, his church membership lapsed, and he became an apostle of pragmatism (and the later "instrumentalism") as the key to the answer to social problems.[55] His major contributions of course came after the turn of the century and are not a part of this study.

George T. Ladd, Congregational minister and long a philosopher and psychologist at Yale, was a profoundly religious man who believed that psychology should be studied as an experimental science grounded in physiology. He had a distinct part in the introduction of such methods from

Germany. Yet, almost inevitably out of such studies a troublesome question arose.

Fundamental to a comprehension of the relation of the new psychology to religion was an answer to the question as to whether the mind could be understood completely by scientific observation. James R. Angell, professor of psychology at the University of Chicago (and later President of Yale), in 1900 asserted that the essential viewpoint of contemporary psychology was "that the consciousness of animals differs from human consciousness in no assignable particular, beyond that of extent and complexity of development."[56] Obviously this position definitely varied from many religious ideas of the uniqueness of the soul of man.

Not only comparative psychology but also the new social psychology aroused real concern in religious circles. George E. Vincent, son of a Methodist bishop and in his own right a professional psychologist, in 1898 reviewed a much discussed volume by Professor James M. Baldwin of Princeton, *Social and Ethical Interpretations in Mental Development: A Study in Social Psychology* (N. Y., 1897). Vincent declared that the volume was typical of the current reaction against "the artificiality" of the older, individualistic psychology. Baldwin stressed the essentially social character of both the ethical and religious life. According to Vincent, Baldwin demonstrated that the individual of the old individualistic psychology was a mere logical abstraction, a phantom without concrete existence.[57]

At Baldwin's own institution, Princeton, with its close associations with organized religion, especially Presbyterianism, there were of course scholars who sensed in this viewpoint a threat to much that seemed precious in the older religious viewpoints. Accordingly, Alexander T. Ormond, long a well-known professor of philosophy at Princeton, approved Baldwin's methods as they kept well within the genetic field of inquiry. He cautioned, however, that the metaphysician as well as the religious teacher tended to look "with some uneasiness on the attempt to trace the natural history of the soul." According to Ormond, the social psychologist should confine his attention (as he indicated that Baldwin did) to the growth of mind as observed "in the sphere of natural operations and causes." According to Ormond, only the metaphysician could professionally deal with "the ultimate ground and first cause, which underlies nature and all natural processes and first cause" and where would be found "the real springs of the existence of the child-soul" and "the secret of its perdurability."[58]

Wilbur M. Urban, son of a Protestant Episcopal clergyman and one who was later professor of philosophy at Dartmouth, subsequently paid tribute to the contributions of both Baldwin and Ormond to his intellectual development at Princeton. From Baldwin he received inspiration, as he found truth in Baldwin's genetic psychology and evolutionary naturalism, but from Ormond he learned the significance of the great speculative systems of philosophy which he declares that he knew in his heart "were right."[59]

Conservative intellectual leaders of organized religion refused to believe that individuality was not "real" and insisted upon the actuality of personality, "the truth that the substance mind exists as self-conscious entities that we designate persons." They held that such belief was necessary to reasoning, to dogmatic theology, to morality, and to social progress in general. They repudiated the Associationist theory of psychology developed by Locke and Hume, according to which a person became merely "a chain of distinct existences." These critics asserted that the Associationist theory held that persons seemed real only because man thinks rapidly enough that the real breaks in the chain of thought are not noted. Conservative thinkers also repudiated William James's "stream" of consciousness theory and the Transcendental Theory (after Kant, Fichte, Schilling, and Hegel), both of which, it was claimed, did not affirm the reality of personal identity.[60]

Accordingly, against new psychological viewpoints, various religious leaders insisted upon the reality of individual persons, each one, from the standpoint of religion, an immortal soul. They also insisted that religion could not be understood wholly in naturalistic terms. Thus, a professor at the University of Chicago, in reviewing a new volume on the psychology of religion in 1900, ventured the belief that it did not speak "the last word." He said:

> It is determinist. It knows no God but the human spirit. It recognizes and traces instinct but can give no hint of its origin. If this essay pretends to give a complete account of religion, we cannot but be dismayed at the havoc it makes in all that religious men hold sacred, such as otherworldliness, mystery, the sanctities and aspirations of the religious life.[61]

Many felt, however, that much might be learned of value in the field of religious education by scientific studies in the psychology of religion. Thus, there was widespread approval of the empirical study of the growth of the religious consciousness by Professor Edwin D. Starbuck of Stanford University. The author, utilizing a large number of cases to draw conclusions regarding such patterns as the age of religious conversion, experiences preceding conversion, and the character of the converted life, was to receive high praise for assembling a systematized body of evidence throwing light on important areas in the spiritual life of man.[62]

Chapter IX

VICTORIAN AMERICA AND RELIGIOUS TRUTH

During the years after 1865, the Roman Catholic Church had, at first, in the viewpoint of many, experienced a conservative reaction. As is pointed out elsewhere, the Syllabus of Errors (1864) and the promulgation of the dogma of Papal Infallibility (1870) had had the effect of tightening the reins on the theological discussions and even on some practical activities of the orthodox.[1] After Pope Leo XIII had taken up the responsibilities of his office, the rather tart E. L. Godkin, in an editorial in *The Nation,* expressed regret that the new Supreme Pontiff did not seem to have a more constructive attitude toward modern problems than his predecessor. Godkin advanced the view that the Papacy had become definitely despondent because of an inability to appreciate "the fact that, whatever the theory may be, Christendom and the Catholic Church are not synonymous terms."

At that time the Catholic and Protestant faiths alike faced what a present day Catholic writer has called "an age of agnosticism, liberalism, and subjectivism," when ideas of the development of dogma, of a demand for reconciling science and religion, of evolutionary thought in the realm of theology, of Biblical criticism and the historical origins of religious institutions were disturbing orthodox circles in Western Christendom.[2]

Catholicism in the United States had enjoyed such a spectacular growth that its sheer activity had subordinated the speculative to the practical. The extensive theological studies of Catholic scholars in countries like France and Germany found no comparable counterpart in the United

States. Here, however, democratic traditions contrasted strongly with political trends in various Roman Catholic countries. Here, too, the spirit of individualism and religious compromise which had sometime been associated with pioneer life and with the isolated situation of parishes and even dioceses in a predominantly Protestant country, had aroused the concern of some bishops. Various Catholic priests tended to extol the blessings of the separation of Church and State and the need for accommodating Catholic practices to the spirit of the age.[3] In contrast, Monsignor Thomas S. Preston of New York contributed an article to the *American Catholic Quarterly Review* in 1891, disapproving some tendencies noted in "American Catholicity." Refusing to accept the idea that separation of Church and State may be desirable, he even pressed the view that all good Catholics must seek the reestablishment of the temporal power of the Pope. The powerful Archbishop Corrigan of New York held similar convictions and refused to write an article for the *Catholic World* so long as it exhibited liberalizing tendencies. Some of these conservative leaders attempted to curb, moreover, such economic views as Cardinal Gibbons and others deemed worthy of toleration.[4]

In 1891, Pope Leo XIII endeavored to give a constructive religious approach to the economic problems of modern life in his encyclical *Rerum Novarum*. Soon, a decided trend toward greater leniency in economic thought was noted when the papal nuncio, Archbishop Francesco Satolli, removed the censures against Father McGlynn who had been a steadfast supporter of Henry George. A leading present day scholar tells us that this "marked a victory for freedom within the Catholic Church, and for freedom in America," although the new attitude "appears to contradict utterly, the secret condemnation of George's works, by the Inquisition, three years earlier."[5]

In the area of religious discussion, however, the trend was definitely toward a conservative position. Archbishop Satolli, who had shown a deep sympathy for the American public school system, in April 1895 began to show a much less liberal attitude.[6] The resignation of the American liberal, Monsignor Denis J. O'Connell, from the rectorship of the American College in the same year, moreover, had not actually been prompted by reasons of health as stated at the time. It was a cruel blow to the tolerant views of Cardinal Gibbons and, as a foremost Catholic historian tells us, "cast a temporary gloom over the spirits of the so-called liberals in the Church in the United States."[7] Actual dismay followed for this group, however, in 1896 with the dismissal of the liberal Bishop John K. Keane from the rectorship of the Catholic University of America. Father Ellis tells us that this meant that for the time being those whose views were deemed philosophically liberal in the Church in the United States seemed to be "in complete rout."

Soon, Archbishop Satolli, as Prefect of the Congregation of Studies was writing from Rome to Archbishop Ireland of St. Paul, who was generally considered liberal in his views, expressing the hope that the Seminary in St. Paul was conforming in doctrine and discipline to the spirit of the Church and was firmly attached to the Papacy. Upon receiving a catalogue of the Seminary, Satolli criticized the program of philosophical studies, contending that too much attention was given to the natural sciences and too little to speculative and moral studies. He expressed amazement that in the Catalogue the name of Aquinas appeared in one place between Spencer and Kant, a situation which made him "think of Jesus Christ placed between two thieves."[8] Later, O'Connell and Keane were given attractive positions within American Catholicism. But, in the meantime, as pointed out elsewhere, the Pope had issued an encyclical against the liberalism associated with so-called Americanism, and the limits of tolerated orthodoxy were officially defined.

In the Jewish community, changes in religious thought had not been primarily of an intellectual nature. Rather, they had been associated with the adjustments of a faith firmly rooted in Old World traditions to the vibrant, ever changing

environments of the United States. Yet, even here the extent
to which Jews in America were willing to accept Reform
Judaism rather than the more orthodox forms was definitely
related to intellectual considerations as to what God had
revealed to them as essential to the preservation of their
faith. Such a young Jewish scholar as Felix Adler, moreover, had been greatly affected by modern intellectual forces
as he had turned his back on the rabbinate and had founded
the Society for Ethical Culture. It is little wonder then that
by the end of the century various Jewish leaders were seeking to curb the broadening tendencies which seemed to
create a bridge leading away from the vital sanctions of the
traditional orthodoxy.

In Protestant thought, drastic changes were in evidence
during the late nineteenth century. One who came to accept
the new trends wrote later that they were not the result "of
any restlessness of spirit, of any frivolity or instability or
wantonness," but were the result of necessary adjustment to
new truth.[9] Professor Charles A. Briggs (a Presbyterian)
spoke for many in the more intellectually sensitive Protestant communions when he wrote in 1891: "Dogmatic theology is in a state of dissolution and reconstruction. . . .
Criticism has made the Bible a new book." Many in the well-
established denominations wished to secure at least a basic
conformity to what they deemed the essentials of orthodoxy.
Yet, the efforts of the Presbyterian denomination to curb
the views of Briggs and others by heresy trials, the struggles
of Congregationalists to stem newer viewpoints which had
crystallized at Andover Seminary, and the demands of conservative Episcopalians that a popularizer of Biblical criticism like Rev. Heber Newton be disciplined had not been
encouraging to the supporters of a theological status quo.

At the very end of the century a leading Presbyterian
minister wrote that much of the contemporary confusion
and unrest theologically was due to a basic concern for religion. To him the struggle was associated with an effort to
find a balance between traditional theology, objective in its

approach and sometimes slow in adaptability to a new day, and the later trends in theology, often so subjective as to fail to garner the lessons of the centuries.[10]

In the adjustment of religious thought during this period many leaders of the various churches had participated, as has been shown in preceding chapters, but the pulpit giants of their day, Brooks and Henry Ward Beecher, were especially important. Both were basically conservative on economic questions. Brooks was undoubtedly the more admirable individual. Children instinctively loved him, and to all he gave an impression of deep sincerity and radiant goodness. James Bryce testified to the quiet earnestness with which he expressed "the thoughts and feelings of a singularly pure and lofty spirit." Brooks preached to large congregations in the intellectually charged Boston area, but he generally did not argue about science or philosophy. Rather, sympathetic to every quest for truth he proceeded with perfect confidence that Faith would not lose through the unraveling of the secrets of the Universe, and that the Church must adjust itself to new interpretations and new modes of living.

This quiet confidence made him less concerned than many avowed religious liberals in regard to such a book as Mrs. Humphrey Ward's *Robert Elsmere,* which pointed to the Christianity of the future as primarily a matter of social concern. He believed that the novel included "unreal dilemmas and alternatives" in the English mind. For him, anyone approaching Jesus in a spirit of experimental religion, attracted by the personality of the humanity of Christ would inevitably be led "through the mystery of manhood into His complete life." There, they would come face to face with "the Christ-miracle" and all else of consequence for real Christianity would be "believable."[11]

When an English bishop declared that cremation tended to do away with the truth of the Resurrection, Brooks became a Vice-President of a Cremation Society "as a protest against such queer ideas."[12] He was emphatic in his rejec-

tion of the doctrine of ecclesiastical apostolic succession, and
he was a Broad Churchman in his love of intellectual freedom, hence when he was chosen Episcopal bishop of Massachusetts in 1891, a determined group accused him of doctrinal unsoundness and dangerous latitudinarianism. His
consecration as bishop was a victory for tolerant views in
American church life.[13]

Beecher doubtless reached a far larger audience than
Brooks. A recent writer describes him thus: "Sentimental,
self-indulgent, egotistical, immensely warm hearted but
sometimes callous, Beecher was as much the embodiment of
nineteenth century as Walt Whitman."[14] He had a strong
sense of the drift of popular opinion, hence he gave to the
American people that which they inarticulately wanted.[15]
He was careful not to stray too far from the paths of orthodoxy. Yet, he realized the appeal which was associated with
keeping "the habitual hearer always wondering what surprise would greet him next Sunday, and the occasional
hearer equally wondering what surprise would greet him in
the next sentence." Much of America was weary of theological controversy and rather attracted to innovation if it
avoided the excesses of iconoclasm. A remarkable pulpit
orator, Beecher was "alternately persuasive, keen, dramatic,
polished, weighty," as he "disregarded the phrases and forms
of religion," stressing what he believed to be its essential
spirit.[16]

At the time of his death in 1887, *Harper's Weekly* asserted that he had been at the moment of his passing "the
greatest preacher of the English-speaking race. . . . The
people heard him gladly, because he was a sturdy, strong,
inspiring preacher, not of theological doctrines, but of
righteousness of life."

Although many of his generation were far from sure
that righteousness had always been exemplified in his private life, and although his preaching was emotional and
optimistic rather than logical and systematic, Beecher's in-

fluence on a rising generation of liberal church leaders was unequalled in American society.

One whose effect on his contemporaries was widespread but had been expressed more largely through his writings rather than his preaching was the liberal Congregationalist, Horace Bushnell. As a youth he had been so impressed by Coleridge's *Aids to Reflection* that in his old age he asserted that he owed more to it than any other book except the Bible. Bushnell developed ideas of the immanence of God in nature and in human personality. The latter relationship he believed enabled man to know God directly and to receive continuous inspiration from him.[17] Bushnell, according to one interpreter, had an intuitive, imaginative mind which had been "ill at ease in the iron cage of Calvinism." In his mature years he had arrived at the view that in relation to spiritual matters, language cannot be exact in meaning but rather must be symbolic and suggestive of truth. Definitive statements of religious ideas, he claimed were, therefore, impossible, and the Church could hold to no fixed dogmas or permanent doctrines. Creeds by such reasoning became no more than "badges of consent."[18]

Bushnell's influence on ideas of Christian nurture had been profound within American Protestantism, and his conception of religious truth may have contributed to an understanding of the problem of "semantics" in theological discussion. Doubtless in some of the well-established Protestant denominations he enabled many people to rest more comfortably within those organizations at a time when numbers of persons were accepting traditional doctrines only with definite reservations. Yet, for those who sought precise answers to what they deemed man's most important queries, Bushnell's voice seemed to be a voice crying in a wilderness of subjectivity.

Bushnell, however, was but one representative of late nineteenth century Protestantism which had been definitely affected, in a time of theological unrest by a number of trends in modern thought. To these we now turn to give consideration in some detail:

1. *Increasing emphasis on Reason in its relation to Revelation.*

In the so-called Ages of Faith, Revelation had been deemed central and Reason had been considered a Handmaiden pointing to Faith in Revelation.[19] In a revolt against this minimizing of the role of Reason the seventeenth and eighteenth century Deists had practically repudiated the whole doctrine of Revelation. Early in the nineteenth century Unitarian thought had experienced a conflict between conservatives who stressed the supremacy of the record of Revelation found in the Scriptures and those who advocated an unquestioned reliance upon Reason. Ultimately, the latter view had been generally accepted by Unitarians. In other denominations, including orthodox Congregationalism, there gradually came to be an increasing reliance upon reason in justifying the ways of God to man. One argument against the rigors of certain interpretations of Calvinism asserted that it was not reasonable to believe that a good and just God would sanction the eternal punishment of some of his creatures. Briggs himself had run afoul of certain conceptions of orthodoxy in his own (Presbyterian) denomination when in 1891 he had given his famous address placing Reason along side of the Bible and the Church as one of the "three great fountains of divine authority."

Deism had spent its force by the nineteenth century, yet the Free Thought movement had popularized an enthusiasm for the role of Reason as a guide to life, and Ingersoll and others had not been without a discernible influence upon certain trends of thought in Church-Going America. In a different way, the philosophy of men like Kant and Hegel had also been significant in emphasizing the role of Reason.

2. *A wider acceptance of the results of Biblical criticism.*

Attention has already been called to the controversy which began long before 1865, and the gradual acceptance by larger numbers of the people of Church-Going America of the results of competent scholarship. This meant that a smaller proportion of American people than formerly adhered to a belief in the verbal inerrancy of the Biblical narrative, as more and more they looked upon the Scriptures as a *record* of God's revelation rather than a Revelation itself which had to be accepted in every detail. A leading Methodist clergyman of Brooklyn, New York, wrote with aggressive optimism of the trends at the very end of the century:

> There are still traces of medievalism in theological opinion and relics of feudalism in ecclesiastical policy, but they are doomed by the law of the survival of the fittest. . . . It means the birth of modern criticism, and since Christianity is the foster mother of criticism we need not fear that the latter will ever become a matricide. . . .[20]

In the strongholds of Christian orthodoxy, however, conservative views of Biblical criticism continued to prevail. The papal encyclical *Providentissimus Deus* of 1893 is a case in point. As has already been pointed out, moreover, various learned scholars, especially Presbyterians at Princeton Theological Seminary, feared that any real concessions in the matter of the plenary inspiration of Scripture would mean a surrender of a belief in its trustworthiness and a decline of substantial interest in it as the Word of God. Representative of such Biblical students was Benjamin B. Warfield (1851-1921) a grandson of the eminent Breckinridge family of Kentucky, and an able, learned, and indefatigable student of Biblical criticism. From 1890 to 1903 he was chief editor of the *Presbyterian and Reformed Review,* and the issues of that periodical testify to his wide learning and his command of ancient and modern languages. In 1881 Warfield had taken an extremely conservative viewpoint, contending, "A proved error in Scripture contradicts not only our doctrine, but the Scripture claims and, therefore,

its inspiration in making those claims." Furthermore, he
sought to throw the burden of proof on those who denied
his views, as he held that Scriptural inerrancy could only
be overthrown by proving that error existed in the original
(and long lost) manuscripts.[21] As the years passed, Warfield
definitely challenged the views of men like Washington
Gladden, who had written in *Who Wrote the Bible?* that
not only was the Bible not "infallible" but that its laws
were "inadequate" and "moral defective" and its religious
teaching such as to give in places "blurred and distorted
ideas about God and His Truth."[22] Warfield believed so
implicitly in Biblical inspiration that seeming errors or inconsistencies he was confident were merely "difficulties"
which the further progress of Biblical criticism would re-
move. Adamant in his convictions, he would assert in 1893:

> No single error has as yet been demonstrated to occur
> in the Scriptures as given by God to his Church. And
> every critical student knows, as already pointed out, that
> the progress of investigation has been a continuous
> process of removing difficulties, until scarcely a shred of
> the old list of 'Biblical errors' remains to hide the naked-
> ness of this moribund contention.[23]

Even, conservatives like Warfield did not hold that the
very existence of Christian faith depended upon traditional
views of Biblical inspiration, but they believed such views
to be "a very important and valuable element" in the Christian faith.

Biblical criticism then was an issue which sharply divided
Christian people even within the same denomination. The
difficulties associated with this problem were well summar-
ized by a leading Methodist editor in the closing year of
the century:

> It would be hard to conceive that greater harm could
> befall the Church of God in any age or clime than to

have padlocks placed upon the lips of its ministry, so as to make sober, intelligent criticism of the Bible impossible or even difficult, for few things have ever impeded either mental or spiritual growth more than a blind adherence to tradition without reflection and inquiry. . . .

On the other hand, reckless criticism, rash speculation, and disregard for holy things are to be regretted no less than blind subscription to articles of faith or systems of creeds.

Pointing out that recent controversy in the Protestant churches had been associated with little spiritual growth, the editor expressed the view that much of the so-called "New Biblical Criticism" was not new, for many of the positions taken by various German Biblical critics had already been voiced by seventeenth century English deists. He then called attention to dangers in the current situation:

The strongest objection to the new criticism is that to-day, as always, it paralyzes growth in experimental religion. The views of these critics have been known in Germany for a century, and the result has been anything but a vigorous spiritual life. And wherever these prevail there is a growing disbelief in the authority of the Bible, the necessity of the atonement, the divinity of Christ, and the efficacy of prayer. Unitarians have proclaimed the same truths in America for fifty years. Have conversions and revivals been numerous among them?[24]

3. An Emphasis on Intuition as a road to religious truth.

An intuitive knowledge of God had traditionally been an important aspect of religious experience. As has been previously indicated, Puritanism was firmly grounded in a mystical experience of the elect who received an influx of divine grace and were conscious of communion with God through a direct infusion of his grace. Yet, Puritans had been concerned about excesses in this direction and endeavored to guard against a fanaticism which tended to be associated with the actions of those who had received instruction from an inner voice or from the presence of God in the landscape. They had further endeavored to frown upon religious views which emphasized an intuitive experience of God unrelated to Christian conduct. Thus, they had banished Anne Hutchinson from Massachusetts in 1636 when she had taught "Antinomianism," boasting that she had received explicit revelations from the Holy Ghost and discrediting moral conduct as an evidence of "justification."[25]

Members of the Society of Friends had of course exhibited a confidence in a belief in the Inner Light of God which, they held, illuminates the heart of every man.[26] Yet, within the Society of Friends, earlier in the century the Hicksite movement, led by a gifted and poetic man, Elias Hicks, who followed the intuitive approach with great emotional power, had aroused conservative Friends because of his disregard of that which was deemed valuable in historic Christianity and in historic Quakerism. A leading present-day Quaker tells us that when Hicks could affirm that the fullness of the godhead dwelt in every blade of grass, he failed to see what he might have learned from the historic creeds if he had allowed the time-honored Christian revelation to have corroborated "the inner revelation of Christ in the heart on which he depended so much."[27]

In New England, a revolt against the "scholastic" logic of Calvinism had led to an emphasis upon intuition, with new views derived, through Coleridge and other writers, from Plato, Kant, and other philosophers and essayists. The result had been the movement known as Transcendentalism. Yet, even William Ellery Channing had perceived the dangers of mystical flights of intuition unchecked by historical experience.

Transcendentalists, and later, many liberal clergymen of various denominations were much influenced by Friedrich Ernst Daniel Schleiermacher, born in Breslau in 1768, who found the heart of religion in a feeling of dependence on God, resulting in a knowledge of the divine that was immediate and self-validating.[28] Many liberal Methodist clergymen were much influenced by this trend, especially as their religious traditions stressed the importance of the "affections" in the religious life. German Reformed clergymen who had felt the impact of German University thought, and Episcopal and Congregational ministers of tolerant sympathies were also much affected by it. Such an influential Congregationalist as Lyman Abbott had shown his unqualified endorsement of this trend in 1880 when he asserted: "God, immortality, Christ, pardon, are not hypotheses reached by laborious arguments; they are facts perceived by the spiritual sense."[29]

The Roman Catholic Church had traditionally placed an important emphasis upon intuition as an indispensable approach to knowledge but insisted upon the Scriptures, church tradition, and reason as necessary guides to truth. Conservative Protestant theologians, moreover, continued to declare that intuition was no substitute for Biblical and theological knowledge. Thus, another area of conflict in religious thought was clearly discernible.

4. *A wider acceptance of Empirical Science as a Road to Truth.*

Just as the Christian Church had long opposed the Copernican theory as one which conflicted with time-honored conceptions of an earth-centered universe but had finally accommodated itself to this theory, so did the Church reluctantly acquiesce in the contentions of the New Geology and in some other aspects of a scientific approach to truth. Gradually, thoughtful religionists in large numbers came to accept what scientists claimed to be the record of geologic ages, even though this meant the discarding of some traditional views. They also tended increasingly to accept a scientific approach to other fields, even the study of the human mind. Yet, by the end of the century a definite conflict was noted in organized religion between conservatives and those

who seemed to endorse a rather radical empiricism and a
rather thoroughgoing reliance upon scientific method. The
division of opinion was well illustrated by the discussion
prompted by an article, "The Significance of Current Religious Unrest," by a Minneapolis Methodist clergyman,
J. F. Chaffee, that appeared in the summer of 1898.[30] Dr.
Chaffee placed great emphasis upon the Natural in religion.
This deeply offended the sentiments of some of his co-religionists, but Dr. Chaffee dismissed their complaint as "a
frantic plea in behalf of the supernatural" by men who
failed to see that modern man found not miracles but law
in the world of nature. Chaffee deplored the idea of taking
"our measure of God from men who lived during the childhood period of the race," though he advised attention to the
revelation in Jesus Christ, who brought many of his most
beautiful illustrations from nature.[31]

This brought forth a rejoinder from a fellow Minne-
sotan, who wondered at any difference between "the results or logical conclusions" from Dr. Chaffee's premises
"and those of Ingersoll or Thomas Paine" and who questioned the grounds for Chaffee's continuing in the Methodist ministry "while believing and uttering doctrines so contrary to her teaching."[32]

Chaffee then boldly replied at length to his critics, insisting:

> Religion can never become thoroughly wholesome
> until it becomes entirely natural. It is not an exotic,
> but has its foundations in the nature of things, having
> had its evolution just as certainly as civilization has had
> its evolution.[33]

Chaffee went on to point out that even John Wesley had
been greatly mistaken in teaching that earthquakes are a
"judicial act of God" in punishing sin. He excused Wesley's
error as unavoidable in one who had lived before geology
had revolutionized human thinking, at a time when men

generally thought that "God made the mountains outright" and did not know "that the cooling of the earth had caused it to shrivel up the mountains."

Chaffee, however, went further, contending:

> But it is not enough to maintain that nature is not disordered and unsympathetic; our contention should be that she is beneficent and absolutely righteous. In fact, she can be beneficent only by being righteous; and, if she be not righteous, it is useless to talk of an Author of nature whom we can Worship. But she is righteous. It is only our ignorance that makes us think the contrary. . . . So, then, everything depends on our keeping in harmony with nature. We must study her laws in order that we may know her secrets.

His conclusion was, "Our point of view, then, must be natural and not supernatural."

Needless to say, from the standpoint of many American theologians, Protestant and Catholic, such views identified God completely with Nature. For them, the Creator had not been thus imprisoned in his handiwork.

5. *A Growing Acceptance of Ideas of Evolution, and an Emphasis on Divine Immanence.*

As has just been shown, the importance of natural law had loomed increasingly larger in the minds of a whole generation, and in this trend evolutionary ideas had played their part. It has already been pointed out that at first the leaders of Church-Going America, both Catholic and Protestant, were generally unfavorable to evolutionary views and their unsettling effect on long established modes of thought. Five main views toward evolution had developed by the end of the century:

(a) Those who continued to hold to the literal Creation story and denounced as Godless any deviation from that explanation. Here were found those who, to the extent that they were Protestant Christians, helped to give life to the Fundamentalist movement of the twentieth century.

(b) Those conversant with scientific and philosophical thought of the time, who insisted on a theistic interpretation of life that retained traditional views of a transcendent God. Moderately conservative theologians of the well-established churches were apt to be found in this camp, particularly by the end of the century. Thus, Rev. James McCosh, president of Princeton and an orthodox Presbyterian, had accepted theistic evolution as early as 1871, insisting that man's spiritual qualities pointed to his special creation rather than to his origin by natural selection. Rev. John B. Adger, long associated with Columbia Theological Seminary (Presbyterian) in South Carolina where he had been associated with Thomas Woodrow,[34] in a famous address in 1882 before the directors of that Seminary held that evolution describes "the mode" in which the world came into its later form and not "the power" by which it was done, the latter question belonging to the field of religion.[35] Similarly, Professor George Macloskie, professor of biology at Princeton University, in 1898 asserted that the main contention of evolution had been generally accepted by biologists and all attempts to weaken its force had failed. He declared, however, that man may have been both created and evolved, for his creation may have been effected under divinely directed evolution, either as a natural development or possibly as a development with supernatural incidents. Macloskie believed that it was "by a sad trip of logic that Darwin and others interpreted the orderly development of nature as negativing the doctrine of Divine Providence."[36]

(c) Those liberal theologians like Lyman Abbott and Washington Gladden who accepted Beecher's view that science was "the deciphering of God's thoughts as revealed in the structure of the World." Such writers proceeded to apply evolutionary principles to the Bible, theology, the Church, society and the soul. The usual distinction between the natural and the supernatural was repudiated by many of this group, and the emphasis of the conservatives on logic, the Bible and the creeds was largely abandoned.[37] Abbott's biographer has pointed out that this reconciliation of evolution and religion was vague and superficial but served to encourage an acceptance of science and a retention of spiritual values in a world of changing sanctions.[38] Closely related to the churches, these liberals did not abandon but reinterpreted the traditional doctrines of the Incarnation, the Atonement, and the Resurrection. To the extent that they espoused the idea of an Immanent God wholly identified with the world, they aroused opposition like that expressed by a Methodist writer in 1900:

> The facility with which speculative writers are transforming the religion of the nineteenth century into pantheism is transcended only by the supreme indifference manifested by the general Church at this sacrifice of old-time orthodoxy.[39]

(d) Those, in the most liberal section of religious life liked the Unitarians who accepted enthusiastically the views of John Fiske. Fiske repudiated the Augustinian idea of God as a being actuated by human passions, who was definitely removed from the universe upon which He was said to act intermittently.[40] Fiske unqualifiedly renounced metaphysics. In place of the old anthropomorphic theism he sought to advocate "Cosmic Theism," based upon the scientific systematizing of the sciences. He stated in his *Outlines of Cosmic Philosophy* (1874) that the evolutionist must throw over much of the "semi-barbaric mythology" in which Christianity had been symbolized but preserve its genuinely religious and ethi-

cal values.[41] Fiske's God was not the "Unknowable" of
Herbert Spencer's philosophy but the Power that is infinite and immanent in the world of nature.

Conservative religious thinkers denied that informed
orthodoxy accepted a crude anthropomorphism. One
even quoted Calvin's answer to those who make God
corporeal because the Bible ascribes to Him mouth, ears,
hands, and feet, "Who of even the least intellectual per-
ception does not know that in these forms of expression
God uses a sort of baby-talk as nurses are wont to talk
to little children?"[42] It was asserted, however, that man
had to endeavor to visualize God in order to bring him
within human consciousness, and the heart of the orthodox objections to Fiske's philosophy was stated thus:

> [True Christianity] teaches that God is apart from
> and above, as well as in and through the cosmos. . . .
> The immanence of God is a great truth, too often
> overlooked in the past, but it is not the only truth.
> If we cannot know God except as the objective world
> makes him known to us, then the communings and
> comfortings of His holy spirit are the dreams of a
> mystic or the crass fancies of a fanatic. If Mr. Fiske
> is right, Providence is a fable . . . and the whole idea
> of Divine Government in nature and in man is un-
> scientific and untrue.[43]

In his latter years, Fiske seemed to move closer to the
orthodox views. In *Through Nature to God* (Boston, 1899)
he defended the idea of an ethical world not visible to the
senses, using it as an argument for theism. Even a conservative Presbyterian could hail it as "the high-tide mark" of
Fiske's intellectual faith and as a work which demonstrated
that he had "grown far away" from his earlier philosophy.[44]

(e) Those who believed that evolutionary thought
pointed to a wholly naturalistic view of life that made

traditional religion an anachronism. This position was not common in the United States, but a reviewer in the *American Journal of Theology* in July 1900 looked with some dismay upon a new German work which endeavored to prove that the "soul" is a myth, that the activities of the mind are entirely mechanical and corporeal in origin and nature, and that instead of a spiritual aspect of man there is only natural egoism like that inherent in every living organism.[45]

CHAPTER X

LIBERAL PROTESTANTISM AND THEOLOGICAL CHANGE

Emphasis on reason, Biblical criticism, intuition, science, and evolutionary thought, had important consequences on generally accepted ideas of God and of Jesus Christ. Much earlier, especially in New England, the rise of Arminianism and then of Unitarianism had been especially important.[1] The rapid decline of Calvinistic views in Congregationalism and the questioning among liberal Unitarians as to whether they should longer retain the "Christian" label were more recently clear indications that the role of God as a Sovereign Judge of mankind and that of Christ as an indispensable Saviour of the lost no longer received their older emphasis in many religious circles.

With the progress of Biblical criticism not only Unitarians but the orthodox churches were affected by the Hegelian David Friedrich Strauss, a German, in his *Life of Jesus* (1835) in which emphasis was placed upon the historical Jesus but the Christ of the Gospels became largely a mythical creation of organized Christianity.[2] Later, in England a group of seven scholars, all but one being ordained clergymen, produced *Essays and Reviews* (1860) which a present-day Episcopalian scholar tells us were generally "so cautious and reverent" that it is hard to "recreate in imagination the angry opposition which they excited."[3] Certainly, many of the orthodox in America were not prepared to accept the view of one of the writers that if miracles had once been the chief supports of Christianity they had come to be one of the main hindrances to a thorough acceptance of it. In his later years one of the contributors, Benjamin Jowett, became even more radical in his views, and in 1899 a Baptist scholar commented that Jowett's views of the person of Christ, the personality of God, immortality, and changes in historic doctrine "gave such offense that some earnest churchmen did not hesitate to characterize his teaching as anti-Christian, and even pagan or infidel."[4] Other English writers such as Frederick Denison Maurice and Charles Kingsley had presented appealingly liberal "Broad Church" views which tended to stress ethical rather than dogmatic views of the significance of Jesus. American churchmen like Phillips Brooks were much influenced by the trend. Almost thirty years later, Charles Gore of Oxford and ten other Anglican priests had issued a volume of twelve essays, *Lux Mundi,* in which Gore declared that Jesus exhibited no signs of transcending the science or history of his age.[5] This volume and Mrs. Humphrey Ward's *Robert Elsmere,* which took a modernistic view of Jesus, were widely read in America. At the same time Protestant religious thought in the United States was much affected by the German Friedrich E. D. Schleiermacher (b. 1768). A Scotch theologian, writing in 1899 in the conservative *Presbyterian and Reformed Review* termed him "the most representative theologian of the nineteenth century," one whose name "shines with brightest lustre in the grateful memory of all the Christian world." He was one who, in a time of excessive rationalism had "championed the peerless worth of personal religion," emphasizing "living piety as itself a norm" and imparting "a new conception of theological science, and one which carried in itself the guarantee of progress." Thus, he had instilled "the breath of a new reverence for living religion into the nineteenth century," thereby rendering "a quite inestimable service" to the whole Christian Church.[6] Schleiermacher, however, had his weaknesses, in the viewpoint of the orthodox world. Dangerous trends were noted in the subjective nature of his religious approach, for he stressed the religious consciousness of the individual and failed to understand the importance of the Scriptures for normative standards of the religious life and the significance of personal immortality, Christ as a Risen Redeemer, and a transcendent God as distinguished from the immanent One. An American scholar found a weakness in the fact that he was too much of a dialectician to be a sound theologian, as he had something "of Calvin's spirit of dependence upon God, but lacked his Scripture principle; . . . a little of Luther's spirit of liberty, without his warm faith in Christ, the crucified Savior."[7]

Thus, Schleiermacher was one who stimulated religious feeling which enabled many to "gain an experience in time of the dashing of the waves of eternity." Yet, his appeal was not to the whole man but rather definitely to the emotions, and this deficiency paved the way for the contribution of Albrecht Ritschl, who tended to recall liberal thought "toward the positive in theology," that of "revelation."[8] Ritschl's influence was just beginning to have marked effect in the United States in the closing decade of the century.

Ritschl's theology laid great stress on the historical revelation and denounced all previous systems of theology as vitiated by metaphysical "subtleties" like the doctrine of the Trinity. It held that Christianity was an experienced fact, verified in the consciousness of the Christian and incapable of being disturbed by metaphysical or natural science. God, to Ritschl, was Love revealed through Jesus Christ, the first and only sinless man. Divine anger, original sin, and mysticism were repudiated, as well as the traditional doctrine of the Incarnation, Christ being viewed as a man by nature but developing into God in value with his divine motive of love. The emphasis was on the moral and the practical as demonstrated in faithful labor, patient endurance, and worth-while service.[9]

Problems, such as whether Ritschlian theology was essentially based on revelation or intuition, were soon found to be inherent in the new doctrines. Extreme critics accepted the comment of a German scholar, that "what in Ritschlianism is true is not new, and what is new is not true."[10] To some this theology seemed to rest "on a subjective idealism which, while a great parade is made of reverence for historical facts, makes the whole ground for accepting the historical facts doubtful or even illusory."[11] Certainly it came to be widely believed that Ritschlianism was a "presentation rather than a solution of problems," a "ferment, not a finality," for on every great doctrine it discussed it "excited more questions than it answered."[12]

Yet, it was a "ferment," emphasizing that Christianity has often been confused with philosophical and metaphysical explanations at the sacrifice of the practical and the ethical. It also commended itself to many who were weary of the conflict between science and religion and who found in it a sympathy for modern thought not always discernible in the orthodox systems. One observer found that Ritschl's view had been teaching the Christian church that theology is not religion and that upholders of faultless theological systems had not necessarily experienced Christ. But, in view of its deficiencies and errors he urged that "neither sloth, nor impatience, nor despair" should dissuade American Christians from replacing the Ritschlian theology "with doctrines that are better."[13]

Further Changing Concepts: Man, Sin, Salvation, and the Church

Attention has been called in many previous chapters to what the liberal Roman Catholic Bishop Spalding of Peoria observed was a "wavering of religious belief" so that nothing seemed "to rest upon a firm and immovable basis."[14] While Roman Catholic scholars were assiduous in their researches, generally the accepted dogmatic answers of the Church Fathers were given to basic religious questions. Accordingly, a not untypical Catholic scholar produced in 1899 a dissertation on *Religion and Morality. Their Nature and Mutual*

Relations Historically and Doctrinally Considered.[15] Such scholarship was not likely to be faced with charges of heterodoxy.

On the other hand, Protestant liberalism during the period had so drastically departed from traditional viewpoints that James H. Tufts who became a professor of ethics at the University of Chicago could later declare that his generation had seen "the passing of systems of thought which had reigned since Augustine" along with the "conception of the world as a kingdom ruled by God, subject to his laws and their penalties, which had been undisturbed by the Protestant Reformation." For him, even the "sanctions of our inherited morality" had gone.[16]

As has likewise been pointed out in earlier chapters, various liberal religious writers greeted these changes with a sense of emancipation. The influential Congregationalist, Lyman Abbott, wrote in 1897 of the need for "a new theology constructed on a new foundation," the evolutionary principle which would mean that scholarship would pursue "the study of a continuous, progressive change, according to certain laws, and by means of resident forces. . . ."[17] Henry Churchill King, long associated with Oberlin College, although more conservative in many respects than Abbott, likewise called for a "Reconstruction in Theology," since the philosophical world had come to be "utterly different from that of the Reformation."[18]

While conservative Protestant, Catholic, and Jewish theologians continued to emphasize the sinfulness of man, the trend of liberal theology, in tune with much of the optimistic spirit of the time, stressed his goodness and even his perfectibility. In previous chapters attention has been called to the earlier trends in this direction associated with the rise of Unitarianism, the abandonment of Calvinistic views of human depravity by many Congregational churches, and the acceptance of less pessimistic conceptions of human nature in liberal Presbyterian circles.

Similarly views of sin were drastically altered. Even the

liberal Horace Bushnell had accepted the sinfulness of man. Indeed, a recent scholar tells us that his view of sin was "much more profound" than his liberal predecessors or his successors, men like Munger, Gladden, and Rauschenbusch.[19] But, with the widespread acceptance of rather optimistic interpretations of evolution, with overtones of inevitable human progress, Lyman Abbott came to view the Genesis account of man's fall as "a beautiful fable" and sin as a lapse into animal nature from which man had risen.[20] Similarly, to Augustus H. Strong, long President of the Rochester Theological Seminary (Baptist), man's sinfulness arising from his Fall was to be interpreted as Man's "revolt against the will of God" after harmony with his environment, typified by the Garden of Eden.[21] To Henry C. King, sin was to be viewed not so much as that which merited punishment by God (as in the older theology) but as that which should be seen "in the light of the suffering love of God, of what it cost the Father's heart," so as to bring home to the offender "the shame of it and the guilt of it as no punishment could possibly do."[22]

Others, as has been indicated elsewhere, now stressed the responsibility of society for much that had been generally deemed unquestionably sinful.

Similarly, the new theology brought in humanistic considerations which altered conceptions of the Atonement of Christ. Conservative theology had held that the Heavenly Father had offered his Son on the cross to make compensation for the sins of man. Thus, divine Justice had been satisfied by the "blood Atonement" of Christ. This "satisfaction theory," held by early New England theologians and, in viewpoint, not unlike earlier views of Anselm, had been supplanted by the "governmental" theory elaborated by Jonathan Edwards Jr. before 1800. Various other theories were developed by the end of the century, liberals being especially attracted by Horace Bushnell's "moral influence" theory (not unlike that of Abelard centuries earlier) stressing the sacrificial love of Christ as an atoning example of

divine power.[23] In his early years as a minister Lyman
Abbott (around 1870) had believed that salvation came
through the blood of Christ, but by 1900 he had repudiated
this aspect of the old orthodoxy.[24] Yet, even Abbott believed
that liberal Unitarians had gone too far, as they had "sometimes ignored or belittled, if they have not denied, the organic sinfulness of man as a racial fact." Abbott had come
to approve Bushnell's moral influence theory, and for this
a conservative could chide him for going too far in embracing a "sentimental doctrine of divine love" that obscured the
sterner Biblical teachings and minimized the sense of personal responsibility for wrong-doing.[25] A Presbyterian scholar
even thought that, in spite of the great constructive influence of Phillips Brooks, in the matter of salvation "as the
free gift of sovereign grace" across which is "written Justification" he seemed as "ignorant as Europe was of America before Columbus."[26]

As the liberal theologians emphasized the immanence
of God, they stressed the naturalness of religion. Lyman
Abbott, carrying out the implications of Horace Bushnell's
viewpoints declared, "We are coming to see that there is
no distinction between the supernatural and the natural;
that the natural is all supernatural, and that the supernatural
is all most natural."[27] Henry Churchill King similarly was
insisting that there was no difference between the sacred
and the secular, for, from the liberal Christian standpoint,
all of life was sacred. For some who were not wholly satisfied with such an abandonment of the special sphere of the
religious life, the acceptance of the views of Abbott and
King would mean that the Church would no longer occupy
a unique place in the life of man. As a reaction against this
tendency we have seen that Abbott's own brother had embraced rather "High Church" viewpoints within the Protestant Episcopal communion. One Methodist leader compared
the liberals in Methodism to the Sadducees who, he said,
had denied the authority of all revelation and were skeptical
of the supernatural, giving themselves up to ease and social

conformity. According to this critic, the prototype of the Sadducee among Methodists of the day had no need for the sacrament of the Lord's Supper, for no Atonement was necessary, since man had fallen "upward, not downward."[28] The implication was clear that for such the Church as a redemptive fellowship was giving way to easy going secularism. Indeed, a liberal theological professor of the last generation (at Union Seminary, New York) tells us that gradually religious liberals were coming to have "little use for the Church" as an effective institution either in the transformation of the lives of individuals or in the radical transformation of society. A direct appeal by liberals to the individual, who was deemed to be both a rational and disciplined personality, minimized the role of organized religion.[29]

CHAPTER XI

THE APPEAL AND PROBLEMS OF CATHOLICISM

Hugh McCulloch, distinguished Secretary of the Treasury under Lincoln and Johnson, was an able Fort Wayne, Indiana, banker and a rather astute observer of human affairs. Liberal in his personal views, in 1887, he commented:

> The church whose claims are the highest will always have the largest following. . . . The growth and permanency of the Catholic Church are largely the result of its claims to infallibility. Admirable as it is in organization—the most perfect that has ever existed—it would lose its hold upon its people if this claim to infallibility were relinquished.[1]

Similarly James Ford Rhodes, the renowned historian, many years later found that the Episcopalian faith in which he had been raised had been eroded for him by the impact of modern thought, and lamented that he feared for the future of Christian civilization, one reason being that the Church had lost its power. But he found an exception in the Catholic Church which he felt would certainly persist.[2]

As many had struggled with personal faith during the nineteenth century some had laid their doubts aside by embracing wholeheartedly the doctrine and discipline of Catholicism. This had been especially noticeable in the middle decades of the century when the question of Apostolic Succession had seemed especially important to many of Anglican affiliation. In England the Oxford or Tractarian movement had led to the conversion (1845) of the gifted and subtle John Henry Newman to the Roman Catholic faith[3] and comparable trends had been noted in America.[4] Three youthful students who were deeply affected by the movement and who were to have much influence in post Civil War America were impelled to embrace Catholicism. The three paid a visit in 1845 to Newman in England and then studied at a Redemptorist College in Louvain, Belgium. One of these, Clarence Augustus Walworth (1820-1900) was the son of Reuben Hyde Walworth, last chancellor of the state of New York and a devoted Presbyterian. The son had prepared for the Episcopal ministry and had unsuccessfully attempted the establishment of an Episcopalian monastery in the Adirondacks. He had an active career as a Catholic missionary, and from 1866 to 1900 was pastor of St. Mary's Catholic Church, Albany, New York.

The second of the trio was James Alphonsus McMaster (1820-1886), a stormy figure in American church history. McMaster's father was a Presbyterian minister, and his two brothers were ministers of the same faith, one serving for a period as President of Miami University, Oxford, Ohio. The father prayed humbly for the return of his son to the faith of the rest of the family.[5] Finding that he had no religious vocation, the young McMaster married and for the rest of his life devoted himself to Catholic journalism, making the *Freeman's Journal* (New York) the outstanding Catholic paper of the time. He was characterized as "a Scotch Highlander with a touch of Calvinism not yet sponged out of him," and a Catholic scholar has recently termed him "a real ultramontane," with "a noisy enthusiasm regarding the Papacy."[6]

The third of the group, Isaac Thomas Hecker (1819-1888), was determined to bring to as many Americans as possible what he believed to be the essentially democratic character of the Catholic Church. He found The Missionary Priests of St. Paul the Apostle (Paulist Fathers) in 1858 and founded the important *Catholic World* (1865). His vigorous leadership was highly influential in the development of so-called "Liberal Catholicism."[7]

Another important individual was Augustus Francis Hewit (1820-97), the son of a Congregational clergyman who had been a founder of Hartford Theological Seminary. He had been ordained in the denomination of his family affiliation but almost immediately became an Episcopalian. Newman's conversion had influenced him to join the Catholic Church in 1846. Thereupon, he had renounced his original name of Nathaniel Augustus Hewit. Editor of the *Catholic World* (1869-74), he succeeded Father Hecker as head of the Paulist Seminary in New York (1888). For twenty years before his death he was a foremost Catholic apologist in the United States.

The period of Newman's conversion had also brought other Episcopalians into the Catholic fold. William Starke Rosecrans (1819-98), later famed Civil War General, embraced Catholicism while a student at West Point. He then influenced his brother, Sylvester Horton Rosecrans (1827-78), who turned to Catholicism (1845) while a student at Kenyon College (Episcopalian) in Ohio, and later became the first bishop of the Catholic diocese of Columbus, Ohio.

Few converts who were turned to Catholicism by the Oxford Movement were more influential than a Vermonter, Rev. William Henry Hoyt (1813-93), who served as Episcopal rector at Middlebury and St. Albans until he joined the Catholic Church in 1846. He was the father of eleven children, all of whom, as well as his wife, were received into the Catholic Church. For thirty years afterwards, he was an indefatigable Catholic layman bringing numerous converts to Rome, and after his wife's death, he became a Catholic priest (from 1877 until his own death).[8] Among the numerous persons whom he influenced to accept the authority of Rome was George Allen (1808-76), a Vermont-born Episcopalian clergyman and educator. Embracing Catholicism in 1847, Allen subsequently had a notable career as a professor of Greek at the University of Pennsylvania.

A member of an old but obscure Maryland family, Alfred Allen Curtis (1831-1908), became an Episcopalian clergyman of influence, serving as pastor of the important Mount Calvary Church, Baltimore. But, doctrinal dissatisfaction led to his entering the Catholic Church under the guidance of Cardinal Newman in 1872. Later he served (1886-96) as bishop of the diocese of Wilmington, Delaware.

Previously mentioned, Thomas Scott Preston (1824-91) had become the priest of the fashionable St. Luke's Episcopal Church in New York City, but in 1849 had entered the Catholic Church, as did eventually three of his four brothers. As vicar-general of the Archdiocese of New York, he was extremely zealous and uncompromising in the enforcement of ecclesiastical discipline, being in a sense "more Catholic than the Pope" and bearing down especially hard upon Father Edward McGlynn and other supporters of Henry George. He experienced deep personal satisfaction in the Catholic Church where he said that he found "humility, purity, and charity" everywhere around him "like the fruits of the heavenly grace" for which his "soul thirsteth."

An illustration of the soul-searching distress involved in some of the personal religious struggles of the time is found in the case of James Kent Stone (1840-1921) who, as president of Kenyon College (1867), was unhappy in the atmosphere of Low Church Episcopalianism. Then he became president (1868) of the High Church Hobart College at Geneva, New York. Following intense grief because of the death of his wife, he became a Catholic (1869) and then a Paulist Father. As "Father Fidelis of the Cross" he spent some years in Argentina and other South American countries. In the United States, he made a most favorable impression on his Catholic co-religionists. When he became a priest, the step involved the adoption of his daughter by others, and his deceased wife's relatives felt that he ought to be placed in a mental hospital. The priest's father, John Seeley Stone (1795-1882), was the first dean and professor of systematic theology (1867-76) at the new Episcopal Theological School, Cambridge, Massachusetts. Although wholeheartedly opposed to Newman's teachings, the elder Stone refused to permit his son to be placed in an insane asylum, and later the son was even permitted to preach a sermon at Appleton Chapel, Harvard College.

A leading present-day Jesuit recalls how as a boy in the 1890's at Newport, Rhode Island, he installed an electric bell in the room of the High Church Episcopal rector, Father Buckey, and took occasion to leave on the clergyman's desk a Catholic pamphlet imputing the validity of Anglican Orders. Two or three weeks afterward the rector said farewell to his congregation and later was received into the Catholic Church, spending his last days as pastor of the fashionable St. Matthew's Church, Washington, D. C.[9]

Besides Episcopalians whose zeal for the doctrine of Apostolic Succession led them to Catholicism, another source of conversions was the disillusionment of some with the liberalism of advanced Unitarianism and Transcendentalism or the narrowness of New England Calvinism. One of the first prominent individuals to take this step was Miss Ruth Charlotte Dana, sister of the author of *Two Years Before the Mast*. She embraced Catholicism in 1846 and continued as an active convert until her death in 1901.[10] Among numerous others, there was Eliza Allen Starr (1824-1901), born to an old Massachusetts family, who had found her Unitarian beliefs seriously disturbed by the advanced thought of Theodore Parker in 1845 and had eventually embraced Catholicism. She spent the rest of her life as a noted contributor to painting, poetry, and writing, with religion providing the central motif.

Those who had followed the Transcendentalist road and found that it did not lead to peace of mind included Isaac Hecker (previously mentioned) who had participated in the Brook Farm Experiment. Another was the Transcendentalist and Brook Farm resident, Orestes Augustus Brownson (1803-76), who had been a Presbyterian, then a Universalist, then a free lance, then a Unitarian, before becoming a Catholic in 1844, a year before Newman. Less subtle and profound than Newman, like the British churchman he came to demand certainty in religion, and the divine mediation of Jesus seemed to each to involve the divine mediation of an authoritative Church.

One important Catholic writer believes that Brownson's mind was the most remarkable one to be found in American Catholicism.[11] He was strong, uncompromising, and often extremely rude. Arthur M. Schlesinger, Jr. contends that humility "was the one Catholic virtue" he never acquired,[12] but Maynard insists that submission to the Church involved a "towering humility" which was exhibited a thousand times when he encountered enemies within the Roman communion.[13] Yet, if this was humility it was like its Protestant counterpart in such a person as Oliver Cromwell, whose fixed Calvinistic faith made him fearless of all opposition. Brownson found in the Catholic Church the norm of his intellectual life which he believed to be independent of human causality.[14] With such an orientation he could be during part of his life a submissive novice in the Church, then an outspoken liberal, and finally a spokesman (1864-76) for an intransigent and narrow orthodoxy. A recent scholar has suggested that what appears like liberalism in one phase of his career was an attempt to make Catholicism less objectionable to Protestant America. According to this view, Brownson's Catholicism was always animated by twin ideals, conservatism and an infallible Church. In the furtherance of these he had sought for a time to adapt church practices to American conditions, and he had also clashed violently with members of the hierarchy. The essential unity of his purpose was grounded on the conviction that only the Church of Rome could prevail against radicalism and preserve civilization.[15]

Brownson was the most noted of scores of New Englanders who found the appeal of a dogmatic answer to every soul-searching question a blissful haven amidst the storms of the vigorous intellectual life of New England. An Irish Dominican priest found in America in 1886 that of all con-

verts to Catholicism the children of New England Puritanism were "the most intellectual, the most fervent, the most
simple-minded and religious, carrying with them the vibrant
energy and determination of their forefathers."[16]

One whose family had especially represented the literary
expression of Puritanism was the daughter of Nathaniel
Hawthorne, Rose Hawthorne Lathrop. A half-hearted Unitarian, she was married to George Lathrop, less than a half-
hearted Episcopalian, and one who had found liquor more
than a match for his power of will. Both had religious na-
tures, and in the late 1880's they found themselves talking
much about religion, especially Catholicism. They discussed
it with Catholics, including Irish servant girls; received instruction in Catholic doctrine; and were taken into the
Catholic Church in March 1891. The Lathrops, however,
had found much incompatibility in their marriage, and Mrs.
Lathrop separated from her husband. She then became a
Dominican lay sister and devoted the rest of her life to the
establishment and maintenance of homes for the victims of
incurable cancer.[17]

Many Catholic converts became more Catholic than most
of those born within that faith in their rigid insistence on
inflexible views. Some converts in addition to those already
mentioned, became bishops. Thus, many years before, Josue
Maria Young (1808-1866), Maine-born and of Congregational and Universalist antecedents, as a youth had argued
religious matters with an old friend and had become a
Catholic in 1828, eight brothers and sisters following him
into that faith. At the time of his death in 1866 he was
bishop of the Erie, Pennsylvania diocese.

One of the most influential bishops of the period was
Richard Gilmour (1824-91), Scottish-born son of covenant-
ing (Presbyterian) parents in Pennsylvania. Irish-American
school chums influenced him to accept Catholicism (1842),
and he became a priest, and then bishop of the Cleveland,
Ohio diocese beginning in 1872. He was extremely zealous,
developing parochial schools, a diocesan newspaper (The

Catholic Universe) and preparing a *Bible History* that received wide acceptance in Catholic schools.[18] Gilmour was a strict disciplinarian and a vigorous apologist whose zealous methods aroused some antagonism among parish priests and, for different reasons, among non-Catholics.

Besides the appeal of the Catholic claims to Apostolic Succession and Infallibility, the sacramentalism of the Mass with its ordered ritual and with the soul-stirring music was not without its attractiveness to many of aesthetic or mystical temperaments. F. Marion Crawford, the well-known novelist and nephew of Julia Ward Howe (a vigorous Unitarian), embraced Catholicism while in India (about 1881). A rather cosmopolitan minded relative who became Mrs. Winthrop Chandler joined the Catholic Church a little later. Her residence in Rome had caused her to absorb the Roman attitude "without reference to textbooks," as she had found the Anglican service "jejune, uninspiring," except for the incomparable beauty of the Book of Common Prayer.[19]

Representing the wealthy, socially inclined society of that day were Bellamy Storer (1847-1922) and his wife. He had been an Ohio congressman and she was a member of the well-known Longworth family of Cincinnati. Storer's first cousin, Horatio Robinson Storer (1830-1922), a noted Boston gynecologist, had become a Catholic following his third marriage in 1876, and in 1896 the Cincinnati couple followed the same path. This step paved the way for Storer's role as minister to three Catholic countries, Belgium, Spain, and Austria-Hungary.

One other representative of Middle Western leadership who became a Catholic convert was the handsome Ross Wilkins (1799-1872) who was said to have resembled Lord Byron in appearance. A devout man, long a federal judge in Michigan (1837-70) he was a prominent Methodist who constantly had a Greek Testament at his side. Late in life, however, he embraced Catholicism.

After the waning of the Oxford Movement, a potent factor in securing conversions to Catholicism was the popular exposition of that religion in the persuasive *Faith of Our Fathers* (1876) by James Gibbons, later to be a Cardinal. Eventually, during three-quarters of a century, more than two million copies were distributed. In 1877 a grand nephew of Chief Justice Marshall, and over a period of years various theological students and ministers of both the Methodist and the Protestant Episcopal Churches were among those who joined the Catholic Church after being influenced by the volume's appealing arguments.[20] By the end of the century another who yielded to its presentation of the Catholic viewpoint was Carleton J. Hayes, destined to be a distinguished professor of History at Columbia University and a rather controversial United States ambassador to Spain.

If, in the intellectual and social adjustments of the nineteenth century, many had found the authority which gave their souls peace, in the Catholic Church, others had left their Mother Church, seeking the greater freedom which they came to believe existed outside its fold. Thus, as has been pointed out elsewhere, Scottish-born James Gordon Bennett had attacked the Church of his fathers with acid-like bitterness and was excommunicated.[21] Mrs. Henry George, baptized a Catholic and with a convent education, quietly ceased to be a practicing member of that Church.[22] Mrs. John William Draper had turned from Catholicism to Episcopalianism. Nicholas Murray (1802-1861), Irish-born Catholic had become a Protestant, with such powers as a preacher that he was often called "the Presbyterian Pope."[23] Theodore Dreiser and his brothers and sisters had rebelled against Catholicism as they experienced it in Indiana,[24] although one brother, Paul Dresser [*sic*], author of "On the Banks of the Wabash Far Away," received such tender ministrations from the Jesuit pastor of St. Francis Xavier's Church, New York City (even when he neglected his religious duties and had to be urged to attend Mass) that at his death he received a church funeral with Requiem Mass.[25]

As pointed out elsewhere, Karl Heinzen (1809-1880), one of the most extreme of anti-religious German-Americans and an avowed materialist had been raised in a devout Catholic family in a distinctly Catholic neighborhood in Rhenish Prussia.[26] Mathilde Franziska Giesler-Anneke (1817-1884), had been carefully educated in the Catholic tradition, but had abandoned all dogmatic religion. Establishing herself in the United States, as founder and head of the girls' school, the Milwaukee Töchter Institute, she became an influential figure in liberal German circles of the Middle West.

Alexander Jacob Schem (1821-81), born in Westphalia, had been ordained a Catholic priest but had abandoned that faith and migrated to the United States. He later became a noted editor and encyclopedist, served as assistant superintendent of the New York public schools (1874-81) and contributed to Methodist periodicals.

William Jay Gaynor (1849-1913), destined to be mayor of New York City, was born in upstate New York, and his Catholic training carried him into the novitiate of a religious vocation as Brother Adrian Dengs. But, after almost five years during which he had taken only annual vows, he definitely returned to secular life. Of a speculative turn of mind, he lost the Catholic faith of his early years and became at least nominally an Episcopalian, although he really no longer definitely accepted Christian doctrines.[27]

Various other prominent persons who had been reared as Catholics definitely broke with that tradition. Ignatius Donnelly (1931-1900), one of the foremost leaders of the Populist movement, had been born a Catholic but never really embraced that faith, and in his later years he was inclined toward Spiritualism. Another agrarian reformer, Mrs. Mary Elizabeth Clyens Lease (1853-1933), who had been educated in a Catholic academy and had even taught in a parochial school and was to electrify farmers' gatherings in the 1890's by calling upon them to "raise more hell and less corn," had left Catholicism, and orthodox religion generally, before she entered upon her part in the "Agrarian Crusade." Terence Powderly, leader of the Knights of Labor, as we have seen, eventually left the Catholic Church.[28]

Mrs. Emma Dorothy Eliza Nevitte Southworth (1819-99), author for a generation of best-selling novels like *Self-Raised* (1876), was baptized a Catholic but became an Episcopalian and in 1883, a Swedenborgian.

Miss Mary G. Caldwell and her sister Lina were instrumental in establishing the Catholic University of America by a gift of $300,000 in 1885, but later left the Catholic Church and the former even published a booklet, *The Double Doctrine of the Church of Rome.*[29]

Some, who for a time found a spiritual home in Catholicism, later renounced their adopted allegiance. Thus, James Hall (1811-98), distinguished geologist and paleontologist, had joined the Catholic Church at the time of his marriage (1838) but later left it. He was destined to be the first president of the Geological Society of America. Rev. John Murray Forbes, rector of St. Luke's Episcopal Church, New York City, for fourteen years, had become a Catholic in 1849 and had received distinct recognition in the Church of his new allegiance. But ten years later he had returned to the Episcopal Church, believing that Rome required that "all individual liberty must be sacrificed." Eventually he became Dean of the General Theological Seminary, New York City.[30]

Some who would have found their family situation much pleasanter by their whole hearted acceptance of Catholicism realized that they could not conscientiously do so. Thus, William Tecumseh Sherman had been baptized a Catholic and had married Ellen Ewing, a devout and energetically aggressive Catholic woman. But, even before his marriage he had plainly told his bride-to-be that, while he believed in the principal doctrines of Christianity, the purity of its influence, and the absolute necessity for its maintenance in all law-abiding communities, "with due reflection" he could not attribute importance to "minor points of doctrine" and ritual. The children of their marriage were raised as Catholics, but when the mother's zeal helped to turn a son, Thomas, to the priesthood, General Sherman was "completely astounded and crushed"[31] and apparently refused to attend the ordination ceremonies. After his wife's death, the General wrote that it had been "simply impossible" for him to accept Catholicism.[32] Upon the death of the General in 1891, the rather adaptable Cardinal Gibbons advised Archbishop Corrigan to allow the General's son who had become a Jesuit to read the Catholic burial service and to grace the occasion with his own presence. To the satisfaction of the family the last rites of the Church had been administered to the General after he had lapsed into unconsciousness.[33]

The mother and sister of James G. Blaine had been devout Catholics, but Blaine had followed the Protestant faith of his father. During his last illness Blaine had asked Cardinal Gibbons to call on "a little matter of pecuniary business." There is some reason to believe that Gibbons hoped that Blaine would wish to die in his mother's faith, but the expiring political leader did not seek to do so.

As many had found the certitude in Catholicism which they had found lacking in Episcopalianism, others found a satisfying spiritual pilgrimage in the opposite direction. Thus, Eugene J. V. Huiginn, who had been raised in a Catholic home and had sought to enter the priesthood, had found in the seminary at Maynooth, Ireland that the professors felt compelled to defend dogmas in spite of their own "unrest of mind." He had come to rebel against Catholic views of Papal Infallibility, the Eucharist, Confession, indulgences, and especially the dogma of the Immaculate Conception which he deemed "a striking instance of Roman developments and innovations." In the Roman Church he had found many devout souls, but in the Anglican Church he had met "with holier and nobler Christians, with more sublime ideas of Jesus Christ and his teachings, and a more practical and Christian observance of the virtues his Gospel teaches." Ordained an Episcopalian minister in the United States, he served parishes of that faith in New York state and Massachusetts until his death.

For those who found a bulwark of faith in the Catholic

Church, it was often easier to hold to such a position because controversy over doctrine was not generally aired in
public fashion in Catholic circles. There much contention
was at times in evidence, but it was prompted to a large
extent by the clash of positive personalities, disagreements
as to educational and economic policies, and friction arising
from diverse racial backgrounds within a single ecclesiastical
organization. The issue of trusteeism (lay control of church
property) that had proved troublesome a generation before,
had been settled in favor of the episcopal authority.[34]

The authoritarian nature of Roman Catholicism did not
permit wide variance in doctrine within its fold as had led
to animated controversy in many Protestant denominations.
Yet, the democratic life of America had contributed to a
freedom which seems to have led to a far from uniform
acceptance of all of the Papal encyclicals. Thus, as has been
indicated previously, an anonymous Roman Catholic in 1886
declared that he had never been able to come to terms with
the Pope's Syllabus of Errors (1864) which had denounced
various modern tendencies, including types of Rationalism,
Socialism, and contemporary Liberalism.[35] The writer asserted that anyone in the United States who was the enemy
of such progressive forces belonged in "some tranquil isle
in the Doldrums" and that if American Catholics would ever
"approve the Pope's anathema of modern civilization" some
method would have to be found to check the growth of
American Catholicity. But, he was sure that American Catholics would do their own political thinking.

Many American Catholics, moreover, looked upon the
Vatican Council (1869-70) as one which aimed at tightening
unnecessarily the reins of orthodox conformity. Newspapers
in American cities gave considerable notice to the meetings
of the Council, and to some extent a revival of anti-Catholic
and especially anti-papal feeling resulted.[36]

Twenty-three American bishops had journeyed to Rome
in 1867 to attend the ceremonies on the occasion of the
eighteenth centenary of the martyrdom of St. Peter and St.

Paul. At that time official announcement had been made of the forthcoming Council. Three years later, forty-six members of the American hierarchy attended the Vatican Council. Twenty of those eligible to participate from the United States did not attend, some of them because of illness or age.[37] Many Americans were far from happy at the trend of events. Dr. James A. Corcoran, the American representative on the Commission of Dogmatic Theology which met in Rome to prepare material for the Vatican Council was deeply distressed by the obligation of secrecy placed upon him. He wrote, moreover (in March, 1869), to Archbishop John McCloskey that in Rome there was a *"mania"* to define as a matter of faith a great mass of propositions on a wide variety of subjects so as to severely limit the degree of tolerated views within the Church. He had constantly opposed such a course as inexpedient and had stated that he thought that American bishops were opposed to a formal definition of the infallibility of the Pope. Bishop McQuaid of Rochester was of similar opinion, believing that the Jesuits had been "at the bottom" of the movement and that a declaration of infallibility would be "a great calamity for the Church."[38]

George Bancroft, noted American historian and at the time United States minister to Prussia, wrote from Berlin in 1870 that the Council had been gotten up "under the influence of the Jesuits," and the plan was to turn the Church from an organization "with the bishops as the aristocracy" into one "under an absolute spiritual monarch."[39]

A leading Episcopalian vestryman of New York City wrote in his diary that the secrecy was more "appropriate to a lodge of Freemasons or a Carlist Club" than a general Church Council, but that the Jesuit influence would prevail over that of a "few independent thinkers."[40]

In the discussion at the Council of the *Schema de Fide Catholica* (prepared to assert Catholic principles against errors of Rationalism, Materialism, and Atheism), French-born Jean Marcel Pierre Auguste Verot (1805-1876) a noted theologian and bishop of Florida, took a prominent part, as did Peter Richard Kenrick (1806-1896), Irish-born arch-bishop of St. Louis. At first uncertainty existed as to whether the question of the infallibility of the Pope should come before the Council, and in January 1870, a large part of the American hierarchy expressed itself against such a move. Twenty-one bishops from the United States signed petitions to the Holy Father to that effect.[41] In the United States, the convert editor, James A. McMaster of *Freeman's Journal,* showed himself a real Ultramonte with "a noisy enthusiasm regarding the Papacy."[42] Three groups of bishops, however, opposed the promulgation of a dogma of papal infallibility: (1) Those representing the Gallican tradition in the Church that did not believe the proposed doctrine but stressed the authority of church councils; (2) Those who believed the doctrine but held that it could not be accurately defined because of the somewhat obscure tradition of the Church regarding it; (3) Those who believed the doctrine and deemed it capable of precise definition but deemed such a declaration at the time perilous for the peace and ad-vancement of the Church.[43]

When the matter of the promulgation of a dogma of the primacy and the infallibility of the Pope did come before the Council, Verot spoke frequently and emphatically against such action. Indeed, he became something of an *enfant terrible* of the Council when he declared that pon-tifical infallibility was not "an apostolic tradition, but an opinion introduced by a piety and a zeal not according to knowledge."[44] He asserted, moreover, that several popes had already erred in matters of faith and morals.[45]

A number of other American bishops including Kenrick, the Spanish-born Michael Domenec of Pittsburgh, and Ber-nard John McQuaid of Rochester, agreed with Verot that a definition of the doctrine was not possible because of a lack of undisputed evidence from Scripture and church tra-dition. They believed, furthermore, that such a definition of dogma would be inexpedient, for it would: (1) Cause dissension within the Church; (2) Hamper conversions; (3) Give Protestants a chance to challenge the immutability of Catholic teaching; (4) Secure no greater obedience from good Catholics but heighten the opposition of other persons; (5) Accentuate the political difficulties of the Papacy. Bishop Domenec asserted that the promulgation of the dogma would prove "an insurmountable obstacle to the conversion of Protestants in the United States." Bishop McQuaid wrote privately that his head was "fairly splitting with pain and anxiety," for hard times would be created for relations between Catholics and Protestants, and reasons would even be furnished to Protestants who wished to drive Catholics from the country.[46]

Bishop Kenrick failed to secure an opportunity of speaking at the Council because of the closure of general debate, but he published his views in a pamphlet, *Concio in concilio habenda, at non habita.*[47] In this Kenrick denied that a single passage of Scripture the meaning of which was uncontested had promised to Peter power not given to the other apostles. To Kenrick, the primacy of Peter was based not on Scripture, but on Christian tradition and was conditioned by the use of "the counsel of the brethren."[48]

The chief American supporter of the viewpoint which came to prevail was Martin John Spalding (1810-72), Kentucky-born archbishop of Baltimore. Upon his arrival in Rome he had inclined to the view that a formal definition of infallibility was unnecessary and perhaps inexpedient. Soon, however, he came to support the proposal as highly desirable and became a leader of those favorable to such action. As the weeks went by, the climate of Rome became "fearful, hot, sultry and enervating," and many were very eager to leave.[49]

When a preliminary vote was taken at the Council, eighty-eight bishops voted negatively (*non placet*). Seven of these were from the United States: Archbishop Kenrick and Bishops Verot, Domenec, Fitzgerald (Little Rock), McCloskey (Louisville), McQuaid (Rochester), and Mrak (Mar-

quette-Saulte Ste. Marie).[50] Bishops Purcell of Cincinnati
and Whelan of Wheeling had already left for home. Thereafter, fifty-five bishops (including Kenrick, Verot, and Domenec) signed a letter to the Pope, explaining their desire
to leave before the taking of a final ballot so as not to create
something of a scandal by voting *non placet* at that time.
On the final ballot, only two bishops, an Italian, and Bishop
Fitzgerald of Little Rock voted negatively. After the official
promulgation of the dogma, Fitzgerald approached the papal
throne and proclaimed his acquiescence, *"Modo credo, sancte
Pater"* (Now I believe, Holy Father) .[51]

Some, like Bishop McQuaid were troubled by the practical difficulty of determining "how, when, under what circumstances, and about what matters" the Pope is infallible.
The Bishop was especially disturbed that the definition was
"as absolute and strict as it was possible to make it," with
unpredictable consequences in various European countries.[52]

A severe test then confronted other Catholics who loved
the Faith of their Fathers but who intellectually found difficulty in honestly accepting the declared dogma that when
the Pope speaks *ex cathedra* as head of the Church he cannot
err in matters of faith and morals. Informed Catholic opinion in the English-speaking world had watched with interest
the activities of Lord Acton, whose family was notable in
Catholic circles both in Britain and on the continent. Lord
Acton himself was the most erudite British historian of his
day. He had gone to Rome to labor against the movement
for infallibility and had written a long essay in the *North
British Review* (October, 1870) systematically analyzing
"the errors and frauds" of which he believed the doctrine
was compounded.[53]

Some of the bishops who had opposed the Vatican decrees
hoped that the Catholic world would reject them because
the Council had been, in their opinion, "neither legitimate
in constitution, free in action, nor unanimous in doctrine."
But, one after another of the bishops submitted, and Acton
wrote to some of them inquiring into their motives and

reasons. One of the bishops who yielded was the scholarly Bishop Hefele of Rottenburg who had written several works on Pope Honorius showing why he believed historically that the Popes had not been infallible. His scholarship had merited the esteem of Protestant church historians such as the distinguished Philip Schaff of Union Seminary, New York City. Schaff declared, "Bishop Hefele had forgotten more about the history of the councils than the infallible pope ever knew." Later, it was explained to Schaff by German friends that Hefele probably had not changed his views of Honorius' pontificate but had submitted to the dogma to conserve the unity of Catholicism in Wurtemburg.[54]

Archbishop Kenrick had also hoped that many would join him in refusing to accept the decrees, thus depriving infallibility of the seal of unanimity and ecumenical authority. The submission of the bishops, one by one, however, seemed to put the rest in the position of defying the established authority of the Church.[55] Hence, Archbishop Kenrick avowed his "entire and unreserved submission" to the dogma "simply and solely" because of his belief in the authority of the Catholic Church.[56] Yet, the stubbornness of Kenrick's personal convictions was not entirely overcome, for he wrote to Lord Acton that he did not intend to issue any pastoral letter on the Council, or publicly to discuss the dogma, or ever to affirm that the dogma was based on indubitable Scriptural authority.[57]

Archbishop Purcell of Cincinnati while still in Rome had written to a Mother Superior in Ohio that the infallibility question had "made many anxious minds and restless nights or nights restless." A fellow bishop wrote that the Cincinnati bishop was "worried almost to death" by the trouble.[58] Leaving Rome before the vote was taken, Purcell continued to be sorely troubled, pacing the floor of his room in Cincinnati and taking his meals in seclusion, and at length only being persuaded by the priests of his household from giving to a great audience his frank opinion of the action of the Council.[59] Purcell believed that many prelates

and schools in his native Ireland had never favored an expressed dogma of papal infallibility and that such a definition was inexpedient.[60] Therefore, although at the public
reception accorded him at Mozart Hall, Cincinnati, he proclaimed the newly declared dogma, a trace of the unbending
tenacity of his convictions seems to have lingered in the
phraseology of his reaffirmation of his personal belief in "the
rights of the Pope and the infallibility of the Catholic
Church."[61]

Chief Justice Salmon P. Chase who had a deep appreciation "of Roman Catholics and Roman Catholicity" believed that the promulgation of the new dogma was a "fearful error."[62] Various groups of "Old Catholics" who rejected
papal infallibility subsequently maintained congregations in
the United States but their combined membership has always been very small numerically.[63]

Godkin of the *Nation* had commented that some Protestants had hoped that the "excesses" of the Council might
rebound to the benefit of Protestantism, but that there was
little ground for such hope. Educated men among Euro-
peans, he found, were not likely to be zealous Catholics, but
those leaving Catholicism were apt to turn to literature and
philosophy rather than to Protestantism. Thus, the effect of
the Council might result "in swelling the ranks" of the
religious indifferent. Yet, he thought that Catholicism might
gain, in the existing world of transition, from among those
who would find in her "rest, not from religious doubt only,
but from social disturbances and disorganization."

Cardinal Gibbons' first important biographer, Allan S.
Will, with the perspective of half a century of time, ventured the opinion that it was probably true that the spread
of Catholicism was impeded for a time, but that the growth
of the Church eventually was such as to indicate that papal
infallibility was not a permanent obstacle to Catholic
progress.[64]

During the rest of the nineteenth century other problems brought drastic differences within the Catholic Church

in America. Among these was that of the relation of the
Catholic Church to public education. For a time this involved the question as to whether the Faribault Plan (for religious instruction after public school hours) would be "tolerated." Also involved was the membership of Catholics in
secret fraternal and in labor organizations, the compatibility
of Henry George's Single Tax with Catholic doctrine, and
the preservation of national cultures within the Church in
America, the last mentioned raising the issue known as
"Cahenslyism."[65] Other issues were the establishment of a
Catholic University of America, the fraternizing of Catholics
with non-Catholics in interfaith meetings, and the participation of Catholic clergy in such meetings. On these questions some bishops took a conservative stand and others a
more liberal one, some bishops being conservative on some
matters and liberal on others. These questions, however,
were more definitely administrative, social, and economic
problems rather than those involving the intellectual foundations of the Catholic faith.

One difference of opinion, however, did relate more
vitally to matters of faith, that of the adaptation of the
Catholic Church to the active tempo of American life. The
tendency toward adjustment was illustrated in the case of
Cardinal Gibbons. In 1891, Theodore Roosevelt, after attending a dinner party in Baltimore at which the Cardinal
was also a guest, expressed the conviction that Gibbons possessed "a thorough knowledge of the fact that his Church
must become both Republicanized and Americanized to
retain its hold in the United States."[66] The Paulist Fathers,
among others, had made aggressive efforts to secure conversions in America, and in France and other European countries some church leaders feared that in some circles a relaxation of the traditional discipline of the Church and a
compromise with the modern age were being employed to
obtain converts.[67] Leading progressive bishops, Archbishop
Ireland and Cardinal Gibbons, endeavored to persuade the
Pope not to send an encyclical definitely condemning alleged

progressive tendencies, but they did not act quickly enough
to do so, and at any rate the alleged influence of American
views on the religious situation in France demanded attention. Accordingly, Pope Leo XIII in January, 1899 issued
an apostolic letter, *Testem Benevolentiae,* condemning what
had become known in a special sense as "Americanism."[68]
The Pope specifically warned against the relaxation of the
severity of church discipline and the adoption of concessions
to new opinions in order to make converts. This general
attitude had led to the views: that external guidance should
be set aside for souls striving for Christian perfection; that
greater importance should be placed upon the natural virtues; that the virtues should be divided into active and passive ones with the idea that the vows of the religious life
were alien to the modern spirit; and that a new method
must be developed for winning back those lost to the Church.
The Pope did not say that the proscribed views were held
in America, and a leader of the "progressive" bishops, Archbishop Ireland, denied that he had ever adhered to the condemned views. On the other hand, "conservative" bishops of
the Province of Milwaukee informed the Pope that they
experienced "pain and just indignation" that some had denied the presence of the erroneous principles which they
said had actually existed in the United States. At any rate,
the Holy See had spoken, and the faithful were warned of
the limits of tolerated views.[69]

One of the conservative leaders, Bishop McQuaid, in a
sermon in the cathedral at Rochester, New York in June
1899 insisted that examples of the type of Americanism
condemned by the Holy Father that had existed in the
United States, included: (a) Participation in the World's
Parliament of Religions; (b) The liberal stand on the Faribault Controversy; (c) The defense of certain secret societies; and (d) The appearance of Keane in clerical robes to
lecture at Harvard University. In recent years a Catholic
scholar has concluded that the first phase of the "Americanism" struggle had ended in a victory for the conserva-

tives, when Bishop Keane had been removed from the rectorship of Catholic University of America. He believes, however, that the second phase of the struggle appeared as a defeat for the liberals in the publication of the encyclical, but that actually the liberals were vindicated when the Pope told Archbishop Ireland to forget the Letter on Americanism, for it had "no application except in a few dioceses in France." The same scholar believes that the third phase resulted in vindication for the liberals when one of their number, Denis O'Connell, was made third rector of the Catholic University of America.[70]

In the meantime, in 1895 the Pope had ruled against the further participation of Catholics in interfaith congresses, and after the turn of the century he spoke out against the theological liberalism known as "Modernism." Catholicism in America was thereafter to continue to express itself in accordance with traditional orthodoxy, and any "Americanizers" certainly would refrain from some actions which were at least possible before 1895. This may have meant that a certain type of convert who had sought a kind of liberalism which Catholic authorities came to deem incompatible with the essential spirit of Rome would no longer join that Church. However that may be, David H. Buel, who had become a convert while a student at Yale (about 1881), then a Jesuit, and was to be President of Georgetown University (1905-8) later left the Church and eventually became an Episcopal clergyman.[71] Similarly, a British Catholic, Professor St. George Mivrat, who had often been quoted by progressive American Catholics as one who had reconciled revealed religion with science, ran into grave difficulties. In 1887, he had taken rather advanced ground in an article for *The Forum* on "The Future of Christianity." He asserted emphatically his belief "that no theism but Christian theism, that is, some form of Christianity, can be the absolute and final religion of mankind," while admitting that the Catholic Church "seems most hampered by the bonds which the bigotry and ignorance of antecedent ages have bound round it, and most imbued with the prejudices and superstitions of pre-scientific ages." Yet, he pointed out that the Catholic Church had adapted itself: (1) To the Copernican revolution; (2) To the new Geology; (3) To theistic ideas of evolution. Hence, there was no reason why it need "be engulfed by the whirlpool of historical science, including Biblical criticism." He espoused a theory of "development" in church doctrine, quoting Lord Acton to the effect that the "slow, silent indirect action of public opinion bears the Holy See along, without any demoralizing conflict or dishonorable capitulation." Mivrat's views, however, came under suspicion and then condemnation. Some of his articles printed in British publications from 1885 to 1892 were put on the *Index of Prohibited Books,* and other articles subsequently led to his excommunication, and at his death, a refusal of Catholic burial.[72] Some faithful friends believed that illness had induced heterodoxy before his death in 1900, but at any rate he had crossed the limits of orthodox tolerated opinion.[73]

The seeds of "Modernism," evident in the late nineteenth century Western world only came to bear what the orthodox considered bitter fruit after the turn of the century. One Catholic historian repeats the often made suggestion that American Catholicism was "saved from those ravages" which afflicted the Catholic Church in Europe by the active, rather than the speculative turn of mind of most Americans. He believes, however, that the fundamental explanation is "that the practicality and good sense typical of Americans proved their chief safeguard."[74] (Yet, a later liberal Protestant theological Dean wrote in 1945 that "private conversation" often revealed "a good deal of residual Modernism in Catholic circles, biding its time. . . .")[75]

At any rate, for many persons religious faith was something deeper and more personal than the pronouncements of science or the assumptions of philosophy. James Gibbons Huneker, born to an old-fashioned middle-class family in Philadelphia, was destined to become a noted musical critic and essayist who personally experienced the intellectual storms of the late nineteenth century. From his mother he had imbibed something of the feeling that to revolt "against Rome meant to revolt against life." Personally he found that he was not of a strong religious temperament, but that there was great fascination in the Hebrew and Catholic ritual. To him the development of the race with its "totem and fetish, tabu, magic, animism, and idols" were represented in the solemn "aesthetic symbolism" of the Mass. Religious feeling was a part of his very being, and, as he looked back years later upon his life he concluded that his parents had not been his enemies in the training they had given him. Rather, he could say, "To them I owe everything."[76] He loved "the odour of incense, the mystic bells, the music, the atmosphere of the altar" and especially the wisdom of the Church. Yet, he also could not resist the inspiration and insight in what some religious people deemed the "powerful and pernicious toxics" of Baudelaire, Whitman, Schopenhauer, and Havelock Ellis.

Huneker, like John La Farge, the distinguished artist, felt a deep emotional attachment to Catholicism, but each possessed something of the individualism of the artistic temperament. A friendly priest referred to him as a "hickory" Catholic, and he and La Farge were not so zealous in their regularity at Mass as devoted relatives wished that they might be.[77]

CHAPTER XII

SOME DIFFICULTIES OF PROTESTANT ORTHODOXY

1. *The Protestant Episcopal Church*

If the Protestant Episcopal Church lost numerous potential leaders to Catholicism as a result of the Oxford Movement, it also gained from other quarters. A part of the reason for this has been illustrated in the personal religious experiences of a man like Richard Henry Dana, Jr., author of *Two Years Before the Mast*. His family had been orthodox Massachusetts Congregationalists, in whose churches the preaching had satisfied his intellect, sounding like the "knell of judgment," but among whom worship carried no aesthetic appeal to the eye and the imaginative sense. The Unitarians also generally lacked visible aids to worship, and he confessed that their attempts at erudite preaching "went over his head." Accordingly, he had found a spiritual home in the Episcopal Church.[1] Many other prominent families were among those who took similar steps. To such persons Unitarianism often seemed little more than arid rationalism, and orthodox Congregationalism appeared overly dogmatic and lacking in the mystical appeal of the older Puritanism. Less austerity, moreover, than had been associated with basic New England traditions, now seemed to be demanded by many of the wealthy and cultured of prospering communities. Thus, as early as 1839 the parents of Phillips Brooks, destined to be a world famous preacher, left Unitarianism for the Episcopalian fold.[2] Robert Traill Spence Lowell, the brother of James Russell Lowell, had abandoned the Unitarianism of his family for the Episcopal ministry. Frederic

Dan Huntington likewise turned from Unitarianism and later (1869) became the first bishop of the Episcopal diocese of Central New York.

Huntington had been born into a Congregational family, but his mother had become a Unitarian, and he was ordained a Unitarian minister. Congregationalism, he believed, was narrow and disproportioned; Unitarianism considered all beliefs "elective" and the sacraments only such "in a figure of speech"; Catholicism's claims to Apostolicity, Catholicity, and papal authority seemed to him "unsustained"; hence he turned to Episcopalianism.

Endicott Peabody (b. 1857) had been raised in a family environment of staunch Massachusetts Unitarianism, but against family objections he determined to become an Episcopalian clergyman. He had found powerful intellectual currents in Unitarianism where reason dominated emotion, but a "certain Stoic coldness" repelled him and he found warmth, color, and form which his soul craved in Episcopalianism. In 1884 he established the famous Groton School which had great influence in molding the character of thousands of boys such as Franklin D. Roosevelt in accordance with the spirit of the Episcopal Church.[3]

In Congregational circles, Edward Abbott, brother of the noted Lyman Abbott, was perplexed by the trend away from the old orthodoxy and became an Episcopalian (1878), later serving for many years as pastor of St. James' Church, North Cambridge, Massachusetts. Melville Fuller, later Chief Justice of the United States Supreme Court, who had been baptized in a Maine Congregational church, was one of a family which revolted against Calvinistic orthodoxy, and he was during the remainder of his life a devoted Episcopalian.[4]

Even Harriet Beecher Stowe, daughter, sister, wife, and mother of Congregational clergymen, found a certain bleakness in New England doctrines, particularly as she experienced for long periods the warm climate of Florida and the acclaim of sophisticated European critics. In later life she joined the Episcopal Church.[5] A biographer has analyzed this as a "phase of the Romanticist's yearning for elegance and permanence and tradition and mystery, an aspect of the Gothic mania." Mrs. Adeline Dutton Train Whitney (1824-1906), author, who was sometimes called the American Maria Edgeworth, followed a similar course.

The tendency toward Episcopalianism was particularly marked among those who rose to positions of wealth and luxury and were no longer wholly comfortable in the austere religious atmosphere of their forefathers. Levi P. Morton (1824-1920), son of a Vermont Congregational minister and destined to be minister to France and vice president of the United States (under Benjamin Harrison's administration) was one of these.[6] William C. Whitney (1841-1904), son of devout Massachusetts Congregationalists, and destined to be one of the richest men of his day as well as Secretary of the Navy under Cleveland, came to believe that in New York the Episcopal Church was taking in "the best classes of society," for "there is less to offend enlightened feelings in it." He was eventually able to win his zealous Presbyterian wife, Flora Payne Whitney, and his Yale college friend, William Graham Sumner, to his adopted Church.[7]

Nicholas Murray Butler, later to be President of Columbia University, was the grandson of a noted Presbyterian minister and was given his early religious training in the First Presbyterian Church, Elizabeth, New Jersey. But, he accompanied his father's relatives often to the Episcopal Church, where "the beauty of the service, particularly the splendid liturgy of the Book of Common Prayer" attracted him strongly, and as a young man he was confirmed as an Episcopalian.[8]

Whitelaw Reid (1837-1912), a son of cultured Ohio Presbyterians of stout religious convictions and destined to be editor of the New York *Tribune* and minister to France, also embraced the Episcopal faith.[9] William G. Thayer born in 1863 and educated as a Presbyterian at Union Theological Seminary[10] became an Episcopalian priest in 1890, and was

later to have a long career at St. Mark's School, South-
borough, Massachusetts.[11]

Charles W. Shields (1825-1904), long a professor of the
harmony of science and religion at Princeton, who had been
largely responsible for the publication of a Presbyterian
Book of Common Prayer (1893), eventually found Episcopalian ritual especially congenial and in 1898-9 took orders
in the Episcopal Church.[12]

Within the Episcopal Church there were members of
deep devotion and consecrated faith. The clergyman who
was perhaps most influential and beloved in Protestant
America in the years around 1890 was Phillips Brooks, rector of Trinity Church, Boston. In many parishes were men
of the character and culture like Robert C. Winthrop (1809-
94) who had succeeded Webster as United States Senator
from Massachusetts. An impressive figure, for sixty years he
was a vestryman of Trinity Church, Boston. There were also
men of moderate means, scarcely known outside of their
own communities, like William W. Dallinger of Cambridge,
Massachusetts who gave generously of his time and money to
his church, its Sunday School, the Y. M. C. A., and many
philanthropic causes.[13]

Yet, the very characteristics which recommended the
Episcopal Church to many people— (the beauty of its ritual;
its appeal to the cultured and those of broad secular interests; its inclusiveness as to varying ecclesiastical emphases;
and its moderation as to dogmatic requirements) —all carried dangers to the cultivation of a vital, enriching faith.
James Ford Rhodes, the historian, later recalled his Episcopalian upbringing in Cleveland, and the familiarity with
the Bible and Book of Common Prayer which never left him,
but somehow he did not acquire a persisting faith in the beliefs of the Church.[14] Often, indeed, the very richness of the
Prayer Book led to a kind of "bibliolatry." One Episcopalian
reported that at the time of the Chicago fire (1871) the
Episcopal General Convention was meeting in Baltimore

and prayers for the suffering city were called for. There being no "Collect for a Burning City," the dignitaries refused to engage in fervent heart-felt ex tempore prayer for their stricken countrymen, as a Methodist or Presbyterian would have done, but went solemnly through the whole Litany "which prays for well-nigh everything except a burning city." Moreover, the reliance on ritual sometimes meant that the congregation was denied a good sermon, and easy-going rectors "got by" with efforts which congregations of other denominations would have protested.

Moreover, as Henry S. Canby, the noted editor, remembered the situation in Wilmington, Delaware, in the 1890's, Episcopalianism had become "a beautiful decorum," faith there having declined into an "apotheosis of esthetic respectability," a ritual perfect "like a movement of a Beethoven symphony," but a ceremony from which, he thought, the heart beat had departed.[15]

The appeal of the Episcopal Church to the cultured and well-to-do often made for definite class-consciousness and more emphasis on social than religious values. It was sometimes the Church of those who "took nothing too hard," as the Presbyterians did with their social service, or the Catholics seemed to do with their rites and ceremonies. Canby says that it was sometimes a gentleman's Church, easy-going but rather snobbish, discouraging extremists and sentimentalists, and suiting the needs of all well-mannered people "except those who insisted on erecting altars in their own hearts." Some Episcopalians, moreover, believed that money and social station were not unrecognizable factors in the choice of bishops.

The Episcopal Church looked upon itself as an inclusive religious organization within which varying viewpoints were permitted. Generally, it did not emphasize doctrinal standards as Lutherans and Presbyterians were apt to do. Theologically, it had within its ranks some who would later have been deemed extreme Fundamentalists, such as Bishop Thomas H. Vail of Kansas and Dr. Stephen H. Tyng and his son who believed in the pre-millennial advent of Christ. But, the chief differences in Episcopalianism were regarding ecclesiastical matters, and there had emerged by the post Civil War period three main groups: (1) The High Churchmen, who stressed church authority and sometimes a tendency toward Catholic ritual; (2) Low Churchmen who stressed a Protestant evangelical approach; and (3) Broad Churchmen who advocated tolerance of differing views.[16] Such differences of opinion, however, led at times to great bitterness which was not conducive to vital faith. After 1865, the General Conventions of the Church were much concerned with the allegedly excessive ritual employed by High Churchmen. Finally, in 1874 a canonical law was overwhelmingly adopted that definitely prohibited certain ceremonies which were not authorized by the Book of Common Prayer.[17] For a long time, a dislike of much ritual was so strong that, for example, in Ohio in 1869 a rector had been tried for the introduction of a surpliced choir.[18] As time went on, however, there was no rigid enforcement of the anti-ritualistic canonical law.

The inclusiveness of the Church meant that in faith and religious practice it was not so closely knit and integrated a body as some other denominations. If Low Churchmen opposed excessive ritual, High Churchmen were distressed by a tendency of other Episcopalians to invite persons not episcopally ordained into Episcopal pulpits. In 1891, when many in New York protested to Bishop Potter against the latter practice, he replied that such a practice was of canonical irregularity and of doubtful edification. When the deeply spiritual Phillips Brooks was chosen as Bishop of Massachusetts, some had opposed him because of his less than strict views on Apostolic Succession. Brooks himself had been born into a Unitarian household, and his distaste for the refinements of dogma had caused him to be deemed rather heretical in some Episcopalian circles. In 1881, when Rev. James O. S. Huntington, son of the Bishop of Central New York, started, with the Bishop's consent, The Order of the Holy

Cross, with vows of chastity, poverty and obedience, some, including Bishop Alfred Lee of Delaware, protested against such "Romish vows." In Toledo, Ohio, when one rector went so far as to introduce auricular confession, the bishop of the diocese advised him to enter the Roman priesthood, a course which he refused to follow.

The relatively undogmatic emphasis of the Episcopal Church provided a church home for many ultra-liberals who might have been excluded elsewhere. Thus, Dr. William W. Mayo, father of the famous Mayo surgeons, according to his son, "was an Episcopalian but didn't work very hard at it." He himself quoted Bismarck, perhaps mistakenly, to the effect that he had never really felt the need for religious faith so had never had any, adding that his religion was to do all the good he could to his fellow men and as little harm as possible.[19]

Yet, the Episcopal Church did not avoid problems of faith relating to sound doctrine. As has been pointed out, in 1865, the House of Bishops authorized the publication of a letter written by Bishop McIlvaine of Ohio censuring certain British scholars and Bishop Colenso of South Africa for denying truths "precious to the sinner's hope of salvation."[20] In 1869 Rev. Charles E. Cheney of Illinois was tried by a church court for omitting the word "regenerate" from the service of baptism, and this led to the formation of the Reformed Episcopal Church.[21] In 1886 the Bishops issued a pastoral letter referring to the "flood of infidelity which is sweeping over our land."[22] The advanced views of the popular Rev. R. Heber Newton of All Souls' Church, New York, on biblical criticism, both in 1883 and in 1891 prompted charges that he had violated his ordination vows.[23]

Rev. Howard McQueary, rector of an Episcopal Church in Canton, Ohio, published a book on evolution in relation to Christianity in 1890. He asserted that he no longer believed in the Virgin Birth or the Physical Resurrection of Jesus Christ, yet he asserted his right to continue in his ministerial position. After a trial he was deposed until his views could be shown to be satisfactory, and he received a call from a Universalist church in Saginaw, Michigan. This created such discussion within the denomination that in 1894 a so-called Pastoral Letter which was later endorsed by the House of Bishops was issued, condemning "two novelties," the denial of the two traditional doctrines involved in the McQueary case. Emphasis was now laid on the absolutely essential importance of the Virgin Birth and on the interpretation of the Resurrection so as to include "the revivification of flesh and bones." The Bishops went further by committing themselves to fixity of interpretation of the facts and doctrines of the Creeds, which viewpoint a recent historian of the Church contends "could have been prompted only by a regrettable ignorance of the past and a somewhat optimistic view of the future."[24]

Such rigidity of doctrine had occasionally sent an Episcopalian seminarian into the Unitarian fold. This pronouncement, moreover, was not acclaimed in some church circles where it was deemed "a warning to the more thoughtful clergy of the Episcopal church not to allow their imaginations to stray beyond the intellectual horizon of the Dark Ages."

Yet, Bishop Lawrence of Massachusetts had felt inclined to believe that many fine young ministerial students could not be expected "to have on a certain date fixed and definite convictions on many questions of the faith which will require years to mature and solidify." When, however, one young man, whose orthodoxy had been questioned, was ordained, it became known as the "Massachusetts Case" and severely distressed conservative Episcopalians.[25]

As has already been pointed out, the noted Rev. Charles A. Briggs, who had been deposed from the Presbyterian ministry for alleged heretical views regarding the inspiration of the Scriptures, was by the end of the century accepted into the Episcopal priesthood, but only after emphatic protests from many in that Church.

2. *The Presbyterian Church*

Attention has already been given to the serious problems
which faced the Presbyterian Church intellectually in a period of scientific inquiry and Biblical criticism. Note has
been taken of the heresy trials which disturbed the peace
of the denomination, and examples have been given of
numerous people born into Presbyterianism who found it
narrow and uncompromising. In some circles it has seemed
a baffling mystery as to how a man like Abraham Lincoln
had found in its ministry the spiritual prop of his troubled
years, though he had never become a communicant member.[26] To many it has seemed strange indeed that during this
period men as diverse as Samuel J. Tilden, Grover Cleveland, Benjamin Harrison, William Jennings Bryan, Woodrow Wilson, John M. Harlan, William G. McAdoo—to men-
tion only a few of the leaders of this and the following generation—found guidance in its sanctuaries. A contemporary
writer analyzed the strength of this "powerful communion,"
in view of its "uncompromising assertion of a rigid dogmatic
system," as a "striking illustration of the decided preference
of a most intelligent section of the American people for a
vigorous and well-administered ecclesiastical system."

Certainly one of the points of strength (as well as of
vulnerability) of Presbyterianism—as of Catholicism—has
rested in its precise system of thought. As many have recognized, the almost insuperable difficulties of finding a flaw in
the theological system of St. Thomas Aquinas, once his
premises are granted, so a recent Scottish theologian has
claimed that, once certain initial premises are assumed, the
Presbyterian theology finds few rival systems of thought
which "hang together in so coherent a whole, or in which
the vulnerable Achilles-heel is so hard to find."[27] Implicit
in the teachings of Catholicism is the premise of an infallible
Church, while in the teachings of (Presbyterian) Calvinism
is the premise of the Scriptures as an infallible guide to

Christian faith and practice. Calvin, as has been shown earlier, had found it unnecessary to insist at length on the authority of the Scriptures in doctrine and morals. It was the commonly accepted teaching of all Christian bodies, Catholic and Protestant.[28] The idea of predestination, moreover, so central to Presbyterian beliefs, was firmly grounded in Scriptural references, and in its moderate forms, is a definite part of Roman Catholic theology.[29]

In 1893, a leading Methodist scholar acknowledged "the utter failure of man to break Calvin's logical chain," though the world had turned "first in aversion and then in terror" from such doctrine.[30]

Calvin had cautioned against the doctrine being used in an injudicial, partial, and reckless manner, and he had protested against assumptions being made by anyone regarding the eternal destiny of any other person. The emphasis was clearly on the sovereignty of God. Yet, as time had gone on, Calvin and even to a greater degree, some of his followers had speculated about the "reprobation" of those who had not been the beneficiaries of the divine initiative in bringing them to salvation. The Continental Reformed creeds had been formulated before the Westminster Confession of Faith (1646) which became the standard for Anglo-Saxon Presbyterians. Formulated at a time when there was a strong tendency toward Arminianism in England, the Westminster Confession tended to put great emphasis on God's sovereignty as expressed in Calvinistic terms. The Westminster Confession of Faith was deemed, not a statement to which all must subscribe, but a careful exposition of correct doctrines. In the American colonies, it became the Presbyterian standard of faith and polity, but a minister was not required to subscribe to it categorically and verbally. Rather, he was to declare his adherence to all of its "essential and necessary articles."[31] Thus, over many generations this had become the basis for Presbyterian orthodoxy, and inevitably as the years had gone by, conservatives and liberals had expressed varying views as to the limits of per-

missible viewpoints while agreeing on "necessary and essential matters." Differences had been accentuated, as New
England Puritans going west of the mountains had become
liberal or "New School" Presbyterians, accepting revivalism
and similar measures, and this had led to a division between
"New School" and "Old School" or conservative Presbyterians in 1837-8. This breach had been healed in 1869, but
there had continued to be liberal Presbyterians, who sought
to adjust their faith to modern thought, and the conservatives who struggled to maintain the traditional faith in unaltered form. The latter point of view was especially dominant at the powerful Princeton Theological Seminary in
New Jersey. There, president for a generation (1859-1900)
was the tall, dignified, dutiful, and personally unassuming
William Henry Green (1825-1900), who at one time refused the presidency of the College of New Jersey (now
Princeton). An unrivalled teacher and a merciless opponent
in controversy he was amazingly adept in his explanations
of discrepancies or apparent contradictions in the Hebrew
Scripture. He was ably seconded in his work by two erudite
and devoted theologians, Charles Hodge (1797-1878), and
the latter's son, Archibald Alexander Hodge (1823-1886).
Both were learned, cultured, sincere, of broad human sympathies, and with a gift for vivid illustration. Both were
devoted to the traditions of Calvinism and helped to perpetuate it as a continuing force in American life. At the
feet of the older Hodge, three thousand seminarians learned
their theology, more than were trained by any other American theologian of the nineteenth century. As a result, one
present-day scholar tells us that no other alumnus of Princeton "possibly excepting Woodrow Wilson, shaped so deeply
the thought-molds of his day."[32]

A distinguished religious leader of the period after 1890
later recalled that when the older Hodge spoke on religious
"grace" in the classroom he did it with such reverence and
love that each student was moved to go out into life hoping
"for usefulness only through that undeserved love, which

is the grace of God." Moreover, such an influential person as Theodore Dwight Woolsey (1801-89), a Greek scholar and President of Yale (1846-71), testified that earlier, as a student in Germany, "doubt had crept into his heart and he was walking in darkness," but Hodge had reverently read passages of faith from his Greek Testament and there had come "brightness instead of darkness and certainty instead of doubt." Woolsey thereafter often had thought that when he died he would be happy to have his Greek Testament placed on his breast in the coffin.[33]

Hodge believed that basic truth had been revealed to man in the Scriptures, hence he could rejoice that "a new idea never originated" in Princeton Seminary. His three-volume *Systematic Theology* (1869-73) was so influential that the piety of thousands who accepted its tenets was manifested in the faith of America. His exposition was one of transparent sincerity, without condescension, with "nothing left at loose ends," and wholly devoid of sarcasm toward those who did not agree with him. It revealed his "glowing, unmistakable personal piety," grounded in views which were "painstakingly upheld by legal, scholastic reasons" and which were based "squarely upon proof texts from an originally inerrant Bible."[34]

Yet, the period was one when great numbers of educated Presbyterians were being greatly influenced by the currents of nineteenth century thought, and gradually Hodge's inflexible system was to become "among most churchmen an honored anachronism." Accordingly, it was a period of tensions, as some looked upon the old orthodoxy as a citadel of faith to be preserved at all costs, and bitterness inevitably developed between those who claimed to be brothers in Christ. One widely publicized episode had developed out of the liberal views of Rev. David Swing (1830-94), professor at McCormick Seminary and pastor of the Fourth Presbyterian Church, Chicago. After the Chicago Fire of 1871, he had preached for a period in a theatre where by his popular and sympathetic approach to fundamental problems he had attracted great crowds, many of whom had not been church-goers.[35] He was in some respects of a poetic mind that disliked rigid bounds of creed,[36] and at length the Rev. Francis L. Patton, a later President of Princeton, brought formal charges of heresy against him in 1874. Swing denied the charges but with the explanation that "a creed is only the highest wisdom of a particular time and place." He be-lieved that in the Church as in the state there is "always a quiet slipping away from old laws without any waiting for a formal repeal." The charges against him had not been formulated in unambiguous specifications, and Swing was extremely popular among his fellow ministers, hence he was acquitted by the Chicago presbytery by a more than three to one vote. When Dr. Patton proposed to appeal the case to a higher Presbyterian jurisdiction, Swing announced that he would withdraw from the Presbyterian Church that his prosecutor might not be able to arraign him "from time to time, on some dead dogma, or over some Sabellian or Mohammedan word."[37] Many sincere Presbyterians were in no mood to condone "heresy hunters" and were deeply of-fended that Swing had been driven from the Church. Swing represented an advancing mood which minimized "doctrines and definitions."[38] His poetic insights caused him to seek more "play of individual taste and judgment" than the Presbyterian Church then afforded. He realized that the "gates which lead out of orthodoxy" without "leading away from Christianity" were few in number, but one such portal he found in a "Spiritual Interpretation" of the Scriptures which would recognize the boldly figurative nature of the Oriental speech in which they were expressed. Another portal was the sentiment of justice found in man which he thought rebelled against a just God decreeing eternal tor-ment for millions. He believed that the time had come when man stressed the miraculous less and the natural more than in by-gone eras and when Christianity would increasingly place Christ at the "center and circumference of its truth and emotions."

Many Presbyterians, especially in New York and in states farther west, had long believed in a rather liberal interpretation of Calvinistic doctrines.[39] A definite demand arose that the confession of faith should be revised to conform to modern views, for, since ministers and lay officers were required to subscribe, at least in a broad way, to the tenets of the Church, many were concerned as to whether they were being guilty of intellectual dishonesty.

Something of the significance of the issues involved is illustrated in the cases of men like Benjamin Franklin Butler (1795-1858) able New York lawyer and Secretary of War under Jackson; his son, William Allen Butler (1825-1902) well known lawyer and author; and Lucius Quintius C. Elmer (1793-1883), long justice of the Supreme Court of New Jersey. All were devoted supporters of the work of the Presbyterian Church, but none could accept all of the inherited viewpoints, and both of the Butlers abstained from serving as church officials. Ray Stannard Baker ("David Grayson") testifies in his autobiography that he felt moved to give a layman's support to the Presbyterian denomination which had nurtured his youthful character, but that the old creeds proved a stumbling block.[40]

Able men, however, worked, in spite of opposition, to eliminate the harsher features of the confession of faith. Among these was Rev. Henry Martyn Field (1822-1907), the ability of whose family is indicated by the fact that one brother (Cyrus West) developed the first Atlantic cable; another (Stephen Johnson) became Justice of the United States Supreme Court; and a third (David Dudley) was one of the leading lawyers and legal reformers of his generation.

Beginning in 1877 at least, Presbyterian churches throughout the world had been endeavoring to agree on acceptable creedal changes. Even Francis L. Patton was quoted as saying that the Westminster Confession had been "written as a guide against the errors of the time" and was "therefore defective and inapplicable at the present time." Yet, he saw dangers in a revision of the creed. He held that, since no

church member not an officer was obliged to subscribe to it
and no minister or officer was required to accept it in every
detail, the whole agitation was "entirely unnecessary."

President McCosh observed "that religious men were
only injuring their cause when they denied" the modern
idea of development in theology, and in later years he continued to be favorable to some revision. Even Dr. Hodge
of Princeton had accepted personally a modifying of the
more severe Calvinistic views, for Princeton Seminary at
that time taught the salvation of all infants dying in infancy,
thus confining eternal punishment to those of responsible
age who were judged for sins actually committed.[41] Hodge
personally believed, moreover, that a majority of the human
race would be saved.

After 1887 there was a definite demand for Revision of
the Confession of Faith,[42] especially to meet objections to
the belief that God "passed by some men and ordained them
to dishonor and wrath for their sin," to clarify the rather
ambiguous reference in the creed regarding "elect infants"
so that Presbyterians would not be accused of teaching "the
damnation of infants," and clearly to affirm the "free offer
of salvation in Christ" to all men.[43] By 1891, it was clear
that the Presbyterian Church as a whole desired revision.
But, Dr. Briggs, who had antagonized many by his stand on
Biblical criticism, took advanced ground in regard to the
need for removing all denominational fences and thereby
irritated many loyal Presbyterians. Church polity, moreover, by requiring a two-thirds majority of all presbyteries
for any change made alteration extremely difficult, especially when a skillful and determined minority was opposed
to any departure from older standards. Thus, in 1893 at a
time when the Church was disturbed by the alleged heretical
views of Dr. Briggs, a majority, but not two-thirds of the
presbyteries favored revision, and for the time being the
movement failed.[44]

But, by the end of the century the movement was re-
vived. In this effort no one was more influential than Henry

Van Dyke (1852-1933) preacher, poet, author, and university teacher. His Presbyterian heritage was unassailable, for his father had been pastor at Germantown, Pennsylvania, and then in Brooklyn, New York, and had been a leader in the earlier movement for revision. The son, as pastor of the influential Brick Church, New York City (1883-99), had an enviable reputation as an opponent of political corruption and a leader in the cause of civic responsibility. In 1890 he had addressed the New York presbytery on, "Is This Calvinism or Christianity?", repudiating implications of church doctrine that endeavored to measure "the mind of God by the logic of the seventeenth century." At the time of the Briggs trial he had published a fervent plea for liberty of investigation within the Church. He then formulated "A Plea for Peace and Work" in opposition to heresy hunters, and the document had been signed by about 235 Presbyterian ministers.[45] By 1900 a denominational committee was appointed to consider the Revision question again, and among its members were ex-President Benjamin Harrison, Supreme Court Justice John M. Harlan, former Secretary of State John W. Foster, and Henry Van Dyke. Changes to meet the principal objections to the older viewpoints were agreed upon, and by 1903 had been overwhelmingly accepted by the Church so as to become part of its official standards.[46]

Thus, the Presbyterian Church had refused to accept the idea of some religious liberals that creeds were mere "poetic interpretations." Rather, it had made a successful effort to resolve the tensions between those who opposed all reinterpretation of belief "because of its unsettling effect upon religious conviction" and those who believed that historic affirmations couched in language taken from the thought of a by-gone age need constant restatement and redefinition in the light of the new knowledge of a new era.[47]

As in other strongholds of a deeply rooted, personally vital faith many intellectual Presbyterians found in what they believed to be a tested way of life something too pre-

cious to be sacrificed on the altar of philosophical speculation. Woodrow Wilson and his wife, Ellen Axson Wilson,
both had come from deeply religious Presbyterian ministerial
families of intellectual interests. As a young woman, Ellen
Wilson had religious perplexities and had read Kant and
Hegel, which brought much "happiness" to her.[48] But, Wilson refused to argue religion.[49] To him, all experience
pointed to the necessity of religious faith without which
life was "a furnace without a fire,—a pursuit without goal,
—a measurement without standard."[50]

3. *The German and Dutch Reformed Churches*

Intellectual problems in the German Reformed Church
in the United States never became so acute as in the sister
Church of Scotch-Irish antecedents, the Presbyterian. The
Reformed Church heritage could be traced back by way of
Heidelberg in the Palatinate area of western Germany to
the contributions of Zwingli in Zurich and Calvin in Geneva.
The Calvinistic tradition, however, had lost definitely some
of its Genevan austerity in the more mellow atmosphere of
the Palatinate, and milder Zwinglian influences had been
subjected to modification by various successors of the early
Zurich reformer.[51] The Heidelberg Catechism, moreover,
was less rigidly Calvinistic than that of Westminster, having been termed "the most sweet-spirited and experiential
of the expositions of Calvinism."[52] Moreover, German Reformed theologians in the United States in the years before
the Civil War had been much influenced by German philosophical thought including that of Hegel and Schleiermacher, though they had endeavored to separate it from the
rationalism of the times and adapt it to orthodox doctrines.[53]
Under the leadership of three Seminary professors, located
then at Gettysburg, Pennsylvania, Frederick A. Rauch,
John W. Nevin, and Philip Schaff, the "Mercersburg Theology" had been developed which taught a Christological
and altar-centered Church against the revivalistic and sub-
jectivistic tendencies of the time.[54]

This theology was an attempt to synthesize the best German scholarship with the distilled thought of the Anglo-Saxon world. It endeavored "to conserve old truth, to accept new truth, and eliminate traditional errors and defects of previous stages, by advancing into a new and higher stage of evangelical Christianity."[55] It emphasized the person of Christ, rather than any doctrine or even work of Christ, as central to Christianity, and this contributed to a confessional Church in maintaining historical continuity without feeling "heavily burdened" by such a Confession.[56] Yet, for a period this had led to a doctrinal, and then a liturgical controversy with Low-Church Reformed scholars. Schaff later joined the faculty of Union Theological Seminary, New York, where his moderate Calvinism was a mediating influence in Presbyterian circles.[57] The irenic influence of the Mercersburg movement is suggested by the motto of some German religious leaders that was popularized by Dr. Schaff: "In essentials, unity; in doubtful points, freedom; in all things love." Thus, he had sought to avoid the excesses of, (1) Confessional literalism; (2) Philosophic rationalism; (3) Pietism.[58] But, occasionally a Reformed clergyman found difficulties within the orthodox household. Thus, Robert Reitzel (1849-98), German-American poet who served as pastor of the First German Reformed Church of Washington D. C., developed views which disturbed many of his congregation, and demands were made for his resignation (1872). Later, he became editor of a radical German weekly in Detroit, *Der arme Teufel.*

The Dutch portion of the Reformed Church ("The Reformed Church in America") also was not without its problems of doctrine and discipline. As early as 1822, a few ministers had seceded because of what they deemed "Hopkinsian errors and looseness of discipline."[59]—matters that were troubling Congregationalism and Presbyterianism at the same time—and soon a separate synod was formed.

A little later, in the Netherlands steadfast Calvinists had protested against the alleged worldliness and doctrinal latitudinarianism of the state Calvinistic Church and had formed the Christian Reformed Church. Some of these Separatists migrated to the United States, particularly to Michigan, but most of such nineteenth century Dutch immigrants were organized in the "Particular Synod of Chicago" (1856) within the Reformed Church in America. Among some of them, however, their fervent orthodoxy and cultural clannishness soon led to protests against the use of hymns rather than psalms, the neglect of catechetical instruction, and a lack of sympathy with doctrinal rigidity on the part of many of the Dutch Reformed people in America. By 1880 some were insistent that Free Masons and other members of secret oathbound societies must be denied church fellowship, a stand which most of the Dutch Reformed denomination would not support. Accordingly, the remnants of the old anti-Hopkinsian conservatives of 1822 received new recruits, and there developed what came to be known as the Christian Reformed Church, an uncompromising defender of old time Calvinism.[60]

Within the more moderate orthodoxy of the main body of the Reformed Church in America, however, other tensions were noted from time to time. In 1876, Rev. Augustus Blauvelt of Kingston, New York, published an article on "Protestant Vaticanism," asserting that "the religion of the Bible" was "by no means synonymous with Christianity" and insisting that "every so-called Christian Confession of Faith, Catholic or Protestant, written or unwritten demands revision." For such views he had been suspended from the ministry, and on appeal, he was tried in the Dutch Reformed Church at Fifth Avenue and Twenty-Ninth Streets, New York City, in June 1877.[61] Dr. Blauvelt admitted having departed from the standards of the Church, but he denied that he had betrayed the cause of Christ. The suspension, however, was confirmed by the ecclesiastical court.

4. *Lutheranism*

The Lutheran Church has generally been a conservative theological force in the United States, with a confessional

basis including the Apostles' and other early creeds of Christendom, the Augsburg Confession (1530), the Larger and
Smaller Catechisms (1529), and the Formula of Concord
(1577).[62] Swedish Lutherans along the Delaware, Dutch
Lutherans along the Hudson, Salzburgers in Georgia during
colonial times had all accepted the Confessions. In the
eighteenth century Henry M. Muhlenberg, sometimes considered the Father of the Lutheran Church in America, had
exhibited a certain liberality of opinion among the Pennsylvania Germans.[63] Hence, some pastors had looked upon his
orthodoxy with suspicion, but he and his co-workers had
not departed from the church creeds. Yet, by the early years
of the nineteenth century the Church had been affected by
cultural currents of the time, and some rationalistic tendencies expressed themselves. Thus, Rev. F. H. Quitman, pastor
at Rheinbeck, New York, and an influential figure in the
denomination had published an *Evangelical Catechism*
(1814) which had omitted all reference to the Trinity.[64] In
Maryland and Virginia some Lutherans assumed a definitely
liberal position. Benjamin Kurtz who became president of
Gettysburg Theological Seminary, believed that modern people had more knowledge, and, therefore, greater insight into
the Scriptures than did St. Paul and the reformers, hence,
the Confessions were not infallible in every respect. He held
much in common with Samuel S. Schmucker (1799-1873),
long professor at Gettysburg Seminary, who publicly stated
that at least portions of six articles of the Augsburg Confession were contrary to Scripture, as he repudiated baptismal
regeneration and the Real Presence in the Eucharist.[65] Kurtz
and Schmucker had believed that an "American" Lutheranism must be developed, emancipated from "full allegiance
to the symbolical books and treatises of the sixteenth and
seventeenth century German theologians" and committed to
"that liberty of thought which all Protestants must retain."
"The General Synod," that part of the Lutheran Church in
America with which Kurtz and Schmucker had been associated, continued to be the most liberal branch of Lutheranism
in the United States, allowing independence in non-essen-

tials and sometimes permitting clergymen of other faiths to occupy their pulpits. In part this liberal position endeavored to mediate between those who were impatient of liturgies and were interested in revivals and other "new measures" and those who sought a confessional basis not only on the Scriptures and the Augsburg Confession but on the whole body of Lutheran symbolic books as presented in the Book of Concord.

In the meantime, the arrival of great throngs of German Lutherans in the United States, many of whom were wholly unacquainted with the cross currents of modern thought led to a conservative reaction. Prussians who had come to the United States in 1839 had founded (1845) a strongly orthodox Buffalo Synod. Similarly, Germans from Saxony who had been repelled by the rationalism of the state Church in their homeland had sought an economic haven and a religious refuge in the United States. In 1839-41, they had founded in Missouri their "Zion on the Mississippi,"[66] and out of this developed the staunchly conservative Missouri Synod Lutheran Church, ever afterwards the unyielding defender of orthodoxy.[67]

In the various conferences and synods of Lutheranism in America, moreover, a conservative reaction was noted after 1865. Clergymen who voiced views such as had been taught at Gettysburg Seminary before the Civil War often found themselves in disrepute. The story has been told by a Lutheran scholar in a volume, *American Lutheranism Surrenders to Forces of Conservatism.*[68] Lutheranism rather generally strengthened its organized life by an emphatic insistence on adherence to the "unaltered Augsburg Confession." This meant, of course, that it made minimum concessions to modern secular thought. Theories like evolution were accordingly looked upon rather definitely as an "unwarranted departure from the Scriptural faith" and accordingly a "modification of historic Lutheranism."[69] In many communities this uncompromising position turned some young people to other Protestant churches.

A Norwegian-born youth, Kristofer N. Janson (1841-1917), indeed had started to study for the Lutheran ministry but had developed liberal views and served for over a decade as missionary and organizer for the Unitarians in Minnesota and Wisconsin. Anton J. Carlson (b. 1875), Swedish-born youth, went to the Lutheran Augustana College to study for the ministry, but changing intellectual currents caused him to turn to science, and he became one of the world's great physiologists.

Doubtless there were numerous cases, moreover, like that of the Swedish-born parents of John Lind, destined to be Governor of Minnesota and special representative of President Wilson to Mexico. At the time of the death of their unbaptized child, Lind's parents were deeply offended by the attitude of the Swedish Lutheran minister and became devout members of the Swedish Methodist Church. The younger Lind, however, was repelled by the seemingly narrow views of frontier pastors and never affiliated with any church. Not an orthodox believer, he could nevertheless give a convincing address on "The Church as a Power of Civilization," stressing the fatherhood of God and the brotherhood of man.[70]

Yet, most German and Scandinavian Lutherans remained faithful Lutherans, and the discipline and strength of their churches were widely recognized.

5. *Congregationalism*

The Calvinistic theological tradition (with its emphasis on the sovereignty of God and predestination) was the basis of doctrinal faith in 1865 for Congregational, Presbyterian, a large part of the Baptist, and the Welsh Methodist churches of the United States. Even many Lutheran synods were definitely affected by it. Scholars today are not wholly agreed as to the extent to which the Puritan Fathers adhered to the "pure Calvinism" of the Genevan reformer. There is some evidence that Elizabethan reformers in England, from whom New England leaders derived their views, had already modified the earlier Calvinism, and apparently further modifications were made in Massachusetts Bay Colony.[71] At least, even before the American Revolution various factors had served to divide New England Puritans into the Old (or Moderate) and the Consistent (or Extreme) Calvinists. The former had been content to know that God did certain things and to define the results. The Consistent Calvinists, however, insisted on trying to explain the method and reasons for God's actions, and after the thought of Jonathan Edwards, stressed the utter helplessness of man.[72] These views had been carried to a rather logical conclusion by Samuel Hopkins (1721-1803) of Newport, Rhode Island and his followers who had urged that even those not elected to salvation should live for the good of all and be willing to be damned for the greater glory of God. These "Hopkinsians" felt that man, however, must not try to place himself in the way of salvation.

In opposition to such extreme Calvinism, Nathaniel William Taylor (1786-1858), had urged sinners to employ every means of grace that their regeneration would be more assured. Lyman Beecher, and other Calvinistic advocates of revivalism followed this form of "evangelical Christianity," but were opposed by the more conservative Calvinists of the new generation who rallied under the leadership of Bennet Tyler. Thus, before 1840 orthodox Congregationalists in the United States had been divided into two camps, at a time when a third group, made up of those who were being known as Unitarians, was discarding Calvinistic theology entirely.[73]

Trends away from a strict Calvinism had paved the way for the work of Horace Bushnell, whose *Christian Nurture* (1846) had revolutionized New England theology by insisting that the child must "grow up a Christian and never know himself as being otherwise." The Church, he believed, had tried too much the method of "conquest" and too little that of "growth."[74]

Adjustments within the Congregational fold were more readily made than in some more closely knit denominational families, for within Congregationalism each local congregation enjoyed a large measure of autonomy. Yet, Congregationalists had been concerned about the need for a close connection between religious profession and "consistency of behavior," and in the midst of Unitarianism, some individual churches had adhered to creedal tests to promote an insistence on really "regenerate" personal character.[75] In June 1865, when a representative Council of Congregationalists had met in Boston, a determined effort had been made to secure the adoption of a creed committing Congregationalists in express terms to a Calvinistic form of belief. The Committee appointed to consider the matter, however, reported that it would be inexpedient to impose such a creed, so endeavored only to characterize in a comprehensive manner the doctrines held in common. Therefore, at an adjourned session of the Council in Plymouth, the Burial Hill Declaration (1865) was adopted. While the prevailing doctrine of American Congregationalism was then essentially Calvinistic, the tolerance of the denomination had been so developed that the Declaration omitted the word "Calvinism."[76] The Declaration was broad enough that it really affirmed nothing "as belonging to the substance of the faith" that was rejected by any Christian.[77] Individual churches, however, often imposed creeds as "tests" rather than as mere "testimonies" to a traditional faith, and some were rather envious of the official solidarity of the Presbyterians. In 1865, moreover, the noted Andover Seminary professor, Edwards Amasa Park, had declared that anyone who had studied theology for three years and had read the Bible in the original languages was either a Calvinist or "not a respectable man."[78] For many years thereafter, Calvinistic teaching held sway in Congregational theological seminaries, but the feeling rapidly became widespread that its vitality had been lost in an absorption in the abstruse issues of a Protestant "scholasticism." The prosperity and ease of Amer-

ican life, moreover, were not conducive to an acceptance of
the rigorous doctrines of Calvinism. In 1871, a further liberalizing of viewpoint was indicated in a new doctrinal statement adopted by the National Council of Congregational
Churches that was understood as definitely extending "a
welcome to those of Arminian beliefs."[79]

A liberally inclined Congregational minister in 1865 lamented that in his congregation at Haverhill, Massachusetts
"the very best Christians" in the congregation stayed away
from church "because of a lumbering creed that only here
and there" touched vital Christianity. Amidst the humanitarianism of the time some revolted against the doctrine of
eternal punishment. In November 1877, this had led to a
famous episode when a Congregational council had refused
to install Rev. James F. Merriam as pastor at Indian Orchard, Massachusetts, because he affirmed that the Scriptures
did not clearly teach the eternal punishment of those who
die unregenerate, and that if the Scriptures did teach it, the
punishment was annihilation. As a result, the Indian Orchard
church exercised the reserved right of Congregational
churches, and proceeded to ordain and install Mr. Merriam,
thus sacrificing its standing in the Congregational fellowship.[80]

In view of the substantial autonomy of the local Congregational church, difficulties that arose among Congregationalists were often associated with policies of educational
institutions. Thus, Noah Porter (1811-92), Congregational
minister and President of Yale, was so solicitous for the
maintenance of the college as one "distinctively and earnestly
Christian" that he precipitated a controversy regarding academic freedom at the college. He objected to the introduction of Herbert Spencer's *Study of Sociology* as a text
book at Yale (1879) by Professor William G. Sumner who
had served in the Episcopal ministry, but it was not suppressed.[81]

A more famous controversy was that involving Andover
(Massachusetts) Theological Seminary. There, a group of

professors had come to believe that a just God would not condemn to eternal punishment those persons, especially in foreign lands, who had never had opportunity of embracing the Christian way of salvation. Andover had been established in 1808 as a means of stemming the tide of religious liberalism. Hence, the charter had provided that each professor must subscribe to a creed (a modified form of the Westminster Confession of Faith) and must reaffirm his position every five years. Obviously, this had led to a firm adherence to orthodox standards. But, when Edwards A. Park, "a brilliant teacher and eloquent preacher," who was essentially an interpreter of the old rather than a prophet of the new, retired in 1881, new men who accepted much of the changing thought of the period had assumed leadership. They had sought not so much to contradict the old orthodoxy as to ignore its concepts. They had accepted particularly the idea of development in theology and the Love of God rather than the rigors of His law. Eventually they came to accept Biblical criticism, the immanence of God, and evolution.[82]

To present their views in the light of modern scholarship, Egbert Coffin Smyth (1829-1904), president of the faculty, along with others had founded the *Andover Review*. Soon they presented the view that there might be "future probation" for those who had never heard the Gospel. Smyth did not definitely affirm this view, but he and four other professors were brought to trial by the Board of Visitors of the seminary, and Smyth was removed from his theological chair. The trustees of the seminary, however, sustained the faculty members, and an appeal to the Massachusetts Supreme Court (1891) resulted in the setting aside of the decision of the Board of Visitors. A later trial resulted in the dismissal of the case.[83]

In the meantime, the issue had come up in a different manner. Conservatives argued that if missionaries believed in a "future probation," the vital nerve that gave impelling urgency to missionary efforts would be cut. Accordingly, in 1886, an attempt was made to prevent the return to India, under the American Board of Foreign Missions, of Robert A. Hume who, on furlough, had made utterances regarding "the larger hope," which had aroused suspicions among the guardians of orthodoxy. At first, conservatives were successful, but eventually Hume was returned to India, as more liberal views prevailed.[84]

As late as 1900, Rev. Edward Chandler, an Andover Seminary graduate who was pastor at Wellesley, Massachusetts, was accused of being unsound in doctrine, but he resigned rather than foster dissension in the congregation. In November of the same year the Visitors and Trustees decided that the Andover creed was to be declaratory and not obligatory, and a newly appointed professor of Christian theology was not required to subscribe to it.

In discussing the gradual modernizing of Andover's position, one journal of opinion commented in 1900:

> First an indispensable principle, then a war-cry, then a bugaboo, then a curiosity—that is the history of many a queer bit of political or theological junk that one finds labelled on some shelf, and thanks Heaven that it can do no more harm.

If the Episcopal Church stood especially for historical continuity and liturgical order, the Methodist Church for evangelistic work in city and country, and the Presbyterian Church for "a unique power to educate in Christian truth a community which has already received the Gospel," the Congregational Church came to express particularly the freedom of the individual congregation. Hence, in Boston one Congregational minister of Methodist background, Dr. Meredith, still employed Methodist religious techniques and another, Dr. Withrow, of conservative Presbyterian antecedents, reflected the strong doctrinal emphasis of his upbringing.

From time to time some liberal Congregationalists, of

whom Rev. M. J. Savage was one of the most prominent, entered Unitarianism. Henry Ward Beecher at Plymouth Congregational Church, Brooklyn, came to advocate such liberal views that he withdrew from the Association of Congregational ministers in 1882.[85]

Many Congregational churches, however, rapidly became more liberal in their viewpoints. Indicative of this trend was the action of Plymouth Church, Indianapolis, during the pastorate of the dynamic Oscar Carleton McCulloch (1843-1891), when new members were merely expected to agree to participate as "friends associated for Christian work and worship."

Old South Church, Boston, under the leadership of George A. Gordon, a most powerful Scottish-born preacher, finally in 1899 formally abolished its Confession of Faith which had been adopted in 1680 and had emphasized the unchanging number of the elect and the hopeless state of all others. Not in use since 1850, the creed had not been accepted by the last two ministers.

Indeed, laymen and clergy alike showed increasingly a departure from traditional views. Elizabeth Stuart Phelps Ward (1844-1911), descended on both sides from orthodox Congregational theologians, showed in her writings a progressive divergence from the faith of her childhood. She tended to minimize the obligation of the sinner to God and to emphasize more and more the definite duty of the Almighty to satisfy the reasonable desires of the human hearts which he had created. In her *The Gates Ajar* (1868) she depicted a rather sentimental Heaven which gave uncertain people "the sort of answer they most wished for," and the volume became so popular that it was translated into French, German, Dutch, and Italian.[86]

In many ways, Congregationalists, with the liberty permitted to individual congregations, led in the movement of those of orthodox traditions into newer ways. Thus, Thomas K. Beecher, younger brother of the famous Henry Ward Beecher, explored new trails as pastor of Park Church, El-

mira, New York. There, Olivia Langdon, beloved wife of
Samuel L. Clemens (Mark Twain), had received her religious nurture, and a son of the congregation has testified
that the Church's gospel was "one of self-reliant revolt
against forms and conventions as such."[87] Thomas Beecher
called himself "Teacher of Park Church," and "a whole
rebel character and thought of life lay behind that choice."
He tried to do in Elmira what he thought a modern Jesus
would do, hence he was iconoclastic in relation to tradition
and "preached no doctrine but the fatherhood of God and
brotherhood of men." His methods infuriated the people
of many other Elmira churches, and when his Sunday evening meetings became too large to be accommodated in the
church, he hired a local theatre. His actions caused him to
be expelled from the Elmira Ministerial Union. Pool tables
were installed in the church parlors, and the church became
a pioneer "institutional" church.[88]

As Congregational churches adapted themselves increasingly to the demands of the prevailing culture, some of the
churches adopted the practice of having Sunday evening lectures with the element of worship almost wholly excluded.
In University communities like Columbus, Ohio and Madison, Wisconsin, the First Congregational Church became an
advanced expression of religious liberalism. But, there were,
in Congregational circles marked tendencies away from institutional religion that naturally raised questions as to
whether the strength of the Church as a continuing religious
body was not being enfeebled. The Yale University Church,
in 1901 renounced its creedal requirements and its denominational character, though continuing to be governed by
Congregational principles. Other churches in New Haven,
the United Church and the historic First Church followed
the same course regarding a creed.[89]

Something of the trend of faith in liberal Congregationalism was shown by the situation in three churches of
cultured and public-spirited members in Hartford, Con-

necticut, where, in the 1870's and 1880's, three younger clergymen were leaders of religious expression and without peers in the pulpits of the community. One was Nathaniel Burton, pastor of Park Church, who had a tremendous personal influence, but who found the strain of a highly intellectual pulpit responsibility very great. He came to have melancholic moods and seriously considered entering the Episcopalian fold. A second was Edwin Pond Parker, pastor of the Second Church, who came to rely in part upon music and ritual. The third was Joseph Hopkins Twichell, who became pastor of Asylum Hill Congregational Church soon after the Civil War and held no other charge during his life time. Handsome, humorous, charming, sincere, he brought to his congregation inspiring messages which were permeated with ideas of Christian brotherhood, of the Christian ethic as the foundation of the good life, of man's relation to a God of love, and of the seeming progressive advance of Christian principles in the world. Presented to a generally prosperous and ethically sensitive people the sermons involved nothing that would irritate or repel. A pleasant social life related to the church involved many purely secular programs, such as lectures on American literature by young Richard Burton. Even Mark Twain took an active part in the affairs of the congregation.[90]

But, the traditions of Horace Bushnell were now implicit in the thought and life of these Hartford congregations. From the conservative viewpoint, Bushnell had minimized institutional religion, emphasizing a personal religious experience not dependent on church discipline, and with the passing of time devoting his energies more largely to secular matters, ceasing to concern himself particularly with the spiritual life.[91] Twichell had, like Bushnell, turned his back on Calvinism, and Twichell found escape from obvious difficulties by avoiding the central problems of religious faith. Hence, when Mark Twain suffered dire personal tragedy, he found no consolation in the faith of the "healthy-minded" that saw no evil, and for many troubled souls, the Church seemed to speak with no real authority as to the ways of God to man.

Similarly, the influential Lyman Abbott, as early as 1880 had come to believe that "God, immortality, Christ, pardon" were not hypotheses reached by laborious argument, but were rather "facts perceived by the spiritual sense."[92] The Calvinistic forefathers had faced the problem of evil and death with answers that were integrated into an intellectual framework, and they had not minimized the authority and purpose of institutional religion. Now, much seemed to hinge upon "spiritual intuition" rather than upon intellectual and institutional bulwarks, and many suspected that much had been lost.

The Asylum Hill Church of course could not be blamed for the plight of Mark Twain. He had early revolted against the staunch Calvinism of his mother and had adopted a skeptical attitude toward many religious matters. Liberal religion, however, in his hours of need had not helped him to find an answer to his soul's quest.[93]

Many Congregationalists, of course, stood in defense of the traditional answers to matters of faith. Thus, Richard Salter Storrs (1787-1873), for almost fifty years pastor of the Congregational Church at Braintree, Massachusetts, had been severely orthodox, refusing to exchange pulpits with any clergyman viewed as possibly unsound in faith. His son, Richard Salter Storrs (1821-1900), for over fifty years pastor of the Church of the Pilgrims, Brooklyn, was a steadfast opponent of some of Henry Ward Beecher's "novelties" and exerted a nation wide influence as a defender of the "faith of the fathers."

Yet, the defenders of orthodoxy were assigned no easy task in an age when many trusted increasingly to science rather than the insights of faith. At Union Theological Seminary, a Congregational minister, William G. T. Shedd (1820-94), represented the tradition of orthodox Puritan Congregationalism, based on Calvinistic foundations. But, amidst the intellectual currents of the day he could not be unmindful of the "Romantic reaction to Enlightenment, empiricism, the new emphasis on historical consciousness, and the prophetic foreshadowing of evolutionary naturalism." All of these new movements contained within them the seeds of heresy, but Shedd ventured forth to explore them all, in every case returning "to anchor his vessel in the safe harbor of orthodox Calvinism." In the process, however, a certain eclecticism was involved, and Shedd's valiant efforts, according to one recent student, could not hold the old "orthodoxy in stable solution."[94] President William De Witt Hyde of Bowdoin College, moreover, expressed a fundamental dissatisfaction with older patterns of thought when at the Second International Council of Congregational Churches in Boston, 1899, he declared:

> Seminaries which will emancipate the minds of their students must themselves be free from the bondage to the letter of antiquated creeds.[95]

For many, an unanswered question was involved in how far liberal thought might go in a liberation from "the letter of antiquated creeds" and still remain essentially Christian. In 1888, something of a stir had been created in England, especially in Anglican circles, and in the United States by the publication by Mrs. Humphrey Ward, a niece of Matthew Arnold, of *Robert Elsmere* and later *The Case of Richard Meynell*.[96] Even the liberal Congregationalist Lyman Abbott, refused to accept her contention that Christianity would be revivified by an abandonment of the miraculous element and an emphasis on the Christian social mission. Abbott's periodical, *The Christian Union,* in 1889 said that the belief in particular miracles was not necessary to being a Christian but the belief in "a supernatural Christ and his supernatural life" was indispensable.[97] Yet, Abbott's views of a "supernatural Christ" seemed not to be wholly clear and settled, and in 1895, his periodical asserted that the Virgin Birth was central to "no practical ethical question, no essential Christian doctrine, no vital Christian experience." Many Congregationalists shared this view, but not all were agreed as to what constituted the hard core of doctrinal Christianity.

CHAPTER XIII

BAPTISTS, METHODISTS, DISCIPLES, AND QUAKERS

1. *The Baptists*

The Baptists in America had early stressed freedom of conscience and had generally not insisted upon elaborate creedal statements, as had the Catholics, Episcopalians, Lutherans, and Presbyterians. Some types of Baptists were strongly Calvinistic in viewpoint, but one observer in 1876 indicated that they were in practice representatives of "a revolt from antiquity, tradition, and church authority." Their emphasis on large autonomy for the local congregation, moreover, had accentuated the trend toward liberty of opinion. One writer in 1891 suggested that Baptists were "if possible, more loosely organized than Congregational churches." The Scriptural interpretation which bound them together in a denominational family was largely the insistence on immersion as the only form of baptism to be sanctioned.[1] In the decades after the Civil War, Baptists were overwhelmingly conservative in their views of the Bible and the traditional Baptist teachings. Dr. Ezekiel G. Robinson, President and Professor of Systematic Theology at Rochester Theological Seminary (1868-72); Dr. Ebenezer Dodge, President and Professor at what is now Colgate University; Dr. George W. Northrup, President and Professor at what later became (1892) the Divinity School of the University of Chicago; and William N. Clarke, Professor at Hamilton College, represented the more advanced currents of thought in the denomination. Later, Lyman Abbott was to testify that Clarke's *Christian Theology* was "the most religious book on systematic theology" he had ever read.[2]

In the South, conservative tendencies were especially marked. Some insisted on claims that the Baptists were in unbroken succession from apostolic times and refused to fraternize with members of other denominations. Even more generally they were uncompromisingly hostile to any denial of the plenary inspiration and inerrancy of Scriptures, to evolutionary teaching, to the recognition of "immersion" performed by other denominations, and to cooperation at home and abroad with other denominational efforts.[3]

One who early accepted new views of Biblical criticism and was forced to resign at Southern Baptist Seminary in 1879 was Crawford T. Toy (1836-1919), who later became professor of Hebrew and other Oriental languages at Harvard. Subsequently, he threw off his earlier reserve, became an advanced Biblical critic, and even withdrew from the Cambridge Baptist Church of which he had become a member, wishing to be known as a Theist, rather than a Christian. At Hamilton College, Dr. Nathaniel Schmidt, a brilliant young Semitic scholar, resigned in 1896, because it was understood the Board of Trustees did not agree with his seemingly radical views on the Old Testament and revealed religion in general.

Baptists often insisted upon a denial of communion to members of other denominations through a policy of "closed communion." Adolphus Julius Frederick Behrends (1839-1900) resigned his pastorate of the First Baptist Church of Cleveland, Ohio, in 1876 because of his opposition to the restrictive practice and later became the noted pastor of Central Congregational Church, Brooklyn. Similarly, Philip Stafford Moxon (1848-1923), pastor of the First Baptist Church, Cleveland (1879-85) and First Baptist Church, Boston (1885-93), revolted against the insistence on immersion and closed communion and became pastor of South Congregational Church, Springfield, Massachusetts.

At a time when many Southern Baptists believed that their churches could be traced to apostolic times, William Heth Whitsitt (1841-1911), president of Southern Baptist

Seminary at Louisville, Kentucky, contributed an article to an encyclopaedia in 1896 in which he stated his view that adult immersion had been abandoned for a long period in England and only restored by the proponents of Baptist views in 1641. The resulting "Whitsitt controversy" led to Whitsitt's resignation as president of the seminary. Among those coming to his defense, however, was William Eldridge Hatcher (1834-1912), influential Baptist clergyman of Richmond, Virginia, who aided Hatcher in securing a teaching post at Richmond College (a Baptist institution). But, for some years the episode involved rancorous divisions within the Baptists of Kentucky.

Many Baptist laymen also chafed under what they deemed the unnatural limitations of Christian fellowship involved in the "closed communion" for the immersed, and some objected to the rigid views of Biblical interpretation and the emphasis on Calvinistic theology and Puritan restraints.

Robert M. La Follette, Sr., as a boy reacted vigorously against what he deemed the Baptist bigotry of his stepfather who implied that La Follette's own father was burning in everlasting hell fire because he had died unbaptized.[4] When Charles Evans Hughes, son of a strict Baptist minister, as a young lawyer in New York started teaching a Sunday School class in the Fifth Avenue Baptist Church of which he was a member, he did so with the understanding that he could teach the Christian message of Jesus. He later explained that he held no brief for distinctive Baptist tenets but cherished their work in the struggle for religious liberty and wished to do what he could to strengthen Christian institutions.[5]

William Rainey Harper, later to become President of the University of Chicago, as a young instructor at Denison University, Granville, Ohio, found that the theological discussions which sorely troubled Ohio Baptists in the 1870's were of absolutely no interest to him.[6] As President of the University of Chicago, he of course was in the vanguard of Baptists of advanced views.

On the other hand, not only in the South but in the

North many Baptists continued to be what later were
known as Fundamentalists. Some believed firmly in the
speedy Second Coming. One minister in Syracuse, New
York, had so little sympathy with the views of the liberal
Congregationalists that he was reported as saying "Lyman
Abbott is doing more for the devil than Ingersoll."[7]

In the struggle in Baptist circles between extreme conservatives and advanced liberals, William H. P. Faunce
(1859-1930) who became President of Brown University in
1899, endeavored to occupy a mediatorial role.

2. *The Disciples of Christ*

The Disciples of Christ likewise have been a predominantly non-creedal Church, based on Biblical doctrine and
with immersion as the required form of baptism.[8] Yet, they
did not escape the tensions of modern thought. One of the
most prominent of nineteenth century laymen among the
Disciples was James A. Garfield, who had been born into
a Disciples household in Ohio, had experienced personal
conversion, and had joined the Church. This background
of his life and experience had a powerful effect on all of his
life, for the Disciples had a certain "manner of thinking"
which was not always shared in highly intellectual circles.
Part of his education was secured at Williams College in
Massachusetts, in an area where the Disciples were very
weak in numbers and influence. Garfield's biographer believes that he may have been kept from the Disciples ministry by some disillusionment with the particular tenets of
Disciple teaching during this college period when he came
in contact with other influences. Later, his life in Washington caused him to believe that perhaps his early beliefs
had been too narrow.[9]

In the Mississippi and Ohio valleys where the Disciples
were particularly strong, there was often much eager search-
ing of Scripture to see what Biblical viewpoint seemed to
be justified. Thus, Richard Bland (1835-99) of Missouri,

destined to be a leader of the Silver Crusade in Congress, had been raised a Methodist, but had become convinced of the truth of the Disciple approach and had even considered becoming a Disciple preacher.[10]

Jeremiah S. Black, one of the great lawyers of his generation, who served as legal advisor to Andrew Johnson and defended Tilden before the Electoral Commission, as a youth had been stirred by a compelling religious quest. He had been baptized in a stream by Alexander Campbell, a founder of the Disciples organization, and remained a faithful member until his death.[11] With a deep Biblical-grounded faith Black was one who took emphatic exception to Robert Ingersoll's assaults on revealed religion. In the same issue of the *North American Review,* each presented his view of "The Christian Religion." Black asserted: "I am no preacher. . . . My duty is more analogous to that of a policeman who would silence a rude disturber of the congregation by telling him that his clamor is false and his conduct an offense against public decency." Some people believed that each partisan had yielded too freely to invectives and personalities.

Much of the Disciple membership was in areas and among people that were practically inclined rather than intellectually minded. Some local churches were distinctly conservative in their Biblical teachings. Quite understandably then, Rev. John William McGarvey (1829-1911) editor of the influential *Christian Standard* beginning in 1890, fought against the Higher Criticism by both argument and ridicule.

But, the non-creedal nature of the Disciple fellowship opened the way for some congregations to be greatly influenced by new philosophical trends. Thus, Edward Scribner Ames (b. 1879), who was a native of Wisconsin, the son of a Disciple preacher who had sought to escape the creedal tests of other denominations, went through such a process of development. As a boy he had lived in a household of such pious earnestness that he was deeply perplexed at fourteen

to meet a young man working in the local store who was
energetic, courteous, and essentially good but, for some
mysterious reason, not a church member.[12] Ames later went
on to the Disciple college (Drake University), to Yale Divinity School, and the University of Chicago. This educative
process brought him in contact with the thought of Schopenhauer and William James and the preaching of highly educated, liberal Congregationalist ministers. Thus, at the close
of the century, as professor at Butler College and then
(1900) pastor of the University Disciples Church, Chicago,
his approach to faith was vastly different than that of many
a grass roots Disciple preacher in Missouri or Arkansas.

3. *Society of Friends*

In the quest for a spiritual haven, some in America had
early found religious expression in the teachings of George
Fox, seventeenth century Englishman who had founded the
Society of Friends (Quakers). "The Inner Light," the creative working of the Divine Spirit in man, was the heart of
this mystical experience. But, by 1865, even among these
people there were differing views toward revivalism, "qui-
etism," and doctrinal standards, and various groups such as
"Orthodox," "Hicksite," and "Conservative" Friends, had
emerged.[13] Except as some congregations partook of spirited
evangelistic techniques, the Friends made few converts. Occasionally, however some individuals found amidst the perplexities of the advancing industrialism, an answer to spiritual needs in the quiet serenity of the Friends meeting.
(During the period immediately after World War I, Roscoe Pound, brilliant Dean of Harvard Law School, joined
the Society).[14] At the same time some choice spirits among
them were to be found, such as Rufus M. Jones, whose spiritual influence was to permeate far beyond the boundaries
of his own denominational circles.[15]

On the other hand, some birth-right Quakers underwent
a loss of faith, as they experienced an agnosticism respect-

ing the workings of the Inner Light, though they might still cherish the liberty, democracy, and non-resistance views of their childhood faith with the precious remembrance of "the quiet kind of religion which sinks deepest into the heart."[16]

Other Quakers were at times distressed that, instead of emphasizing their special insights and virtues, the Society of Friends seemed inextricably caught up in the secularizing trends of the day.

4. Methodism

Methodism has always been a religious organization that has stressed religious experience rather than doctrinal conformity. The Wesleyan movement had arisen in England as a protest against the low state of morals and the degradation of social life, as well as the cold formality of the Established Church. Accordingly, Methodists have often declared that they have little or no theology, and John Wesley had placed the emphasis on other than intellectual considerations, when he had early asserted that "the distinguishing marks of a Methodist are not his opinions of any sort."[17] Yet, Wesley had realized the need for minimum conformity and discipline. As early as 1783 he had advised leaders of the movement in America: "Let all of you be determined to abide by the Methodist doctrine and discipline, published in the four volumes of 'Sermons,' and the 'Notes upon the New Testament,' together with the large 'Minutes of Conference.'" He also warned against the acceptance of certain doctrines like those of Calvinism.[18]

These writings, therefore, were to be known in America as the Methodist "Standards" and came to be accepted as Methodist doctrine, along with the "Articles of Religion," adopted in 1784.[19] Wesley himself distinguished between the "essential doctrines" in his *Notes* and the mere "opinions" expressed in his sermons.[20] Ministers, however, by the time they are ordained have been required to answer questions regarding their own spiritual experience and be examined on the subject of doctrine and discipline. They are also required to express belief that the Methodist doctrines are in harmony with the Holy Scriptures. Thus, certain standards were set up which admitted of great flexibility.

In the movement toward orthodox standards, however, in various denominations the Northern Methodists joined the procession. One observer in 1880 complained that a provision had been adopted by the last General Conference requiring that a minister must accept not only the "Articles of Religion" but the "standard authorities" as well. This writer said that such works were voluminous and contradictory and would result in making "church trials more easy and convictions more difficult."[21] Another wrote that uncertainty would arise because Wesley himself had believed in literal fire and brimstone, which apparently many of the Methodist clergy did not accept.

In 1840, moreover, the earlier procedure granting admission to lay membership in a Methodist church to any one (upon recommendation of a leader) who would express his faith in Christ and his intention to lead a Christian life, was modified. Thereafter, it had been required that an applicant "pass a satisfactory examination" as to "the correctness of his doctrine and his willingness to observe the rules of the Church."[22] Later, Methodists had been specifically required to assent to the doctrines of the Scriptures "as set forth in the Articles of Religion" of the Methodist Church.[23] One writer in 1886 stated that one of the Articles contained an historical error, for it was not true that the authority of all the canonical books of the Old and New Testament had never been doubted in the Church.

In 1876, the Bishops had submitted a report on a revised creed for Methodism, but constitutionally there can be no alteration in the "Twenty-Five Articles of Religion," hence no change seemed possible. Yet, in view of the degree of doctrinal conformity required in the Methodist Church, rather amazingly a leading ecclesiastic could assert in 1878 that the "Articles of Religion" are "the product of the thought and controversies of other times. They are fragmentary and incomplete. They speak with great distinctness on subjects that are not now discussed, and omit some of the most fundamental questions on doctrines of religion. As a creed, they fail to represent the belief of Methodists, and exert but little influence. They ought to be amended, but the letter of the 'constitution' forbids—a clear instance of bondage to a form of words."[24]

Methodist orthodoxy was particularly strong in the Southern states. In 1882 the *New Orleans Christian Advocate* declared: "The isms and heresies of the North cannot live and thrive in the South. Universalism, Unitarianism, Agnosticism et *id omne genus* have scarcely a name in our borders." The *Christian Advocate* of Nashville, moreover, asserted that the Methodist Church South had been "so busy cultivating the fields it occupies that it has no desire to waste its energies in fitting out North Pole expeditions of ecclesiastical or doctrinal discovery."[25]

Many Southern Methodists were frankly suspicious of the higher learning, and when the remarkable Bishop Holland N. McTyeire endeavored to secure a definitely trained ministry by the establishment of a central theological seminary, Bishop George F. Pierce announced his belief that "every dollar invested in a theological school" would prove damaging to Methodism.

Methodists like others of course often found their faith challenged by various phases of modern thought. Thus, Thomas Roberts Slicer (1847-1916), son of one of the best known Methodist clergymen in the country, was ordained to the ministry of that Church, but joined the Unitarians, serving after 1881 as minister of Unitarian churches in Providence, Buffalo, and New York. Edward Eggleston (1837-1902), author of the *Hoosier Schoolmaster* (1871), had been a Bible agent, Methodist circuit rider, and pastor previous to 1866. His views became more liberal, and even-

tually his religious enthusiasm waned during his pastorate
of the non-sectarian Church of Christian Endeavor in Brooklyn   (1874-9) .[26]

Dr. Hiram W. Thomas, pastor of Centenary Methodist
Episcopal Church, Chicago, came to espouse the moral influence theory of the Atonement and liberal views of the inspiration of the Scriptures. Expelled from the ministry after a
trial in 1881, he had already founded (1880) "The People's
Church of Chicago."[27]

The Hoosier father of David Graham Phillips (1867-
1911), novelist and Muckraker, not only taught Sunday
School but often conducted Sunday services in the pastor's
absence. The younger Phillips went to the denominational
college, De Pauw, for two years. Later, as a Princeton student, he declared, as we have seen, that he was an agnostic.
Yet, his persistent moral fervor, based on his early training,
added zest to his career as a "Muckraker."[28]

Lew Wallace (1827-1905) whose *Ben Hur* was to receive almost unreserved acclaim from religious publications,
as a boy had often accompanied his mother to the Methodist
Church at Covington, Kentucky, and later he had sometimes
attended the Methodist Church at Crawfordsville, Indiana.
He later maintained that the writing of *Ben Hur* had converted him to "a conviction amounting to absolute belief
in God and the divinity of Christ." But Wallace stubbornly
refused to become a church member.[29]

Rutherford B. Hayes, during all of his life, was a faithful church attendant and reader of the Bible. He was active
in the affairs of the Methodist Church and subscribed generously for its work. He even planted trees to beautify the
grounds of the Methodist Church at Fremont, Ohio. He
lauded the contributions to civilization of the Christian religion on innumerable occasions. Yet, he never joined the
church and referred to himself as a "non-church member,
a non-professor of religion."[30] Early in life (1851) he had
expressed a disbelief in the "gloomy theology of the orthodox" (especially Calvinism) and in orthodox views of "the

divinity of the Bible," and had asserted that "in *spite* of my wishes, . . . none but the most liberal doctrines can command my assent." To the end of his life he remained a Christian in his principles but one who felt that he could not accept the orthodox creeds.

Something of the travail of soul which came with intellectual adjustments was experienced by Walter Hines Page who was to be ambassador to Great Britain at the outbreak of World War I. His father was a fervent North Carolina Methodist with a religion of "rugged Old Testament virility and perhaps an Old Testament harshness," undisturbed "by the refinements of the theologians." To him, "God was God, heaven was heaven, and hell was hell; and in all three he most fervently believed." When the younger Page showed signs of marked intellectual ability the family began to consider the sacrifices that might be made to give him the education for the Methodist ministry. In the 1870's he and others went through a trying period of doubt at Randolph-Macon College, and many found great consolation in Tennyson's *In Memoriam*. When he went on to the new Johns Hopkins University for further study, Thomas Huxley gave a series of lectures (1876), with no clergymen in attendance to offer prayer, at this opening of the year's work. Religious people were seriously disturbed, and Page was "sorry" that prayer had not been offered. During this period the dogmatic interpretation of Scripture was to him "the one absorbing subject" of his life's thought, causing him "much grovelling darkness of mind." Worst of all, he was utterly alone in his reverent perplexity, for devout people were overwhelmingly orthodox while "unbelievers" had no sympathy for his deepest concerns. The divinity of Christ seemed but a myth to him, yet he wished above all things to be able to minister to people of "the blessing of the Beauty of Holiness." He could not subscribe to the doctrines of his denomination, so he thought of becoming a Unitarian minister. That course, however, presented insuperable objections, for he well knew that his beloved South was not congenial to unorthodox teachings and his dear mother would doubtless be wounded by such action.[31]

Methodist theological institutions, of course, felt the tension of new intellectual currents. One of these was Drew University in New Jersey.[32] There, as professor of systematic theology, after 1868, and president (1870-72), Randolph Sinks Foster (1820-1903) showed a distinct indifference to authority in religion. It was later said of him that "he would have as soon appealed to the Fathers for the truth of the multiplication table as for the truth of anything depending on reason." But, in 1872 he became a bishop and was therefore devoting himself to administrative duties rather than strictly intellectual activities as the Church faced a period of intellectual transition. James Strong (1822-94), who served as professor of exegetical theology (1868-93), had travelled widely and was well acquainted with the archaeological and literary scholarship of his day. Yet, he presented no problem to conservatives in Methodism, for his biblical position was of the traditional stamp. He believed in the Mosaic authorship of the Pentateuch, the accuracy of the Mosaic account of creation, the view that there was but one Isaiah, and that Paul wrote the Epistle to the Hebrews. But, coming to Drew Seminary in the year of Strong's retirement was a highly trained Orientalist, Robert William Rogers (1864-1930), who had been raised as an Episcopalian in Philadelphia. He accepted whole-heartedly the modern critical view of the Old Testament, but he taught with such consummate tact that he escaped the ecclesiastical censure which was visited by the Methodist Church upon some of its Old Testament scholars.

At Boston University, the transition from the old to the new was facilitated by the administration of William Fairfield Warren, acting president, 1869-73, and president, 1873-1903. Conservative, but convinced of the fundamental soundness of the modern approach to the Bible, he helped develop a faculty who trained Methodist ministers by enlightened scholarship so as to aid the Church in passing with a minimum of stress through the intellectual storms created by the writings of Darwin, Spencer, and the Biblical critics. Naturally, his insistence on academic freedom aroused concern among Old Guard Methodists, and one of the ablest teachers brought to Boston University by Warren was tried for heresy. This was Borden Parke Bowne (1847-1910), philosopher and theologian, who headed the department of philosophy for almost thirty-five years after 1876. He was tried for heretical views by his own New York East Conference but was never really in danger of conviction, and he courageously rose to the defense of his own colleague, Professor Hinckley G. Mitchell, on similar charges.

At Garrett Biblical Institute, Evanston, Illinois, Milton Spencer Terry (1840-1914), who became a department head in 1884, personally went through a development of viewpoint. In 1887 he attended lectures at the University of Berlin and became acquainted with the Higher Criticism. Courageously revising his own ideas, he steadfastly stood for what he had come to believe to be true and valid, but he was therefore the object of much determined opposition within his Church. In this adjustment of thought in the denomination his calmness, clearness, and unfailing Christian charity reaped rich rewards.

Two later leaders of the denomination illustrate the slow transition which was taking place in the denomination. Harris F. Rall, born (1870) in a German Methodist parsonage in Council Bluffs, Iowa, came of deeply devout and pious parents, who were not disturbed by theological controversy. Rall went on to the University of Iowa, then to Yale, Berlin, and Halle. But his faith had never been bound to a dogmatic system, hence he never experienced a severe intellectual crisis.[33] Similarly Albert C. Knudson, born (1873) in a Minnesota parsonage and destined to be Dean of Boston University School of Theology, attended the state University of Minnesota where the emphasis on natural science helped to develop an empirical viewpoint, but where a balance was attained by studies in the humanities and philosophy. Later, studying at Boston University, he was distinctly helped by Bowne and others who endeavored to synthesize the old and the new, and a year in Germany introduced him to the advanced scholarship of the generation.[34]

CHAPTER XIV

GROUPS OF THE THEOLOGICAL LEFT

1. *Universalism*

In the midst of a rising humanitarianism in the late eighteenth century, one avenue of revolt against Calvinistic orthodoxy was Universalism, a doctrine that it is the purpose of God through Jesus Christ to save every member of the human race from sin. This basic Universalist concept had appeared earlier from time to time in Christian thought and had found expression in the views of some people in orthodox circles before 1800.[1] The first church of Universalism in the United States had been organized at Gloucester, Massachusetts (1778) by John Murray, born in England. Later, Hosea Ballou, excommunicated by the Baptists, had joined the Universalists, and a more aggressive policy developed. Thus, Universalism became militant thirty years before Unitarianism asserted itself.[2] By 1800 about thirty-five churches had been established, chiefly in New England, and the movement had developed further, as the Old New England theology lost its grip on much of the population.

Among early Universalists there was the view that sin would reap its reward, hence a term of limited punishment in the future life need not be questioned. Universalism itself, however, yielded to sentimental demands of optimistic thought, and after 1793 a doctrine that received increasing support denied all future punishment. Among New Englanders who sought a "liberal" religion, Unitarianism proved to be to a noticeable degree a Church of the consciously intellectual and socially arrived classes, while Universalism was to a great degree a grass roots, homespun protest against orthodoxy. Hence, after 1865, Universalism continued to be something of a spiritual haven for some religious folk of unorthodox bent, and in 1870 there were in Vermont some sixty Universalist societies in contrast to only four of the Unitarian persuasion.[3] After 1865, with Congregational churches becoming increasingly less Calvinistic in emphasis, Universalism no longer represented so definitely a means of protest against the older faith. Some, indeed, thought that Universalists had come to spend too much time in "knocking" orthodox groups and in taking pains to disjoin themselves from historic Christianity. In some places it was asserted that "easy-going optimists" among Universalists had failed to grasp a fundamental thought of earlier Universalism that each man must work out his own salvation. As a result, in later times they had been very ineffective often in reaching those most desperately needing salvation.

Some Universalist churches, however, continued to appeal to many who found orthodoxy unacceptable. At the Church of the Divine Paternity in New York were found leading parishioners like Horace Greeley and Phineas T. Barnum,[4] as well as other "men whose faces betokened active brains." Perhaps there was some truth in the witticism of Longfellow's brother-in-law, Thomas G. Appleton, who said that Universalists "believed that God was too good to damn them," while Unitarians believed themselves "too good to be damned."

2. *Unitarianism*

For those who revolted against old-time orthodoxy, Unitarianism had early been another avenue of departure from traditionalism. According to Benjamin R. Curtis (famous dissenting United States Supreme Court Justice in the Dred Scott case), this religious development in New England had been "no exotic transplanted from abroad," but a spontaneous, indigenous revolt and protest against Calvinism on the part of "a more cultivated and reasoning generation" which could no longer accept the older theology.[5]

Landmarks in the development of American Unitarianism had been: The renunciation of the doctrine of the Trinity by King's Chapel, Boston (the first Episcopal church in New England) as it became the first Unitarian Church in America (1785); the appointment of Henry Ware to the chair of divinity at Harvard (1805); William Ellery Channing's discussion of Unitarian principles at the installation of Jared Sparks as minister of the Baltimore Unitarian Society (1819); Emerson's departure from the ministry (1832) and his Divinity School Address (1838); and over a period of years the taking over of much church property of older parishes by the Unitarian congregations.[6]

At first, those later calling themselves Unitarians, were relatively conservative, most of them believing that Jesus was "more than man" and that he "literally came from heaven to save" mankind. Others among them rejected the doctrine of the Trinity without formulating a doctrine as to the nature of Jesus and his work, while a third portion believed in the "simple humanity of Christ." For a time, leaders like Andrews Norton had defended the doctrine of "revelation proved by miracles," and such conservative Unitarians believed that in cases of an apparent disagreement between reason and the Bible, the latter must be followed. Later, however, with the development of Biblical criticism and of scientific studies, many like Theodore Parker had come to deny the final authority of the Bible and the reality of external revelation. All Unitarians, however, were apt to differ from orthodox Protestants on four points:

1. The unitarian rather than the trinitarian nature of God.
2. The nature of Christ. During the time of William Henry Channing who died in 1884, most Unitarians were probably Arians, believing that Jesus was more than a man and a Saviour of mankind. Some, however, were Socinians, believing in the simple humanity of Jesus; and all laid the emphasis on his humanity.
3. The nature of man. Renouncing the Calvinistic idea

of the total depravity of man, they stressed the fundamental dignity of man.

4. The doctrine of salvation. All agreed that God aids human effort by allying Himself with reason and conscience.[7]

During the last two-thirds of the nineteenth century Unitarianism moved gradually from fixed beliefs so that to many of the orthodox they seemed to be definitely rationalistic in viewpoint and to have discarded almost completely the idea of revelation.

Oliver Stearns (1807-85), Unitarian theologian, who had been President of Meadville Theological School (1856-63) and then Professor at Harvard Divinity School (1863-78), was perhaps the first theologian in the United States to assert a belief in evolution as a cosmic law (even before Herbert Spencer advocated it), though his own concern was to establish a theory of historical development for Christian thought. Orthodoxy among Unitarians, according to one observer, came to be rather like the "soundness of a legal decision that depends not upon statute but upon the common law."[8] During the later nineteenth century, moreover, the trend of Unitarian teaching (always highly intellectual) moved farther away from the older doctrines. Something of the change may be noted in the preaching of two of the leaders of the Church in the years after 1865. Among conservative Unitarians was the noted Henry W. Bellows, pastor of the First Unitarian Church of New York City after 1839. He frequently surprised his congregation with some theological heresy, and when he emphasized spiritual, as opposed to material values, the term "spiritual" meant largely the influence of the intellect. Yet, Unitarians like Bellows were sometimes disturbed by reports of sermons by other Unitarians such as Octavius B. Frothingham of the Third Unitarian Society of New York (as conservative Unitarians had been distressed by the discourses of Theodore Parker of Boston before his death in 1860). Frothingham was viewed by many as Parker's successor in the leadership of the more

radical Unitarianism. One contemporary who considered
Parker's vital force superior to Frothingham's, believed that
Parker tended to view the older doctrines of orthodoxy as
"pernicious" while Frothingham respected them for the
services they had "rendered to earlier generations." The
same observer believed that Frothingham "had a much larger
bump of reverence and a clearer sense of the continuity of
human thought and of human belief." Yet, Frothingham
moved farther and farther from traditional Christianity, and
by 1867 he found himself outside the bounds of the Unitarian orthodoxy of his day. In *Creed and Conduct* (New
York, 1877), he repudiated ideas of a personal God and
immortality. Even his cousin, Henry Adams, felt that his
faith was that of "skepticism."[9]

Some Unitarians continued to be supernaturalists believing in the miracles and the resurrection of Jesus Christ.
Such was personally the position of the noted Syracuse, New
York pastor, Samuel J. May.[10] Even the well-known Unitarian, James Freeman Clarke, who seemed to eliminate the
dogmatic and the miraculous from religious faith, confided
to Julia Ward Howe that he personally believed in the
Resurrection of Christ and felt that something had happened
on the first Easter morn that could not be explained in a
merely rational way.[11]

Unitarianism was at its best far from merely a negation
of orthodoxy. Some Unitarian clergymen who valued their
denominational affiliation largely because of the freedom of
its fellowship served their congregations with glowing faith
and constructive resourcefulness. There were some mystics
among them, including Edmund Hamilton Sears (1810-76),
pastor at Weston, Massachusetts from 1866 to 1874. Even
today he is remembered throughout Protestantism for his
beautiful hymns, "Calm on the Listening Ears of Night"
and "It Came Upon a Midnight Clear." Similarly, Frederick
Lucius Hosmer (1840-1929), associated with the church at
Northboro, Massachusetts (1869-72), became, during the
course of a long life, the author of more than thirty hymns,

many of which are found in Protestant hymnals of the present day. The gifted Rev. Edward Everett Hale, a Unitarian
who served as pastor of South Congregational Church, Boston from 1856 to 1909 believed that religious faith came
through revelation transmitted by the Church. According to
his biographer, his stirring faith was revealed in sermons
which were "like a beautiful and perfect sphere, perhaps of
crystal, of which every part demands every other part."[12]

Likewise, among others in the Boston area was Cyrus
Augustus Bartol (1813-1900), who succeeded James Russell
Lowell's father as pastor of West Church, serving from 1837
to 1889. He was a man who radiated faith, hope, and love,
and it was said that his "mind was like a mint continually
striking off bright coins of thought and speech."

Certainly, many found faith and courage in the sermons
of such a Unitarian preacher as the English born Robert
Collyer (1823-1912) who (born as Anglican and for a time
a Methodist) was pastor of the Unitarian church in Chicago
(1859-1879) and the Church of the Messiah, New York
(1879-1903). He invariably preached on the basic themes of
personal religious life, using English "of Anglo-Saxon purity"
and expressing with his whole personality the conviction,
sweetness, and light which illuminated his character.

Unitarianism with its highly intellectual approach was
influential far beyond what its numbers might have indicated. Jefferson had written in 1822: "I trust that there is
not a *young man* now living in the United States who will
not die a Unitarian."[13] But the faith of Unitarianism made
little progress outside of New England, and even in Connecticut it had few adherents. In the area South of the Poto-
mac it was feeble indeed. In 1865, William Henry Channing
had left the pastorate of the First Unitarian Church of Washington, D. C., commenting that "an angel could not have
drawn an audience to the dreary, mildewed, tumbledown
edifice of the Unitarian society."[14]

In New England itself, as has been suggested, there were
numerous illustrious preachers, some of whom had left more

orthodox bodies. These included Samuel M. Crothers (1857-1927) who had studied for the Presbyterian ministry, had become a Unitarian clergyman (1882), and after 1894 served as distinguished pastor of the First Parish Church, Cambridge. The renowned Julia Ward Howe, author of the "Battle Hymn of the Republic," was frequently a stimulating preacher at Unitarian services.

Justin S. Morrill, Vermont Senator and sponsor of the significant Morrill Act, had gone through a liberalizing of his faith and had emerged a Unitarian.[15] Thomas B. Reed, Republican leader and known as "Czar Reed," had planned to become a Congregational minister but had later experienced a change in religious views and, following his death he was buried from the State Street Unitarian Church, Portland, Maine.[16] Hannibal Hamlin (1809-91), Vice President, United States Senator, and Minister to Spain, was a constant church attendant and for some years President of the Unitarian Society of Maine.[17] Two distinguished statesmen at a time when public morals were at low ebb were the incorruptible Ebenezer R. Hoar (1816-1895), Congressman from Massachusetts and United States Attorney-General, and his brother, Senator George Frisbie Hoar (1826-1904), both of whom were leaders in Unitarian circles.

In some Middle Western cities Unitarian circles included men like Frederic Huidekoper (1817-92) whose Holland-born father had revolted against Calvinism. The son had enjoyed a thorough education and was long time professor of theology at Meadville Theological Seminary in Pennsylvania. Also a prominent Unitarian layman was the Cincinnatian, Alphonso Taft (1810-91), judge, secretary of war, attorney general and diplomat. In Wisconsin, where Unitarians were few in number, Robert M. La Follette, Sr. and his liberal wife were married by a Unitarian minister.[18] In Indiana, the noted reformer, George W. Julian, had early identified himself with the radical wing of Unitarianism, demanding absolute freedom in religious thought.[19]

But, the struggle of faith with many Unitarians was not

over beliefs which seemed outmoded but rather to attain a satisfying faith strong enough for life's vicissitudes. Thus, we have seen that many New England families, including the parents of Phillips Brooks had left Unitarianism for the Episcopal Church. The same had been the case of Frederick Dan Huntington (1819-1904) Unitarian clergyman who later became Protestant Episcopal Bishop of Central New York. United States Supreme Court Justice Benjamin R. Curtis left the Unitarian Church and became an Episcopalian.[20] Robert Trent Paine (1835-1910), noted Boston philanthropist, in 1870 changed from Unitarianism to Episcopalianism.

William Edward Huntington (1844-1930), nephew of Frederick Dan (mentioned above) became a Methodist, and long served as Dean and, after the turn of the century, as President of Boston University. Henry Boynton Smith (1815-77), raised a Unitarian, eventually became an acknowledged intellectual leader in Presbyterian circles.

Conservative Unitarians had looked upon themselves as definitely within the Christian fold, but when a National Conference was organized in 1867, there were those like Francis E. Abbot (1836-1903) who would not subscribe to the constitution of the group which referred to its members as "disciples of the Lord Jesus Christ," and the result was the establishment of the Free Religious Association. With Abbot went men like Emerson, Thomas W. Higginson, Rev. O. B. Frothingham, and Rev. William J. Potter, the last-mentioned for more than thirty years a vigorous pastor at New Bedford. Thus, a group was definitely discarding the distinctive doctrinal attributes of Christianity, and within the Unitarian churches some thought that a vigorous religious faith was often emasculated by a trend toward humanism and by the old New England "dissidence of dissent." At any rate, Jenkin Lloyd Jones (1843-1918) long pastor of All Souls Church, Chicago, devised as a bond of union for his congregation the statement: "We join ourselves together in the interest of Morality and Religion as interpreted by the growing thought and purest lives of Humanity, hoping thereby to bear one another's burdens and to promote Truth, Righteousness and Love in the World."

As early as 1867, Harvard professor Charles Eliot Norton, whose father had been a pillar of Unitarianism, stated that, as an organization, Unitarianism held no "worth and interest" for him. Certainly there was no zeal sufficient for the mere preservation of a religious body in his further statement that "the deepest religious thought, the wisest religious life" was outside of Unitarianism and outside the limits of any churches.[21]

The famous Hungarian leader, Louis Kossuth, still alive in 1884, wrote at that time, "The Unitarians are the most educated men in America, and as to morality also they are excellent." Therefore, he could not understand why they were losing ground in America. One answer was that other denominations had gradually been assimilating some of the liberalism of Unitarianism. But one who had embraced Unitarianism as a boy of fourteen found that its leaders, journals, and organizations faced "nowhere in particular, and stood for nothing definite and thorough and complete." To him, Unitarianism seemed to waver between its tradition and its destiny, and he thought that, at its best, it attempts no final definitions of Truth, sees Christ only as a simple man however divine in the reach of his mind to God, and the Bible as only imperfect literature.

Thus, Unitarianism, to many who were not of conservative stamp, seemed hardly to have a Gospel for a troubled world. Rev. Frederic Henry Hedge (1805-1890), Unitarian minister and professor at Harvard Divinity, was personally disturbed by the audacities of western Unitarians in their departure from tradition. Yet, he himself was complacently doubting personal immortality, important as it was to traditional Christian teaching. Certainly it was less than a clarion call to a vital faith expressed by John D. Long, then Speaker of the Massachusetts House of Representatives and later

Secretary of the Navy.[22] In addressing the Unitarian Annual
Festival in Boston in 1876, he said:

> I take it that any man is a Unitarian who believes
> in New England, in good morals, in liberal culture, in
> Channing for his divine and Whittier for his poet, in
> the duty of every citizen to purify politics and attend
> the primary meetings, and in the sacred right of bolt-
> ing. . . .

And Senator George F. Hoar, in addressing the National
Unitarian Conference in Washington in October 1899,
spoke eloquently but hardly with a soul-compelling message
when he said that Unitarianism cannot be defined, but Unitarians "are men and women for whom Faith, Hope, and
Charity forever abide; to whom Judea's news are still glad
tidings; who believe that one day Jesus Christ came to this
earth, bearing a Divine Message and giving a Divine example."[23]

From an "easy-going Unitarianism" in which Moorfield
Storey, noted Massachusetts liberal said he had been nurtured, it was for him, as for others we have noted, but a
step to a kind of humanitarianism into which he carried
"many serviceable standards" of his earlier faith and which
took the place of a "purely religious faith."[24] Many, perhaps, were like Ezra Cornell, founder of Cornell University,
who had little faith in dogma but regularly attended the
Unitarian Church and found satisfaction in frequently quoting from Alexander Pope's "Universal Prayer":

> Teach me to feel another's woe,
>   To hide the fault I see;
> The mercy I to others show,
>   That mercy show to me.[25]

Those who forsook the orthodoxy of their fathers often
felt a certain emancipation from what they had come to look

upon as outworn traditions. But, at times there was a sense
of bewilderment and even despair. The noted poet, James
Russell Lowell, indeed was an outstanding example of the
spiritual uncertainty of the times. His father had been a
liberal New England clergyman, but the son had early
broken with the Church as an institution. Since no creed
satisfied him, he was rather inclined toward the religious
faith of his father, but his mother had been an Episcopalian,
and he wrote in 1875, that although not much of a churchgoer, occasionally he attended Episcopalian services.[26] His
own private letters show that he was constantly vexed by
doubts as to the Providence of God, the divinity of Christ,
and the immortality of his soul. Since he had discarded the
Church and the Bible as basic standards for religious truth,
reason, science, and feeling remained as possible guides to
spiritual reality.[27] But, when he turned to reason he found
no sure answer to his quest, and he confessed in 1876 that
he was resolutely shutting his eyes in certain speculative
directions. Later, in 1879 he declared that science seems
like a "poor substitute for the Rock of Ages," by which he
meant those "higher instincts" which had given mankind
a solid foundation "under their feet in all weathers."[28]
Hence, he sought a religious criterion in his feelings, as he
found "solace in certain intimations that seem to me from
a region higher than my reason." But, feelings are change-
able, and his moods were not conducive to a stable intellectual basis for his faith.

Yet, a poet must have faith, and though God for him
seems to have been "reduced to a figure of speech, to a useful symbol," the moralist in him preached with the fervor
of his Puritan forefathers to his contemporaries, and a
Catholic teacher tells us that many Catholic priests have
found consolation in his poetic messages.

Intellectually Lowell could not accept much of traditional Christianity, but practically he could not live without
the spiritual foundation which it had provided. Hence, in
a nostalgic glance backward toward the certainty of his

Puritan ancestors, he confessed that as he grew older, he had "a strong lurch towards Calvinism (in some of its doctrines)."

Edward Rowland Sill (1841-87), poet and professor at the University of California, had been a student at Harvard Divinity School (1867) but came to look upon the Church as "a great fraud and nuisance." His was the deeply personal tragedy of one who entertained skepticism concerning the validity of Christianity, yet needed the assurance of a vital faith. Thus, he was "one of the authentic voices of the age's malady." Likewise, William Mackintire Salter (son of Rev. William Salter, who had been a member of the famous Andover band of pioneer home missionaries to Iowa) [29] studied theology at Yale, only to find that article after article of his former faith became clouded with uncertainty. Later (1873), he entered Harvard Divinity School in the hope that he might hold to enough of a creed to be a Unitarian minister, if not an orthodox one. Eventually, he became a leader in the Ethical Culture Society in Chicago and Philadelphia.

3. *The Ethical Culture Society*

The Ethical Culture Society itself was the result of the transition in the faith of the son of an influential New York rabbi. Felix Adler, whose father was the religious leader of Temple Emanu-El, New York City (sometimes called "America's Cathedral Synagogue"), had gone to Germany to study to be a Reform rabbi. There, however, the liberal religious traditions of his youth had felt the impact of historical scholarship, secular philosophy, economic questioning, and ideas of nationalism. Having secured his Ph.D. in Germany, he returned to New York and was invited to deliver a sermon from his father's pulpit. The discourse clearly revealed to the congregation and to the preacher of the occasion that he could not conscientiously serve as their rabbi. Naturally the father was keenly disappointed that his brilliant son could not succeed him.[30] For a time (1874-76) the younger Adler taught Oriental languages and literature at Cornell University, but this left his spiritual zeal unsatisfied.

He became interested in the Free Religious Association which had been largely inspired by New England Transcendentalism, but he sought more than a merely rationalistic emancipation from traditional religion in what he hoped would be a positive, practical approach to the problems of life.

In the meantime he had led a group of New York people of Jewish or Christian background in the formation of the Ethical Culture Society (1876), "the new religion of morality, whose God was The Good, whose church was the universe, whose heaven was here on earth and not in the clouds." At the same time he had sought to cooperate with the Free Religious Association.

Adler was an agnostic who could hold none of the usual theistic assumptions as essential to religion, but the Free Religious Association accepted all who felt the compulsion of an inward ethical imperative, and he served as President, 1879-82. When he could not turn the Association from involved discussion to a commitment to a policy of good deeds and social reform as an antidote for skepticism, he resigned the Presidency of the Association.[31]

Earlier in his career Adler had organized a group of young men of his own age into "A Union for the Higher Life," based on three tacit principles: (1) Sex purity; (2) The idea of using the surplus of one's own income, above genuine personal needs, for elevating the working class; (3) Continuing intellectual development. The Ethical Culture Society now sought to lead similarly minded men and women, whether theists or agnostics, into a vital fellowship.[32]

The Ethical Culture Society proceeded on the basis that the good life is possible without the previous acceptance of a creed. Bound together by an emphasis on "righteousness," which Adler said was written in the Society's "Holy of Holies," the members were committed only to the promotion of right living. Adler urged, "Try to live your life in such a way that other people will live their lives better."

For members of the Society, traditional religious practices were largely abandoned. The Society sought "to teach the supremacy of moral ends above all other human ends and interests," holding that the moral law has "an immediate authority not contingent on the truth of religious beliefs or of philosophical theories." It was called the "Ethical" rather than the "Moral" Culture Society, however, because an effort was made to understand the underlying principles of human relations and to develop powers of discrimination in ethical conduct rather than merely to obey accepted rules of morality.[33]

Affiliated organizations were established in Chicago, St. Louis, Philadelphia, Brooklyn, and Boston, as well as in several foreign cities, as some sensitive souls believed that they could not honestly endorse the affirmations even of liberal Unitarianism. One such individual, as we have seen, was William M. Salter.[34] Another was S. Burns Weston, a graduate of Antioch College and Harvard Divinity School who, as pastor of the Unitarian Church at Leicester, Massachusetts, had been deemed heretical and had been dropped from his pastorate. Thereafter, he studied for two years at the University of Berlin before undertaking the leadership of the Society in Philadelphia, organized in 1885.

Another outstanding leader was Walter L. Sheldon, who served for many years beginning in 1886, as head of the Society in St. Louis. Sheldon confessed that he was a deeply religious person who had been educated in the ways of the orthodox but had gradually abandoned many of the traditional views. The Ethical Culture movement had "met the cravings" of his religious nature and had given him "something to live for and believe in."[35] Sheldon was concerned "not only with conduct, but with the soul whence conduct springs and on which it reacts." He believed that Ethical

Culture people were "called upon to discover and develop methods for cultivating the spiritual self, the soul we all believe in when divested of its metaphysical trappings." Accordingly, Sheldon himself sought to disseminate "Methods for Spiritual Self-Culture," which included meditative attention to a "Bible" which was not limited to the Books of Sacred Scripture.

The influence of the Society far transcended its numerical strength. In New York its first president was Joseph Seligman, who because of his wealth, social position, and character was able to contribute distinction to the early development of the movement. In the branch at Philadelphia, Joseph Fels, who was of a Jewish immigrant family and had prospered in the soap industry, served for a number of years as trustee of the local Society. At the same time he was a sponsor of numerous worthy causes, as he associated with those who "viewed mankind's future optimistically with overtones of utopianism."[36] He ultimately became influential in the Single Tax movement of Henry George.

For some, the attractiveness of the movement was based in part on the belief that traditional religion seemed somewhat irrational in a world of science and that a faith in Providence made men indolent, as they were prone to rely upon God to do things for them.[37] Another element of attractiveness of the Society was the opportunity it gave to prosperous Jews to "escape the odium of the Jewish badge and the Jewish name" without formally renouncing Judaism.[38]

Adler himself was a man of vigorous enthusiasm, and his faith in righteousness is eloquently expressed in the famous hymn, "Hail the Glorious, Golden City" (1878), which he composed and which is often used in Protestant churches set to the music of Franz Haydn's "Austrian Hymn." A distinguished professor of philosophy at the University of Michigan later testified that Adler's *Creed and Deed* (1877) had fortified him in the youthful crisis of his life and had permanently affected him.[39] The movement has resulted, moreover, in significant accomplishments in settlement work and social reform.[40]

Adler had the fire of an ancient Hebrew prophet but, unlike such a prophet, he meditated perhaps excessively, and qualified and philosophized in true scholarly fashion. Thus, his ethical imperative might, and did, convince men. Yet, this ethical emphasis seemed lacking in power to stir and move other than the rather exceptional individual. Correctly sensing that modern man could less frequently be influenced to live on a spiritual plane without intellectual consent than had been the case in previous generations, he seemingly did not wholly realize that sustained action generally depends on "a passion and a power transcending the limitations of the mind."[41]

Hence, one critic has found in the movement "a juicelessness, a love of humanity rather than man, a lack of the warmth of unreflecting love about it, which, despite its manifold good works and its manifest worth, alienate and repel rather than draw and win men to it." The liberalism of the movement, moreover, was too dogmatic for some members. When Adler maintained that certain basic questions had been settled in ethics, such as that virtue is better than vice, a minority withdrew, holding that a spirit of inquiry rather than affirmation must be followed. The offshoot organization became known as the Fellowship for Ethical Research.

Understandably, for most Americans the "old altars" of the time-honored churches continued to have far greater appeal, and the federal census of 1890 had reported only four Ethical Culture Society branches with 1064 members in all.[42]

4. *Free Thought*

The line of demarcation between the beliefs of many people found in Unitarian and other liberal churches and those in avowedly secularly-minded free-thinking organizations was often difficult to determine. Indeed, there existed here a "twilight zone," and individual affiliation was frequently determined by less than rigidly logical considerations. Few orthodox clergymen, moreover, approached the ethical intensity and moral fervor usually associated with a religious prophet as did the agnostic, Felix Adler of the Ethical Culture Society. The devotion to traditional forms, furthermore, was well illustrated by the fact that Adler himself found that at funeral services for members of the Ethical Culture Society, far from infrequent were requests for a recitation of the Kaddish, the time-honored Jewish prayer for the dead.[43]

Thus, among many religious liberals there was a deep-seated devotion to some of the traditions and forms of historic organizations. The tensions between speculative freedom and a devotion to time-honored landmarks of faith had for many years been acute within Unitarianism. Theodore Parker in spite of his seemingly radical views had successfully struggled to retain his Unitarian connections, but by 1865 Henry W. Bellows of New York and others had sought a national Unitarian organization embracing disciples of "the Lord Jesus Christ," dedicated to the furtherance of His kingdom.[44] Younger rationalists in Unitarian circles had sought an empirical faith with a universal appeal to include those who did not acknowledge Jesus as their Saviour. As the more orthodox views had prevailed, Octavius B. Frothingham persuaded his Third Unitarian Society of New York to change its name to the Independent Liberal Church, and Francis E. Abbot of Dover, New Hampshire began to move more decisively toward a point of view which gave full sway to private judgment and which prompted him in 1868 to realize that he could no longer minister to a congregation which was avowedly "Christian."[45]

Already, in 1866, with the organization of "The National Conference of Unitarian and other Christian Churches" at Syracuse, New York, Abbot had been convinced that Unitarianism had abandoned the principle of freedom and that thereafter Christianity and freedom must be uncompromising foes. After preliminary conferences, a public meeting in Boston, attended by left-wing Unitarians, progressive Universalists, Spiritualists, Quakers, free religionists, Jews, Transcendentalists, and scientific theists, led to the formation of The Free Religious Association in May 1867. Its objects were "to promote the interests of pure religion, to encourage the scientific study of theology, and to increase fellowship in the spirit." One of the sessions had been closed with a speech of endorsement by Ralph Waldo Emerson.

Practically, the functioning of the organization soon revealed a basic contradiction. Some members like Abbot wanted to test theological doctrines "scientifically" and then promote them with ardent zeal. Others held that religion must find sanction only in the mind and heart of the individual. For the latter, any pronouncements of scientific theism were wholly unacceptable.

The founders of the Association were all theists, but in 1872 an amendment to the constitution of the organization specifically renounced any "test of speculative opinion or belief" for membership. This paved the way for affiliation with the Association of Felix Adler and Benjamin F. Underwood, two of the most noted non-theists of the period.

By 1885 Underwood was insisting that an Association really free could not serve, as the Constitution provided, for the promotion of "the practical interests of pure religion." As a "materialist" he found that he had different conceptions of such "practical interests" than did humanistic theists. The result was that the constitution of the Association was altered in 1886 to meet this objection, and the Association became thereafter virtually "a debating society."

In general, the Free Religious Association was made up of those who found in genuine religion the ennoblement of man's life, regardless of theoretical or "theological" presuppositions. Most members disagreed with those secularists who deemed that positive knowledge made religious faith unnecessary, but they asserted that Christianity was no longer adequate intellectually or morally. In the quest for a satisfactory faith, absolute freedom must be permitted the individual. One of the Free Association leaders, John W. Chadwick, held that all truths were to be found by observation, experiment, and reflection. Generally, members of the Free Religious movement agreed in an emphasis on reason, natural law, the basic similarities of the many historic faiths, evolutionary progress, and faith in humanity. They were not agreed, however, upon the existence of God, and if Deity exists, whether in personal or impersonal form. They also found no unanimity of opinion on the question of personal immortality and on how far experimentalism in ethics meant the hasty modification of traditional moral sanctions. They failed to agree, furthermore, on the question of whether local societies ought to be formed after the manner of churches.

A mainstay of the organization, William J. Potter, who served as secretary for fifteen years, continued as pastor of the First Congregational Society of New Bedford, Massachusetts until his death in 1893, although he refused to administer communion and was dropped from the list of ministers in the Unitarian Year Book after 1867. Hence, although the Free Religious Association was influential in calling attention to the need for a greater reasonableness and a greater spirit of humanity in organized religion and to the need for the linking of religion with social reform, it proved to be a veritable "voice without a hand."[46] By the end of the century the movement had largely spent its force.

Radical as the Free Religious Association seemed to many of the orthodox, a present day scholar has termed it "Conservative Freethought," for its founders were chiefly discontented liberal churchmen who had sought to establish a "scientific theism."[47] Some of its leaders had been highly skeptical of Auguste Comte's positivism which "made mankind the only God man can know."[48] Some, moreover, though radical in their own views, looked upon the popular leader of free thought, Robert Ingersoll, as untutored in scientific and philosophical matters and as old-fashioned in basing his criticism of Christianity on the older concepts of Voltaire and Paine rather than those of Darwin and Spencer.

Among German-Americans there were religious liberals who sought unorthodox church life in organizations called *Freie Gemeinde,* but radical German leaders had sought to emancipate their fellow German-Americans from all traditional religion in freethinking groups, *Freimännervereine.*[49]

On the national scene there were avowed secularists, moreover, who had founded the National Liberal League in 1876 (called after 1884, the American Secular Union) with the aim of stripping the religious connotation from American life and thought.[50] Other groups likewise wished to decimate the forces of traditional religious life.[51]

David Goodman Croly (1829-89), Irish-born editor of the New York *World* (1862-72), was one of the chief advocates of Auguste Comte's "Positivism" as a substitute for orthodox religion. D. M. Bennett of Paris, Illinois published the free thinking *The Truth Seeker* from 1873 until his death in 1883, and as an outspoken atheist did much lecturing. Especially the terror of the churches was Benjamin F. Underwood (1839-1914) who, denying even the immanence of God, lectured from Maine to California five or six times a week for nine months of the year on "The Positive Side of Liberal Thought," "What Free Thought Gives Us in Place of the Creeds," and kindred topics.[52] Unlike Ingersoll he was of the logical rather than the rhetorical type and was possessed of no little philosophic acumen, as something of an orthodox materialist. He challenged the clergy of the large cities to meet him in public debate (three to thirty meetings). Only the boldest of the clergy, however, ventured to oppose his forensic skill. Although a member of the Free Religious Association, he was "religious" only in the sense that he sought a naturalistic basis for humanitarian morality.

James Parton (1822-91) who has been called the "Father

of Modern Biography" because of his lives of Burr, Jackson, Franklin, Jefferson and Voltaire, and who was also a leading lecturer and essayist, was likewise an aggressive free thinker.[53] He was associated with Abbot, Frothingham, and others in the Free Religious Association which had a certain respectability in conventional circles, but he moved toward more radical associations like the Society of Humanity, the National Liberal League, and the Free Thinkers Society. At a convention of the last mentioned organization in 1878, Parton defined religion as falling in love with duty, loving human welfare, and practicing the homely moralities. Factionalism developed among the societies, and to some degree there was involvement in opposition to the Comstock Crusade against obscenity in the mails.

The popular spokesman for the Free Thought movement, however, was Robert G. Ingersoll. With great personal charm, unquestioned moral rectitude, and a "gift of silver oratory," he commanded huge fees as capacity crowds came to hear spell-binding lectures on themes like "The Gods," "Why I am an Agnostic," or "Superstition." He lectured in every state of the Union except North Carolina and Mississippi. One New York newspaper reported that he wiped the stage "with the Christian religion, tore the Bible into shreds and shook his fist in the face of the Creator in a way that delighted a large and seemingly intelligent audience and kept it alternately laughing and applauding for upward of two hours." After an Ingersoll lecture in Utica, New York, seventeen clergymen there devoted sermons to him.[54]

Under the changing currents of the times men like Samuel Calvin Tate Dodd (1836-1907), leading American lawyer, who had had a strict Presbyterian boyhood and who provided the legal acumen for the organization of the Standard Oil Trust (1882) became a reverent free thinker. Oliver Perry Morton (1823-77), governor and senator from Indiana, who had had a very orthodox Presbyterian boyhood, became known for very heterodox views. Joseph Cannon (1836-1926), long time speaker of the national House

of Representatives after 1901, had been born a Quaker, but
in adult life he gave up his connection with the Society of
Friends, and never afterwards was he a church member.[55]

Gerrit Smith (1797-1874), long time reformer of New
York state, had been a Presbyterian, and while continuing
to aspire "to be perfect after the standard set up in the New
Testament" had come to be heterodox and rationalistic
in his intellectual views.[56] The fiery William Lloyd Garrison
in antebellum days had, as he thought, freed himself from
a belief in the supernatural sanction of the Bible and in
the "divine nature and atoning mission of Jesus." Yet, he had
continued to use the Bible "as a moral engine" and had
urged the reading of it on his children. He also, according
to Mrs. Elizabeth Cady Stanton, suffrage leader, had early
helped to free her from "the darkness and gloom of a false
theology."[57] During the period other reformers like Susan
B. Anthony and Matilda Joslyn Gage became known for
their agnostic views, and the freethinking views of Thomas
A. Edison, David Starr Jordan, Mark Twain, and Andrew
Carnegie received much attention.[58]

There were some who believed that the Church had out-
lived its usefulness and that ideological impulses should
now find expression outside of organized religion. Professor
Charles E. Norton (1827-1908), whose father had been a
kind of "Unitarian Pope," had long been professor of art
and literature at Harvard. He had come to "an open profession of free thinking, believing God and immortality to
be inconceivable" but that "the motives which impel an
intelligent man . . . to virtuous conduct, are the strongest
which can be addressed to a human being, because they appeal directly to the highest qualities of his human nature."[59]

Thus, in the intellectual trends of the period, liberal Unitarianism and Universalism had felt the impact of more
radical dissent, and finally, even more extreme leaders
arrived at a position which denied both God and the usefulness of organized religion.

Chapter XV

QUESTIONINGS WITHIN JUDAISM

Those who had been raised in the traditions of the Jewish faith found that the "acids of modernity" were having a dissolving effect upon the traditional standards of that religious community, and some tendency to revert to more orthodox viewpoints was noted when the effects of the trend became evident. Here, the problem had not been primarily theological, but questions of Biblical criticism had aroused differing opinions concerning previously accepted norms. An intimate connection, moreover, between Jewish traditions and religious patterns had meant that when traditional customs were sacrificed to the devastating demands of modern urban Americanization, the vitality of religious concepts was immeasurably weakened.

Long before the American Civil War, certain Jewish congregations had departed from the strict observances of their fathers, establishing "Reform" synagogues which endeavored to interpret Judaism by modifying ancient practices to conform to modern intellectual and cultural standards.[1] As early as 1824 a Reform Jewish congregation had been organized in Charleston, South Carolina. The movement had been accelerated by the migration of large numbers of German Jews, many of whom had been trained in the universities of the Old World.

One of the foremost leaders of this movement was Bohemian-born Isaac Mayer Wise (1819-1900), rabbi in Albany (1846-54) and in Cincinnati (1854-1900). In the latter city he established the *American Israelite,* and in 1875 helped found Hebrew Union College (Reform) which graduated the first rabbis ever to be consecrated in America. In New

York City, Samuel Adler (1809-1891), German-born rabbi of the congregation Emanu-El, revised the Reform prayer book and otherwise sought the adaptation of his people's religious life to American ways. In the same city, Bavarian-born David Einhorn (1809-79), became rabbi of a Reform congregation which was merged (1874) with an orthodox one to become the important congregation Beth-El. During Einhorn's lifetime he was undoubtedly the leading Reform theologian in the United States.

Einhorn's son-in-law, Kaufman Kohler (1843-1926) also a native of Bavaria, became his successor at Temple Beth-El. Earlier, in Chicago Kohler had introduced Sunday services to supplement those of Saturday evening, and the same practice was followed in New York, beginning in 1879.

The innovations of Reform Judaism of course diminished the distinctiveness of Judaism as a faith, and in the opinion of many, impoverished it to a disastrous degree.[2] The fears of many that Reform Judaism might lead away from a definite Jewish faith were confirmed in the case of Felix Adler (1851-1933), son of the noted Reform rabbi. The younger Adler, in connection with others of Jewish or Christian background, as we have seen, founded the humanistic Society for Ethical Culture in New York City (1876).

Marcus Jastrow (1829-1903), German-born rabbi in Philadelphia after 1866, engaged in an unremitting struggle against what he considered the occidentalizing of the historic faith. Similarly, Hungarian-born Alexander Kohut (1842-94), upon coming to the United States in 1885, was astounded by what he deemed the extreme vagaries of the Reform movement. Almost at once he launched into a series of sermons on "The Ethics of the Fathers," insisting that the Mosaic-rabbinical tradition was essential and that extravagant "reform" meant religious "suicide." These views received a reply from Kohler in a series of lectures (1885) published as *Backwards or Forwards*. Kohut's friends, however, believed that traditional Judaism was at stake, and the orthodox Jewish Theological Seminary of America was established (1887). Kohler's supporters, on the other hand, held the Pittsburgh Conference and adopted a Pittsburgh Platform (1885) as a statement of Reform principles.[3]

For a time, however, some Reform rabbis felt that too extreme a departure from tradition would lead to atheism and result in a generation of Jews to whom the Jewish heritage would be no more meaningful than that "of the Hindus." Such essentially was the viewpoint of Bernard Felsenthal (1822-1908), rabbi of Zion congregation (Reform), Chicago, and Isidor Kalisch (1816-1886) who had served as rabbi of numerous Reform organizations.

Another rabbi, Solomon Schindler (1842-1915) who had really introduced Reform Judaism to New England through a Boston congregation (1874) long afterwards preached a famous sermon, "Mistakes I Have Made," in which he expressed regret for some of his more radical views within Judaism.

Between the Scylla of extreme Orthodox rigidity and the Charybdis of a radical Reform spirit, some rabbis and their congregations followed a Conservative or middle course, as a means of compromise between the older and younger elements in a synagogue, and "Conservative" congregations were the result. Among leaders of such congregations were Benjamin Szold (1829-1902), Hungarian-born rabbi in Baltimore (1859-92), and Aaron Wise (1844-1896), German-born rabbi (1875-96) at the influential Temple Rodeph Sholom, New York City.[4]

Even Felix Adler who had left the Reform Jewish faith had found a haven in the Ethical Culture Movement. Some, however, of both Orthodox and more liberal Jewish backgrounds, were influenced by trends of modern thought to embrace a wholly secular position in their alienation from religious organizations of even the most untraditional type. Thus, Morris R. Cohen, born and raised in an orthodox

Jewish family in Russia, as a youth in New York City became interested in the Socialist Labor Party, and reading in
economics and philosophy led to changed viewpoints which
caused him to reject supernaturalism and to become a materialist of the type of Hobbes and Spinoza.[5]

CHAPTER XVI

NEW APPROACHES THROUGH MYSTICISM
AND IDEALISM.

1. *Swedenborgianism*

A type of mysticism which involved rather esoteric doctrines was the expression of the teachings of Emmanuel Swedenborg, Swedish mystic-philosopher of the eighteenth century. Jacob Duché (1738-1798), Anglican minister who was a rector of Christ Church, Philadelphia, and chaplain of the Continental Congress, in his latter days became a convert to the faith. After the War of 1812 some Harvard students had become interested in the doctrines, and by 1823 societies of what came to be called "The Church of the New Jerusalem" had been organized in Baltimore, Philadelphia, Cincinnati, New York, and Boston.[1] Its appeal was related to a rather abstruse philosophy (based in part on the "law of correspondence," every natural object being the expression of a spiritual cause) so that its following was always severely limited numerically, yet during a time of religious readjustments it was a bulwark for a number of unusual Americans.

John Bigelow, political leader and minister to France, had reacted strongly against the Calvinistic God of his Presbyterian boyhood and against the Episcopal faith which permeated the Trinity College (Connecticut) life of some of his college career.[2] He had become an agnostic, but from 1854 on, during a period of almost sixty years until his death in 1911, he was so intensely influenced by "Biblical standards of faith and conduct along with Swedenborg's interpretation of them" that his life can only be understood by bearing in mind "the religious exercises to which he devoted himself regularly."

New England, ever receptive to changing intellectual currents, had more than an average number of Swedenborgian enthusiasts. The largest church of the faith, indeed, was at Boston, where James Reed (1834-1921) served as assistant pastor and then pastor from 1860 to 1919, firm in the belief that Swedenborgian doctrines contained the truth by which humanity might be guided to a new era. Theophilus Parsons (1797-1882), long professor at Harvard Law School, was an active member of the "New Church."

Henry James, Sr. (1811-1882) born in a strict Presbyterian family had reacted strongly against orthodox religion and had found solace and inspiration in the writings of Swedenborg. He never became a doctrinaire Swedenborgian, but he found in this interpretation of Christianity the framework and method for his thought and writings, as in *The Secret of Swedenborg, being an Elucidation of his Doctrine of the Divine Natural Humanity* (1869).[3]

William James, the philosopher and psychologist, was profoundedly influenced by his father's attitude toward religion, although he did not share at all his father's enthusiasm for the Swedenborgian approach. Yet, his sympathy for his father's views may have increased somewhat as he grew older.[4] Both were alike in that they were vitally interested in religion but had no enthusiasm for organized church life. The older James had so revolted against the ministration of the churches that he proposed before his death that the clergyman officiating at his burial should say only that here was a man who all through his life had believed "that the ceremonies attending birth, marriage and death were all damned nonsense." But even a liberal Unitarian clergyman would not proceed with such directions.[5]

Robertson James, unfortunate brother of the famous philosopher and of the famous novelist, was given to moody depression, and then overindulgence in alcohol. In his personal tragedy he found "a measure of peace and amendment" in Swedenborgianism. Yet, eventually he concluded that this mysticism could not be satisfying to more than a very few, and he developed a serious interest in the appeal of Catholicism.[6]

Sometimes it seems to have been but a step from Swedenborgian mysticism to Spiritualism. Andrew Jackson Davis (1826-1910), who was to give to modern Spiritualism the first formulation of its underlying principles and much of its phraseology, believed that Swedenborg guided his life personally from the time when he was twenty-one.

2. Spiritualism

During the Civil War Period and the developing industrial expansion thereafter, some people, not always within the organized churches, found solace from the personal loss of a beloved relative in the War or relief from the seeming stark materialism of the time through Spiritualism. The movement in America had arisen near Rochester, New York, under the leadership of Margaret Fox and her sister, Kate. It arose, as traditional anthropomorphism, with its vivid ideas of beings in the world beyond, tended to yield to vaguer concepts of reality transcending the material world. Especially those bereaved sought assurance of life persisting beyond the grave. In Washington, D.C., Joshua R. Giddings, vigorous anti-slavery Congressman from Ohio. had attended Spiritualist meetings with keen interest.[7] Several of the socially prominent literary groups at Hartford, Connecticut, were among those who developed unusual concern for psychical activity. After 1887, Isabella Beecher Hooker (half-sister of Henry Ward Beecher) and her husband left Park Street Congregational Church, Hartford, and for Isabella Spiritualism became a definite obsession. In 1876-7, Isabella had come to believe that within a year she would be summoned to the Presidency of a matriarchal government which would spread from the United States throughout the world and under her guidance be merged

with the Kingdom of Jesus Christ in a great millennial period.[8] In 1885, she drew up a general confession of her
faith. She came to the belief that on New Year's 1877, announcement of her great election would be made from on
high so she arranged a New Year's Eve Party with people
like Mark Twain and his wife as guests. The mediums invited, however, came in very unsuitable attire and created
an awkward social situation, especially as the guests apparently knew nothing of the great expectations. Of course the
evening passed without the looked-for revelation. After the
Hookers lost a daughter in 1887, Isabella thought that she
could talk with the departed one in moments of vivid con-
centration. Her patient husband accepted her belief more
willingly as time went on. Another of the Hartford circle,
Mrs. Charles D. Warner, wife of the famous essayist and
novelist, as she grew older, began to listen to the promptings
of spirit messages.

In the same community Calvin Stowe, theologian and
husband of the noted novelist, received phantom visitors
who increasingly became more numerous and more vivid.
He believed that his first wife and his dead son, Henry,
visited him by plucking the strings of a guitar. Harriet
Beecher Stowe came to share her husband's interest, especially as age brought losses and the fading of hopes.[9]

Mark Twain found no allurement in Spiritualism, for
he had developed increasing agnosticism regarding personal
immortality. Yet, he found a fascinating interest in mental
telepathy.[10]

In the Boston area, men like William James were interested in Spiritualism, and in the 1880's he became a member
of the Society for Psychical Research, though personally he
does not seem to have had "a belief in the existence of departed spirits."[11] One of the most noted mediums of later
years, Mrs. Piper, came under some research by James, who
concluded that she had "supernormal knowledge in her
trances," but as late as 1907 he was not sure of the source
of it. For a time, certainly she had extraordinary influence
upon many gifted people. Thus, Lilla Cabot Perry (wife

of the Harvard professor, Thomas Sargent Perry), who was proficient in the classics, would not, it was said, even pack a trunk, without first consulting Mrs. Piper's "control," the mysterious Dr. Phinuit, and she influenced her husband and daughters somewhat in the same direction.[12]

William Lloyd Garrison, moreover, had come in his later years to believe in "spiritual manifestations."[13] Robert Dale Owen (1801-77), eldest son of the founder of New Harmony Community and a social reformer of note in his own right, at length became a Spiritualist. During the post Civil War period his books, including *The Debatable Land Between This World and the Next* (1872), were read in some church-going circles. A vestry man of Trinity Church, New York, deemed *The Debatable Land* "less irrational than most books of its very low class."[14]

In Madison, Wisconsin, Lyman C. Draper, the famous collector of historical manuscripts, had long been a leader and for many years a deacon in the First Baptist Church. In his extended trips throughout the older sections of the country in search of manuscript collections, in Kentucky and southern Indiana he encountered Spiritualist seances in 1868. Three deaths in his immediate family having occurred in a relatively short time, he was in a mood to find solace in Spiritualism. He came to believe that the spirits of the old pioneers could be communicated with so as to furnish "useful matter and correct errors." He became convinced that George Rogers Clark and other spirits gave him information apparently known only to research students. At length, he told his Baptist brethren of the change in his beliefs, and finally in 1869 he was expelled from membership in the Baptist Church.

Draper, an organizer by nature, sought to promote Spiritualist societies in Wisconsin and converted J. Fletcher Williams of the Minnesota Historical Society to the faith. He, moreover, eagerly attended seances and sought the advice of mediums on matters of health, personal finances, and his own remarriage.[15]

The unsettled atmosphere of the time is illustrated by

the fact that the father of John R. Commons, the noted economist, turned from the philosophy of Herbert Spencer to Spiritualism, and then later to Christian Science.[16]

In distinct opposition to Spiritualist views were those of some rationalistic Unitarians, such as Rev. Moncure D. Conway, who called for a discarding of "unreal supernaturalism" and the substitution of "the supernaturalism of science, art and wealth," which he asserted could "work miracles beyond all dreams and traditions of the past."

Yet, far different was the attitude of another leading Unitarian, Minot J. Savage, who had discarded a supernatural interpretation of man's salvation, as he had found faith in an immanent God working through natural law and understood by means of scientific principles. Accordingly, the revelation of immortality in the New Testament had come to mean little to him, and he had turned to psychic research to demonstrate the assurance of a future life. This even explained for him on a natural basis the credibility of the gospel narratives of the resurrection of Jesus. Such a belief he held to be a crying need to satisfy the doubts and answer the cravings of the human heart. Savage reiterated his theme in books like *Religion For Today* (Boston, 1897) and *Life Beyond Death* (N. Y., 1899), but his critics were to suggest that the world had grown weary of "dishonest" Spiritualism and had not yet discovered that which could be trusted.[17]

3. *Theosophy*

Related in some measure to Spiritualism was Theosophy, founded in the United States by Henry Steel Olcott (1832-1907) who has variously been considered "a fool, a knave, and a seer." His interest in Spiritualism led to an acquaintance with Helena Petrovna Hahn Blavatsky (1831-1891) which developed into intimacy. He became the first president of the Theosophical Society, founded in 1875, and he aided the Russian-born Madame Blavatsky by editing the imperfect English of her two-volume *Isis Unveiled,* a largely unacknowledged assembly of quotations on occultism. These "Theosophic Twins," as the feminine member called them, sailed for India in 1878, in an attempt to carry the philosophy of Hinduism to the Hindus. Much contention developed with native leaders, but cordial relations with many were later established. Having formally adopted the Buddhist religion, Olcott devoted himself energetically to the task of developing the Theosophical Society. He was chiefly responsible for the fact that at his death the Society was represented by more than six hundred branches in forty-two different countries. A New York lawyer, William Quan Judge (1851-96), became an enthusiastic member of the Society in America. For a time Henry Jotham Newton (1823-1895), New York manufacturer and inventor, who became a millionaire through real estate investments, showed great interest. Deeply concerned about Spiritualism, he helped to found the Theosophical Society, as he thought, as an organization for the scientific study of occultism. But, after the publication of *Isis Unveiled,* essentially the Bible of Theosophy and hostile to Spiritualism, he withdrew in great bitterness. In spite of the chicaneries of some of the leaders, Theosophy made definite appeal to thousands of Americans, although a Unitarian minister commented that if theosophy were carefully studied it would "appear that Mrs. Blavatsky's art has consisted chiefly in drawing about her people of means and influence, but without the critical instinct, and contriving to get abler persons too deeply committed to dare open their eyes."

4. *Christian Science*

When, for some people, orthodox religion lost something of its vitality, numerous persons turned to Christian Science. Views of the personality of its founder held by faithful Christian Scientists and those held by others have been in marked contrast, hence she is a rather controversial

figure in American biography.[18] In the closing year of the
Civil War, Mrs. Mary Morse Baker Eddy was a middle-aged
woman of forty-four, far from vigorous in health, who believed that she was receiving much help from a rather remarkable and unworldly faith healer, Phineas Parkhurst
Quimby (1802-66). In 1866, however, Quimby died, much
to Mrs. Eddy's distress. Separating from her husband, an
itinerant dentist, Mrs. Eddy lived for a time with at least
seven different families in as many different towns. She supported herself by teaching and by practicing the new method
of healing, and she slowly departed from a reliance on her
former teacher and his principles. Although unlearned in
philosophical concepts she was enabled by her extraordinary
will to carry to completion *Science and Health* (1875). At
once small groups using this as a study book began to call
themselves Christian Scientists, and by the summer of 1879
"The Church of Christ, Scientist" had been organized. *Science and Health* was improved in some respects by a literary
editor, Rev. James Henry Wiggin, a one-time Unitarian
minister who had served as an editor for the Harvard University Press. Subsequently, it went through various editions
and became one of the most widely read religious volumes
of modern America. Based upon a type of idealism which
denies the reality of disease, sin, and death, the new religious
faith spread gradually with rather remarkable success.

A half century ago a noted American philosopher claimed
to have traced the rather "inextricably confused" sources
of the movement. He then asserted that its doctrines came
partly from the Yankee mesmeric "healer," Phineas P.
Quimby of Maine, partly from the Shaker prophetess,
Mother Ann Lee of New Hampshire, and partly from the
orphic sayings of the Massachusetts Transcendentalist, Bron-
son Alcott.[19] Reasons for the rapid development of the movement, the same philosopher found, in an analysis of conditions in the East, the Middle West, and the Far West, where
Christian Science received its greatest number of supporters.
He claimed to have discovered in these areas the following

aspects conducive to the expansion of Christian Science: (1) These were the centers of urban life, with many large cities producing tensions, strains and nervous disorders, and numerous people being in mountain and health resorts in the hope of personal benefits; (2) To many the traditional Christian doctrines seemed "dry" and lacking in vitality, and to those unacquainted with the history of thought, Christian Science brought what seemed like the fresh breath of a new discovery, and urban people especially were apt to "think for themselves" in arriving at what they deemed to be the truth; (3) America has traditionally taken a liberal, open-minded attitude toward new, unconventional views, and this was especially true in Massachusetts (long a hot-bed of heresies), in Illinois (with its variety of faiths among the foreign-born), in Colorado (where woman suffrage won an early victory), and in California (land of Buddhism and strange cults); (4) America, particularly in the region proximate to the fortieth parallel, has been highly prosperous, and Christian Scientists generally appeared to be prosperous people who were reacting amidst their own economic well-being against an exaggerated emphasis on things material; (5) Geographically, the movement was related to the areas where New England Transcendentalism (with its emphasis on personal experience) and the St. Louis School of Hegelian idealism had been widely accepted; and (6) This was an area where women and business men were accustomed to some degree of speculative thought and sought a practical answer for their problems, yet frequently were not prepared to test it by the criteria of academic philosophy, and the movement seemed to appeal especially to women and business people.[20]

Coming at a time when the evolutionary hypothesis led to questions concerning the time-honored creeds, the devotional literature of Christian Science enabled thousands to have a quiet confidence in a God that seemed to bring them a feeling of strength, confidence, and serenity. Especially from those who had dwelt too constantly upon the thought of real or imagined ailments and among the distraught of a highly mechanized generation, testimonials of great benefits were frequent and often highly enthusiastic.

Harper's Weekly in 1895 asserted that at least nine-tenths of all Christian Scientists were women. It elaborated that for such it seemed to become

> . . . their first interest in life, as perhaps must be the case with any form of religion which really takes hold of the believer. It makes them happy, too, as any controlling enthusiasm does while it lasts, and Christian Science in many cases seems to last very well. But it is hard in this world to get anything for nothing. No one gets much out of Christian Science who does not put a good deal in it. Whether the gain is worth the investment is a question. . . .

Bishop William Lawrence of the Episcopal Church in Massachusetts later expressed the belief that Christian Science had performed a type of work which "the historic churches have somehow neglected to do."[21]

Yet, the inroads made by Christian Science upon the membership of the established churches were not well received by orthodox clergymen, and in 1888 a leading Congregational minister, Leonard Woolsey Bacon, took occasion to criticize "the novelties that are just now most talked about" under the titles of "Mind Cure" and "Christian Science" and "Faith Cure." He thereupon expressed what he believed to be the orthodox Christian view of healing, although disclaiming any intimate knowledge of Christian Science:

> We have learned from the Apostle James that all healing is divine; that when the trained sagacity of experienced physicians has been employed, and the treatment which the best science of the time approves has been fully applied, with trustful and filial prayer, we are

still to remember that not the physician nor the treatment has been the supreme and deciding cause, but a Power above and behind and in them all; that is the prayer of faith that has healed the sick.

A conservative Presbyterian scholar contended that Christian Science was open to the same objections which philosophers had raised against pantheism and idealism and that its attitude toward sin and the Atonement meant that it was hardly Christian in the traditional sense. He felt, moreover, that it contradicted the facts of life, for, according to its principles, food would be unnecessary. Hence, he deemed it unscientific. This writer believed that its saving truth was its emphasis on the "reality and power of spirit" and that it was essentially a protest against late nineteenth century materialism.[22]

Even among Christian Scientists, there developed questions of orthodoxy. Mrs. Augusta Emma Simmons Stetson (c. 1842-1928), whose husband's health had failed in the post Civil-War years, had endeavored to support herself and her husband as an elocutionist in Boston. There she had attracted the attention of Mrs. Eddy, who was so impressed with her talents that she was sent to New York City late in 1886 to open up Christian Science activities in that community. After initial difficulties had been overcome, amazing success attended Mrs. Stetson's efforts, and by 1899 property was secured that led four years later to the completion of a magnificent building costing over a million dollars at Ninety-sixth Street and Central Park West. Animosities developed between the two women leaders, however, and later (1909) Mrs. Stetson was formally excommunicated, after her opponents had charged that she taught the sinfulness of physical procreation.

CHAPTER XVII

AT THE DAWN OF A NEW CENTURY

As Professor Arthur M. Schlesinger, Sr. has pointed out, and as has been illustrated in this volume, the impact of scientific thought and the advancing industrial revolution had created a "Critical Period in American Religion," especially after 1875.[1] Another distinguished historian has suggested that the problems were more difficult of solution than any which had faced the Christian Church since the Protestant Revolt.[2] The latter scholar believes, however, that "it speaks volumes for the virility and adaptability of the Christian Church" that it was able to "survive the strain so well."

Certainly, various aspects of the Free Thought movement had, directly and indirectly, important effects upon the organized faith of the churches. There had been four important phases of this: (1) Scientific (represented by men like Huxley and John Fiske); (2) Metaphysical or philosophical (with Theodore Parker as a spokesman); (3) Sociological (represented by men like Lester F. Ward); and (4) Iconoclastic (with Robert G. Ingersoll as a central figure.) [3]

As a result, A. L. Rawson, writing in *The Truth Seeker* (New York), June 25, 1881 could claim that religious beliefs and church attendance had weakened more during the preceding twenty years than during any similar period. Such views were confirmed by leading newspapers such as the New York *Times,* March 12, 1881, which asserted as "an undeniable fact that the number of churchgoers was not keeping pace with increase in population." The New York *Daily Tribune* proposed in May of the same year that un-

belief arising from recent scientific progress should be met
by reasoned argument showing the reconciliation of the
old faith and the new science.

In a somewhat similar mood, an able journalist and devout churchman like Henry W. Grady of the Atlanta *Constitution,* could deem "The Atheistic Tide Sweeping Over
the Country" as the great "dread of the times."[4] He deplored the way in which novelists, scientists, and essayists
were arraying themselves on the side of skepticism and could
find no comfort in what Henry Watterson of Louisville had
told him, that Ingersoll's effect on an audience in the Kentucky city was "no more than a theatrical presentation."
Grady believed that he had "never seen a man who came
away from an Ingersoll lecture as stout of faith and as strong
of heart as he was when he went there." He did not know,
he said, that this "spirit of irreligion" had made much in-
road on the churches but was "simply eating away the material upon which the churches must recruit and perpetuate
themselves." If this continued, Grady believed, the masses
of Americans would be demoralized and debauched, "loosed
of the one restraint that is absolute and imperious . . . and
bringing confusion and ruin." Yet, when Ingersoll asserted
that the church was dying out, a Methodist Church Exten-
sion leader, Charles C. McCabe (1836-1906), replied that
the Methodists alone were building an average of one new
church for every day in the year and proposed to double the
number.

Nevertheless, the intense devotion to church life which
had characterized many of the older generation did not always carry over into the lives of younger members of the
family. A physician's family in Cleveland was perhaps a not
unusual case in point. There, after the Civil War, Erastus
Cushing (1802-93) was a prominent physician and a devout
churchman, faithful in his attendance at the Old Stone
(First) Presbyterian Church. His religious spirit carried
over into his every day life, and "his declining years were
blessed by the same gracious charm which had ever made

him beloved." A son of the next generation, Henry Kirke Cushing (1827-1910), also a Cleveland physician, was known for the rectitude of his conduct and his steadfast interpretation of ethical principles and was one of the most highly regarded members of his profession in his home city.[5] In his family, prayers, Sunday School and church were essential parts of the spiritual life of its members. But, as time went on, morning prayers and grace at meals were given up, the father ceased to teach a Sunday School class, and after a time he ceased going to church altogether. After college two of the boys, one of them, Harvey Cushing, destined to be the distinguished brain surgeon of Boston, ceased to attend church. For a time several younger members of the family attended regularly, but after the turn of the century, the beloved mother, still a pillar in the family church, was the only one to go with regularity.

Another instance was Joseph B. Eastman, distinguished coordinator of Railroads under Franklin D. Roosevelt. He was the son of a Presbyterian minister who served in New York and Pennsylvania and who was known for his democratic, unselfish public-spirit associated with a lively sense of humor. The family traditions "were those of plain living and high thinking, simplicity, conscientiousness, and devotion to duty."[6] When the son was asked (about 1890) by his father to declare his love for Jesus and join the church, the son replied, "But I don't know Jesus." The younger Eastman to the end of his days refrained from joining a church, although he recognized that the early training he had received was of the best and that religion constituted a primary need of humanity.

A further example of changing viewpoints was the mother of Eugene V. Debs, later Socialist leader. She had been raised as a practicing Roman Catholic in France, but after the removal of the family to Terre Haute, Indiana, had failed to find the serene security in the local parish church that she had known in the cathedral at Colmar, France. Her doubts had been fostered by her Protestant husband (also a native of France), and although her older children had been baptized as Catholics, when Eugene was born (1855) the family had severed its ties with organized religion. Accordingly, Debs began life without the sacrament of infant baptism, and only once, according to his biographer, did he ever venture inside a church. When as a young man he had found his way into St. Joseph's Cathedral in his home city, his reactions were such that he later recalled the episode:

> The priest delivered an address on Hell. I shall never forget it as long as I live. He pictured a thousand demons and devils with horns and bristling tails, clutching pitch forks steeped in brimstone, and threatening to consume all who did not accept the interpretation of Christianity as given by the priest. I left that church with a rich and royal hatred of the priest as a person, and a loathing for the church as an institution, and I vowed that I would never go inside a church again.[7]

Yet, Debs was much influenced by the life and example of Jesus, and years later, when in Atlanta Penitentiary because of his views during World War I, he kept a large portrait of Jesus on the wall of his room.

E. L. Godkin, the Anglo-Irish son of a clergyman and one of a deeply religious nature, was a very influential figure as editor of the *Nation*. In private correspondence he wrote Professor Charles E. Norton, showing his distrust of the orthodox with "their certainty that they have the truth, and that *their* truth is necessary to salvation." He indicated that he believed that the world especially needed the preaching and proving of the possibility of Christian life outside of the Church and that Norton was one of the few men he knew who seemed to lead such a life, most others being "pagans to all intents and purposes."[8]

Also, as in the case of Norton, at Harvard, Professor George Santayana, who had had important Catholic influences in his training, as professor of philosophy took such a broad view of religious matters that he seriously disturbed Catholic students.[9] In the *Harvard Monthly* (December 1892) he had suggested that the organized religious forces had a "right and natural" function, but "beneath these specifically religious forces, and permeating the whole community" there was "a vaguer but deeper religion,—the faith in enlightenment, the aspiration to be just, the sympathy with the multiform thoughts and labors of humanity."

Charles F. Thwing, later President of Western Reserve University, raised the question as to whether this was "not a bit vague to be worthy of being made the doctrine of a religion." He stated his own belief that the "one great need" of the education offered at Harvard was "the one great need of modern life . . . a more vital spiritual impulse and inspiration." Christianity at Harvard, he thought, would be improved, "not by being made less broad, but by being touched by an ethical and religious enthusiasm." Hence, "a vigorous enthusiasm for a broad-church Christianity would do more for the University, and through the University, for humanity than all else."

Indeed, everywhere people generally found that the faith of the Church seemed necessary to the cultivation of the moral and spiritual life. Godkin showed a great esteem for the Church as an historic institution, for, as he said, he had "not entirely got rid of the medieval faith in forms." Accordingly, he had never left the Episcopal Church, though paradoxically he had "never been able to muster courage" to have his own children christened.[10] Godkin himself contended that Christianity had lost its power over conduct, partly because of a decline in faith in the dogmatic part of Christianity, and he believed that only as church members developed "a good deal of the ascetic about them without any withdrawal from the world" would they prove to be a vital force. Incidentally, a correspondent from Ithaca, New York, replied vigorously to this editorial, denying that morals were highest when dogmas were most rigidly held.

He cited as evidence the Middle Ages, the religiously orthodox brigands of Southern Europe, and the contemporary
dogmatic Roman Catholic Church which he said was "the
one which furnishes our State prisons and our haunts of vice
and ignorance with a large part of all their inmates." Yet,
he found that Unitarians were not at all noted for vice.
This correspondent deemed it the work of the Church not
only to teach piety but, with equal enthusiasm, "honesty,
goodness, truth, sobriety, and personal righteousness." Godkin, in reply, asserted that dogma did not make men good
but that great faith had kept the Church alive and given it
vigor, and that church membership had come to involve no
personal sacrifice of any kind but often had contributed
socially and otherwise to one's personal pleasures.

In practically every phase of American life there were
many of those who looked upon the Church as a great
channel of personal piety and righteousness. Thus, as a student at Harvard, the energetic Theodore Roosevelt had
taught for three and a half years in an Episcopal Sunday
School until, as he said, he was discharged by the rector for
the "heinous crime of being a Presbyterian."[11] Representative of the many less distinguished students at Harvard at
a little later time was Frederick W. Dallinger, who subsequently testified that during his undergraduate days (1889-
93) nothing had occurred to shake his faith. As a Freshman
he had joined the St. Paul Society (for Episcopalian students) and the Y.M.C.A., each of which had a fortnightly
religious service and address in the parlor of Lawrence Scientific School.[12] At one of the St. Paul Society meetings he sat
next to a student who had the reputation of being "very
wild and dissipated," but after Phillips Brooks had addressed
them, the undisciplined youth said, "Gee, when you were
in the room with *that* man you not only couldn't do anything wrong but you couldn't *think* anything wrong!"

Even those whose faith in the churches had been shaken
often realized that, as Matthew Arnold had said, it was the
only organized institution for promoting goodness, and that

without faith society could scarcely survive. Edward A. Ross, later a distinguished sociologist at the University of Wisconsin, during the late nineteenth century gave up his religious connections, but he came to refrain from attacking organized religion because of "the momentous social significance of the teachings of the great Hebrew Prophets" and because the cardinal Christian doctrines, he believed, were "capable of affording great consolation and inspiring much good will." Clergymen, he found to be "sincere, simple and saintly" in comparison with many of their contemporaries, and Christian worship even at its dullest making a distinct appeal to "conscience and reason."[13]

Henry Holt, the publisher, had only disgust for "the imbecile dogmas with which Christianity" had been "smothered," but he later came to see the effect of the breakdown of religion on the youth, resulting in frivolity and excessive drinking, and he had noticed the need for religion among the Catholic servant girls of Larchmont when sailors were numerous on nearby yachts. Moreover, he had come to have "added appreciation of Nature and the moral order," as well as an "enthusiasm for the morality on which all religions pretty well agree," and he had come to see how, along with forms surviving from times of ignorance and brutality, "much beautiful literature and art" had also been the inheritance of religion.[14]

Daniel Willard, destined to be a great railroad president, had as a youth lost the dogmatic religion in which he had been reared. Humbled by the experience, he had given up an expectation in this life of knowing absolutely "where God is, or how He looks, or how He works." His own intelligence, he thought, told him that every design must have a designer and that such a view of the world was more sensible than to think that it all "just happened." And practical religion seemed to him to call for "decent and upright living and fair and honest dealing between men" as expressed in the great teachings of Christ.[15]

A man like John G. Carlisle, Secretary of the Treasury

under Cleveland, was a generous and kind individual, who took no interest during most of his life in religion and looked upon death as an eternal sleep. Yet, in his last years, he turned for faith to the Church.[16]

Moreover, if some lost the faith of their fathers, some descendants of a man like Robert Owen, free-thinking New Harmony communitarian, became church leaders. Apparently, Owen had raised no objection to his children being given religious education according to their mother's Presbyterian standards. One son, Richard Owen (1810-90), noted scientist and later first President of Purdue University, regularly conducted a Sunday School class in the Bloomington, Indiana, Presbyterian Church.[17] A granddaughter of Robert Owen, Constance Faunt Le Roy Runcie (1836-1911), a composer of some distinction, was the wife of an Episcopal clergyman.

Yet, as has been pointed out earlier in this volume, life after 1865 in the United States had become increasingly complex and secular in much of its activities. Doubtless this meant that the churches would not easily occupy so central a place in daily life as they had in an earlier period. One writer reviewing the cultural change in the Connecticut Valley pointed out that before the Civil War, Dr. Peabody of the Unitarian Church, Springfield, Massachusetts, in his black pulpit gown, represented the public teacher, though somewhat austere in his own personality. A third of a century later, however, guidance of thought and opinion had in large measure passed to the high-strung journalist, spokesman for the world's teeming activities, though the Church still functioned for the personal "cure of souls," and for inspiration, mutual help, and moral solidarity.[18]

In the struggle with intellectual forces, as has been shown, there had been some "spiritual suicides." Adjustments had taken place moreover, that had involved widespread transference of religious loyalties. As one historian has said (and the present volume had explained) : "Unitarians sought refuge in the glamour of Episcopal symbolism, and men with a wealthy lineage of anti-Catholicism bowed to the authority of Rome. Cultured scholars of scientific tastes looked to spiritualism for the solution of life's mysteries, and the new faith called Christian Science to whom the name alone afforded shelter."

Doubtless theological squabbles and heresy trials among Protestants and strong antagonisms among Catholic leaders had not contributed to the onward "march of faith." In Protestant and Catholic circles there was often a feeling that the active life of America hardly was conducive to the development of a devotional spirit of faith. In 1873, an observer reported having visited Congregational, Unitarian, and Presbyterian gatherings and having been constantly disappointed by the lack of concern for prayer and communion. At a meeting of Unitarian leaders, for example, he found "a rich array of communion silver, but a beggarly show of communicants."[19] In 1894, a leading religious leader found that many influential members had more of the philanthropic than the devotional spirit and that an even larger group believed that the one important service of the Church was as a social institution, "making men less selfish and ignorant, less vicious and idle, and therefore better members of society and better citizens." The same leader, however, was optimistic as to the spiritual life of the churches being stronger than before. He felt that theological changes, Biblical criticism, the larger emphasis on reason, and changing attitudes toward "the heathen" had not resulted in less faith in the Church but rather more.

Yet, at the end of the century, a leading American educator submitted to the freshmen at Western Reserve University (Cleveland) and then to the first year class of an Eastern women's college, twenty-two Biblical allusions from Tennyson's poems, and from the results concluded that the Bible had ceased to be a force in American literature. Forty out of eighty-five knew nothing of the story of Esau or that of Ruth. At about the same time a doctoral dissertation at Clark University concluded that it was "a matter of common observation that the church of today exercises less control over the masses of the people than was the case two or three decades ago."[20]

During the 1870's and 1880's in many leading Protestant denominations lagging faith had often received at least a temporary infusion of vitality by the famous revival meetings of the period. The most renowned team had been that of Dwight L. Moody, and his song leader, Ira David Sankey. Moody's son recalled that at one series of meetings his father had spoken two hundred and eighty-five times to audiences averaging over seven thousand.[21] Moody had concentrated on the cities, asserting with some sagacity that "water runs down hill, and the highest hills in America are the great cities. If we can stir them we shall stir the whole country."[22] For some years he and other evangelists attained a considerable measure of success. In the Protestant churches moreover, a vital connection with organized religion on the part of the youth had often been preserved by the establishment of young people's societies, such as that of Christian Endeavor. In 1892, this one organization boasted a membership of 1,200,000, and when a national convention was held, thirty thousand persons taxed the capacity of the three largest halls in New York City. Two years later, the Christian Endeavor Societies enrolled 1,724,460 members, and fifteen of Cleveland's largest churches were secured for simultaneous meetings at their annual convention. Thus, in the late 'eighties and early 'nineties the organized Church in America manifested great vitality. In 1886 the Presbyterian Church had received more new members than in any year in its history, and the Methodist Episcopal Church had raised a million dollars for missions alone.

But, by the end of the century, the *fin de siècle* spirit was evident in the churches of the country. As Professor Commager had pointed out, intellectual currents around 1890 for many had swept away some of the older forms of religious certitude, and a period of great insecurity in matters of faith had followed.[23] Professor Merle Curti had indi-

cated that in American thought there had been a definite
"delimitation of the supernatural,"[24] as more phenomena
were explainable in terms of natural law. Animosities between factions in both Protestantism and Catholicism, with
heresy trials plaguing some Protestant circles, and a decreas-
ing interest in revivals, had dulled the edge of religious
faith. As a result, leading observers of church affairs asserted
that 1899 had witnessed a definite lack of spiritual vigor
with a net gain numerically in most of the churches, including the Roman Catholic, approaching the vanishing point.
The northern Methodist Church apparently lost in membership, and the Southern Methodists encountered "an ar-
rested movement," the first experience of that kind in thirty-
three years.[25]

Thus, organized religion had indeed faced a Critical
Period in its development in the United States. For the
time being it was apparently a bit stunned by some of the
impacts of currents of the age, and for the moment was doing
little more than "marking time."

But the faith of the Church in America which would
develop in the twentieth century would not be the same as
that of the Civil War period. Certain notable developments
had taken place:

1. *Faith was based upon a theology in which there had
come to be important adjustments.* For Roman Catholics and
many conservative Protestants, the Revelation which had
been a heritage from the Apostolic Age might be clarified,
but the basic "Deposit of Faith" could not be altered. Even
for many liberally inclined Protestants, such as the well-
known poet and essayist, Henry Van Dyke, a leading Presbyterian, scientific thought had not modified the fundamental
teachings of the Gospel. W. H. P. Faunce, a later president
of Brown University, in reviewing Van Dyke's popular *The
Gospel for an Age of Doubt* (New York, 1896), declared:

The gospel which the author has for the age of doubt
is essentially the teachings of the Westminster Confes-

sion, held unequivocally and tenaciously; yet, held so generously, winsomely and tenderly that one does not note their sharpness.[26]

Van Dyke found in Calvinism a place for human freedom and for a reconciliation of miracles with the workings of natural law. More conservative Calvinists were among those who listened to a series of lectures in 1898-9 at Princeton Theological Seminary by the Dutch theologian, Abraham Kuyper, in which he portrayed Calvinism as one of the five great intellectual systems in world history, of which Paganism, Islam, Roman Catholicism, and Modernism were the others.[27] To him, Calvinism represented the ripest substance of Christianity with beneficent applications for all phases of human activity.[28] At the same time Calvinists in America were somewhat disturbed by the development among French Protestant scholars of a symbolic interpretation of Christianity known as "Symbolo-Fideisme."[29]

As has been pointed out elsewhere, the precisely developed theological viewpoints of Catholicism and Presbyterianism often were vigorously attacked by religious liberals during this period, but neither was willing to surrender basic religious insights to the theological fashions of the moment. In this effort American Presbyterianism was greatly aided by the gifted intellectual leaders of Scotch Presbyterianism who stoutly defended historic Christianity. Thus, a leading professor of philosophy at the University of Michigan could write approvingly in 1899 of the way in which Scotch Presbyterians had retained traditional standards but with such an emphasis on Christ and on a social and ethical spirit as to unite "what is best in the new spirit with what is most stable in the old orthodoxy."[30] Similarly, an American Presbyterian scholar was cautioning, "Whenever the Church has treated lightly the historical record, it has fallen into scholasticism or mysticism," the former lacking in inspiration, the latter lacking reality and balance.[31] Because of this tenacity perhaps the Presbyterian Church was already earning for itself the reputation which the Dean of Harvard Divinity School attributed to it at the close of World War II, when he suggested that it was "in some ways the theological stronghold of orthodox Protestantism."[32]

Yet, all religious organizations, as has been pointed out elsewhere, were feeling the impact of new emphases on Reason, Biblical criticism, Intuition, Empirical Science, Evolutionary Thought, and changing theological concepts. This was so much the case that in 1900, a University of Chicago professor could declare:

> Ours is an age of deep-seated revolt against dogmas, creeds, and confessions in religion. In the rebound we have gone so far that we are in danger of overlooking an important side of historical and profitable truth, as it is expressed in the creeds of Christendom. Writers of true historical sense and sound judgment, who can keep to the *via media,* and do it with largeness and sweetness of spirit, have an important mission to fulfil.[33]

In the effort to reconcile newer views of historical criticism with traditional Christianity many liberals sponsored a return to the Christ of the Gospels and came forth with the widely accepted belief:

> . . . [not] that Jesus knew all the occurrences on earth and through the universe and was conscious that He created the stars, and knew more, not only than the ancients but than the moderns of science and philosophy; but it is the belief that God was in Christ as far as God can manifest his life in a human personality at a given period in history, and for the purpose of bringing in his grace and love for the renewal and perfection of man.[34]

To some, this emphasis on the Divine Love of Christ would revive the interest of the masses in the Church by rejecting the "unethical form" in which the Gospel had been presented as a result "either of a series of formal ceremonies imposed by the church, or of a series of legal fictions floating in the mind of God."[35]

Many objected, however, to the attempt to give greater significance to the words of Jesus in the Gospels than to the teachings concerning Christ and his kingdom as given in the Epistles, it being held that the two must stand or fall together.[36] Some were no doubt confused when a leading Congregational theologian asserted that, "Jesus was always perfect, yet his perfection constantly developed from more to more."[37] Certainly, not only conservative Presbyterians but many Congregationalists, Methodists, and Baptists protested against "sentimental doctrines" of divine love which obscured the sterner Biblical teachings, minimized the sense of personal responsibility for wrong doing, and tended to regard Jesus as a product of natural evolution.[38]

The Baptist president of Rochester Theological Seminary, A. H. Strong, could lament:

It is very plain that the Christ to whom recent theology bids us go back is not the Christ on whom the Church has believed, and who has wrought the transformations which have been witnessed in individual lives and in Christian history. It is not such a Christ as this to whom the penitent has looked for forgiveness and the sorrowing for comfort. It is not for such a Christ as this that the martyrs have laid down their lives.[39]

In the welter of theological controversy some were apt to lose their bearings. Some found in works like Adolph Harnack's *History of Dogma* a failure to give due emphasis to some phases of Biblical study and to the Church's understanding of the human heart in all ages.[40] Yet, a Congregationalist scholar could declare that Harnack had shown for all future generations that political, racial, social, moral, re-

ligious, intellectual, and philosophical conditions had profoundly affected the development of the doctrines, discipline
and life of the Church in its early centuries.[41]

For most Protestants, at least for those of intellectual
inclinations, at the end of the century, the status of theological interpretations was perhaps well expressed by Professor
Ernest D. Burton of the University of Chicago:

> Till the perfected theology came, dogmatic theology
> must give to each generation of the church a report of
> progress which shall distinguish certainties from proba-
> bilities and probabilities from problems, laying bare the
> unshakable rock on which Christian faith can stand . . .
> [especially as to the truths which are revealed in the
> Bible and established by experience], and giving a clear
> air in which Christian scholarship may solve its prob-
> lems.[42]

2. *Faith was less definitely based on uncompromising
denominational loyalties.* In 1900, a leading Presbyterian
spokesman said, "Denominational acerbities are giving place
to church federation." The assertive Rev. Charles A. Briggs
had declared in 1893 that "denominational dogmas are to
a great extent esoteric to the ministry. The people know
little about them and care less for them." Certainly, this
was an exaggeration, but doubtless there were many like
John Sherman, long congressman and senator, Secretary of
the Treasury, and later Secretary of State, who had followed
the Episcopal faith of his mother but who declared that he
had a "firm belief in the Bible as the only creed of religious
faith and duty" and willingly granted to everyone the right
to worship according to his own judgment.[43]

Charles Evans Hughes, destined to be a Presidential nomi-
nee, Secretary of State, and Chief Justice of the United States,
was the son of very devout parents, the father being a Baptist
clergyman. Yet, when the younger Hughes as a fledgling lawyer joined the Fifth Avenue Baptist Church, New York City

(1889) , and soon agreed to teach a Sunday School class, he undertook the instructional task with the understanding that he would deal with the teachings of Jesus. He was definitely uninterested in ritual and in tests of orthodoxy, and later explained that he attached no importance to the distinctive tenets of the Baptists, though he cherished their traditions of religious liberty and wished to throw his personal influence "in support of Christian institutions."[44]

It might appear that there was an unbridgable denominational gulf between a Massachusetts Episcopalian like Phillips Brooks and a Quaker like John Greenleaf Whittier. But, each had a certain quality of Christian mysticism in his religious experience; and the author of the hymn, "O Little Town of Bethlehem," and the author of "Dear Lord and Father of Mankind" both came to feel that the very doctrines of their sects were non-essential as compared to the serious work of godly lives and deeds. At the time of the death of the famous Boston Unitarian minister, James Freeman Clarke, in 1888, Brooks, moreover, in a sermon paid the highest tribute to him as "a living epistle to the Church of Christ" and one, who as a real servant and true saint of the Heavenly Father "belonged to the whole Church of Christ."[45]

In other ways Brooks had exhibited a strong ecumenical spirit. In 1887, at a meeting of Methodist ministers where "Christian Unity" was discussed, his address deepened the conviction that a basic Christian unity already existed. When, moreover, he spoke the same year at the consecration of a new Episcopal Church in Andover, Massachusetts he paid tribute to the deep faith embodied in "the Church of Christ in other forms" in the town. He decried any effort on the part of Episcopalianism to attempt an "arrogant presentation of herself as the only Church of Christ" to which all church life must conform. Rather, he looked upon his communion "as one contribution to the Church of the future which is to be larger, deeper, wiser, holier than any Church existing in the land today."[46]

Of Leland Stanford, famous California railroad builder and philanthropist it was noted that, although a churchgoer and a religious man, "in each confession of faith he found something to which he could not subscribe." Yet, at his funeral (1893) at Stanford University, denominational differences were submerged in a service conducted by the Episcopal bishop, a San Francisco Episcopalian rector, and the minister of the First Unitarian Church, San Francisco.[47]

In the efforts to serve as wide a constituency as possible, denominational emphases had often been minimized. Thus, for example, Rev. J. W. Hamilton, a Methodist minister, had secured the erection of a "People's Church" in Boston with a maximum seating capacity of 3250. No pew rent was collected, and membership was on a broad basis.

Even members of the older generation often mellowed in their interest in denominational niceties. Nicholas Murray Butler later recalled how his mother, who was reared in the old school of Calvinist theology both as to faith and practice, "broadened enormously with the years" and became "as catholic and as liberal a spirit as one could imagine."[48]

The same attitude even permeated somewhat the leadership of Roman Catholicism. A remarkable ecumenical spirit certainly was voiced in March 1900, by Bishop John L. Spalding, one of the most gifted intellectuals who has arisen in the Roman Catholic Church in the United States. Speaking at Notre Dame University he said in part:

> The old controversy between Catholics and Protestants has, to a large extent, lost its meaning, because problems of more radical import have forced themselves on our attention. . . . Too long have we all, Catholics and Protestants alike, busied ourselves with disputations about the meaning of texts, while we have drifted away from the all-tender and all-loving Heart of Christ.[49]

Yet, Bishop Spalding was looked upon in some Catholic

circles as a dangerous liberal, if not actually a venturer in a domain beyond the bounds of orthodoxy. Certainly the papal injunction (1895) against Catholic participation in inter-faith meetings had not been conducive to better understanding between Catholics and members of other religious faiths, however much it may have been justified by Catholic views of the unique authority of their Church. Furthermore, the action of the Vatican Council of 1870 in approving the dogma of papal infallibility had pointed up a seemingly insuperable barrier between intelligent and fair-minded Catholics and similarly disposed members of other communions. Thus, before the promulgation of the decrees of the Vatican Council, a Catholic student of church history like Archbishop Kenrick of St. Louis, might take a certain common position with many Protestant scholars in attacking the "motives of credibility" advanced by the supporters of papal infallibility as "either insufficient or utterly worthless." But, once the dogma had been promulgated, faithful Catholics were required to recognize that "an all-sufficient motive of credibility as well as the true and only motive of Christian faith" had been furnished by the authoritative voice of the Church which had proclaimed, "It is revealed doctrine."[50] Non-Catholic historians, however, who had not been able to accept the authority of Rome, found themselves unable to endorse this approach to the credibility of a religious principle.

The Catholic Bishop McQuaid of Rochester had believed at the time of the Vatican Council of 1870 that an official pronouncement of papal infallibility would give "good reasons" to Protestants to wish to drive Catholics from the country. At any rate, many Protestant leaders of distinguished reputations felt that papal authority was a genuine challenge to traditional American freedom. A scholarly Presbyterian New York minister, Charles H. Parkhurst, declared:

> We can love Catholics, and in very many particulars
> admire them and their system, but . . . we can never

forget that a thorough Catholic accords his supreme
earthly loyalties to the Pope, and that an American
Catholic is primarily a papal subject living on American
soil.

John H. Vincent, Methodist bishop and founder of the
Chautauqua movement, asserted that Americans must maintain "sleepless vigilance" and "uncompromising and unre-
lenting antagonism" toward the principles of Roman author-
itarianism, though defending with life itself the right of
Catholics to freedom of worship.

When in 1893 the new Apostolic Delegate, Francisco
Satolli, for a time showed support for liberal Catholic views
on various questions of church administration, a prominent
Congregationalist, Leonard W. Bacon, declared that all this
was "in flat inconsistency with the solemnly declared principles," set forth in various papal encyclicals, though Protestants could be glad of the "good sense" displayed. Such
comments led Catholics to deprecate liberal Protestantism as
a vague "Undogmatic Christianity" scarcely distinguishable
from agnosticism and to predict that fifty years later Catholic
teaching in the United States would be "blooming and
vigorous," while the peculiar tenets of Protestant sects would
be "as extinct as the pterdactyl."

In less urbane circles, moreover, the religious prejudice
which many Protestants had been manifesting in the American Protective Association movement of the 1890's indicated
that tolerance had yet a far road to travel in the United
States.[51] A realistic approach to the spirit of the times would,
moreover, not be able to minimize the acerbities which still
marked relations between various Protestant groups. Dwight
L. Moody in 1899 decried the dangers of liberal, "destructive theology," but he found that, on the other hand, extreme
intolerance had likewise "wrought wide dissensions" in many
communities in America. He elaborated:

> . . . Instead of fighting error by the emphasis of truth,
> there has been too much 'splitting of hairs,' and too

often an unchristian spirit of bitterness. This has frequently resulted in depleted churches, and has opened
the way for the entrance of still greater errors.[52]

3. *Faith found an aid in a greater emphasis upon the
aesthetic approach to religion.* Not only were Roman Catholic churches and cathedrals often decorated with murals and
works of art, but Protestant churches took a course which
meant that "the bare order of service which characterized
the Puritan worship" had disappeared with the Puritan Sabbath. "Various forms of music, the elaboration of ritual,
church decorations and church architecture" had been introduced "to change the service of worship from its earlier simplicity to one of elaborate aesthetic import."[53] Episcopalian
clergymen would no longer be disciplined for using a robed
choir and for introducing the communion table. Presbyterians who had long been concerned in certain congregations
about the ritualistic trend associated with the use of responsive Scriptural readings, had become definitely interested in
a *Book of Common Worship.*

For some, rituals might seem an attempt at escape from
intellectual perplexities, but there may have been a wisdom,
in a period of waning orthodoxies, to insist, as did the mother
of a latter-day author, that one might find comfort "in a
heritage of beauty in word and feeling, in a habitual concern for the better order of earth," and in a regular infusion
"of an element of poetry into the prose of life."[54]

4. *Faith was aroused less by revivalistic method and more
by the "Christian nurture" of the home and Church.* In
Roman Catholic circles increased emphasis had been placed
on the role of parochial schools. In Protestant groups, revivalistic efforts as late as 1882 had prompted the President
of Amherst College to report that the chief blessing of the
year had been "a deep and pervasive religious revival."[55]
There too in 1895, B. Fay Mills, evangelist, had held four
days of intensive meetings. Yet, gradually, both in the colleges and in the urban community, revivals appeared less

central to the life of the Church.

5. *The Faith of the churches demanded a more effective expression of Christian faith in the life of the world.* As late as 1876, organized Protestantism in the United States had presented "a massive, almost unbroken front" in defense of the social and economic *status quo.*[56] The essentially conservative attitude of Catholicism at the time was soon evidenced by the attitude of many priests and bishops in opposition to the theories of Henry George. Yet, two decades later, social and economic criticism had penetrated deeply into every religious denomination, and after 1895 the new ideas of Social Christianity had come to dominate increasingly the most articulate sections of the Protestant Church. Without such vigorous faith rooted in religious values the Progressive movement might have been impossible. During the same period, moreover, Pope Leo XIII had implemented Catholic views of a more Christian social order in his encyclical of 1891.[57]

Thus, at the end of the century, the church was in a period of adjustment. In the midst of difficulties twenty years before Henry W. Grady, journalist and active Methodist layman, had predicted that the faith of the Church founded on the rock of a high consistency of its members, a warm and earnest evangelistic spirit, and the purity and gentleness of its apostles, would eventually win.[58] Many were confident by 1900 that such a faith had never spoken more eloquently in the life of the times than it did at that juncture, for, it was asserted, "The Christ walks more perceptibly among the haunts of men and is oftener in the market place, in the court-room and at the fireside" than ever before.

James Parton, the famous biographer, who called himself "a pagan," had written in 1867 that if "anything can be predicated of the future with certainty, it is, that the American people will never give up that portion of their heritage from the past which we call Sunday, but will always devote its hour to resting the body and improving the soul."[59]

Many confidently believed that the very conflict of faith had emancipated it from that which was childish and even untrue. The development of the views of Edward Francis Baxter Orton (1829-1899), first president of the Ohio State University, shows in remarkable fashion much of the transition in thought during the period. Orton himself was the son of an upper New York state Calvinist minister, and he himself had become a Presbyterian minister in 1856. He had, however, pursued scientific studies at Harvard University, and while teaching at the State Normal School at Albany had expressed to a Sunday School class, ideas which at the time were deemed heterodox. Therefore, to prevent public scandal he felt constrained to resign his teaching position (1859), and his religious views during the remainder of his life were much more liberal than those in which he had been nurtured.[60]

Orton became a distinguished geologist, and in an address before the Alumni of Hamilton College in June 1888, he pointed to "the immense and inestimable service that modern science had rendered to Christian theology, how much it has done to broaden and rationalize it and thus to perpetuate and strengthen its hold on the world." He proclaimed with joy the way in which man had been freed from the narrow literalism of the Creation story, from the idea of an arbitrary God who visits pestilences and destruction to manifest his wrath, from the ideas of witches and of insanity induced by evil spirits, and from views which turned "all the heathen into hell." On the positive side, he maintained, modern theology could now find strength in:

(a) A realization of "the reign of law" in both the "worlds of matter and mind." This meant that "the earthquake shock is a part of the force that fashions the dry land and builds upon it the mountains that are its strength and glory," and that the religious man could confidently "rely upon this integrity of nature."

(b) The revolutionary doctrine of the divine immanence. This meant that the "power that rules the world has

not retreated into the depths of a distant heaven" but is
"present here and now, in all that we call the forces of
nature, nearer to us than aught else can be."

(c) A more "natural and rational" view of the Bible as
a book "charged with fresh and original spiritual life, giving
light to all that are in the house when set on its own candle-
stick and not covered by the bushel of fictitious claims."

(d) An understanding of "how central and potent a factor religion has always been in all the progressive races of
men and how much in common all these religions have."

Thus, Orton found in the method of science "the best
gift that God has given to the mind of man." But, for him
there could be no conflict with true religion since,

> Beyond the final and all-comprehending law of reason
> and righteousness which was laid down by Jesus of Naza-
> reth, it is impossible to go. The whole was uttered then,
> and any other statement is but a repetition.[61]

Orton personally was a very spiritually-minded man on
whose desk one might often find a book of devotions.[62] For
many persons, nevertheless, views of men like Orton partook
too definitely of "scientism" and placed too little emphasis
on older views of divine Revelation. Yet, such conceptions
as those held by Orton had definitely affected the thought of
a whole generation of church-goers.

Certainly, however little or much personal views had
been altered, the faith of the Church lived on in the hearts
and lives of men. Perhaps no one expressed it more poign-
antly than Dr. Oliver Wendell Holmes, the poet, who personally was definitely a rebel against the old theology, and
who had come to believe in one loving God, revealed "in-
fallibly in creation," in nature, and in Jesus, and in religion
consisting in "holy affections, the evidence of which is in
the righteous life." He had written in 1888:

> . . . But my natural Sunday home is King's Chapel, where

a good and amicable and acceptable preacher tries to make us better, with a purity and sincerity which we admire and love. In that church I have worshipped for half a century, there I listened to Dr. Greenwood, to Ephraim Peabody, often to James Walker, and to other holy and wise men who have served us from time to time. There, . . . I was married, there my children were all christened, from that church the dear companion of so many blessed years was buried. In her seat I must sit, and through its door I hope to be carried to my resting-place. . . .[63]

Thus, the faith of the churches and the definite cultivation of it were deeply rooted in the common joys, disappointments, and tragedies of life. The storms of intellectual controversy might threaten the very foundations, and the winds of new doctrine might assail this bulwark of the common life. Yet, for millions of Americans, the experience of Holmes, varying as to time, place, and cultural background, carried with it a deep-seated loyalty amidst a changing world.[64] What might happen in the twentieth century still awaited the unfolding of time and circumstance.[65]

General note: Further details regarding individuals mentioned in the text can be found, in most instances, in *Dictionary of American Biography* ed. by Allen Johnson, Dumas Malone, *et al.*, 20 vols. and supplements (N. Y., 1928-   ).

NOTES FOR INTRODUCTION

1. *Democracy in America,* 2 vols. (N.Y., 1945), I, 300-14.
2. "The American Acta Sanctorum," *American Historical Review,* XIII (1907-8), 286-302.
3. Paul S. Mower, *The House of Europe* (Boston, 1945), 394-5.
4. *Proceedings of the Massachusetts Historical Society,* LXIV (1932), 523-37.
5. Spalding, *Things of the Mind* (Chicago, 1894), 211-12.
6. Introduction to Sidney Warren, *American Free Thought, 1860-1914* (N.Y., 1943).

NOTES FOR CHAPTER I

1. Bascom N. Timmons, *Portrait of An American: Charles G. Dawes* (N. Y., 1953), letter on p. 9.
2. Perry Miller, *Orthodoxy in Massachusetts, 1630-1650. A Genetic Study* (Cambridge, 1933); Raymond P. Stearns, "Assessing the New England Mind," *Church History,* X (1941), 246-62.
3. Herbert W. Schneider, *A History of American Philosophy* (N. Y., 1946), 3.
4. William W. Fenn, "The Revolt Against the Standing Order," *The Religious History of New England* (Cambridge, Mass., 1917).
5. Robert H. Lord, *et al., History of the Archdiocese of Boston,* 3 vols. (N. Y., 1944), II.
6. *Letters of James Russell Lowell,* ed. by C. E. Norton, 2 vols. (N.Y., 1894), I, 348.

7. Merle Curti, "Human Nature in American Thought," *Pol. Sci. Quart.*, (Dec., 1953), LXVIII, 492-510.

8. Goldwin Smith, "Will Morality Survive Religion?" *The Forum*, XI (April 1891), 155.

9. "The Cultivation of Theology in Colleges," *The Nation*, XXIX (July 3, 1879), 6-7.

10. Samuel E. Morison, ed. *The Development of Harvard University . . . 1869-1929* (Cambridge, 1930), 108 ff.

11. Edward E. Hale, Jr., *The Life and Letters of Edward Everett Hale*, 2 vols. (Boston, 1917), II, 10-11, 15, 30-1.

12. Lyman Abbott, "The Growth of Religious Tolerance in the United States," *Forum*, XXIII (Aug. 1897), 653-660.

13. M. A. DeWolfe Howe, *A Venture in Remembrance* (Boston, 1941), p. 90.

14. Geo. Herbert Palmer, *The Life of Alice Freeman Palmer* (Boston, 1908), 90-92.

15. L. Clark Seelye, *The Early History of Smith College, 1871-1900* (Boston, 1923), p. 60-1.

16. Louise Fargo Brown, *Apostle of Democracy: The Life of Lucy Maynard Salmon* (N. Y., 1943), p. 65.

17. Frederick C. Waite, *Western Reserve University: The Hudson Era . . . 1826 to 1882* (Cleveland, 1943), 139, 433-4.

18. W. W. Sweet, *Revivalism in America* (N. Y., 1944), 169-70; Paul D. Moody, *My Father* (Boston, 1938), 124.

19. David Schaff, *Philip Schaff* (N. Y., 1897), 252-8.

20. *The Memoirs of William Jennings Bryan and His Wife Mary Baird Bryan* (Philadelphia, 1925), 47 ff., 450.

21. *The Autobiography of William Allen White* (N. Y., 1946), 60-1.

22. Champ Clark, *My Quarter Century of American Politics*, 2 vols. (N. Y., 1920), I, 33-5.

23. Isaac F. Marcosson, *"Marse Henry": A Biography of Henry Watterson* (N. Y., 1951), 38.

24. Victor L. Albjerg, *Richard Owen* in *Archives of Purdue*, No. 2 (March, 1946), 97.

25. Paul Sayre, *The Life of Roscoe Pound* (Iowa City, 1948), 15-6, 53, 389.

26. Colin B. Goodykoontz, *Home Missions on the American Frontier* (Caldwell, Idaho, 1938), 335-6, 350.

27. Angie Debo, *Prairie City, The Story of an American Community* (N. Y., 1944), 28-36.

28. Absent from such an occasion often were local Catholic families who might drive on some Sundays a distance of fifteen or twenty miles to the nearest Catholic chapel.

29. John T. Morse, Jr., *Life and Letters of O. W. Holmes* 2 vols. (Boston, 1896), I, 280 ff.

30. M. A. DeWolfe Howe, *Portrait of an Independent, Moorfield Storey, 1845-1929* (Boston, 1929), 361.

31. George L. Austin, *The Life and Times of Wendell Phillips* (Boston, ed. of 1901), 385.

32. Carl Swisher, *Roger B. Taney* (N. Y., 1935), 50-1, 395. Sophia, one of the six daughters, rather late in life voluntarily became a Catholic.

33. Eric F. Goldman, *Charles J. Bonaparte, Patrician Reformer: His Earlier Career* (Baltimore, 1943), 17-8; T. Harry Williams, *P. G. T. Beauregard, Napoleon in Gray* (Baton Rouge, 1955), 36, 327.

34. D. R. Sharpe, *Walter Rauschenbusch* (New York, 1942), 13, 41, 45.

35. James H. Moynihan, *Archbishop Ireland* (N. Y., 1953), 8.

36. Allen S. Will, *Life of Cardinal Gibbons,* 2 vols. (N. Y., 1912), I, 182.

37. John T. Ellis, *The Life of James, Cardinal Gibbons,* 2 vols. (Milwaukee, 1952), II, 581-92.

38. *Ibid.,* II, 592-5; Robert D. Cross, *The Emergence of Liberal Catholicism in America* (Cambridge, Mass., 1958).

39. Indeed, when the future Bishop of Savannah, Benjamin Keiley, heard of the action of the Baltimore prelate he wrote privately that Gibbons had "outeroded Herod in wanting Catholics to recognize the damnably Puritan substitute for Christmas." *Ibid.,* II, 5.

40. Will, *op. cit.*, I, 208-9.

41. Royal Cortissoz, *John LaFarge: A Memoir and a Study* (Boston and New York, 1911), 260, 258.

42. *The Forum,* XXIII, 659. Of course, all enlightened Catholics knew that Protestants who in complete sincerity held to their beliefs were not considered to be eternally lost, and many Protestants were not unmindful of the virtues of Catholicism.

43. Kenneth R. Andrews, *Nook Farm: Mark Twain's Hartford Circle* (Cambridge, Mass., 1950), 10, 11 and note, 250.

44. George Stewart Stokes, *Agnes Repplier, Lady of Letters* (Philadelphia, 1949), 260, 107.

45. Ellis, *Gibbons,* II, 492.

46. Maurice F. Egan, *Recollections of a Happy Life* (N. Y., 1924), ix.

47. Belle Case LaFollette and Fola LaFollette, *Robert M. LaFollette,* 2 vols., (N. Y., 1953), I, 12.

48. Egan, *op. cit.*, 161-3, 170.

49. *Memoir of Samuel J. May* (Boston, 1882), 294.

50. Ellis, *Gibbons,* I, 167; II, 582.

51. William Cardinal O'Connell, *Recollections of Seventy Years* (Boston, 1934), 5-6. Francis A. Christie, noted scholar, who also had been raised in Lowell, took definite exception to the accuracy of these recollections in, "An Historical Footnote on Cardinal O'Connell's *Recollections,*" *N. E. Quarterly,* VIII (1935), 268-62.

52. John LaFarge, S. J., *The Manner Is Ordinary* (N. Y., 1954), 37.

53. Ellis, *Gibbons,* I, 322.

54. P. H. Ahern, *The Catholic University of America, 1887-1896* (Washington, D. C., 1948), 61.

55. David Schaff, *op. cit., passim.*

56. Ahern, *op. cit.*, 62.

57. Ahern, *op. cit.*, 65-66; and Ellis, *Gibbons,* II, 12-13.

58. David Schaff, *op. cit.*, 490.

59. Moynihan, *op. cit.*, 39-40; Ellis, *op. cit.*, II, 13 ff.

60. Ahern, *op. cit.*, 67-69.

61. *The World's Parliament of Religions* (Chicago, 1893), II, 1559-60, quoted in Ahern, 69 note. For a fuller account of Keane's career, see P. H. Ahern, *Life of John J. Keane* (Washington, 1953).

62. Thos. T. McAvoy, "Americanism, Fact and Fiction," *The Catholic Hist. Review*, XXXI (1945), 133-54; Ahern, *Catholic University of America, 1887-1896*, 162-181.

63. Hogan, *Catholic University of America, 1896-1903*, 18.

64. Henry Morgenthau, *All in A Lifetime* (N. Y., 1922), 15-6, 128-9.

65. Geo. Haven Putnam, *Memoirs of a Publisher, 1865-1915* (N. Y., 1916), 13.

66. Octavius B. Frothingham, *Recollections and Impressions, 1822-1890* (Boston, 1891).

67. Hamilton Schuyler, *The Roeblings* (Princeton, 1931), 325.

68. George Hodges, *Henry C. Potter* (N. Y., 1915), 183.

69. Jacob Riis, *The Making of An American* (N. Y., 1901), 85-6.

70. Mary Earhart, *From Prayers to Politics* (Chicago, 1944), 27-39.

71. Elmer T. Clark, *The Small Sects in America* (Nashville, 1937), 92 ff.

72. William Lawrence, *Memoirs of a Happy Life*, 186.

73. *Harper's Weekly*, Oct. 21, 1893.

74. Bacon, *Munger*, 313.

NOTES FOR CHAPTER II

1. *The Heritage of the Reformation*, ed. by Elmer J. F. Arndt (N. Y., 1950), 23; Harold J. Grimm, *The Reformation Era* (N. Y., 1956).

2. Arthur C. McGiffert, *The Rise of Modern Religious Ideas* (N. Y., 1915), 5 ff.

3. Ralph B. Perry, *Puritanism and Democracy* (N. Y., 1944), 82 ff.

4. See *e. g.,* Whitney R. Cross, *The Burned-over District . . . 1800-1850* (Ithaca, N. Y., 1950).

5. *Life and Letters of E. L. Godkin,* ed. by Rollo Ogden, 2 vols. (N. Y., 1907), II, 37.

6. George S. Merriam, *The Life and Times of Samuel Bowles,* 2 vols. (N. Y., 1885), II, 48-9.

7. Henry Adams, *Education of Henry Adams* (Boston, 1918), 35.

8. See discussion in Chapter IX and in Chapter XI.

9. Phillips Brooks, "A Sermon on the Nature of the Church" (Dec. 19, 1886), printed in *Theology Today,* XII (April 1955), 57-67.

10. Riis, *op. cit.,* 32-3.

11. Oliver Carlson, *The Man Who Made News: James Gordon Bennett* (N. Y., 1942), 10-18, 140-175. He had been excommunicated after a quarrel with Bishop Hughes in 1841. P. 213 f.

12. The best biography is Stephen Bell, *Edward McGlynn, Rebel, Priest and Prophet* (N. Y., 1937).

13. A fine account of the resulting controversy, by a Catholic scholar, is Ellis, *Gibbons,* I, 547-95. See also Charles A. Barker, *Henry George* (N. Y., 1955), 464-67; *Harper's Weekly,* Apr. 16, 1887.

14. Anna George de Mille, *Henry George* (Chapel Hill, 1950), 118-9.

15. Ellis, *Gibbons,* I, 550; Barker, *H. George,* 486-87.

16. Ellis, *Gibbons,* I, 552.

17. De Mille, *Henry George,* 156-8.

18. Ellis, *Gibbons,* I, 559, 585.

19. De Mille, *op. cit.,* 159.

20. Ellis, *op. cit.,* I, 568.

21. Moynihan, *Ireland,* 230-232.

22. Ellis, *op. cit.,* I, 571; Barker, *H. George,* 489.

23. *The Independent,* XLIII (Nov. 26, 1891), 1754.

24. Ellis, *op. cit.,* I, 590; Barker, *H. George,* 576-77.

25. De Mille, *op. cit.,* 241; Barker, *H. George,* 619.

26. Maurice F. Egan, *op. cit.,* 133.

27. Ellis, *op. cit.,* II, 460, 469.

28. Sister Mary A. Kwitchen, *James Alphonsus McMasters: A Study in American Thought* (Washington, 1949), 184-9.

29. Ellis, *op. cit.,* I, 599; II, 323 f. See also Moynihan, *Ireland,* 16-18.

30. Gordon A. Riegler, "The Story of Religion in Toledo, 1865-1900," Part Two, *Northwest Ohio Quarterly,* XXVI, 85 f.

31. Ellis, *Gibbons,* I, 10-11; Cross, *op. cit.*

32. Ellis, *The Formative Years of the Catholic U. of America,* 288-9.

33. Moynihan, *Ireland,* 36. For a later discussion of these tendencies, see chapter XI.

34. W. J. McNiff, *Heaven on Earth: A Planned Mormon Society,* (Oxford, Ohio, 1940); Ray B. West, Jr., *Kingdom of the Saints* (N. Y., 1957); Thomas F. O'Dea, *The Mormons* (Chicago, 1957).

35. Allan Nevins, *The Emergence of Modern America, 1865-1878,* (N. Y., 1927), 141-43.

36. William A. Linn, *The Story of the Mormons* (N. Y., 1902), 560 ff.

37. Nels Anderson, *Desert Saints: The Mormon Frontier in Utah* (Chicago, 1942), 301.

38. Linn, *op. cit.,* 566.

39. Anderson, *op. cit.,* 302.

40. Nevins, *op. cit.,* 144.

41. Robert J. Dwyer, *The Gentile Comes to Utah: A Study in Religious and Social Conflict, 1862-1890* (Washington D. C., 1941), 248-49.

42. Anderson, *op. cit.,* 330.

NOTES FOR CHAPTER III

1. Perry Miller, *The New England Mind: The Seventeenth Century* (N. Y., 1939), 59.

2. Hunter D. Farish, *The Circuit Rider Dismounts: A Social History of Southern Methodism, 1865-1900* (Richmond, Va., 1938), 30-2.

3. Francis B. Simkins and Robert H. Woody, *South Carolina During Reconstruction* (Chapel Hill, 1932), 396.

4. Cincinnati *Gazette*, June 16, 1865, quoted in E. M. Coulter, *The Civil War and Readjustment in Kentucky* (Chapel Hill, 1926), 394.

5. Lewis G. Vander Velde, *The Presbyterian Churches and the Federal Union* (Cambridge, 1932), 183 ff.

6. Farish, *op. cit.*, 40-41.

7. E. M. Coulter, *The South During Reconstruction 1865-1877* (Baton Rouge, 1947), 332.

8. W. B. Hesseltine, *Confederate Leaders of the New South* (Baton Rouge, 1950), 70-72.

9. Coulter, *op. cit.*, 335.

10. Robert H. Elias, *Theodore Dreiser: Apostle of Nature* (N. Y., 1949), 12-13.

11. *Challenging Years: The Memoirs of Harriot Stanton Blatch,* by Harriot S. Blatch and Alma Lutz (N. Y., 1940), 21.

12. Aaron I. Abell, *The Urban Impact on American Protestantism* (Cambridge, 1943), 21-3.

13. Henry F. May, *Protestant Churches and Industrial America* (N. Y., 1949), 54.

14. John T. Ellis, *The Formative Years of the Catholic University of America* (Washington, 1946), 65.

15. George S. Hellman, *Benjamin N. Cardozo, American Judge* (N. Y., 1940), 10-3.

16. Cincinnati *Daily Commercial*, Nov. 6, 1874, quoted by H. C. Hubbart, *The Older Middle West* (N. Y., 1936), 273.

17. *Atlantic Monthly*, XIX (Jan. 1867), 40.

18. Theodore C. Smith, *Life and Letters of James A. Garfield*, 2 vols. (New Haven, 1925), II, 774-5.

19. Emory K. Lindquist, *Smoky Valley People: A History of Lindsborg, Kansas* (Lindsborg, 1953), 25, 190-1.

20. Ira V. Brown, *Lyman Abbott* (Cambridge, 1953), 113-5.

21. Quoted in Abell, *op. cit.*, 63.

22. Gladden, *The Church and Modern Life* (Boston, 1908), 145.

23. Harold L. Ickes, *The Autobiography of a Curmudgeon* (N. Y., 1943), 21-2.

24. John T. Ellis, *op. cit.*, 66.

25. Carl Wittke, *Against the Current: The Life of Karl Heinzen, 1809-80* (Chicago, 1945). His views were related to the intellectual adjustments of the time, to be discussed later.

26. Ellis, *Gibbons*, I, 332-43.

27. This will be discussed in more detail later. See John J. Meng, "Cahenslyism: The First Stage, 1883-1891," *Catholic Historical Review*, XXXI (Jan. 1946), 389-413, and "Cahenslyism: The Second Chapter, 1891-1900," in *ibid.*, XXXII (Oct. 1946), 302-40.

28. Rev. Henry J. Browne, "The Italian Problem in the Catholic Church of the U. S., 1880-1890," Catholic Historical Society, *Historical Records and Studies*, XXXV (N. Y., 1946), 46-72.

29. Giovanni Schiavo, *Italian-American History, II: The Italian Contribution to the Catholic Church in America* (N. Y., 1949), 477.

30. Rev. Henry J. Browne, *loc. cit.*, 55.

31. Wellington G. Fordyce, "Immigrants' Institutions in Cleveland," *Ohio Historical Quart.*, XLVII (1938), 89.

32. Wittke, *We Who Built America* (N. Y., 1939), 425.

33. Edward A. Ross, *Seventy Years of It: An Autobiography* (New York, 1936), 115.

34. Cyrenus Cole, *I Remember, I Remember* (Iowa City, 1936), 48.

35. Wittke, *We Who Built America*, 211 f.

36. *The House of Europe* (Boston, 1945), 6-9.

37. For the success of the churches in overcoming this tendency in one community see William W. Howard, "The Modern Leadville," *Harper's Weekly*, Dec. 1, 1888.

38. John P. Hylan, *Public Worship: A Study in the Psychology of Religion* (Chicago, 1901), 6.

39. Augustus J. Thebaud, *Forty Years in the United States of America* (N. Y., 1904), 305.

40. Harold S. Jacoby, *Remember the Sabbath Day? The Nature and Causes of the Changes in Sunday Observance Since 1800* (a Summary), (Philadelphia, 1945), 10.

41. Mark D. Hirsch, *William C. Whitney, Modern Warwick* (N. Y., 1948), 6, 44.

42. Noel P. Gist, "Secret Organizations: A Cultural Study of Fraternalism in the U.S.," *U. of Missouri Studies*, XV (Oct. 1940), No. 4, 1-184.

NOTES FOR CHAPTER IV

1. A popular summary, perhaps overly dogmatic in viewpoint is John H. Randall, *The Making of the Modern Mind* (Boston, 1926). See also Arthur C. McGiffert, *The Rise of Modern Religious Ideas* (N. Y., 1915).

2. Herbert M. Morais, *Deism in Eighteenth Century America* (N. Y., 1934); Gustav A. Koch, *Republican Religion* (N. Y., 1933).

3. Clement Eaton, *Freedom of Thought in the Old South* (Durham, N. C., 1940), 280.

4. Albert Post, *Popular Free Thought in America* (N. Y., 1943), 226 ff.

5. Donald Fleming, *John W. Draper and the Religion of Science* (Philadelphia, 1950) .

6. Edward A. White, *Science and Religion in American Thought: The Impact of Naturalism* (Stanford, 1952) , 2.

7. *National Academy of Science, Bibliographical Memoirs* (Washington, 1886) , II, 375.

8. Sidney Warren, *American Free Thought, 1860-1915* (N. Y., 1943) , 60.

9. White, *op. cit.,* 30.

10. Incidentally, Godkin was the son of an Irish Presbyterian minister of English blood, who had lost his pulpit in 1848 for writing a prize essay favoring Home Rule. See Louis Filler, "The Early Godkin," *The Historian,* XVII (Autumn, 1954), 43-66.

11. May 11, 1885, quoted in John T. Ellis, *The Formative Years of the Catholic University of America,* 150-1.

12. B. W. Bacon, *Theodore T. Munger* (New Haven, 1913) .

13. Kenneth R. Andrews, *op. cit.,* 50-1.

14. Walter P. Rogers, *Andrew D. White and the Modern University* (Ithaca, N. Y., 1942) , p. 83.

15. Edward A. White, *op. cit.,* 34-36.

16. Moynihan, *Ireland,* 104.

17. Rogers, *op. cit.,* 76.

18. Andrew D. White, *Autobiography,* I, 425-6.

19. Edward A. White, *op. cit.,* 35-36.

20. Quoted in John T. Ellis, *op. cit.,* 288-9.

21. H. W. Conn, in *The Methodist Review,* LXXII (N. Y., 1890) , 79-92.

22. Chas. C. Gillespie, *Genesis and Geology* (Cambridge, Mass., 1951) , 224.

23. Conrad Wright, *The New England Quarterly,* XIV, 338 f.

24. Daniel C. Gilman, *Life of James Dwight Dana* (N. Y., 1899) , 188.

25. Wertenbaker, *Princeton, 1746-1896,* 312-3.

26. Nevins and Thomas, *Diary, Geo. T. Strong, 1865-75,* 155-6.

27. Gillespie, *op. cit.*, viii.

28. Victor L. Albjerg, *op. cit.*, 62-3.

29. Washington Gladden, "Professor Edward Orton, 1829-1899," *Ohio Archaeological and Historical Publications*, VIII (Columbus, 1900), 416-417. For further discussion of Orton, see pp. 317-18.

30. See Chapter VII.

31. Chas. H. Page, *Class and American Sociology: From Ward to Ross* (N. Y., 1940), 31.

32. Review of G. Frederick Wright, *The Ice Age in North America and its Bearings on the Antiquity of Man*, in *The Presbyterian and Reformed Review*, II (April 1891), 365-66.

NOTES FOR CHAPTER V

1. Robert Scoon, "The Rise and Impact of Evolutionary Ideas," in Stow Persons, ed., *Evolutionary Thought in America* (New Haven, 1950), 4-43.

2. Bert J. Loewenberg, "Darwinism Comes to America, 1859-1900," *Miss. Valley Historical Review*, XXVIII (Dec., 1941), 343.

3. Bert J. Loewenberg, "The Reaction of American Scientists to Darwinism," *American Historical Review*, XXXVIII (1933), 687 f.

4. Hofstadter, *Social Darwinism in American Thought* (Philadelphia, 1945), 15.

5. Daniel C. Gilman, *James Dwight Dana*.

6. Windsor Hall Roberts, *The Reaction of American Protestant Churches to the Darwinian Philosophy*, 1860-1900 —*A Summary*— (Chicago, Ill., 1938), 1-2.

7. Frank H. Foster, *The Modern Movement in American Theology* (N. Y., 1939), 41-42.

8. Windsor H. Roberts, *op. cit.,* 3-4.

9. Windsor H. Roberts, *op. cit.,* 5.

10. Hofstadter, *op. cit.,* 12-13. Yet, even Hodge in 1873 expressed the possibility of a theistic interpretation of evolution. (Loewenberg, in *N. E. Quarterly,* VIII, 247.) Between 1831 and 1871, actually, Darwin's personal views had changed from strict Christian orthodoxy to an undogmatic skepticism. Maurice Mendelbaum, "Darwin's Religious Views," *Journal of the History of Ideas,* XIX (June, 1958), 363-78.

11. This was in spite of a rather tolerant attitude toward evolution in the *Catholic World,* 1865-6. Information furnished the author by Mrs. Elizabeth Gleason.

12. Hofstadter, *op. cit.,* 12-13.

13. Windsor H. Roberts, *op. cit.,* 6-7.

14. Yet, another Unitarian minister, Moncure D. Conway, who edited a literary magazine, *The Dial,* in Cincinnati, offered in 1860 a favorable review of *Origin of Species.* E. H. Roseboom, *The Civil War Era* (Columbus, O., 1944), 148.

15. Edward Hungerford, *Daniel Willard,* 22-24.

16. Abbott, *Beecher,* 317.

17. Stow Persons, *op. cit.,* 428 ff.

18. Roberts, *op. cit.,* 9-10.

19. Hofstadter, *op. cit.,* 13.

20. Schneider, *op. cit.,* 373-4.

21. Merle Curti and Vernon Carstensen, *The University of Wisconsin,* 2 vols. (Madison, 1949), I, 277-78.

22. Arthur J. Hope, *Notre Dame: One Hundred Years* (Notre Dame, Ind., 1943), 174, 260-61; John Lee Morrison, "A History of Catholic Opinion on the Theory of Evolution, 1859-1950," *Microfilm Abstracts,* XI (1951), 1007-1008.

23. William M. Agar, *Catholicism and the Progress of Science* (N. Y., 1940), 88 ff. The Catholic Church announced no official stand on evolution.

24. Hofstadter, *op. cit.,* 14.

25. Nevins and Thomas, *op. cit.,* 155-6, 355.

26. James T. Addison, *op. cit.,* 246-7.

27. For a summary of his views from the philosophical standpoint, see W. H. Werkmeister, *A History of Philosophical Ideas in America* (N. Y., 1949), 95-103. For analysis of his religious views, see H. Burnell Pannill, *The Religious Faith of John Fiske* (Durham, N. C., 1957).

28. John Spencer Clark, *The Life and Letters of John Fiske* 2 vols. (Boston, 1917), 66, 84-5, 88 ff., 110-115.

29. Ethel F. Fisk, ed. *The Letters of John Fiske* (N. Y., 1940), 35 ff.

30. Edward A. White, *op. cit.*, 37-40.

31. Clarke, *Fiske*, II, 39-40; Pannill, *op. cit.*, *passim*.

32. Fisk, *Letters*, 378-9.

33. Sidney Warren, *American Free Thought, 1860-1915,* 46-7.

34. Clark, *Fiske*, II, 155, 170.

35. Fisk, *Letters*, 511.

36. Ferm, *op. cit.*, I, 341.

37. Paxton Hibben, *Henry Ward Beecher* (N. Y., 1927).

38. Ira V. Brown, *Lyman Abbott*, 75.

39. See W. W. Quillian, Jr., "Evolution and Moral Thought in America," in Stow Persons, ed. *Evolutionary Thought in America*, 398-421.

40. Maurice F. Egan, *op. cit.*, 95.

41. Eugene W. Lyman in Ferm, *Contemporary American Theology*, II, 106-7.

42. Ferm, *op. cit.*, I, 56.

43. W. H. Werkmeister, *op. cit.*, 87-95.

44. Windsor H. Roberts, *op. cit.*, 13 note.

45. Werkmeister, *op. cit.*, 83-4.

46. Edward Mims, *History of Vanderbilt University* (Nashville, 1946), 100-102.

47. Sidney Warren, *op. cit.*, 59.

48. Hunter D. Farish, *op. cit.*, 297-8.

49. Ferm, *op. cit.*, II, 245.

50. Windsor H. Roberts, *op. cit.*, 18-19.

51. Windsor H. Roberts, *op. cit.*, 25.

52. *The Methodist Review*, LXXV (N. Y., 1893), 866.

NOTES FOR CHAPTER VI

1. Joseph H. Allen and Richard Eddy, *A History of Unitarians and Universalists in the U. S.* (N. Y., 1913), 209.

2. James T. Addison, *The Episcopal Church in the U. S. 1789-1931* (N. Y., 1951), 246; Geoffrey C. Faber, *Jowett, A Portrait with Background* (Cambridge, Mass., 1957).

3. B. Harvie Branscomb, "The Study and Interpretation of the Bible," *The Church Through Half a Century,* (N. Y., 1936), 165.

4. James T. Addison, *op. cit.,* 246-7.

5. Walter Phelps Hall, "The Three Arnolds and the Bible," *Essays in Intellectual History Dedicated to James Harvey Robinson* (N. Y., 1929), 74-8.

6. A brief summary is found in George Ernest Wright, "The Study of the Old Testament," in Arnold S. Nash, *Protestant Thought in the Twentieth Century* (N. Y., 1951), 47 f.

7. Edward Hungerford, *op. cit.,* 22.

8. George Harris, *A Century's Change in Religion* (Boston, 1914), 10.

9. A. Mitchell Hunter, *The Teaching of Calvin: A Modern Interpretation* (London, 1950), 63-5.

10. Harris, *op. cit.,* 77-8.

11. *Op. cit.,* 288.

12. John T. Morse, Jr., *op. cit.,* II, 296-7.

13. Washington Gladden, *Recollections* (Boston, 1909), 260-1.

14. Frank D. Ashburn, *Peabody of Groton: A Portrait* (N. Y., 1944) 37 f.

15. George F. Parker, *Recollections of Grover Cleveland,* (N. Y., 1911), 382.

16. William R. Moody, *The Life of Dwight L. Moody* (N. Y., 1900), 494 ff.

17. *Op. cit.,* 60-1; 107.

18. Vergilius Ferm, ed., *Contemporary Theology,* II, 345-6; *Ibid.,* I (1932) , 88.

19. Abbott, *Henry Ward Beecher,* 438-42.

20. C. H. Cramer, *Royal Bob: The Life of Robert G. Ingersoll,* (Indianapolis, 1952) , 123-7, 108-9.

21. Gladden, *Recollections,* 320-1.

22. *Who Wrote the Bible?,* 1.

23. Gladden, *Recollections,* 321.

24. Alexis Cope, *History of Ohio State University* (ed. by Thos. C. Mendenhall), I, (Columbus, 1920) , 187.

25. Edward A. Ross, *op. cit.,* 116.

26. Eric F. Goldman, "David Graham Phillips," in Willard Thorp, ed., *The Lives of Eighteen From Princeton* (Princeton, 1946) 318-20.

27. Ferm, *Contemporary Theology,* II, 105.

28. Hunter D. Farish, *op. cit.,* 100 and note.

29. For an appraisal of his career, see W. F. Albright, "James Henry Breasted, Humanist," *The American Scholar,* V (1936) , 287-99.

30. Philip Schaff, *The Creeds of Christendom,* 3 vols. (N. Y., 1877) , III, 604.

31. Robert E. Thompson, *A History of the Presbyterian Churches in the U. S.* (N. Y., 1907) , 261-2.

32. David Schaff, *op. cit.,* 430.

33. Thompson, *op. cit.,* 265.

34. George L. Prentiss, *The Bright Side of Life,* 2 vols. (n. p., 1901) , II, 378.

35. An excellent discussion of the Briggs case is in Lefferts A. Loetscher, *The Broadening Church: A Study of Theological Issues in the Presbyterian Church since 1869* (Philadelphia, 1954), 48-62.

36. John J. McCook (compiler) , *The Appeal in the Briggs Heresy,* 51.

37. Lyman Abbott, *Reminiscences,* 453.

38. Hodges, *op. cit.,* 302 f.

39. David Schaff, *Philip Schaff,* 436; Philip Schaff, "Other

Heresy Trials and the Briggs Case," *The Forum* (Jan., 1892) , 621-34.

40. Thompson, *op. cit.,* 265.

41. Loetscher, *op. cit.,* 52.

42. Walter R. Bowie, *The Master of the Hill: A Biography of John Meigs* (N. Y., 1917) , 257-8.

43. Loetscher, *op. cit.,* 52; Charles H. Parkhurst, *My Forty Years in New York* (N. Y., 1923) , 50.

44. David Schaff, *op. cit.,* 431.

45. Loetscher, *op. cit.,* 55.

46. *Minutes of the General Assembly of the Presbyterian Church in the U. S. A., 1892* (Philadelphia, 1892) , 119 ff.

47. Bowie, *op. cit.,* 260 f.

48. *Minutes of the General Assembly of the Presbyterian Church in the U. S. A., 1893* (Philadelphia, 1893), 163 ff.

49. David Schaff, *op. cit.,* 434.

50. Theron G. Strong, *Joseph H. Choate* (N. Y., 1917) , 152.

51. Lefferts A. Loetscher, "C. A. Briggs in the Retrospect of Half a Century," *Theology Today,* XII (April 1955) , 42.

52. David Schaff, *op. cit.,* 434, 440; T. C. Hall, *John Hall, Pastor and Preacher* (N. Y., 1901) , 289, 288 note.

53. Loetscher, *op. cit.,* 63-68.

54. Thompson, *History of the Presbyterian Church,* 270-2.

55. Loetscher, *op. cit.,* 71-4.

56. Philip Schaff, *loc. cit.,* 633.

57. Robert H. Nichols, "Leader of Liberal Presbyterianism," in R. Niebuhr, ed., *This Ministry: The Contribution of Henry Sloane Coffin,* (N. Y., 1945) , 42.

58. This was declaratory and not a part of the Church's constitution.

59. Vergilius Ferm, ed., *Contemporary American Theology,* I, (N. Y., 1932) , 4.

60. Carl S. Patton, "The American Theological Scene: Fifty Years Ago in Retrospect," *Journal of Religion,* XVI (1936), 447.

61. Harper, *Religion and the Higher Life* (1904).

62. Hodges, *op. cit.*, 135 ff.; Alexander V. G. Allen, *Phillips Brooks* (N. Y., 1907), 407.

63. James T. Addison, *op. cit.*, 252.

64. Ferm, ed., *Contemporary American Theology*, I, 143-4.

65. George Harris, *op. cit.*, 84.

66. Cited in B. Harvie Branscomb, "The Study and Interpretation of the Bible," in *The Church Through Half a Century: Essays in Honor of Wm. Adams Brown* (N. Y., 1936), 169.

67. Wm. O'Connell, *Recollections of Seventy Years* (Boston, 1934), 120-122.

68. Raymond Corrigan, S. J., *The Church and the Nineteenth Century* (Milwaukee, 1938), 268-9.

69. Moynihan, *Ireland* (Ireland afterwards expressed his total rejection of Loisy's theories), 340 ff.

70. *Challenging Years: The Memoirs of Harriot Stanton Blatch.* By Harriot S. Blatch and Alma Lutz (N. Y., 1940), 22.

71. "What Does Revelation Reveal?" CXXXIV, 476.

72. Thomas W. Goodspeed, *William Rainey Harper* (Chicago, 1928), 93-4.

73. Allan Nevins, *John D. Rockefeller*, 2 vols. (N. Y., 1941), II, 219 ff.

74. Ferm, ed., *Contemporary American Theology*, I, 143.

75. William W. Sweet, *Makers of Christianity, from John Cotton to Lyman Abbott* (N. Y., 1937), 320.

76. Ira V. Brown, *Lyman Abbott*, 55.

77. Lyman Abbott, *Reminiscences*, 460.

78. Brown, *Abbott*, 74.

79. John Poucher in *The Methodist Review*, LXXV (N. Y., 1893), 964-5.

80. *Op. cit.*, 112.

81. Ellis, *Gibbons*, II, 495 f.

82. Discussed in Ellis, *Gibbons*, II, 571. The article was an introduction to the English text of Pope Leo XIII's en-

cyclical, *Praeclera gratulationis publicae* on the reunion of
Christendom, carried in the same number of the *Review.*
The date of the issue of the *Independent* was Nov. 1, 1894.

83. *The Letters of Franklin K. Lane: Personal and Political,* ed. by Anne W. Lane and Louise H. Wall (Boston,
1922), 10-1.

84. Daniel D. Williams, *The Andover Liberals: A Study
in American Theology* (N. Y., 1941) .

85. Ira V. Brown, *Lyman Abbott,* 132.

86. J. H. Allen and Richard Eddy, *op. cit.,* 195-7; 205-6.

87. Chas. F. Adams, *Richard Henry Dana,* II, 202.

88. Arthur S. Bolster, Jr., *James Freeman Clarke,* (Boston, 1954) , 293.

89. *Garfield-Hinsdale Letters,* ed. by Mary L. Hinsdale
(Ann Arbor, Mich., 1949) , 188.

90. Stow Persons, *Free Religion,* 63, 23-24. Johnson's
work comprised Vol. I, *India* (1872) ; II, *China* (1877) ; III,
Persia (1885).

91. *Autobiography,* II, 567.

92. Loewenberg, "Darwinism Comes to America," 348.

93. *Autobiography,* 107.

94. Alexander V. G. Allen, *op. cit.,* 167.

95. Ira Brown, *Lyman Abbott,* 137.

96. Quoted in *Cambridge History of American Literature* (N. Y., 1921) , III, 212.

97. *The Christian Conquest of Asia* (N. Y., 1899) .

98. Galusha Anderson in *American Journal of Theology,* IV (Jan. 1900) , 450-52.

99. Barrows, "Is Christianity Fitted to Become the World
Religion?", *Amer. Journal Theology,* I (April 1897) , 404-
423.

100. The striking difference was later noted by Lyman
Abbott in his *Reminiscences,* 481.

101. Quoted in *The Cambridge History of American
Literature,* III, 214.

NOTES FOR CHAPTER VII

1. Henry F. May, *Protestant Churches and Industrial America* (N. Y., 1949), 62-3.

2. See Robert E. L. Faris, "Evolution and American Sociology," in Stow Persons, ed. *Evolutionary Thought in America*, 160-81.

3. Richard Hofstadter, *op. cit.*, 19-36.

4. Harris E. Starr, *William Graham Sumner* (N. Y., 1925).

5. Hofstadter, *op. cit.*, 37, 41 note, 51.

6. Henry F. May, *op. cit.*, 147.

7. Allan Nevins, *John D. Rockefeller*, II, 545.

8. Hofstadter, *op. cit.*, 53-69.

9. Windsor Hall Roberts, *op. cit.*, 34-5.

10. Hofstadter, *op. cit.*, 80-2.

11. Windsor H. Roberts, *op. cit.*, 36-37.

12. Hofstadter, *op. cit.*, 87-8.

13. The history of the change is thoroughly discussed in Henry F. May, *op. cit.*

14. Aaron I. Bell, "The Reception of Leo XIII's Labor Encyclical in America, 1891-1919," *Review of Politics*, VII (Oct. 1945), 464-95.

15. Hofstadter, *op. cit.*, 88.

16. Earl D. Babst and Lewis G. Vander Velde, *Michigan and the Cleveland Era* (Ann Arbor, 1948), 23-5.

17. Edward A. Ross, *op. cit.*, 115-120.

18. *Young Ward's Diary*, ed. by Bernhard J. Stern (N. Y., 1935), *passim*.

19. Emily P. Cape, *Lester F. Ward: A Personal Sketch* (N. Y., 1922).

20. For a summary of his views, see "Lester Ward and the Science of Society," in Henry S. Commager, *The American Mind* (New Haven, 1950), 199-226.

21. Arthur E. Morgan, *Edward Bellamy* (N. Y., 1944), 5-18, 22-36, 63, 135-7.

22. Anna George de Mille, *op. cit.,* 5-7; Charles A. Barker, *Henry George,* 3-16.

23. Dores R. Sharpe, *Walter Rauschenbusch* (N. Y., 1942), 63-5, 393 ff.

24. Aaron I. Abell, *op. cit.,* 78 ff.; Charles H. Hopkins, *The Rise of the Social Gospel in American Protestantism* (New Haven, 1940), 184 ff.

25. W. S. Rainsford, *The Story of a Varied Life: An Autobiography* (Garden City, 1922).

26. Henry J. Browne, *The Catholic Church and the Knights of Labor* (Washington, 1949), *passim.*

27. *The Path I Trod, The Autobiography of Terence V. Powderly* (N. Y., 1940), 371 ff.

28. Ellis, *Gibbons,* I, 486-547.

29. Powderly, *op. cit.,* 317 f.

30. Henry J. Browne, *op. cit.,* 355.

31. Micah, VI, 8.

32. Aaron I. Abell, *op. cit.,* 3-6.

33. Charles H. Hopkins, *The Rise of the Social Gospel in American Protestantism* (New Haven, 1940), 6.

34. Henry F. May, *op. cit.*

35. Issue of Feb. 27, 1878 in *ibid.,* 96.

36. See page 118.

37. May, *op. cit.,* 140.

38. C. Howard Hopkins, "Walter Rauschenbusch and the Brotherhood of the Kingdom," *Church History,* VII (1938), 145.

39. Gladden, *Reminiscences.*

40. Maurice C. Latta, "The Background for the Social Gospel in American Protestantism," *Church History,* V (1936), 260.

41. May, *op. cit.,* 171-175.

42. Dores R. Sharpe, *op. cit.,* 41-60.

43. C. Howard Hopkins, in *Church History,* VII, 138 ff.

44. Sharpe, *op. cit.,* 144-286.

45. For a discussion of some of these, see May, *op. cit.*, 177-181.

46. Hopkins, *The Rise of the Social Gospel*, 173-183.

47. Abell, *op. cit.*, 78-9.

48. See p. 123.

49. Henry F. May, *op. cit.*, 182.

50. R. V. Hunter, "The Church and The Masses," IV, 78-93.

51. Hopkins, *Rise of the Social Gospel*, 32-34.

52. *The Presbyterian and Reformed Review*, IV (Oct. 1893), 710-11.

53. Rainsford, *The Story of a Varied Life, passim*.

54. May, *op. cit.*, 188.

55. See, for example, Walter B. Posey, *The Presbyterian Church in the Old Southwest* (Richmond, Va., 1952).

56. Hunter D. Farish, *op. cit.*, 10-15.

57. Abell, *op. cit.*, 118-126.

58. J. C. Jackson, "Preaching Both Sides of the Gospel," *Methodist Review*, LXXXIII (Mar.-Apr. 1900), 295-96.

59. Whitney R. Cross, *op. cit.*, 287-321.

60. See review in *American Journal of Theology*, III (Apr. 1899), 354-56 by W. H. P. Faunce (later president of Brown University) of one such book, Samuel J. Andrews, *Christianity and Anti-Christianity in Their Final Conflict* (N. Y., 1898).

61. Elmer T. Clark, *The Small Sects in America* (N. Y., 1937), 25-36; LeRoy E. Froom, "Seventh-Day Adventists," in V. Ferm, ed. *The American Church of the Protestant Heritage* (N. Y., 1953), 371-388. For the rise of those later known as Jehovah's Witnesses, see Life of Charles T. Russell in *D.A.B.*, XVI, 240.

62. Arthur Mann, *Yankee Reformers in the Urban Age* (Cambridge, Mass., 1954), 26.

63. Sharpe, *Rauschenbusch*, 43-44.

64. Aaron I. Abell in *The Catholic Historical Review*, XLI (Jan. 1956), 385-407; Almont Lindsay, *The Pullman Strike* (Chicago, 1942), 53-54.

65. For contributions of mid-nineteenth century revivalism to this development see Timothy L. Smith, *Revivalism and Social Reform* (Nashville, 1957) .

NOTES FOR CHAPTER VIII

1. Herbert Schneider, *A History of American Philosophy* (N. Y., 1946) , 5.

2. W. W. Fenn, *op. cit.*, 120-124.

3. Henry A. Pochmann, *German Culture in America* (Madison, 1957) , 109 ff.

4. Perry Miller, *The Transcendentalists: An Anthology* (Cambridge, 1950) , 8.

5. Clarence L. F. Gohdes, *The Periodicals of American Transcendentalism,* (Durham, 1931) , 10.

6. Perry Miller, *The Transcendentalists,* 11.

7. Clarence H. Faust, "The Background of the Unitarian Opposition to Transcendentalism," *Modern Philology,* XXXV (1938), 297-324.

8. Ronald V. Wells, *Three Christian Transcendentalists: James March, Caleb Sprague Henry, Frederick Henry Hedge,* (N. Y., 1943) .

9. Herbert W. Schneider, "The Intellectual Background of William Ellery Channing," *Church History,* VII (1938), 22.

10. A sympathetic appreciation of Channing is found in Robert Leet Patterson, *The Philosophy of William E. Channing,* (N. Y., 1952) . Even more recent is David G. Egdell, *William Ellery Channing* (Boston, 1955) .

11. Perry Miller, *The Transcendentalists,* 315-16.

12. *Autobiography,* II, 535.

13. Schneider, *op. cit.,* 263-64.

14. Perry Miller, *The Transcendentalists,* 14.

15. George H. Palmer, Introduction to *Contemporary American Philosophy*, ed. by G. P. Adams and W. P. Montague, I (1930), 15-62; I, 169-70.

16. Richard Hofstadter, *The Development and Scope of Higher Education in the U. S.* (N. Y., 1952), 33-36, 167-68.

17. John Dewey, *The Influence of Darwin on Philosophy* (N. Y., 1910).

18. James McCosh of Princeton had been a leading advocate of this position. He took exception to the views of some Scottish realists (Reid, Stewart, Hamilton) who seemed to him dubious about man's ability to perceive things. McCosh, *The Prevailing Types of Philosophy: Can They Logically Reach Reality?* (N. Y., 1890).

19. W. B. Greene, Jr., "The Metaphysics of Christian Apologetics," *Presbyterian and Reformed Rev.*, IX (Jan. 1898), 60-69.

20. Adams and Montague, eds., *op. cit.*, II, 13-27. Apparently, Torrey was actually an "undogmatic disciple of the Kantian philosophy." Lewis S. Feuer, "H. A. P. Torrey and John Dewey: Teacher and Pupil," *American Quarterly*, X (Spring, 1958), 34-55.

21. W. B. Greene, Jr. in *Presby. and Ref. Rev.*, IX (Apr. 1898), 261 ff.

22. Werkmeister, *op. cit.*, 80.

23. Robert B. Warden, *An Account of the Private Life and Public Services of S. P. Chase* (Chicago, 1874), 793-94.

24. W. M. Urban in Adams and Montague, eds., *op. cit.*, II, 356-381.

25. *Presby. and Ref. Rev.*, IX, 264-69.

26. George W. Howgate, *George Santayana* (Philadelphia, 1938).

27. W. P. Montague in *Contemporary American Philosophy*, II, 138.

28. Santayana, "Brief History of My Opinions," in *ibid.*, 239-257; Howgate, *op. cit.*, 292.

29. *Presby. and Ref. Rev.*, IX, 269-71. During this period, William T. Harris (1835-1909) and his "St. Louis

School" were influential Hegelians. For the religious aloofness of this group, see Pachmann, *op. cit.*, 262.

30. Marc E. Jones, *George S. Morris* (Philadelphia, 1948) ; Adams and Montague, eds., *op. cit.*, II, 15-21.

31. W. P. Montague in Adams and Montague, ed., *op. cit.*, II, 140-141.

32. J. W. Buckham and G. E. Stratton, *George H. Howison*, (Berkeley, 1934) .

33. Adams and Montague, eds., *op. cit.*, II, 189.

34. The scholar was Walter G. Everett.

35. Albert C. Knudson in Ferm, ed., *Contemporary American Theology*, I, 220-223.

36. Review by William N. Clarke of G. R. Pike, *The Divine Drama: The Manifestation of God in the Universe* (N. Y., 1898), in *Am. Jour. Theol.*, III (Oct. 1899) , 752-3.

37. *Ibid.*, IV (Oct. 1900) , 807-9.

38. *Ibid.*, (Jan. 1900) , 135-138.

39. *Ibid.*, III (July 1899) , 580-581.

40. Adams and Montague, eds., *op. cit.*, II, 389, 85.

41. *Am. Jour. Theol.*, III (Jan. 1899) , 301.

42. Adams and Montague, eds., *op. cit.*, II, 389.

43. C. A. Strong, *A Creed for Skeptics* (London, 1936) .

44. Adams and Montague, *op. cit.*, II, 109-132. The younger man was Evander B. McGilvary. James's views owed much to Chauncey Wright (1830-1875) and Charles S. Peirce (1839-1914) .

45. Frederick J. E. Woodbridge in, Former Students of Charles E. Garman, *Studies in Philosophy and Psychology* (Boston, 1906) , 137.

46. Adams and Montague, eds., *op. cit.*, II, 13-27.

47. Edward A. White, *op. cit.*, 5.

48. Herbert W. Schneider, *op. cit.*, 232-37.

49. Edwin G. Boring, "The Influence of Evolutionary Theory upon American Psychological Thought," in Stow Persons, ed., *Evolutionary Thought in America*, 268 ff.

50. Lorine Pruette, *G. Stanley Hall: A Biography of a Mind*, (N. Y., 1926) , appendix, 264.

51. C. Hartley Grattan, *The Three Jameses* (N. Y., 1932), 21-109.

52. Julius S. Bixler, *Religion in the Philosophy of William James* (Boston, 1926), 117.

53. Ralph Barton Perry, *The Thought and Character of William James*, 1 vol. ed. (Cambridge, 1948), 40-41, 266.

54. *The Letters of William James*, ed. by his son, Henry James, 2 vols. (Boston, 1920), I, 296-97.

55. George Dykhuizen, "An Early Chapter in the Life of John Dewey," *Journal of the History of Ideas*, XIII (Oct., 1952), 563-73.

56. Review in *American Journal of Theology*, IV (July 1900), 565-66.

57. *Ibid.*, II (July 1898), 712-15. Apparently Horace Bushnell approached this conclusion, for a recent scholar tells us that Bushnell believed "that man exists only in the processes of social interaction." E. Clinton Gardner, in *Theology Today*, XII (April, 1955) 17.

58. Review by Ormond in *Presbyterian and Reformed Review*, X (Jan. 1899), 177-181.

59. Urban, "Metaphysics and Value," in Adams and Montague, eds., *Contemporary American Philosophy*, II, 356-381.

60. William B. Greene, Jr., "The Metaphysics of Christian Apologetics: Personality," *Pres. and Reformed Rev.*, IX (Apr. 1898), 472-99.

61. G. S. Goodspeed, review of Henry R. Marshall, *Instinct and Reason . . . with some Special Study of the Nature of Religion* (N. Y., 1898), in *Am. Jour. of Theology*, IV (July 1900), 566-68.

62. Nathaniel Butler, review of *The Psychology of Religion: An Empirical Study of the Growth of Religious Consciousness* (N. Y., 1899) in *Am. Jour. of Theology*, IV (Oct. 1900), 809-11.

NOTES FOR CHAPTER IX

1. See Chapters II and XI.

2. Moynihan, *John Ireland,* 104.

3. Ellis, *Gibbons,* II, 10.

4. See Chapter II; see also Cross, *Emergence of Liberal Catholicism.*

5. Charles A. Barker, *Henry George,* 576-77.

6. Moynihan, *Ireland,* 301.

7. Ellis, *Gibbons,* II, 31-39.

8. Moynihan, *Ireland,* 305.

9. Frank Hugh Foster, *The Modern Movement in American Theology* (N. Y., 1939), 12-13.

10. William Pierson Merrill, *Faith and Light, Essays on the Relation of Agnosticism to Theology* (N. Y., 1900). For a concise review of this see G. B. Foster in *Amer. Jour. Theol.,* IV (Oct. 1900), 891-892.

11. Alexander V. G. Allen, *op. cit.*

12. William Lawrence, *op. cit.,* 94-95.

13. Alexander V. G. Allen, *Phillips Brooks,* 584 ff.

14. Henry F. May, *op. cit.,* 67.

15. Paxton Hibben, *op. cit.*

16. Lyman Abbott, *Reminiscences* (Boston, 1915), 351.

17. David E. Roberts and Henry P. Van Dusen, eds., *Liberal Theology* (N. Y., 1942), 118-19.

18. See discussion in Roberts and Van Dusen, *op. cit.,* 116-117. For a favorable evaluation of Bushnell's influence, see Barbara Cross, *Horace Bushnell: Minister to A Changing America* (Chicago, 1958).

19. Edward C. Moore, *An Outline of the History of Christian Thought Since Kant* (N. Y., 1922), 110-111.

20. Rev. J. H. Willey, Ph.D., "Christianity and Race Evolution," *Methodist Review*, LXXXII (Nov.-Dec. 1900), 869-878.

21. Lefferts A. Loetscher, *The Broadening Church* (Philadelphia, 1954), 30-31.

22. *Who Wrote the Bible?* (Boston, 1891), 21, 154.

23. "The Real Problem of Inspiration," *The Presbyterian and Reformed Review*, IV (1893), 220.

24. "The New Criticism," *Methodist Review*, LXXXII (March-April 1900), 311.

25. Perry Miller, *D. A. History*, I, 82-83.

26. Thomas E. Drake, *ibid.*, IV, 386-87.

27. D. Elton Trueblood, "The Career of Elias Hicks," *Byways in Quaker History*, ed. by Howard H. Brinton (Wallinford, Pa., 1944), 77-93.

28. Edward C. Moore, *op. cit.*, 74 ff.

29. Quoted in Ira V. Brown, *Lyman Abbott*, 74.

30. *Methodist Review*, July 1898.

31. *Ibid.*, LXXXII (Jan.-Feb. 1900), 127-130.

32. H. G. Bilbie in *ibid.*, (Sept.-Oct., 1900), 802-3.

33. J. F. Chaffee, "First, That Which is Natural," in *ibid.*, (Nov.-Dec. 1900), 898.

34. See p. 78.

35. John B. Adger, *My Life and Times* (Richmond, Virginia, 1899).

36. "Theistic Evolution," in *Pres. and Reformed Rev.*, IX (Jan. 1898), 1-23.

37. Ira V. Brown, *Lyman Abbott*, 141. See also Stow Persons, "Evolution and Theology in America," in Persons, *Evolutionary Thought in America*, 422 ff.

38. Brown, *Abbott*, 149.

39. H. H. Moore, "Idealistic Theism," *Methodist Review*, LXXXII (Sept.-Oct. 1900), 798-800.

40. Edward A. White, *op. cit.*

41. J. S. Clarke, *Life and Letters of Fiske*, II, 1, 39. See also W. F. Quillian, Jr., "Evolution and Moral Theory in America," in Stow Persons, ed., *Evolutionary Thought in*

America, 398 ff, and Pannill, *The Religious Faith of John Fiske.*

42. *Calvin's Institutes,* Book I, ch. XIII, 1.

43. Henry P. Minton, *Presby. and Reformed Rev.,* X (Jan. 1899), 1-24.

44. Minton, in *ibid.,* XI (Jan. 1900), 151-2.

45. Review of Von F. Hanspaul, *Die Seelen theorie* (Berlin, 1899) in *op. cit.,* IV, 569-71.

NOTES FOR CHAPTER X

1. Conrad Wright, *The Beginnings of Unitarianism in America* (Boston, 1955).

2. James T. Addison, *op. cit.* For an appraisal of Strauss's work by a German scholar, see *Am. Jour. Theol.,* IV (July 1900), 514-35. Also controversial was the humanistic *Life of Jesus* (1863) by the French skeptic, Joseph Ernest Renan.

3. Addison, *op. cit.,* 244-45.

4. Benjamin O. True in *Amer. Jour. Theol.,* III (April 1899), 394-96. See also Faber, *Jowett.*

5. Addison, *op. cit.,* 251.

6. James Lindsay in X (Jan. 1899), 56-68.

7. Nicholas M. Steffens in *Am. Jour. Theol.,* IV (Jan. 1900), 204-206.

8. Lindsay, *loc. cit.,* 67-8.

9. C. M. Mead, "Ritschl's Theology," *Presby. and Ref. Rev.,* III, 1-21; F. H. Foster in *ibid.,* VIII, 381.

10. Quoted in *Am. Jour. Theol.,* III (Apr. 1899), 401-2.

11. Mead, *loc. cit.,* 21.

12. J. H. W. Stuckenberg in *Am. Jour. Theol.,* II (Apr. 1898), 268-292.

13. Hugh R. Macintosh, in *Am. Jour. Theol.,* III (Jan. 1899), 22-44.

14. See Introduction.

15. A dissertation for the S.T.D. degree at the Catholic University of America by Rev. James T. Fox, published in New York.

16. James H. Tufts, "What I Believe," in Adams and Montague, *Contemporary American Philosophy*, II, 333-53.

17. Lyman Abbott, "The Need of a New Theology," *Am. Jour. of Theology*, I (April 1897), 460-64.

18. In *ibid.*, III (Apr. 1899), 295-323.

19. E. Clinton Gardner, "Horace Bushnell's Doctrine of Depravity" in *Theology Today*, XII (April 1955), 10-26.

20. Ira V. Brown, *Lyman Abbott*, 145.

21. *Christ in Creation and Ethical Monism* (Philadelphia, 1899).

22. *Am. Jour. Theol.*, III, 320.

23. A liberal writer commented in 1900: "Doubtless there is a sense in which each of the theories of the cross—the substitutionary, commercial, governmental, sympathetic, ethical, vital—may subtend some arc of the infinite circle of truth." Charles J. Baldwin in *American Journal of Theology* IV (Jan. 1900), 218-19. See also Cross, *Horace Bushnell*.

24. Ira V. Brown, *Abbott*, 55.

25. *American Jour. Theology*, IV (July 1900), 627-29.

26. John Fox in *Presbyterian and Reformed Review*, XXI (July 1895), 393-413.

27. *American Journal of Theology*, I (Apr. 1897), 460-64.

28. A. B. Leonard, "The Sadducees in Methodism," *Methodist Review*, LXXXII (May-June, 1900), 473-74.

29. William Adams Brown in *Liberal Theology: An Appraisal*, ed. by D. E. Roberts and H. P. Van Dusen (N. Y., 1942), 255 ff. Brown asserts that a marked emphasis of recent times has been in increased belief in the importance of the Church.

NOTES FOR CHAPTER XI

1. *Men and Measures of Half a Century* (N. Y., 1889),
32-3.

2. M. A. De Wolfe Howe, *James Ford Rhodes* (N. Y.,
1929), 30, 321.

3. Charles Frederick Harrold, *John Henry Newman*
(N. Y., 1945), 266-90.

4. William W. Manross, *A History of the American Episcopal Church* (Milwaukee, 1935).

5. Sister Mary A. Kwitchen, *James Alphoneus McMaster:
A Study in American Thought* (Washington, 1949), 10-11
and notes.

6. Kwitchen, *op. cit.*, 192.

7. Walter Elliott, *The Life of Father Hecker* (1891);
Cross, *Emergence of Liberal Catholicism.*

8. Lord, *et al., op. cit.*, II, 734-42.

9. John La Farge, S. J., *op. cit.*, 44-5.

10. Lord, *et al.*, II, 359.

11. Theodore Maynard, *The Story of American Catholicism,* (N. Y., 1941), 580.

12. *Orestes A. Brownson, Pilgrim's Progress* (Boston,
1939), 188.

13. Maynard, *op. cit.*, 581-2.

14. Stanley J. Parry, C. S. C., "The Premises of Brownson's Political Theory," *The Review of Politics,* XVI (Apr.,
1954), 194 f.

15. Carl F. Krummel, "Catholicism, Americanism, Democracy, and Orestes Brownson," *American Quarterly,* VI
(Sept., 1954), 19-31.

16. A discussion of numerous conversions to Catholicism
is found in Lord, *et al., op. cit.*, II, 354-60, 722-43; III, 407-
15.

17. Vernon Loggins, *The Hawthornes* (N. Y., 1951), 317 ff.

18. Michael J. Hynes, *History of the Diocese of Cleveland* (Cleveland, 1953), 113 ff.

19. Mrs. Winthrop Chandler, *Roman Spring* (Boston, 1935), 61, 128 ff.

20. Ellis, *Gibbons*, II, 582 ff.

21. Oliver Carlson, *James Gordon Bennett*, 10-18, 140-75. He was given the sacraments of the Church on his death bed but was not buried from St. Patrick's Cathedral, and the body was interred in a non-sectarian cemetery.

22. De Mille, *op. cit.*, 31 ff, 50.

23. Nevins and Thomas, *op. cit.*, p. 84, note. His grandson, Nicholas Murray Butler, became a noted President of Columbia University.

24. Robert H. Elias, *op. cit.*, 3-6, 12-13.

25. Carmel O'Neill Haley, "The Dreisers," *The Commonweal*, XVIII (July 7, 1933), 265-67.

26. Carl Wittke, *Against the Current: The Life of Karl Heinzen.*

27. Mortimer Smith, *William Jay Gaynor, Mayor of New York* (Chicago, 1951), 2-9, 44.

28. Browne, *op. cit.*, 355.

29. *Under Orders: The Autobiography of William L. Sullivan* (N. Y., 1944), 56-7, 175.

30. James T. Addison, *op. cit.*, 161.

31. Anna McAllister, *Ellen Ewing, Wife of General Sherman* (N. Y., 1936), 10-11, 33, 328 ff.

32. Lloyd Lewis, *Sherman, Fighting Prophet* (N. Y., 1932) 54, 58, 627-28, 649.

33. Ellis, *Gibbons,* II, 504 note.

34. Patrick J. Dignan, *A History of the Legal Incorporation of Catholic Church Property in the U. S., 1784-1932* (Washington, 1933).

35. For a discussion of the Syllabus, see Raymond Corrigan, *The Church and the Nineteenth Century,* (Milwaukee, 1938), 175 ff.

36. J. Ryan Beiser, *The Vatican Council and the American Secular Newspapers, 1869-70* (Washington, 1941) .

37. Raymond J. Clancy, "American Prelates to the Vatican Council," U. S. Catholic Historical Society, *Historical Records and Studies*, XXVIII (N. Y., 1937) , 11, 15-19.

38. Farley, *Life of John Cardinal McCloskey*, 276 ff.; H. J. Browne, ed. "The Letters of Bishop McQuaid from the Vatican Council," *Cath. Historical Rev.*, XLI (Jan. 1956) , 412-13.

39. Sister Mary P. Trauth, S.N.D., "The Bancroft Despatches on the Vatican Council and the Kulturkampf," *The Catholic Historical Review*, XL (July 1954) , 178-90.

40. Nevins and Thomas, *op. cit.*, 283.

41. Clancy, *op. cit.*, 42.

42. Sister Mary A. Kwitchen, *op. cit.*, 192.

43. Sister Mary Agnes McCann, *The History of Mother Seton's Daughters, III* (N. Y., 1923), 32-3.

44. Dom Cuthbert Butler, *The Vatican Council,* 2 vols., (London, 1930) , II, 53.

45. Clancy, *op. cit.*, 61.

46. Butler, *op. cit.*, II, 54; H. J. Browne, ed., in *Cath. Historical Rev.*, XLI, 430-31.

47. *Catholic Encyclopaedia*, XV, 306; H. J. Browne, ed., *loc. cit.*, 437-39.

48. The English translation is printed in Clancy, *op. cit.*, Appendix, 93-111.

49. Clancy, *op. cit.*, 40-41; Browne, ed., *loc. cit.*, 439-40.

50. Clancy, p. 65 and Butler, *op. cit.*, II, 151. *The Catholic Encyclopaedia*, XV, 307 differs from some other Catholic authorities in omitting Mrak and Domenec.

51. Butler, *op. cit.*, 11, 152, 158-160; 164.

52. Browne, ed., *loc. cit.*, 439-41.

53. Gertrude Himmelfarb, *Lord Acton: A Study in Conscience and Politics* (London, 1952) , 111.

54. David Schaff, *op. cit.*, 411-12.

55. Himmelfarb, *op. cit.*, 112.

56. Clancy, *op. cit.,* 66-7.

57. Butler, *op. cit.,* II, 176.

58. Sister Mary Agnes McCann, *op. cit.,* III, 33; H. J. Browne, ed., *loc. cit.,* 425-27.

59. William L. Sullivan, *Under Orders* (N. Y., 1944) p. 68-9.

60. Clancy, *op. cit.,* 54.

61. Butler, *op. cit.,* II, 176. In England Lord Acton made a statement of submission in 1874, at Cardinal Manning's insistence, but in 1875 he believed that he would ultimately be excommunicated. A recent scholar asserts that he underestimated the prudence of Rome, for he was too influential and as a peer and associate of Gladstone too valuable to be excommunicated. Himmelsfarb, *op. cit.,* 126.

62. Robert B. Warden, *op. cit.,* 793-94.

63. 22,240 in 1936. *Bureau of the Census: Religious Bodies, 1936* (Washington, 1941) , 18-19. For the background of this movement, see Willibald Beyschlag, "The Origin and Development of the Old Catholic Movement," *The American Journal of Theology,* II (July 1898) , 481-526.

64. Will, *Gibbons,* I, 131.

65. A discussion of these matters is contained in Ellis, *Gibbons,* I, II (indexed). The problem is treated in some detail by John J. Meng in the *Catholic Historical Review,* XXXI (Jan. 1946) , 389-413, and XXXII (Oct. 1946) , 302-40.

66. *Letters from Theodore Roosevelt to Anna Roosevelt Cowles, 1870-1918* (N. Y., 1924) , 113.

67. See Vincent F. Holden, "A Myth in 'L'Americanisme,' " *Catholic Historical Review,* XXXI (July 1945) , 154-71.

68. A scholarly summary, with emphasis on Cardinal Gibbons' attitude, is in Ellis, *Gibbons,* II, 1-80.

69. See Thos. J. McAvoy, "Americanism, Fact and Fiction," *The Catholic Historical Review,* XXXI (July 1945) , 133-54.

70. Peter E. Hogan, "Americanism and the Catholic University of America," *ibid.*, XXXIII (July 1947), 183-84.

71. Sullivan, *Under Orders*, 173.

72. Sullivan, *Under Orders*, 185.

73. *The Catholic Encyclopaedia*, X, 407-8. The body was exhumed and placed in a Catholic cemetery (1904).

74. Theodore Maynard, *op. cit.*, 549-50.

75. Willard L. Sperry, *Religion in America* (Cambridge, England, 1945), 137.

76. James Gibbons Huneker, *Steeplejack*, 2 vols. in 1, (N. Y., 1922), 34-5, 52.

77. Maurice F. Egan, *Recollections of a Happy Life*, 121; John La Farge, S. J., *The Manner Is Ordinary*, *passim*.

NOTES FOR CHAPTER XII

1. Charles F. Adams, *Richard Henry Dana* [Jr.], (Boston, 1890), 2 vols., I, 19-21.

2. Alexander V. G. Allen, *op. cit.*, and William Lawrence, *op. cit.*, 74-5.

3. Frank D. Ashburn, *op. cit.*, 33.

4. Willard L. King, *Melville Weston Fuller* (N. Y., 1950), 13-14.

5. Catherine Gilbertson, *Harriet Beecher Stowe* (N. Y., 1937), 310 f. For a careful study of Mrs. Stowe's attitude toward Puritanism and toward the Episcopal Church, see Charles H. Foster, *The Rungless Ladder* (Durham, N. C., 1954), 169-171, 180-183, 236-238.

6. Robert McElroy, *Levi P. Morton* (New York, 1930).

7. Mark D. Hirsch, *William C. Whitney* (N. Y., 1948), 6, 44-45.

8. Nicholas Murray Butler, *Across The Busy Years*, 2 vols. (N. Y., 1939), I, 27, 39-42.

9. Royal Cortissoz, *op. cit.*

10. William Lawrence, *op. cit.,* 106.

11. Albert E. Benson, *History of St. Mark's School* (n.p., 1925) , 138-150.

12. An additional factor in his leaving the Presbyterian Church was the opposition of many in that Church to the serving of beer and wines at the old Princeton Inn. Wertenbaker, *Princeton, 1746-1896,* 284-5, 374-5.

13. Frederick W. Dallinger, *Recollections of an Old Fashioned New Englander* (N. Y., 1941) , 30.

14. M. A. De Wolfe Howe, *James Ford Rhodes,* 321.

15. *American Memoir* (Boston, 1947) , 72-4.

16. James T. Addison, *op. cit., passim.*

17. Chas. C. Tiffany, *A History of the Protestant Episcopal Church in the United States* (N. Y., 1916), 533-4.

18. George Hedges, *op. cit.,* 75.

19. Helen Clapsattle, *The Doctors Mayo* (Minneapolis, 1941) , 92-3.

20. J. T. Addison, *op. cit.,* 246-7.

21. Hodges, *op. cit.*

22. Addison, *op. cit.,* 248.

23. Hodges, *op. cit.,* 135 ff.

24. Addison, *op. cit.,* 252-3.

25. Lawrence, *op. cit.,* 99-101.

26. Benjamin F. Thomas, *Abraham Lincoln* (N. Y., 1953) , 478.

27. John Baillie, "Confessions of a Transplanted Scot," Ferm, *op. cit.,* II, 35.

28. A. Mitchell Hunter, *The Teaching of Calvin* (London, 1950) , 63.

29. The confusion of a layman in regard to matters of concern to theologians is suggested by the fact that in Roman Catholic theology a denial of the articles of faith which affirm a belief in "predestination" is heresy, but on the other hand, "predestinarianism" is heresy. The distinction between the two is, of course, significant. *The Catholic Encyclopaedia,* XII (N. Y., 1911) , 376-84.

30. Daniel A. Goodsell, *The Methodist Review*, LXXV (N. Y., 1893), 12.

31. Lefferts A. Loetscher, *The Broadening Church* (Philadelphia, 1954), 2 ff.

32. John O. Nelson, "Charles Hodge, Nestor of Orthodoxy," in Willard Thorp, ed., *The Lives of Eighteen From Princeton* (Princeton, 1946), 192.

33. James G. McClure of McCormick Theological Seminary in *Semi-Centennial Celebration, Garrett Biblical Institute* (Evanston, Ill., 1906), 171-72.

34. Nelson in Thorp, *op. cit.*, 209.

35. Loetscher, *op. cit.*, 13.

36. J. F. Newton, *David Swing, Poet-Preacher* (Cedar Rapids, 1909).

37. Loetscher, *op. cit.*, 14. Swing then organized Central Church (undenominational), Chicago, and served as pastor, 1875-94.

38. Wertenbaker, *Princeton, 1746-1896*, 344.

39. Loetscher, *op. cit., passim*.

40. Baker, *American Chronicle* (N. Y., 1945), 56-58, 216-17. Baker's concern in a way was wholly unnecessary, for the Presbyterian Church did not require subscription to a formal creed by its members. Yet, his gift for leadership would probably have led to his being presented as a possible church officer.

41. Philip Schaff, "The Calvinistic System," *The Independent*, XLIII (July 2, 1891), 971.

42. Loetscher, *op. cit.*, 41.

43. David Schaff, *op. cit.*, 423-27.

44. Loetscher, *op. cit.*, 47.

45. Tertius Van Dyke, *Henry Van Dyke* (N. Y., 1935), 122 ff.

46. Loetscher, *op. cit.*, 83-90.

47. William Adams Brown, "Seeking Beliefs That Matter," in Ferm, *op. cit.*, II, 79-80.

48. Ray Stannard Baker, *Life and Letters of Woodrow Wilson: Youth* (Garden City, 1927), 243-4.

49. Ray Stannard Baker, *American Chronicle* (N. Y., 1945), 59-60.

50. Baker, *Life and Letters, Youth,* 67-8.

51. David Dunn, "The Evangelical and Reformed Church," in Ferm, *The American Church of the Protestant Heritage,* 295 f.

52. Milton J. Hoffman, "The Reformed Church in America," in Ferm, *op. cit.,* 136.

53. J. H. Dubbs, "A History of the Reformed Church, German," in *American Church History,* VIII (N. Y., 1902), 357 ff.

54. *Ibid.,* 368 ff.

55. Geo. Warren Richards, "The Mercersburg Theology Historically Considered," *Papers of the American Society of Church History,* Second Series, III (N. Y., 1912), 117-49.

56. Dunn, in Ferm, *The American Church,* 305.

57. David S. Schaff, *op. cit.*

58. Maurice C. Latta, "The Background of the Social Gospel in American Protestantism," *Church History,* V (1936), 131.

59. E. T. Corwin, "A History of the Reformed Church, Dutch," in *American Church History* Series, VIII (N. Y., 1902), 211-12.

60. Hoffman, "The Reformed Church in America," *loc. cit.,* 142-45.

61. This was the very church where Rev. Norman Vincent Peale later popularized the so-called "Positive Thinking."

62. Rev. John Nicum, "The Confessional History of the Evangelical Lutheran Church in the United States," *Papers of the American Society of Church History,* IV (1892), 93-109.

63. Paul A. W. Wallace, *The Muhlenbergs of Pennsylvania* (Philadelphia, 1950).

64. Henry E. Jacobs, *A History of the Evangelical Lutheran Church in the U. S.* (N. Y., 1907), 309 ff.

65. Nicum, *loc. cit.,* 104-5.

66. Walter O. Forster, *Zion on the Mississippi* (St. Louis, 1953).

67. Walter A. Baepler, *A Century of Grace: A History of the Mo. Synod, 1847-1947* (St. Louis, 1947).

68. Carl Mauelshagen, *op. cit.*

69. Paul W. Spaude, *The Lutheran Church Under American Influence* (Burlington, Iowa, 1943), 244 ff.

70. George M. Stephenson, *John Lind of Minnesota* (Minneapolis, 1935), 125-26.

71. Raymond P. Stearns, "Assessing the New England Mind," *Church History,* X (1941), 249-52.

72. Sidney Earl Mead, *Nathaniel William Taylor, 1786-1858, A Connecticut Liberal* (Chicago, 1942), 97-98, 114-17.

73. Joseph H. Allen and Richard Eddy, *op. cit.*

74. Theodore T. Munger, *Horace Bushnell* (N. Y., 1899); see also Benjamin W. Bacon, *Theodore T. Munger;* Barbara Cross, *Bushnell.*

75. Benjamin W. Bacon, *Theodore Thornton Munger,* 182 ff.

76. Williston Walker, *A History of the Congregational Churches in the U. S.* (N. Y., 1916), 397-8.

77. Bacon, *Munger,* 186.

78. John W. Platner, "The Congregationalists," *The Religious History of New England* (Cambridge, 1917), 66-67.

79. Walker, *op. cit.,* 409-11; Ira V. Brown, *Lyman Abbott,* 129 ff.

80. Bacon, *Munger,* 160-62.

81. Harris E. Starr, *William G. Sumner* (N. Y., 1925).

82. Daniel Day Williams, *The Andover Liberals* (N. Y., 1941); Ira V. Brown, *Lyman Abbott,* 131-35.

83. Ira V. Brown, *Lyman Abbott,* 135-36.

84. Bacon, *Munger,* 293 ff.

85. For Beecher's views, see Paxton Hibben, *Henry Ward Beecher.*

86. Mary Angela Bennett, *Elizabeth Stuart Phelps* (Phila., 1939), 115.

87. Max Eastman, *Enjoyment of Living* (N. Y., 1948), 107-12.

88. Lyman Beecher Stowe, *Saints, Sinners, and Beechers* (Indianapolis, 1934), 354-384.

89. Bacon, *Munger*, 283.

90. Kenneth Andrews, *op. cit.*

91. Andrews, *op. cit.*, 27-8, 29-30. For a favorable view of Bushnell's influence, see Barbara Cross, *Horace Bushnell.*

92. Ira V. Brown, *Lyman Abbott*, 74.

93. Andrews, *op. cit.*, 67-76.

94. Cushing Strout, "Faith and History: The Mind of W. G. T. Shedd," *Journal of the History of Ideas*, XV (Jan. 1954), 153-63.

95. Charles T. Burnett, *Hyde of Bowdoin* (Boston, 1931), 247-8.

96. Walter Phelps Hall, "The Three Arnolds and Their Bible," in *Essays in Intellectual History, Dedicated to James Harvey Robinson* (N. Y., 1929), 83-5.

97. Ira V. Brown, *Lyman Abbott*, 157-58.

NOTES FOR CHAPTER XIII

1. Albert H. Newman, *A History of the Baptist Churches in the U. S.* (Revised edition, N. Y., 1915).

2. *Reminiscences*, 485.

3. Newman, *op. cit.*, 520.

4. Bella Case La Follette and Fola La Follette, *op. cit.*, I, 17.

5. Merlo J. Pusey, *Charles Evans Hughes*, 2 vols. (N. Y., 1951), I, 110.

6. Thos. W. Goodspeed, *op. cit.*, 36-39.

7. Ira V. Brown, *Abbott*, 157.

8. Ronald E. Osborn, "The Disciples of Christ," in

Vergilius Ferm, ed. *The American Church of the Protestant Heritage* (N. Y., 1953), 389.

9. Theodore C. Smith, *The Life and Letters of James Abram Garfield,* 2 vols. (New Haven, 1925) I, 32-34.

10. Wm. V. Byars, ed., *An American Commoner: The Life and Times of Richard Parks Bland* (St. Louis, 1900), 273.

11. William N. Brigance, *Jeremiah Sullivan Black,* (Phila., 1934), 4, 11, 21-22.

12. Vergilius Ferm, ed. *Contemporary American Theology,* II, 1-2.

13. Vergilius Ferm, ed. *The American Church of the Protestant Heritage,* (N. Y., 1953), 225 ff.

14. Paul Sayre, *op. cit.,* 389.

15. Rufus Jones, "Why I Enroll with the Mystics," in Ferm, ed. *Contemporary American Theology,* I, 191 ff.

16. William Dudley Foulke, *A Hoosier Autobiography* (N. Y., 1922), 219-21.

17. Vergilius Ferm, ed. *The American Church of the Protestant Heritage,* 313, 320.

18. J. M. Buckley, *A History of Methodists of the United States* (New York, 1897), 196.

19. William W. Sweet, *op. cit.,* 111.

20. Ferm, ed., *The American Church,* 323.

21. Austin Bierbower, "Unfortunate Methodist Legislation," *The Independent* XXXII (July 22, 1880), p. 1.

22. Osman C. Baker, *A Guide-Book in the Administration of the Discipline of the M. E. Church,* (N. Y., 1855), p. 24.

23. Bishop Harris, ed., *The Doctrines and Discipline of the M. E. Church,* (Cincinnati, 1880), 281.

24. *Methodist Quarterly Review,* LX (N. Y., 1878), 390-91.

25. Quoted in Hunter D. Farish, *op. cit.,* 100 note.

26. William P. Randel, *Edward Eggleston* (N. Y., 1946).

27. Bessie Louise Pierce, *A History of Chicago,* III (N. Y., 1951), 432-33.

28. Isaac F. Marcosson, *David Graham Phillips and His Times* (N. Y., 1932), 11-20; Eric F. Goldman, "David Graham Phillips, Victorian Critic of Victorianism," in Willard Thorp, ed. *The Lives of Eighteen From Princeton,* (Princeton, 1946), 318-20.

29. Irving McKee, '*Ben Hur' Wallace: The Life of General Lew Wallace* (Berkeley and Los Angeles, 1947), 164, 173.

30. Charles Richard Williams, ed., *Diary and Letters of R. B. Hayes,* 5 vols. (Columbus, 1926), I, 122, 188; IV, *passim.*

31. Burton J. Hendrick, *The Training of an American: The Earlier Life and Letters of Walter Hines Page* (Boston, 1928).

32. Chas. F. Sitterly, *The Building of Drew University* (N. Y., 1938).

33. Rall, "Theology, Empirical and Christian," in Ferm, ed., *Contemporary American Theology,* II, 245-50.

34. Knudson, "A Personalist Approach to Theology," in Ferm, ed. *Contemporary American Theology,* I, 219-23.

NOTES FOR CHAPTER XIV

1. Joseph Henry Allen and Richard Eddy, *op. cit.,* 255 ff.

2. John Coleman Adams, "The Universalists," in *The Religious History of New England* (Cambridge, 1917), 300-304.

3. Francis A. Walker, *A Compendium of the Ninth Census* (Washington, 1872), 524-25.

4. Don C. Seitz, *Horace Greeley* (Indianapolis, 1926), 23.

5. *A Memoir of Benjamin Robbins Curtis,* ed. by his son, Benjamin R. Curtis (2 vols., Boston, 1879), I, 18-19.

6. Allen and Eddy, *op. cit.,* 175 ff.

7. W. W. Fenn, "The Revolt Against the Standing Or-

der," in *The Religious History of New England* (Cambridge, Mass., 1917) , 125-26.

8. Geo. H. Putnam, *op. cit.,* 17-19.

9. As Unitarians became more rationalistic, in his declining years Frothingham resumed (1890) attendance at Unitarian services. Stow Persons, *Free Religion* (New Haven, 1947) , 155.

10. *Memoir of Samuel Joseph May,* 285.

11. Mrs. Winthrop Chandler, *op. cit.,* 118.

12. E. E. Hale, Jr., *op. cit.,* II, 217-18.

13. Ford, ed., *Writings of Thos. Jefferson,* X, 220-1.

14. Clarence Gohdes, "Some Notes on the Unitarian Church in the Ante Bellum South," in David K. Jackson, ed., *American Studies in Honor of W. K. Boyd* (Durham, 1940) , 349.

15. William B. Parker, *The Life and Public Services of Justin S. Morrill* (Boston, 1924), 356.

16. William A. Robinson, *Thos. B. Reed* (N. Y., 1930) , 5, 385.

17. Chas. E. Hamlin, *The Life and Times of Hannibal Hamlin* (Cambridge, 1899) , 574.

18. La Follette and La Follette, *op. cit.,* I.

19. Grace Julian Clarke, *George W. Julian* (Indianapolis, 1923) , 70-2, 407.

20. *Memoirs of Benjamin Robbins Curtis,* I, 323.

21. *Letters of Charles E. Norton: With Biographical Comment* by Sara Norton and M. A. De Wolfe Howe, 2 vols. (Boston, 1913) , I, 294 ff.

22. *America of Yesterday. The Journal of John Davis Long,* ed. by Lawrence S. Mayo (Boston, 1923), *passim.*

23. George F. Hoar, *Autobiography of Seventy Years,* 2 vols. (N. Y., 1903) , II, 436 ff.

24. M. A. De Wolfe Howe, *Portrait of an Independent: Moorfield Storey, 1845-1929* (Boston, 1932) , 361.

25. *Autobiography of Andrew Dickson White,* I, 327-28.

26. Richard C. Beatty, *James Russell Lowell* (Nashville, 1942) , 233-34.

27. Leo M. Shea, *Lowell's Religious Outlook* (Washington, D. C., 1926), 41.

28. Beatty, *op. cit.*, 252.

29. Philip D. Jordan, *William Salter, Western Torchbearers* (Oxford, Ohio, 1939).

30. Henry Neumann, *Spokesmen for Ethical Religion* (Boston, 1951), 4.

31. Stow Persons, *Free Religion*, 70-71, 96.

32. Henry Morgenthau, *All In a Life Time* (N. Y., 1922), 95-97.

33. Neumann, *op. cit.*, introduction, xvii.

34. See page 270. See also Neumann, *op. cit.*, 90-97.

35. Sheldon, *An Ethical Movement* (N. Y., 1896), VII.

36. Arthur P. Dudden, "Joseph Fels of Philadelphia and London," *The Pennsylvania Magazine of History and Biography*, LXXIX (April 1955), 143 ff.

37. Otto Pfleiderer, "Religionless Morality," *American Journal of Theology*, III (April 1899), 225-250.

38. "Analyticus" [James W. Wise] *Jews Are Like That* (N. Y., 1928), 133-136.

39. DeWitt H. Parker in *Contemporary American Philosophy*, ed. by G. P. Adams and W. P. Montague, II, 163.

40. Horace J. Bridges, ed., *Aspects of Ethical Religion* (N. Y., 1926).

41. "Analyticus," *op. cit.*, 141.

42. Harry K. Carroll, *Report on Statistics of the Churches, Eleventh Census, 1890* (Washington, 1890), 765.

43. Analyticus, *Jews Are Like That*, 134-37.

44. Stow Persons, *Free Religion*, 15.

45. *Ibid.*, 35; Ralph H. Gabriel, *The Course of American Democratic Thought* (N. Y., 1956), 183-207.

46. Persons, *op. cit., passim*.

47. Sidney Warren, *American Free Thought, 1860-1915*, 96-116.

48. Persons, *op. cit.*, 66.

49. Wittke, *We Who Built America*, 222-225.

50. Warren, *op. cit.*, 34-35, and 156-183.

51. For a discussion of "Atheism: the Left Wing of the Free thought movement," see Warren, *op. cit.*, 184-205.

52. Warren, *op. cit.*, 39-40.

53. Milton E. Flower, *James Parton: The Father of Modern Biography* (Durham, N. C., 1951) .

54. Clarence H. Cramer, *Royal Bob: The Life of Robert G. Ingersoll* (Indianapolis, 1952), 110, 122.

55. L. White Busbey, *Uncle Joe Cannon* (N. Y., 1937) , 3, 33 ff.

56. Octavius B. Frothingham, *Gerritt Smith* (N. Y., 1877) , 359.

57. *William Lloyd Garrison . . . The Story of His Life Told by His Children,* 4 vols. (Boston, 1894) , IV, 337.

58. Warren, *American Free Thought,* 42-3. Yet, Mark Twain was long associated with the life of the liberal Asylum Hill Congregational Church, Hartford, Connecticut, and Mrs. Andrew Carnegie was an active Universalist and later a zealous Presbyterian.

59. *Letters of Charles E. Norton,* II, 364.

NOTES FOR CHAPTER XV

1. David Philipson, *The Reform Movement in Judaism* (Revised Ed., N. Y., 1931) , 329 ff.

2. But, for a highly favorable discussion of Reform Judaism in the United States, see Joseph Leiser, *American Judaism* (N. Y., 1925) , 123-43.

3. David Philipson, *op. cit.,* 355 ff.

4. David Philipson, *op. cit., passim.*

5. Cohen, "The Faith of a Logician," in G. P. Adams and W. P. Montague, eds. *Contemporary American Philosophy,* I, 221-47.

NOTES FOR CHAPTER XVI

1. William L. Worcester, "The Swedenborgians," in *The Religious History of New England* (Cambridge, 1917), 325-28.
2. Margaret Clapp, *Forgotten First Citizen* (Boston, 1947), 5-6, 84 ff.
3. An extensive discussion of James' thought is found in Frederic Harold Young, *The Philosophy of Henry James, Sr.,* (N. Y., 1951).
4. Julian S. Bixler, *op. cit.,* 2, 156, 196-97.
5. *Alice James, Her Brother, Her Journal,* ed. by Anna Robeson Burr, (Cornwall, N. Y., 1934), 238-39.
6. Francis O. Matthiessen, *The James Family* (N. Y., 1947).
7. Giddings MSS., Ohio State Museum, Columbus, Ohio.
8. Kenneth R. Andrews, *Nook Farm,* 54 ff.
9. Catherine Gilbertson, *op. cit.,* 263-64.
10. Andrews, *op. cit.,* 65-66.
11. Julius S. Bixler, *op. cit.,* 146 ff.
12. John La Farge, S. J., *op. cit.,* 71-72.
13. *William Lloyd Garrison, 1805-1879: The Story of His Life Told by His Children,* 4 vols. (Boston, 1894), IV, 338.
14. *D.A.B.,* XIV, 118-20; *The Diary of George T. Strong, 1865-75,* ed. by Allan Nevins and Milton H. Thomas (N. Y., 1952), 411.
15. William B. Hesseltine, *Pioneer's Mission: The Story of Lyman C. Draper* (Madison, 1954) 115-116, 229-236, 274, 284, 312-15.
16. John R. Commons, *Myself* (N. Y., 1934), 7-10.
17. Moncure D. Conway, "Contemporary Supernaturalism," *The Forum,* I (Mar. 1886), 293; Franklin Johnson in *American Jour. of Theol.,* IV (July 1900), 641-42.

18. The official biography by Sibyl Wilbur, *The Life of Mary Baker Eddy* (4th Edition, Boston, 1913) is endorsed by the Church. Some others, especially E. F. Dakin, *Mrs. Eddy, the Biography of a Virginal Mind* (N. Y., 1930) are unacceptable. *The Harvard Guide to American History* (Cambridge, 1954) suggests only the Dakin volume; E. S. Bates and J. V. Dittemore, *Mary Baker Eddy* (N. Y., 1932); and L. P. Powell, *Mary Baker Eddy* (N. Y., 1930).

19. Woodbridge Riley, "The Personal Sources of Christian Science," *Psychological Review*, X (Nov. 1903), 593-614.

20. Woodbridge Riley, *American Thought: From Puritanism to Pragmatism and Beyond*, (N. Y., 1915), 44-53.

21. *Memories of a Happy Life*, 186.

22. W. B. Green, Jr., "Christian Science or Mind Cure," *Presbyterian and Reformed Review*, I (January 1890), 88-95.

NOTES FOR CHAPTER XVII

1. *Proceedings of Massachusetts Historical Society*, LXIV (1932), 523-537.

2. Harold U. Faulkner, "American Christianity and the World of Everyday," in *Essays in Intellectual History Dedicated to James Harvey Robinson*, (N. Y., 1929), 128.

3. Sidney Warren, *op. cit.*, 9.

4. An article by Grady for his paper reprinted in Joel C. Harris, *Life of Henry W. Grady* (N. Y., 1890), 230-7.

5. John F. Fulton, *Harvey Cushing: A Biography*, (Springfield, Ill., 1946), 2-14.

6. Claude M. Fuess, *Joseph B. Eastman: Servant of the People*, (N. Y., 1952), 5-6, 10-11.

7. Quoted in Ray Ginger, *The Bending Cross: A Bi-*

ography of Eugene V. Debs (New Brunswick, New Jersey, 1949), 6-7, 10.

8. *Life and Letters of Edwin Lawrence Godkin,* ed. by Rollo Ogden, 2 vols., (N. Y., 1907), II, 35-36.

9. John La Farge, *op. cit.*

10. *Life and Letters of E. L. Godkin,* II, 241, 37.

11. *Letters of Theodore Roosevelt to Anna Roosevelt Cowles, 1870-1918,* (N. Y., 1924), 37.

12. *Op. cit.,* 253 ff.

13. Edward A. Ross, *op. cit.,* 117 ff.

14. Henry Holt, *Garrulities of an Octogenarian Editor,* (Boston, 1923), 415-437.

15. Edward Hungerford, *Daniel Willard,* 24-25.

16. James A. Barnes, *John G. Carlisle: Financial Statesman,* (N. Y., 1931), 9.

17. Victor L. Albjerg, *op. cit.,* 16, 61 ff.

18. Geo. S. Merriam, *op. cit.,* II, 394-95, 402.

19. Rev. Edward C. Towne, "What Does It Mean?", *The Independent* XXV (July 3, 1873), 836.

20. John P. Hylan, *Public Worship: A Study in the Psychology of Religion,* (Chicago, 1901), 5.

21. Paul D. Moody, *My Father* (Boston, 1938), 124.

22. W. R. Moody, *op. cit.,* 263.

23. Commager, *The American Mind.*

24. See chapter under that title in Curti, *The Growth of American Thought* (N. Y., 1943), 531-54.

25. *The Independent,* LII (Jan. 4, 1900), 20-57.

26. *Am. Jour. of Theol.,* I (Apr. 1897), 522-24.

27. *Calvinism, Six Lectures Delivered in the Theological Seminary at Princeton* (Chicago, n. d.).

28. See review by William N. Clarke in *Am. Jour. Theol.,* IV (July 1900), 634-5.

29. A. C. Zenos in *Pres. and Ref. Rev.,* XI (July 1900), 397-413.

30. R. M. Wenley in *Am. Jour. Theol.,* III (Jan. 1899), 207-8.

31. Henry C. Minton, *Pres. and Ref. Rev.,* XI (Jan. 1900), 192-5.

32. Willard L. Sperry, *op. cit.,* 137.

33. J. W. Moncrief in *Amer. Jour. Theol.,* IV (Jan. 1900), 213-15.

34. George Harris, *A Century's Change in Religion,* 96-97.

35. W. Rupp, a Reformed theologian, in *Am. Jour. Theol.,* III, (Oct. 1899), 654-78.

36. E. V. Gerhart, in *ibid.,* (Apr. 1899), 275-94.

37. C. J. H. Ropes in *ibid.,* II (Jan. 1898), 80-96.

38. See *e.g.,* George N. Boardman, *A History of New England Theology* (N. Y., 1899).

39. "Recent Tendencies in Theological Thought," *Amer. Jour. of Theol.,* I (Jan. 1897), 118-136.

40. Franklin Johnson in *ibid.,* IV (Oct. 1900), 865-66.

41. Edwin K. Mitchell, *Am. Jour. of Theol.* I (Oct. 1897), 1077-79.

42. "The Function of Interpretation in Relation to Theology," *Am. Jour. of Theol.,* II (Jan. 1898), 52-79.

43. John Sherman, *Recollections of Forty Years,* 2 vols., (Chicago, 1895), I, 26.

44. Merlo J. Pusey, *op. cit.*

45. Whitman Bennett, *Whittier: Bard of Freedom* (Chapel Hill, N. C., 1941), 305-311; Allen, *Phillips Brooks,* 508-509, 486.

46. Allen, *Brooks,* 491.

47. Geo. T. Clark, *Leland Stanford* (Stanford U., Cal. 1931), 469.

48. Nicholas Murray Butler, *Across The Busy Years,* 2 vols. (N. Y., 1939), I, 40.

49. *The Independent,* LII (Sept. 20, 1900), 2285-87.

50. Rev. John Rothensteiner, "Archbishop Peter Richard Kenrick and the Vatican Council," *Illinois Catholic Historical Review,* XI (July 1928), 3-27.

51. Carl Wittke, *We Who Built America,* 500-505.

52. William R. Moody, *op. cit.,* 496-97.
53. John P. Hylan, *op. cit.,* 7.
54. M. A. De Wolfe Howe, *A Venture in Remembrance,* 34-5.
55. Thomas Le Duc, *Piety and Intellect at Amherst College,* (N. Y., 1946) , 34.
56. Henry F. May, *op. cit.,* 91.
57. See chapter on "The New Sociology and Economics and the Social Gospel."
58. Joel C. Harris, *Grady,* 237.
59. *Atlantic Monthly,* XIX (Jan. 1867) , 49; Milton E. Flower, *James Parton,* 202.
60. Samuel C. Derby, "Edward Orton," *The Old Northwest Genealogical Quarterly,* III, (January 1900) , 1-14.
61. *The Method of Science and its Influence Upon the Branches of Knowledge Pertaining to Man* (Columbus, Ohio, 1898) , p. 26.
62. *In Memoriam: Edward Orton* (Columbus, Ohio, n. d.) , 50.
63. John T. Morse, Jr., *op. cit.,* I, 280 ff.
64. Holmes's own son, Oliver Wendell Holmes, Jr., the distinguished jurist, however, broke away from the traditional concepts of absolute values and all-embracing moral codes, and from all organized religion. Highly individualistic, he embraced a large element of Stoicism in his personal philosophy, and pragmatism became, for him, central as a basis of judgment. Thus, in three generations the family had moved from orthodox Calvinism to liberal Unitarianism and then to thorough-going secularism. Mark De Wolfe Howe, *Justice Holmes, The Shaping Years, 1841-1870* (Cambridge, Mass., 1957) and Silas Bent, *Justice Oliver Wendell Holmes* (N. Y., 1932) .
65. In spite of the significant intellectual changes, during the twentieth century liberal churches like the Unitarians, Universalists, and Society of Friends declined absolutely, while it was "the Calvinistic, the Evangelical, and the

Catholic churches that increased steadily in membership and authority." Commager, *The American Mind*, 163. Unitarianism, in the period after 1940, seems to have benefited by the so-called "Return to Religion," though the greatest numerical gains apparently have been made by those organizations with a strong doctrinal appeal.

INDEX

Date